Reception Theory
and Biblical Hermeneutics

Princeton Theological Monograph Series

K. C. Hanson, Charles M. Collier, and
D. Christopher Spinks, Series Editors

Reception Theory
and Biblical Hermeneutics

DAVID PAUL PARRIS

PICKWICK *Publications* · Eugene, Oregon

RECEPTION THEORY AND BIBLICAL HERMENEUTICS

Princeton Theological Monograph Series 107

Pickwick Publications
A Division of Wipf and Stock Publishers
199 W. 8th Ave., Suite 3
Eugene, OR 97401

www.wipfandstock.com

ISBN 13: 978-1-55635-653-7

Cataloging-in-Publication data:

Parris, David Paul

Reception theory and biblical hermeneutics / David Paul Parris.

xviii + 326 p. ; 23 cm. — Includes bibliographical references.

Princeton Theological Monograph Series 107

ISBN 13: 978-1-55635-653-7

1. Bible—Reading. 2. Bible—Hermeneutics. 3. Bible—Criticism, interpretation,
etc.—History. 4. Bible—History and criticism—Theory, etc. I. Title. II. Series.

BS476 P365 2009

Manufactured in the U.S.A.

To Anthony and Rosemary Thiselton
Who not only taught me scholarship
but modeled what it means to be a scholar.

And my deepest appreciation to my wife
and co-laborer, Catherine.

Contents

Introduction

RECEPTION THEORY OFFERS INTERPRETIVE RESOURCES AND INSIGHTS that can serve the valuable role of providing a hermeneutical model that relates biblical exegesis, the history of biblical interpretation, and church history to each other. From an exegetical perspective, reception theory rescues the Bible from being approached like other ancient texts, as a relic from the past. At the corporate level, it provides a means for us to engage our rich heritage of biblical interpretation in a manner that not only allows us to grasp how our tradition has shaped who we are, but also to realize that we are active participants in the ongoing process of that living tradition. The call for an approach along these lines is a rather recent development in church history that began less than one hundred years ago and is just now being taken seriously.

A Voice Crying in the Wilderness

Ernst von Dobschütz was a man ahead of his time. In 1909, he wrote an article entitled "The Bible in the Church" in which he asked the question: what effect has the Bible had upon the church?[1] Dobschütz found it rather incredulous that even though more has been written on the Bible than any other book "no one as yet has made a comprehensive investigation of the influence which it has exerted upon the Christian Church and the life of the Christian peoples as a whole."[2] While others before him had examined the exposition of the Bible and the history of texts and translations, Dobschütz asked what exactly has been the effect or influence of the Bible upon the church. Martin Kähler's, *Die Geschichte der Bibel in ihrer Wirkung auf die Kirche, ein Vorschlag* (1902), precipitated Dobschütz's work, but it was too general in nature and confined itself to demonstrating the significance of the Bible as a whole for the church. Dobschütz proposed to refine Kähler's idea by

1. Dobschütz, "Bible in the Church," 2:579–615.
2. Ibid., 2:579–80.

working out the details through the application of a purely historical method.[3] Some of the most significant material in his article concerns the effect of the Bible on worship, public and private reading of the Bible, and the Bible's influence on language, art, and law.[4] A half century would pass before the questions that Dobschütz raised would be given serious consideration again.

Ebeling, "Church History as the History of the Exposition of Scripture"

It was not until 1964 that questions about the post-history of the biblical text or its *Wirkungsgeschichte* received any degree of meaningful discussion. The turning point came with the publication of Gerhard Ebeling's book, *Wort Gottes und Tradition*. According to Ebeling, the most significant contribution to theology since the Enlightenment "has been the result of historical work, both in the field of exegesis and in the field of Church history and the history of doctrine."[5] This returned theology back to its real subject matter—Jesus Christ and protected theology from sliding into Scholasticism or Gnosticism, and from the intrusion of outside schools of philosophical thought.[6] However, the real significance of historical study is found in the concept of *Geschichte*, "the dialogue between the objective event in the past and the subjective understanding of the past event in the present."[7] This means that not only will church history always remain an unfinished exercise, but biblical exegesis will as well.

This idea should not be foreign to theology. The seed for such an approach dates back at least to the Reformation and is evidenced in the manner that the framers of the Augsburg Confession's made an explicit link between the Bible, the church, and history in Article VII.[8]

3. Ibid., 2:580.

4. Ibid., 2:601–15.

5. Ebeling, *Wort Gottes und Tradition*, 14.

6. Ibid., 14–15.

7. Ibid., 17.

8. *"Es wird auch gelehrt, daß allezeit müsse eine heilige christliche Kirche sein und bleiben, welche ist die Versammlung aller Gläubigen, bei welchen das Evangelium rein gepredigt und die heiligen Sakramente laut des Evangelii gereicht werden. Denn dieses ist genug zu wahrer Einigkeit der christlichen Kirche, daß da einträchtiglich nach reinem Verstand das Evangelium gepredigt und die Sakramente dem göttlichen Wort gemässe*

The church is guided by its interpretation of the Bible, is actualized by its obedience to the Word of God, and as a result, is an assembly that is constantly constituted anew in each historical horizon. Since the church is constantly being instantiated in new historical and cultural settings it is constantly being reshaped and renewed by its interpretation of Holy Scripture. This is not something that occurs in the abstract but involves actual readers, teachers, preachers, and hearers who implement their understanding of the Scriptures.

Geschichte weds church history to the Bible and biblical interpretation to the church. On the side of church history, the traditional approach which emphasizes the history of doctrines, events, and movements must "be corrected by a fresh attention to the history of hermeneutics and the exegesis of Scripture."[9] On the exegetical side, the interpretation of the Bible needs to be expanded from commentaries that focus on what the text meant to its original audience to include church policies, organizational structures, politics, and the "doing and suffering" of the church. "The concept of interpretation has therefore a range whose extent cannot be grasped."[10]

Ebeling also realized that this view of history (*Geschichte*) raised the question of how we could posit any form of continuity to the Christian tradition since its history is characterized by both continuity and discontinuity. Models of church history or history of interpretation based on a cumulative understanding of the Scriptures were no longer tenable. Evolutionary models of theological development were being replaced by views that take the situatedness of the interpreter more into account and highlight aspects of historical discontinuity. Ormond Rush testifies to the implications of this shift and the need to address them:

> Emerging out of a nineteenth century understanding of history, the evolutionary notion of development, with its emphasis on and confidence in continuity, unity, clarity, and normativity, breaks down when we read doctrinal history from our twentieth century, post-modern horizon. A more adequate model is

---

gereicht werden. Und ist nicht not zu wahrer Einigkeit Zeremonien, von der Menschen eingesetzt, gehalten werden; wie Paulus spricht Eph. 4, 5.6 "Ein Leib, ein Geist, wie ihr berufen seid zu einerlei Hoffnung eures Berufs; ein Herr, ein Glaube, eine Taufe." Augsburg Confession, Article VII, "Of the Church," in Dau and Gente, *Concordia Triglotta*.

9. Ebeling, *The Word of God and Tradition*, 29.

10. Ibid., 28.

required that enables us to face the issues of discontinuity, plurality, ambiguity, and relativity that persist in our Christian past, present and future.[11]

For Ebeling, the continuity of Christianity is constituted by the self-same subject-matter of the tradition: Jesus Christ, who is the same yesterday, today, and forever. At the same time, the church's understanding of Jesus is characterized by manifold developments and diverse expressions in its history because the church always understands Jesus from a particular historical perspective.[12]

> From the theological point of view the remarkable thing about this course of events is that the church, although she remains one and the same, undergoes a manifold change of form; thus the witness to Jesus Christ in the history of the Church does not consist in the mere repetition of Holy Scripture and in the imitation of the way in which the disciples followed him; but in interpretation, that is, in ever new usages and forms, thoughts and decisions, sufferings and victories, and hence in an unfolding of the richness and power of the Word of God, and in ever new victories for the hidden kingdom of God.[13]

Froehlich, "Church History and the Bible"

The call for biblical exegesis and church history to include the *Wirkungsgeschichte* of the Bible was echoed in the Anglo-American tradition by Karlfried Froehlich in his article "Church History and the Bible."[14] Like Ebeling, Froehlich retrieves the Reformer's position that there could be no church without the Bible and that there could be "no Bible without the church—the church which received the apostolic witness, selected the canon, and gave the biblical witness unity by its interpretation."[15] While the historical critical method might have made the most significant contribution to theology in the past two hundred years, it is also responsible for the artificial division between church

---

11. Ormond Rush, "Reception Hermeneutics and the 'Development' of Doctrine," 126.

12. Friedrich De Boor, "*Kirchengeschichte oder Auslegungsgeschichte?*" 406.

13. Ebeling, *The Word of God and Tradition*, 31.

14. Froehlich, "Church History and the Bible," 1–15.

15. Ibid., 7.

history and biblical exegesis. According to Froehlich, Ebeling's revolutionary contribution to theological studies was his thesis that we need to grasp the normative power of the biblical language and its interaction with the diverse horizons of understanding that comprise the history of the church. This should "encourage a style of history writing that would expose this normative power of the biblical language not only as past-factum reflection or rationalization but also as the historical start for thought and action."[16] The Christian tradition is not a barrier to understanding Jesus Christ but serves to point to him. In order to realize this church history and the history of biblical interpretation must be incorporated into biblical hermeneutics, and the biblical interpretation into church history. While Froehlich speaks positively of Ebeling's proposal, he thinks the results of the research that Ebeling's work stimulated have been rather disappointing so far.[17] One of the weaknesses of Ebeling's approach is that the interpreter did not know what he or she should be looking for in the post-history of a text. As a result, the "tracing of random texts in their history of exposition yield at best interesting details and the impression of a bewildering zigzag course."[18] This dilemma is unavoidable. Because of the vast amount of material written on the Bible, there will be a disproportionate number of false starts and dead-ends as in any new field of research. Simultaneously, Froehlich argues that studies on the *Wirkungsgeschichte* of a text should attempt to illuminate the historical development of understanding the text. The success of diachronic studies such as this will depend to a large extent on the careful selection of texts. "The success, it is maintained, depends entirely on the selection of a good passage, one which has made history rather than just having one."[19]

16. Ibid., 13.

17. Ibid., 9; de Boor, "*Kirchengeschichte oder Auslegungsgeschichte?*" 406–9.

18. Froehlich commends Childs's commentary on Exodus as an example but criticizes it for the manner in which he thinks that Childs has contrived his sources and does not demonstrate from them any form of development in the exegetical understanding of the book. Froehlich, "Church History and the Bible," 10; Childs, *The Book of Exodus*.

19. Froehlich, "Church History and the Bible," 10. De Boor is more critical, claiming that if one attempted to pursue an approach that considered the history of the influence of the Bible in other fields besides the history of interpretation, one will "sink in the material." de Boor, "Kirchengeschichte oder Auslegungsgeschichte?" 409.

The rewards of this approach outweigh the difficulties inherent in attempting to study the reception of a particular biblical text for Froehlich. At the institutional level, this type of approach helps to overcome the artificial divisions between biblical studies and church history. At the corporate and personal levels, this type of research will hopefully assist the contemporary church to arrive at a deeper self-understanding of its position in the Christian tradition. Incorporating the history of biblical interpretation into church history and our exegetical practices "holds out the promise of something really new, of seeing really new light, of becoming open to truly new horizons, of experiencing change in ourselves, precisely because we cannot change the past. History itself in its inexhaustible universal horizon is the given, and as such the best dialogue partner to help us discover that life never needs to be dull."[20]

A Traditional Way to Write a Commentary

In the past few years there have been several very promising developments that would probably appease Froehlich's earlier frustrations. At least two commentary series devote their attention to the history of how the Bible has been interpreted. *The Ancient Christian Commentary* series (InterVarsity Press) offer a collection of patristic commentaries and homilies on the various biblical texts. *Blackwell Bible Commentaries* (Blackwell) focuses on the influence and impact of the various biblical texts on history. Anthony Thiselton's commentary on 1 Corinthians is an excellent example of how the posthistory of the text, from the church fathers to the present, is incorporated directly in the exegetical discussions of the Greek text. Specific sections that examine the reception history of pivotal passages in 1 Corinthians (such as 2:6–16 where two different trajectories of interpretation that focus on either the Holy Spirit's deity or role in illumination are compared) are presented in the Extended Note sections.[21]

Perhaps the most promising of these recent developments has been the publication of the *Evangelisch-Katholischer Kommentar zum Neuen Testament* series in which the post-history of the text occupies a central element of the discussion of the text's meaning. Ulrich Luz's three volumes on the Gospel of Matthew has been one of the more suc-

---

20. Froehlich, "Church History and the Bible," 6.
21. See Thiselton, *The First Epistle to the Corinthians*, 276–86.

cessful commentaries at achieving this goal than the other volumes in the series. Luz not only practices a *wirkungsgeschichtliche* approach but he is a strong advocate and apologist for it as well. Hermeneutically, Luz's model is based on Hans-Georg Gadamer's work and stands within the trajectory of thought launched by Ebeling.

The Bible and the history of its effects are related in two primary ways according to Luz. First, the biblical texts are the products of the history of effects themselves. The New Testament is the result of the early church's interpretation and preaching of God's revelation in the life, death, and resurrection of Jesus Christ. Second, "the biblical texts have a history of effects, namely, the history of the churches and their confessions after them and, through them, the history of the whole Christian world."[22] Texts possess a potential for meaning that is disclosed or concretized in the history of their reception. As such, both the New Testament and the history of its effects are witnesses to the creative power of the transmission of the gospel message in new historical situations.

> A biblical text is not a reservoir or cistern, with a fixed amount of water in it that can be clearly measured. Rather it resembles a source, where new water emerges from the same place. This means that the history of interpretation and effects that a text creates is nothing alien to the text itself, as if the text with its meaning existed at the beginning and then only afterward and secondarily had consequences and created a history of interpretation.[23]

The history of a text's effects and interpretation should be an integral part of a commentary and should not be treated as material to be tucked away into an appendix or serve as occasional illustration to make the commentary more readable or interesting. The reception history of the text exposes the interpreter to the "great treasury of experience" that other Christians have found in the Bible.[24] This not only helps

---

22. Luz, *Matthew in History*, 23.

23. Ibid., 19. At another point he explains the same idea in this manner. "I would propose to understand the meaning of a biblical text as an interaction of a 'kernel of meaning,' which corresponds to the given structure of a text, and a 'directional meaning,' which gives a present direction to the readers on their way to new lands." Ibid., 20.

24. Luz, *Matthew 1–7*, 99.

us to learn from previous interpretations, but it also reveals to us why we approach the text the way we do. History reveals to us what we owe to those who preceded us. We find ourselves in a position similar to someone "who must investigate the water of a river while sitting in a boat which is carried and driven by this same river."[25] Or to cite another metaphor, one that has a rich history of reception, we are like the far-sighted dwarf standing on the shoulders of giants.[26]

Where Does Tradition Go from Here?

The need for building upon the contributions of Ebeling, Froehlich, and Luz is important for two reasons. First, if the post-history of the text functions as a hermeneutical bridge between our contemporary understanding of the Bible and the text itself, then we ignore this historical dimension at our own peril. Markus Bockmuehl complains about the inattention bestowed upon the Christian tradition's rich history of biblical interpretation. He contrasts the situation with civil engineers who know that when they are constructing a new road it is often wisest to follow the route of the old road and thus build upon their ancestors' knowledge of the land. It is not uncommon to find modern motorways in Europe following in the same route Roman roads did. Biblical studies followed an analogous approach until the rise of the historical critical method. "For the last century and a half, however, we have not been building and improving a road on which to travel back and forth, but have attempted to slash a wide swath through the woods with picks and machetes and, one suspects, often without much sense of direction or sensitivity to the terrain."[27] The history of the Bible's reception presents a challenge to contemporary biblical scholarship that is dominated by questions concerning the origin of the text. This is not to deny the value of such research, but we need to ask why such a disproportionate amount of research in biblical studies is devoted to historical

---

25. Ibid., 96.

26. This metaphor can be traced all the way back to Bernard of Chartres in the twelfth century. Parris, *Reading the Bible with the Giants*, viii–xiii.

27. Bockmuehl, "A Commentator's Approach to the 'Effective History' of Philippians," 58.

reconstruction while so little is given to the history of a text's interpretation and effects.[28]

Second, while the contributions of Ebeling, Froehlich, and Luz's work are impressive, I think that they can be strengthened and advanced by incorporating recent work in philosophical hermeneutics and literary theory, specifically the work of Hans Robert Jauss. Is it worth the effort to examine the history of the Bible's interpretation and influence in our exegetical practices? "If, . . . the answer is yes, great care should be devoted to the construction of a proper theoretical framework for the pursuit."[29]

Structure to This Study

The goal of this study is to examine critically the hermeneutical resources of reception theory to see whether it can provide an adequate theoretical framework to achieve these goals. To facilitate this, I have divided my argument into three sections. The first three chapters will consist of an exploration of the philosophical concepts and theories behind reception theory. Because Hans Robert Jauss studied under Hans-Georg Gadamer, Gadamer's philosophical hermeneutics played a major role in shaping Jauss's thought. Because the range of Gadamer's hermeneutics is vast and has generated numerous studies on various aspects of his thought, it is not possible to discuss the entire breadth of his thought. Therefore, I have had to limit my discussion of his work to those aspects that are particularly relevant to reception theory. I have also attempted to select areas of Gadamer's work that have not received the same amount of attention as other areas have. The first chapter will focus on Gadamer's rehabilitation of tradition and, more specifically, how we actually engage tradition in a dialogue and what type of knowledge we can hope to ascertain from such a dialogue. The second chapter will build upon this and will probe two issues; the role that the logic of question and answer plays in Jauss's hermeneutic, and the epistemological nature of hermeneutical understanding. The third chapter explores the categories of play, performance and provocation in regard

---

28. "Of course, some people should always specialize in origins, but is it reasonable that thousands do it all the time?" Räisänen, "The Effective 'History' of the Bible," 323–24.

29. Ibid., 324.

to whether a tradition of interpretation is constituted by continuity or diversity in to how it understands its past.

Chapter 4 marks a major turn in this study. From that point forward the focus will be primarily on select aspects of Hans Robert Jauss's literary and hermeneutical theory of *Rezeptionsgeschichte*. Because of its importance, the fourth chapter will concentrate on Jauss's seminal lecture "Literary Theory as a Challenge to Literary Theory." Chapter 5 will assess three facets of reception theory as Jauss's work matured. These his development of the concept of horizons of expectations, three different levels of reading, and the role that aesthetic experience plays in hermeneutical understanding.

And finally, lest I become guilty of Jeffrey Stout's complaint that all too often modern theology has "been reduced to seemingly endless methodological foreplay," I shall attempt to demonstrate the relevance of reception theory for biblical studies.[30] Chapters 6 and 7 not only examine a conceptual feature of reception theory but also include case studies that are related to those concepts. Chapter 6 focuses on how Thomas Kuhn's work on paradigm shifts was appropriated by Jauss to explain why the history of a text's interpretation is marked by radical shifts in how it is understood. The second half of this chapter explores the reception history of the "moon-struck" boy in Matthew 17. The summit-dialogue of authors is a concept that Jauss developed to explore the living dialogue that takes place between significant interpreters of a work. This idea takes center stage in chapter 7 and will be applied to the post-history of the parable of the Wedding Feast from Matthew 22. Finally, chapter 8 considers the relevance of the classic for biblical hermeneutics. If chapter 6 investigated the reception history of a word's interpretation, and chapter 7 explored a passage, the eighth chapter expands our attention to consider the entire Bible and authoritative interpretations.

---

30. Stout, *The Flight from Authority*, 147.

1

The Cultivation of Tradition

THE FLUX AND FLOW OF TIME CREATES AN INTERESTING SET OF PROB-
lems when we try to interpret something. These challenges were perceived as early as Heracleitus, who was quoted by Socrates as saying,
"all things move and nothing remains still, and he likens the universe to
the current of a river, saying that you cannot step twice into the same
stream."[1] René Descartes, however, believed that he could climb out of
the river and onto solid land. As such, he thought he found a place to
stand outside and above the flow of history and tradition on the firm
ground of reason and doubt. Gadamer marks a return to Heracleitus.
There is no solid ground on which an observer can stand alongside
this river; we are always captives of its current. In *Truth and Method*,
Gadamer has two goals. On the one hand, he wants to demonstrate that
there is no solid ground from which one could gain an objective view-
point to look down and survey the flow of history. On the other hand,
he attempts to construct a hermeneutic that is not only cognizant of
our being carried along in the river, but also to show how this situation
is actually constitutive of how we understand our world and what is
handed down to us from the past.

To raise the question about Gadamer's significance for any hermeneutical theory may seem almost facile. Richard Bernstein writes,
"Building on the work of Heidegger, or rather drawing on themes that
are implicit in Heidegger and developing them in novel ways, Gadamer's
book is one of the most comprehensive and subtle statements of meaning and the scope of hermeneutics to appear in our time."[2] Gadamer's
work plays two extremely important roles in reception theory. First,

---

1. Plato *Cratylus* 402b.
2. Bernstein, *Beyond Objectivism and Relativism*, 34.

I

Gadamer laid the philosophical foundation that all contemporary hermeneutical theories either build upon or engage in dialogue. Second (perhaps more significant for this study), he was Hans Robert Jauss's mentor. Thus, we must understand Gadamer as a prelude to Jauss.

The primary goal of this and the following chapter is to answer the question, "What does our knowledge of the past consist of and how is this shaped and handed down within a tradition according to Gadamer?" In order to answer this question I have selected four lines of thought in Gadamer's work. I hope to show how Gadamer rehabilitates the concept of tradition from the antithesis that the Enlightenment set up between tradition and reason. The second section will focus on Gadamer's appropriation of Hegel's ideas of experience and sublation and the role they play in how knowledge is historically transmitted. Hegel's thought on the open nature of dialogue is appropriated by Gadamer to illustrate how we should approach our tradition and the texts that are handed down in it. The relevance of Collingwood's logic of question and answer for hermeneutics is the subject of the first half of the next chapter. This plays a central role not only in Gadamer but also Jauss's hermeneutical frameworks. The final section of the next chapter will examine the question, what are the characteristics of hermeneutical understanding?

The Rehabilitation of Tradition

An Ontological Approach to Tradition

Tradition has not enjoyed a very positive reception in philosophical thought since the dawn of the Enlightenment. For Descartes, errors in thought, irrational ideas, and prejudices were the result of either the hastiness of thought or were un-examined ideas passed down through tradition. Because these prejudices lacked methodological justification, they were an unreliable and unfounded source of knowledge. Gadamer summarized this view toward tradition and the prejudices contained in it: "there is one prejudice of the Enlightenment that defines its essence: the fundamental prejudice of the Enlightenment is the prejudice against prejudice itself, which denies tradition its power."[3] This view is not limited to the period of the Enlightenment; it reverberates to this day. "The category of tradition is essentially feudal. . . . Tradition is opposed to

---

3. Gadamer, *Truth and Method*, 270.

rationality, even though the one took shape in the other."[4] The irony
is that the Enlightenment "launched the tradition of living without a
tradition."[5] The result of this line of reasoning has been that we have lost
the innocence by which we once appropriated traditional concepts and
are alienated from our past.[6]

In contrast, Gadamer views prejudices as a constitutive element
of human existence and, as such, the prejudices we inherit are neither
negative nor positive in nature. The hermeneutical concept of prejudice
comes from the German *Vorurteil* (pre-judgement). Gadamer defined
Vorurteil as the cognitive processes and ways of understanding the world
that function in our thinking at a pre-conceptual or pre-reflective level.
An example of these prejudices may be how close we stand to another
person when we talk to them, our cultural ideas on what it means to be
a human, or what counts as real. Every act of understanding involves
and calls upon these pre-judgments that we possess before we enter
into that act of interpretation. Georgia Warnke encapsulates Gadamer's
thoughts in this area when she writes, "before I begin consciously to
interpret a text or grasp the meaning of an object, I have already placed
it within a certain context (*Vorhabe*), approached it from a certain
perspective (*Vorsicht*) and conceived of it in a certain way (*Vorgriff*)."[7]
And in a manner similar to Heidegger's analysis of the fore-structure
of understanding, prejudice has a three-fold character in Gadamer's
work: (1) we inherit them from our tradition, (2) they constitute who
we are now, and (3) they have an anticipatory nature in that they allow
us to project possibilities for understanding.[8] As, such tradition is an
ontological category.

> [H]istory does not belong to us; we belong to it. Long before we
> understand ourselves through the process of self-examination,
> we understand ourselves in a self-evident way in the family, so-
> ciety, and the state in which we live.... The self-awareness of the
> individual is only a flickering in the closed circuits of historical
> life. That is why the prejudices [*Vorurteil*] of the individual, far

4. Adorno, "On Tradition," 100.

5. Lundin, "Interpreting the Orphans," in *The Promise of Hermeneutics*, 3.

6. Gadamer, *Truth and Method*, xxiv.

7. Warnke, *Gadamer*, 77.

8. Bernstein, "From Hermeneutics to Praxis," 90.

more than his judgments, constitute the historical reality of his being.[9]

In this sense, prejudice is the pre-conscious cumulative effect of all the judgments we have made and inherited from our tradition that we may not be aware of, but which constitute our horizon of understanding.[10] The important point is that we become aware of that we dwell within a tradition. Once we accept this premise we can begin to appreciate how our prejudices both enable and shape how we understand the past. Every act of understanding takes place within the constraints of our customs, language, and tradition, and invokes possible projections for understanding. Thus, understanding is, as Gadamer would say, an act of *effective historical understanding*.[11]

One of the major challenges that Gadamer seeks to address is the notion that everything is historically conditioned and, as a result, historical knowledge is reduced to a relativity of competing opinions.[12] This fragmentation of the past is an inheritance bequeathed to us from nineteenth-century historicism. History, as a discipline, adopted a positivistic approach and rejected Hegel's notion that there is a higher order of rationality governing history.[13] It focused on the individual events or elements of history, not universal history. "Historical consciousness is interested in knowing, not how men, people, or states develop in general, but, quite on the contrary, how *this* man, *this* people, or *this* state became what *it* is; how *each* of these particulars could come to pass and end up specifically there."[14] Because of the attention given to the particulars we suffer from an historical self-estrangement from our own past and the chain of tradition is fragmented into a series of unrelated, broken segments.[15]

9. Gadamer, *Truth and Method*, 276–77.

10. A horizon of understanding can be defined as all that can be conceived of or understood by someone at any particular time in history.

11. Gadamer, *Truth and Method*, 264; Gadamer, "The Heritage of Hegel," in *Reason in the Age of Science*, 41.

12. Gadamer, "The Problem of Historical Consciousness," 110.

13. Gadamer, "Hegel's Philosophy and Its Aftereffects until Today," in *Hegel's Dialectic*, 26.

14. Gadamer, "The Problem of Historical Consciousness," 116, emphasis added.

15. Gadamer, "The Heritage of Hegel," in *Reason in the Age of Science*, 44; Auerochs, "*Gadamer über Tradition*," 295.

One of the more significant ways that Martin Heidegger shaped Gadamer's thought is the way in which he interpreted human existence and history by means of absolute temporality. Heidegger fully developed the historical nature of human existence and provided a phenomenological epistemology to justify such an approach. He pushed the idea of our temporal existence to its logical conclusion: "What being is was to be determined from within the horizon of time . . . But it was more than that. Heidegger's thesis was that being itself is time."[16] History is not something that we can transcend; rather, we exist historically. It is not something like a book that can be possessed. History possesses us. Our historical existence not only allows us to study the past, but is also the common ground between the knower and the known. This does not mean that there is some form of "homogeneity" between the past and the present (which would lead to a psychological hermeneutic along the lines of Schleiermacher or Dilthey). Heidegger's epistemology is grounded in the idea that both the knower and the known share a common mode of being, "they both have the mode of being of historicity."[17] It is precisely because we "belong" to history and a tradition that we have an interest in studying history and are capable of carrying that desire out.

The tradition a person belongs to constitutes his or her self-understanding. As a result every interpretative act is performed in a certain historical horizon with prejudices that are related to that horizon. Tradition is part of our "thrownness" and it is essential that we recognize our place in our tradition and cultivate it, according to Gadamer. "Even the most genuine and pure tradition does not persist because of the inertia of what once existed. It needs to be affirmed, embraced, cultivated."[18] To understand a text from the past is to participate in an event of tradition, a process in which the past and the present are mediated. Following Heidegger, Gadamer shows how every act of understanding is also projective by nature. The interpreter projects a meaning from the possibilities that he sees from within his horizon.[19] "The general structure of understanding is concretized in historical

16. Gadamer, *Truth and Method*, 257.

17. Ibid., 261.

18. Ibid., 281.

19. Ibid., 264.

understanding, in that the concrete bonds of custom and tradition and the corresponding possibilities of one's own future become effective in understanding itself."[20]

The Rehabilitation of Prejudice and Tradition

The conclusion that Gadamer reached is that the artificial antithesis between tradition and reason or historical research should be cast aside.[21] The mistake made in the Enlightenment's doctrine of tradition was to assume that it was not a trustworthy source of knowledge. Our respect for those who came before us and their authority could lead us into error just as effectively as hastiness in thought. The impact of this line of thought on biblical hermeneutics was profound. The radical thrust of the Enlightenment movement was to "assert itself against the Bible and dogmatic interpretation of it." This movement was not primarily aimed against tradition, but rather its goal was to understand the Bible "rationally and without prejudice."[22] As a result, reason became the ground for authority and the arbiter of the truth claims of the Bible and the Christian tradition.

The influence of the Enlightenment in this area is still felt today even though nineteenth-century Romanticism transfigured it. In contrast to the Enlightenment's striving to free itself from the dogma of tradition, Romanticism embraced the earlier ages of myth as reflecting Christian chivalry and a society closer to nature. "These romantic revaluations give rise to historical science in the nineteenth century. It no longer measures the past by the standards of the present, as if they were absolute, but it ascribes to past ages a value of their own and can even acknowledge their superiority in one respect or another."[23] However, in broad terms, Romanticism shared the same goal as the Enlightenment: the objective knowledge of the historical world which was "on par" with the objective knowledge in the natural sciences. The result was the same for both movements: a break in the continuity of meaning passed down

---

20. Ibid., 264; Pannenberg, *Theology and the Philosophy of Science*, 163–65.

21. Gadamer, *Truth and Method*, 282.

22. Ibid., 272. This criticism of the Enlightenment can be traced as far back as Hegel. Hegel, *Phenomenology of Spirit*, 329–34.

23. Gadamer, *Truth and Method*, 275.

in tradition. What could not be accepted as true according to reason was perceived as reflecting the values of a previous age.[24]

Gadamer further criticized Romanticism for the manner in which it viewed a text as an expression of the genius of the author. Texts were reduced to objectified residues left behind by a creative spirit, like footprints in the sand. "Texts, works of art and the like were thus no longer considered claims to truth but rather seen as the concrete embodiment of creative genius."[25] A text was an objectified construct that was always less than the creative thought that produced it. Understanding a text was a matter of retracing the path from the text back to the creative thought of the author. Friedrich Schleiermacher exemplified this approach in Gadamer's opinion. "Schleiermacher's particular contribution is psychological interpretation. It is ultimately a divinatory process, a placing of oneself within the whole framework of the author, an apprehension of the 'inner origin' of the composition of a work, a re-creation of the creative act."[26] The influence of Schleiermacher's hermeneutic can still be heard today in the work of authors such as E. D. Hirsch and numerous biblical interpreters who follow his lead. Instead of using the term "divination," contemporary authors use the term "authorial intention." In order to correctly understand the meaning of the Bible we must understand what the author intended when they composed it.

There is an underlying Cartesian program in Romantic hermeneutics. By objectifying what ought to confront you (the text) you emasculate it. The text is detached from the creative act by defining it as an artifact of someone's thought. On the one hand, Gadamer praises the Romantic tradition's stress on creativity. On the other hand, he criticizes Romanticism, because in the end, it leaves us only with traces or relics of the creative mind, like the vapor trails of a jet in the sky. This objectification of what has been handed down to us from the past was adopted by nineteenth-century historiography. The result was the same for both Romanticism and historicism when it came to interpreting a text: "The individual text has no value in itself but only serves as a source—

24. Ibid., 275–76.

25. Warnke, *Gadamer,* 73.

26. Gadamer, *Truth and Method,* 187. This criticism is valid of Schleiermacher's later work, but Kimmerle's edition of Schleiermacher's notes on hermeneutics from 1805–1819 reveal that his earlier work was more concerned with the identity of thought and language. Schleiermacher, *Hermeneutics,* edited by Kimmerle.

i.e., only as material conveying knowledge of the past historical context, just like other silent relics of the past."[27] The legacy of Romanticism and historicism's objectification of the text is still felt today in biblical studies. "The best modern commentary series continue to produce technical studies of biblical books as ancient texts and as objects of detached critical analysis."[28] This raises two questions that we need to wrestle with if we adopt this approach. Is the New Testament just an artifact from the era of the primitive church? And, is this the primary interpretive approach in which we should train the next generation of theologians and church leaders?

The Enlightenment perceived a "mutually exclusive antithesis between authority and reason."[29] This assumption was justified if authority displaced one's use of reason, but it overlooked the fact that truth can be found in authority. This was the mistake of the Enlightenment; it understood authority as blind obedience. While it is true that distortions and false prejudices may be handed down through a tradition, a tradition also preserves what is true. In a sense, Descartes himself admitted this when he accepted that our parents and teachers instilled ethical values in us. However, he missed how the very manner by which he narrated his argument in the *Meditations* employed "representational forms of thought" that were part of his tradition.[30] Even his *Cogito ergo sum* ("I think, therefore I am") was from Augustine.[31] As Alasdair MacIntyre writes, we live our lives on "a stage we did not design."[32]

The acceptance of the authority of tradition is not blind obedience but the acknowledgement that those who precede us may have had better insights and judgments than we do. It is an acknowledgement of our finitude and that the knowledge passed down in tradition may contain

27. Gadamer, *Truth and Method*, 198, emphasis added. "The great achievements of romanticism — the revival of the past, the discovery of the voices of the peoples in their songs, the collecting of fairy tales and legends, the cultivation of ancient customs, the discovery of world views implicit in languages, the study of the 'religion and wisdom of India'—all contributed to the rise of historical research, which was slowly, step by step, transformed from intuitive revival into detached historical knowledge." Ibid., 275

28. Bockmuehl, "A Commentator's Approach to the 'Effective History' of Philippians," 57.

29. Gadamer, *Truth and Method*, 277.

30. Gebauer and Wolf, *Mimesis*, 145; MacIntyre, "Epistemological Crisis," 58–60.

31. See MacIntyre, *Three Rival Versions of Moral Enquiry*, 98.

32. MacIntyre, *After Virtue*, 213.

a wider perspective or be better informed about the subject-matter than we are.[33]

> It [authority] rests on acknowledgment and hence on an act of reason itself which, aware of its limitations, trusts to the better insight of others. Authority in this sense, properly understood, has nothing to do with blind obedience to commands. Indeed, authority has to do not with obedience but rather with knowledge.[34]

Underpinning this concept of authority and tradition is the idea that what is passed down is not irrational or arbitrary but contains truth claims that can be validated.[35] In this manner, Gadamer presents an apology for tradition based on epistemological and phenomenological considerations.

If the Enlightenment represents one extreme in respect to tradition, Romanticism represents the opposite. Romanticism defended the authority that tradition has over our behavior and attitude. For example, morality was not based on reason but was handed down in tradition and received by us. Tradition was the antithesis to the Enlightenment's concept of the freedom that reason delivered. In this respect, tradition was a constitutive element of human life, much like nature was. "And in fact it is to romanticism that we owe this correction of the Enlightenment: that tradition has a justification that lies beyond rational grounding and in large measure determines our institutions and attitudes."[36]

However, once again, there is an underlying antithesis between reason and tradition that makes this position untenable.[37] Romanticism held to a faith in the growth and development of tradition that was independent of and superior to reason. In reply to this, Gadamer argues that reason operates within a tradition and that tradition is not as dominant as Romanticists believed. Even the best traditions do not exist simply because they possess some sort of internal force or quality

33. Gadamer, *Truth and Method*, 278–80.

34. Ibid., 279.

35. Ibid., 280.

36. Ibid., 281.

37. Weinsheimer, *Gadamer's Hermeneutics*, 169. Habermas follows the Enlightenment's concept of reason in that reason is what frees us from the repression of tradition and other forms of domination and distortion in communication. Misgeld, "Modernity and Hermeneutics," 167–72.

based on the fact that they come from the past. Traditions need to be preserved and this requires that reason and freedom are operative in the transmission of a tradition.

There is some debate over how to understand Gadamer at this point. Jürgen Habermas criticized Gadamer for subordinating the power of reason and reflection to tradition. For Habermas, prejudices are shackles on our mind that need to be submitted to critical scrutiny.[38] Thus, there needs to be a separation between reason and tradition, if we are going to have any possibility of criticizing our tradition.[39] Richard Rorty basically agreed with Habermas's idea that prejudice constrains reason, but celebrated it. Because of the temporal and cultural conditioning of all knowledge, he argued that there is no common ground on which rationality can operate. Therefore, philosophical discourse is reduced to talking about what looks like reason from our cultural perspective.[40]

Both of these views miss Gadamer's position concerning the operation of reason in tradition. I will discuss this area in greater depth in the next section of this chapter, but for now it is enough to say that Gadamer rejects any form of polarization between reason and tradition. Evidence for this can be seen in the way he defends tradition by means of an epistemological argument. Tradition is a valid form of knowledge because it is reasonable to accept that someone may possess more and better information than we do.[41] Our relationship to tradition is not one of passive obedience but active dialogue, which requires the use of reason. According to Gadamer, the goal of reflection is not to undermine tradition's influence but to connect us with it in a more appropriate manner.[42]

To a large degree, Gadamer's hermeneutical endeavor is an attempt to find an approach that does justice to both tradition and reason. There must be a unity between the "effect (*Wirkung*) of a living tradition and

38. Nicholson, "Answers to Critical Theory," 156.

39. Habermas, "A Review of Gadamer's *Truth and Method*," 358–63. This is not to suggest that Habermas wants to undermine tradition; rather, he wants to allow some manner by which to judge tradition.

40. Rorty, *Philosophy and the Mirror of Nature*, 364–65.

41. Kisiel, "Ideology Critique and Phenomenology," 152–57.

42. Gadamer, "The Problem of Historical Consciousness," 111; Gadamer, "Truth in the Human Sciences," 29.

the effect of historical study."[43] In order to do justice to this concept, we cannot conceive of tradition as a new hermeneutical innovation. Rather, we must regard it as "what has always constituted the human relation to the past. In other words, we have to recognize the element of tradition in historical research and inquire into its hermeneutic productivity."[44] Historical research is not an abstract discipline but is organically connected with its subject matter.

Gadamer's Appropriation of Hegel's Dialectic

Hegel's Dialectic: Experience and Sublation

One of the challenges that confronted Gadamer was how to overcome the notion that a historian was a detached, objective interpreter who approached tradition as an object and to reinstate a living relationship between the interpreter and their tradition. One hundred years earlier Schleiermacher and Hegel had also addressed the problem of estrangement from tradition, which resulted from the Enlightenment and Romanticism. However, they proposed two very different solutions. Schleiermacher maintained that whenever we interpret a text we must reconstruct the original context in which the work was originally understood. Because the intelligibility of any work is tied to its original context of communication, some of the text's potential for meaning is lost if we do not take into consideration this aspect of the text's history. If we accept the premise that a text or work of art is not a timeless aesthetic object, but its significance is grounded in its belonging to a "world," then this would appear to imply that we must reconstruct the original context in order to reveal the true meaning of the text or work.

Historical reconstructions along these lines offer two interpretive contributions. First, they allow us to recover what may have been lost or forgotten about that text (why it was written, what questions or situations it was originally written to address). And second, this type of study can offer corrections to mis-readings or distortions that may have crept into the interpretive history of that text.

43. Gadamer, *Truth and Method*, 282.

44. Ibid., 283, emphasis added. This is important since Gadamer defines hermeneutics in the following manner: "Hermeneutics may be precisely defined as the art of bringing what is said or written to speech again" (*Reason in the Age of Science*, 119).

However, the historicity of our existence makes Schleiermacher's solution an illusion. What we end up with is a second creation—we do not arrive at how the original readers understood the text but rather an interpretation that arises from our historical and cultural horizon. It is like a painting that was removed from its original setting to become part of a museum's collection and then returned to the medieval church from which it was taken. What is reconstructed is not what once was but a tourist attraction.[45] Any attempt to reconstruct the original context in which a text was written will always be a reconstruction from within the horizon of the interpreter and will not be the same as the original context of understanding.

Hegel, in contrast to Schleiermacher, took the perspective that our relationship to works from the past are analogous to fruit picked from a tree. Fate presents these works to us like "beautiful fruit already picked from the tree, . . . as a girl might set the fruit before us." They are no longer connected to the "tree which bore them" but are handed to us through "the veiled recollection of that actual world."[46] Historical reconstruction of the past neither recreates the text's original context nor creates a living relationship with the past. "They [texts] remain fruit torn from the tree." This does not mean that Hegel denies the value of historical research. What Hegel is claiming is that tradition is not handed down to us through the process of historical reconstruction because it does not allow us to "enter into their very life."[47] Gadamer followed Hegel in this area. Historical reconstruction of the original context of a text can play an important function in helping us understand a text, but it is not the ground or primary means for understanding that text. "Integration, not restoration, is the true task of hermeneutics."[48]

Hegel fancifully compared the manner by which works of art and texts are transmitted through a tradition to a maid who serves us fruit from a platter. Just as she is "more and higher" than nature, which produced the fruit, so also "the Spirit of Fate that presents us with those works of art is more than the ethical life and the actual world of that nation, for it is the *inwardizing* in us of the Spirit which in them was still

45. Ibid., 167.
46. Hegel, *Phenomenology of Spirit*, 455.
47. Ibid., 456.
48. Palmer, *Hermeneutics*, 186.

[only] *outwardly* manifested."[49] Like most of Hegel's work, his thoughts in this area are very poetical in nature, if not a bit enigmatic. Gadamer understood Hegel to be claiming that the problem of understanding was not solved by means of historical reconstruction as Schleiermacher thought. The meaningfulness of past art, culture, and religion was lost by taking such an approach. This is because history studied the past in an external, lifeless manner in order to build up snapshot images of the outward manifestations of the past.[50] According to Hegel, what is alive cannot be known by objective methods and self-understanding arises from our involvement in life.

> Hegel quite rightly derives self-consciousness from life. What is alive is not such that a person could ever grasp it from outside, in its living quality. The only way to grasp life is, rather, to become inwardly aware of it. . . . Life is experienced only in the awareness of oneself, the inner consciousness of one's own living.[51]

In contrast to the objective goals of historicism, Hegel asserts that our connection with the past is constituted by remembering and internalizing it. For Hegel, this remembering and internalizing took place at the philosophical level of absolute mind or knowledge. The self-consciousness of the spirit grasps the truth of a text or work of art in a "higher way" than the contextual relationships in which it was originally penned. Just as the maid who served the fruit is "more and higher" than the fruit on the platter, so a living connection with the past is "more and higher" than a methodological study of history. It is the self-penetration of the spirit through history which performs the process of passing on this understanding.[52] Thus, our interpretation of the past is more significant than the past itself. This is an important point for Gadamer. "Here Hegel states a definite truth, inasmuch as the essential nature of the historical

---

49. Hegel, *Phenomenology of Spirit*, 456; Gadamer, *Truth and Method*, 168.

50. Hegel, 454–56; see especially the analysis of the text by Findlay in *Phenomenology of Spirit*, 585.

51. Gadamer, *Truth and Method*, 253. For a fuller explication of Hegel's thought here in relation to the concept of self-consciousness, see Gadamer's article, "Hegel's Dialectic of Self-consciousness," in *Hegel's Dialectic*, 54–74.

52. Gadamer, *Truth and Method*, 167–68.

spirit consists not in the restoration of the past but in thoughtful mediation with contemporary life."[53]

Hegel's Dialectic

The means by which the past is remembered and internalized in the
present is achieved through a dialectical process. Hegel's dialectic involves bringing two antithetical ideas into relationship with each other
in such a manner that it yields a synthesis of the two. "For Hegel the
point of dialectic is that precisely by pushing a position to the point
of self-contradiction it makes possible the transition to a higher truth
which unites the sides of that contradiction: the power of spirit lies
in synthesis as the mediation of all contradictions."[54] Beginning with
concept A, we find that it contains the contradictory concept B when
we conceptually analyze A. In the same manner concept B is antitheti-
cally related to A. The dialectical synthesis that results from this form of
analysis is concept C which unites concepts A and B.[55] Both A and B are
sublated into the higher concept C.

For Gadamer, Hegel's concept of sublation provides an explanation for the continuity we encounter in history.[56] While Hegel realized
that the term sublation, *Aufhebung*, possessed a broad semantic range
of meaning from "negating" to "preserving," he primarily used of it to
focus on how concepts, ideas, or truth were preserved through this process of negation.[57] "For Hegel, however, the meaning shifts and comes to
imply preservation of all the elements of truth, which assert themselves
within the contradictions and even an elevation of these elements to a

---

53. Ibid., 168–69.

54. Gadamer, *Hegel's Dialectic*, 105.

55. Forster, "Hegel's Dialectical Method," 131–32. "In a wide sense Hegel's dialectic
involves three steps: (1) one or more concepts or categories are taken as fixed, sharply
defined and distinct from each other. This is the stage of understanding. (2) When we
reflect on such categories, one or more contradictions emerge in them. This is the stage
of dialectic proper, or of dialectical or negative reason. (3) The result of this dialectic is
a new, higher category, which embraces the earlier categories and resolves the contradiction involved in them. This is the stage of speculation or positive reason." Inwood,
"Dialectic," in *A Hegel Dictionary*, 81–82.

56. Weinsheimer, *Gadamer's Hermeneutic*, 98.

57. Inwood, "Sublation," in *A Hegel Dictionary*, 284. For an example of how Hegel
uses this term in different manners, see Hegel, *Hegel's Science of Logic*, 106–8.

truth encompassing and uniting everything true."[58] Contradictions and oppositions in thought were capable of being mediated and sublimated through the power of synthesis in reason. The process of sublation resulted in a modification to the original meaning or sense of the original categories (*A* and *B*). It was this modification in meaning that both allowed the original categories or ideas to no longer be contradictory, and also allowed the new category (*C*) to contain them.[59] Hegel's dialectic provided an explanation for diversity (and contradictions) in history while, at the same time, it provided an impulse through the dialectical process toward the creation of unity. There is a continuity to history because reason is capable of reconciling "the most alien, inscrutable, and inimical forces of history."[60]

Hegel's dialectic also avoided the problem of Romanticism that reduced a text to an externalized, objectified relic from the past—the fruit on the plate. By contrast, Hegel's dialectical method is always moving forward. An idea or thought is overtaken in sublation before it is objectified. In his system, a text is never reduced to a relic but is part of the ongoing dialectical process of history. The strength of Hegel's dialectic is its reflexive and integrating power which overcame the problems inherent in hermeneutics of reconstructing the original meaning of a text.

Gadamer Sublates Hegel

In his appropriation of Hegel, Gadamer is not interested in reinstating Hegel's philosophy but in attempting to learn something from him.[61] This can be seen by the manner that Gadamer adapts Hegel's ideas in all three parts of *Truth and Method*. In part one, Hegel's concept of *Aufhebung* was incorporated in Gadamer's concept of *Bildung*, the term Gadamer chose to best express the type of understanding involved in the humanities. The concept of the hermeneutic circle, which includes an outward and returning movement, is employed to explain how understanding takes place. In the outward movement, we recognize ourselves in what is alien: we find a place to be at home in it. In the returning movement, we realize that we have changed in the process of

58. Gadamer, *Hegel's Dialectic*, 105.
59. Forster, "Hegel's Dialectical Method," 132–33
60. Gadamer, *Hegel's Dialectic*, 105.
61. Gadamer, "Hegel's Philosophy and Its Aftereffects," in *Hegel's Dialectic*, 27.

understanding and are no longer the same, our horizon has shifted or expanded. Like Hegel's concept of *Aufhebung*, *Bildung* is not fixed but involves a movement of alienation (negation) and reversal in which our understanding is expanded or transfigured.[62] All life is characterized by the hermeneutical circle of excursion and return, differentiation and assimilation.

> Life is defined by the fact that what is alive differentiates itself from the world in which it lives and with which it remains connected, and preserves itself in this differentiation. What is alive preserves itself by drawing into itself everything that is outside it. Everything that is alive nourishes itself on what is alien to it. The fundamental fact of being alive is assimilation. Differentiation, then, is at the same time non-differentiation. The alien is appropriated.[63]

Thus, experience is dialectical in nature. It is characterized by the hermeneutical circle of excursion and return, differentiation and assimilation. When we assimilate the alien, our preconceptions are negated, restructured, or expanded. Our awareness, understanding of the world, and self-understanding is constantly restructured in this hermeneutical circle.[64]

Gadamer repeats many of these themes in part two of *Truth and Method* where he develops the concept of the fusion of horizons. The basic movement of understanding is the hermeneutical circle, a constant movement from whole to the part and then back to the whole again. We construct a provisional understanding of a sentence or text before we read it. This expectation is open to correction as we read the text and a new expectation of the text is shaped in the interaction between the reading process and our prior expectations.[65] In our encounter with a text, our prejudices are called into question and we encounter a tension between our present and the past of the text. Understanding occurs

---

62. Ibid., 10–18. "Thus what constitutes the essence of Bildung is clearly not alienation as such, but the return to oneself—which presupposes alienation, to be sure. However, Bildung is not to be understood only as the process of historically raising the mind to the universal; it is at the same time the element within which the educated man (Gebildete) moves." Ibid., 14

63. Gadamer, *Truth and Method*, 252.

64. Gadamer, *Hegel's Dialectic*, 54–74.

65. Gadamer, "*Vom Zirkel des Verstehens*," 24, 28.

when we are able to experience a fusion of two horizons which involves our rising to a wider horizon, one in which we are able to encompass both horizons. Understanding is, therefore, primarily not an act of *re-constructing* the past, but is a *constructive* activity through the fusion of horizons. "In a tradition this process of fusion is continually going on, for the old and new are always combining into something of living value, without either being explicitly foregrounded from the other."[66]

Part three of *Truth and Method* centers on Gadamer's philosophy of language. Language surrounds us like the air we breathe and is what allows us to be at home in or familiar with the world. Heidegger referred to language as the "house of Being." Language is not only the locus of our belonging in the world, it is also the medium through which every act of understanding occurs.[67]

> The more language is a living operation, the less we are aware of it. Thus it follows from the self-forgetfulness of language that its real being consists in what is said in it. *What is said in it constitutes the common world in which we live and to which the whole great chain of tradition reaching us from the literature of foreign languages, living as well as dead.* The real being of language is that into which we are taken up when we hear it—what is said.[68]

While our experience of the world is bound to our language, this does not mean that our language prescribes a circumference to the limits of what or how we can understand. Instead, language is what gives us the "capacity to embrace the most varied relationships of life."[69]

Gadamer uses the analogy of what occurs in translation to explain the linguistic nature of understanding. Understanding always involves the arriving at some form of agreement about the subject-matter in the medium of a language. For the translator, this task is complicated by the fact that she must bring into one language the subject-matter that the text is referring to in another language. In doing this, the translator must make a linguistic choice since she realizes that she is not able to express in her translation all the nuances conveyed in the original language's

66. Gadamer, *Truth and Method*, 306.

67. Ibid., 389; Gadamer, *Philosophical Hermeneutics*, 239; Gadamer, *Hegel's Dialectic*, 97.

68. Gadamer, *Reason in the Age of Science*, 33, emphasis added.

69. Gadamer, *Truth and Method*, 448.

words. She must decide which elements to highlight, flatten, or clarify in the translation.[70] In this process of translation, or interpretation, understanding "takes place in the medium of language that allows the object to come into words and yet is at the same time the interpreter's own language."[71] As a result, the language of the interpreter is transposed, or mediated, with the subject-matter that was expressed in the text's original language. The words and terms that the interpreter possessed before the act of translation undergo an expansion of meaning as they are utilized in the translation to express the subject-matter of the text. The use of the word "sublation" previously in this chapter is an example. When we use this English term to translate Hegel's works from German into English the meaning of the English term "sublation" is mediated with and expanded to include the philosophical nuances that Hegel was arguing with his use of the German *Aufhebung*. Thus, "understanding always includes an element of application and thus produces an ongoing process of concept formation."[72]

There are several conceptual problems in Hegel's system that Gadamer sought to resolve. For Hegel, the dialectical process of history is a dialectical movement of the Spirit (*Geist*) of knowledge in history. In our experience of the world, we continually undergo a reversal of consciousness as part of the dialectical process. For Hegel, this experience of consciousness naturally leads to a higher form of knowledge in which there eventually will be nothing other or alien to itself. "That is why the dialectic of experience must end in that overcoming of all experience which is attained in absolute knowledge—i.e., in the complete identity of consciousness and the object."[73] Gadamer appeals to Heidegger to correct Hegel at this point. Heidegger opposed the seductive appeal of dialectic that domesticated every conflicting concept into a higher form of knowing, absolute Spirit. Against Hegel's concept

---

70. Ibid., 385–87.

71. Ibid., 389.

72. Ibid., 403, emphasis added. "Words are the tradition of their application: they preserve the occasion and subject matter of specific occasions of utterance. The historical world leaves an indelible mark on the word, so that language cannot be understood if divorced from what it says." Weinsheimer, *Philosophical Hermeneutics and Literary Theory*, 113–14.

73. Gadamer, *Truth and Method*, 355.

of absolute knowledge, Heidegger juxtaposed the finitude of human knowledge and existence.[74]

While there is a great deal of insight in Hegel's concept of experience, Gadamer contends that the dialectical process should be seen in terms of "the linguistically of human being in the world," not in terms of self-consciousness.[75] History does not demonstrate any form of movement toward absolute knowledge. Instead it reveals aspects of both progress and regression. We seem to forget as much as we learn. For Heidegger, the manner by which the Western philosophical tradition forgot the question of Being is the most significant demonstration of this point. Just because we come chronologically later in history does not mean that we can claim to know more or have better knowledge than those who preceded us. "In this light Heidegger's historical self-consciousness appears as the most extreme counterthrust possible against the project of absolute knowledge . . . the project which Hegel makes basic to his philosophy."[76]

According to Gadamer, the historical nature of human existence is characterized by experiences that negate our expectations. "Real experience is that whereby man becomes aware of his finiteness. In it are discovered the limits of the power and the self-knowledge of his planning reason. . . . Genuine experience is experience of one's historicity."[77] Experience is part of the historical nature of human existence and, as such, it is part of the finite nature of human existence and should reveal this finitude to us. Experience should teach us to be open to new experiences and equip us to learn from them. In this way, we gain the insight that the future is open to us (since our expectations and plans are limited) and that we should be open to the past as well. "Hermeneutical experience is concerned with tradition."[78]

Tradition (and the knowledge it passes down) is not a cumulative process for Heidegger or Gadamer. It is not a steady march towards a higher, 'truer' understanding of a text or the past. The knowledge tradition passes down takes a serpentine path, with twists, turns, and dead

74. Heidegger, *Being and Time*, 79–80, 385–87.

75. Palmer, *Hermeneutics*, 165–66.

76. Gadamer, *Hegel's Dialectic*, 107.

77. Gadamer, *Truth and Method*, 357.

78. Ibid., 359.

ends taking place as a result of how the past and present are mediated in the finitude or human existence. As a result, Gadamer declares, "It is enough to say that we understand in a different way, if we understand at all."[79]

I/Thou and Slave/Master

We do not experience tradition as we experience an object or process that we can learn to govern (or place on the lab table and examine scientifically). A better analogy to explain how we experience of tradition is that of a dialogue. In a conversation we come to realize how different our dialogue partner is from us. In a similar manner, as we study a text from the past we should be struck by the historical and cultural distance between us and the original author and readers. We realize the otherness, or the Thou addressing us through the text. "In the hermeneutical sphere the parallel to this experience of the Thou is what we generally call historical consciousness."[80] Weinsheimer summarized Gadamer's argument in the following manner:

> Tradition is not simply a series of events that one comes to know; it is expression that one comes to understand. Historical tradition is language and expresses itself like a Thou who is the other that self-knowledge requires for self-understanding. Hermeneutic experience consists in dialogue with tradition . . .[81]

In order to clearly explicate his position, Gadamer discusses three different kinds of I/Thou relationships. The first is where we learn to make predictions about the other's character based on our experiences of them and use this knowledge to govern our relationship with them. The problem with this is that we reduce the other to a means to reach our ends and runs into Kant's categorical imperative that the other should never be treated as a means to an end. We objectify tradition if we approach it in this manner. Since this approach can only recognize

---

79. Ibid., 297.

80. Ibid., 360. "As one experiences the meaning of a text, he comes to understand a heritage which has briefly addressed him as something over against him, yet as something which is at the same time a part of that nonobjectifiable stream of experiences and history in which he stands." Palmer, *Hermeneutics*, 197.

81. Weinsheimer, *Gadamer's Hermeneutic*, 205.

what is typical or regular, it limits what we can learn from tradition. The result is that it flattens out and constrains the possibilities for learning in the hermeneutical experience.

The second form of the I/Thou relationship occurs when we claim to know what the other is saying from their point of view or even claim to understand our conversation partner better than they understand themselves. This robs the other of his or her individuality and is a reflection of our effort to dominate them. "The claim to understand the other person in advance functions to keep the other person's claim at a distance."[82] Jeremy Begbie concisely summarizes the second form of the I/Thou relationship: "In 'monologue' the individual manipulates or is manipulated: one person treats the other as a means to an end, such that the other becomes self-confirmatory. The other's otherness becomes 'a repetition of a previously private co-ordinated understanding.'"[83]

We fall into the second form of I/Thou relationship with the past when we presuppose that history is governed by our preconceptions of what is possible and do not allow the past to make unique truth claims. This type of relationship with tradition characterized the work of many nineteenth-century thinkers and is clearly seen in the works of David Hume, who sought to deny the rationality of belief in miracles. He asserted that the belief a wise person placed in any event was proportional to the evidence for that event's occurrence. Being a Deist, he defined a miracle as a violation of the natural laws as he understood them. Because experience teaches us that the laws of nature operate in a consistent and reliable manner, an analogy to a miracle could never be found in the contemporary world. Therefore, Hume concluded, no matter how strongly an event like Jesus' resurrection was attested to by historical evidence, the probability of its occurrence would never approach the certainty we have from our daily experience of the world. In other words, we know from experience that dead men do not rise from the dead, therefore any account of this happening in the past must be questioned. As he put it, "Which is more likely—that a man rose from the dead or that this testimony is mistaken in some way?"[84]

---

82. Gadamer, *Truth and Method*, 360.

83. Begbie, *Theology, Music and Time*, 205.

84. Hume, *An Enquiry Concerning Human Understanding*, 10.1.118–123.

The spirit behind the second form of the I/Thou relationship is clearly felt within certain quarters of biblical interpretation. One hundred years after Hume, Rudolf Bultmann provides us with another example of how contemporary interpreters domesticate the biblical texts by placing their presuppositions about the world in a position that determines the validity of what the text may be claiming.

> All of our thinking today is shaped, irrevocably, by modern science. Blind acceptance of the New Testament mythology would be arbitrary.... Man's knowledge and mastery of the world have advanced to such an extent through science and technology, that it is no longer possible for anyone seriously to hold to the New Testament view of the world. It is impossible to use electric light and the radio, to avail ourselves of modern medical and surgical discoveries, and at the same time believe in the New Testament world of spirits and miracles.[85]

The late British historian R. G. Collingwood argued that if one took such a monological relationship to the past it precluded the possibility of learning anything new from the past. To claim that every event in the past must be analogous to how we understanding the world means that the entire range of every possible event occurs in the present (and every generation by extension of this line of thought). If this were the case, then what point would there be to study the past since all of those experiences would also be analogous to contemporary life? In other words, the past would have nothing to teach us that we didn't already know.[86]

The reduction of historical understanding to the second category of the I/Thou relationship is a criticism Gadamer levels against the dominance of a methodological approach to history. Taking a methodological approach means that we project in advance what could or could not have happened historically. The historian now has history in his or her power.[87]

If we are to remain open to the truth claims that a text like the Bible makes, then we cannot enter into dialogue with that text based on this second type of I/Thou relationship. To do so means that we know what the text is claiming better than the author did and shuts down any

---

85. Bultmann, *Kerygma and Myth*, 5. It is hard to imagine how insufferable Bultmann would have been if he had owned a personal computer or cell phone.

86. Collingwood, *The Idea of History*, 138–40.

87. Gadamer, *Truth and Method*, 452–53.

possibility of truly listening to, learning from, and being confronted by the truth claims of the text.

Effective-historical consciousness is characterized by the third variety of the I/Thou relationship. In this kind of relationship, we recognize the Thou by letting the other truly address us. This involves a two-way openness. Experience of this type is based on Hegel's thoughts concerning the independence and dependence of self-consciousness on others. According to Hegel, self-consciousness is independent and dependent in its relationships with others, to the extent that the other is acknowledged. This takes place through two hermeneutical movements. In the outward movement we find ourselves at home in the other when we recognize them for who they are. When self-consciousness returns to itself it cancels out the otherness of the other and its own "other self-consciousness." Thus, the final movement sublates (cancels out and yet still preserves) the outward and returning movements of self-consciousness in relation to the other person.[88] In coming to know the other, the self comes to a greater realization and more complete self-understanding of both the other and themselves.

In the transmission of this concept from Hegel to Gadamer, we can see that the importance of this was not lost on Heidegger.

> Hearing is constitutive for discourse ... Listening to ... is *Dasein's* existential way of Being-open as Being-with for Others. Indeed, hearing constitutes the primary and authentic way in which *Dasein* is open for its ownmost potentiality-for-Being—as in hearing the voice of a friend whom every *Dasein* carries with it ... Being-with develops in listening to one another [*Aufeinander-hören*], which can be done in several possible ways: following, going along with, and the privative modes of not-hearing, resisting, defying, and turning away.[89]

According to Gadamer, we should engage tradition in a manner similar to the way in which we genuinely engage someone in dialogue. The result is that the interpreter, in reading or studying a text (or any other element of tradition), comes to a greater realization and more complete understanding not only of the text but also of himself and his horizon.

---

88. Hegel, *Phenomenology of Spirit*, 111–12.
89. Heidegger, *Being and Time*, 206.

However, an individual cannot carry out this process by him or herself. It requires two participants.[90] The master/slave relationship exemplifies what happens if this dialectical relationship between two people is unbalanced.[91] One of them is reduced to that of a thing, or servant. The master's self-consciousness is related to their consumption of the things that are produced by the servant.[92] The servant, on the other hand, is held in subjection by the power of the master over the thing and over himself. While Hegel was interested in providing a sociological critique of human interaction (a person is fully self-conscious only when they recognize the consciousness and freedom of the other), Gadamer embraced these ideas to illustrate our relationship to tradition.[93] The reduction of the other person to a thing, Hegel's master/slave relationship, illustrates the first two categories of the I/Thou relationship. This reduction takes place through the imposition of the methods, such as the principles of historicism.

Gadamer comments, "When two people understand each other, this does not mean that one person 'understands' the other. Similarly, 'to hear and obey' (*auf jemanden hören*) does not mean simply that we do blindly what the other desires. We call such people slavish (*hörig*)."[94] A methodological approach to history and blind obedience to tradition are forms of the slavish attitude according to Gadamer. By contrast, the third form of the I/Thou relationship is characterized by a mutual openness and interaction between each of the partners. It means that we must be open to the claims that the other makes.

> Historically effected consciousness rises above such naive comparisons and assimilations by letting itself experience tradition and by keeping itself open to the truth claim encountered in it. The hermeneutical consciousness culminates not in methodological sureness of itself, but in the same readiness for experience that distinguishes the experienced man from the man captivated by dogma.[95]

---

90. Hegel, *Phenomenology of Spirit*, 112.

91. Ibid., 116.

92. Ibid., 115.

93. Kisiel, "Ideology Critique and Phenomenology," 154.

94. Gadamer, *Truth and Method*, 361.

95. Ibid., 361–62.

When we study a text like the Bible we must be open to the truth-claims it makes. This does not mean we simply acknowledge what it is claiming. Rather we must be open to the Bible in such a manner that it has something to say to us. To engage the Bible in an interpretive dialogue characterized by the third form of the I/Thou relationship means that we must be open to the claims of the text and that we must allow our preunderstandings and presuppositions about what the text means to be resisted and/or negated. This receptiveness to the text entails that we must be ready to allow the text to transform us as we engage in this dialogue.

It is interesting to note how both Jürgen Habermas and Gadamer developed Hegel's thought on the master/slave relationship in two different directions. For Habermas, the idea that "A man is not free until all men are free" is the utopian impulse to his critique of ideology.[96] Gadamer uses this same concept in Hegel to illustrate our relationship to tradition. We must be open to the claims of tradition and must be wary of method since it constrains the possibilities for understanding. Habermas starts from a position which views tradition negatively, as dominating and distorting our understanding.[97] Gadamer rejects this because it is a form of slavishness. Rather he grants tradition its position based on an epistemological argument. In any genuine relationship we must acknowledge that the other person may possess knowledge that is superior to our own. Habermas claimed that by taking such a stance Gadamer was being too naïve in his approach toward tradition. However, a careful reading of Gadamer's appropriation of Hegel's three categories of the I/Thou relationship allays most of Habermas's criticisms. In our dialogue with tradition, we must be alert to instances in which our dialogue with the past may have degraded into a pseudo-dialogue in which we are no longer experiencing the third category of I/Thou relationship.[98]

In summary, the hermeneutical approach to tradition that Gadamer is positing is distinguished by its fundamental openness to the truth

96. Habermas, "Knowledge and Interest," 295. According to Forster, Habermas follows a Marxist reading of Hegel, while Gadamer takes a much more balanced approach to Hegel's work. Forster, "Hegel's Dialectical Method," 168–70.

97. Nicholson, "Answers to Critical Theory," 156.

98. A similar point is brought out by Paul Ricoeur in his essay, "Hermeneutics and the Critique of Ideology," 300–39.

claim of tradition that is illustrated in the third variety of experience of the Thou. While Habermas criticizes Gadamer for not including any form of ideological critique, we can see that Gadamer's adoption of the I/Thou relationship to illustrate our relationship to tradition does contain the seeds for such a critique. The ideal of the authentic I/Thou experience functions as a regulative principle in Gadamer's hermeneutic, an ideal that an interpreter should always be hoping to achieve. Before I turn to Gadamer's appropriation of Collingwood's logic of question and answer in the next chapter, I would like to probe the problem of universal history.

The Hitch in Universal History

Gadamer found the philosophical resources to explain our relationship to and understanding of the past in a living and active manner that takes place in a "thoughtful mediation with contemporary life" in Hegel's dialectic.[99] However, in favor of Hegel's teleological premise that grounded the particulars of historical knowledge in the whole of universal history, Gadamer followed Heidegger and espoused a hermeneutical model of mediation between the past and present in a dialogical process that was both historically and linguistically finite.[100] Experience does not eventually culminate in absolute knowledge, but is characterized by a fundamental openness to the other that results in a continual dialogue between ourselves and tradition.[101]

According to Hegel, a historian did not study the particulars of history but universal world history. Dilthey and others rejected Hegel's *a priori* universal history but maintained the idea that historical understanding of the parts should lead to some form of universal history, the whole.[102] There were two main difficulties with Hegel's position in Gadamer's estimation. First, the concept of absolute spirit that drew every position into itself through dialectical sublation, was not justified.[103]

99. Gadamer, *Truth and Method*, 168.

100. DiCenso, *Hermeneutics and the Disclosure of Truth*, 94–95.

101. "If anything does characterise human thought, it is this infinite dialogue with ourselves which never leads anywhere definitely and which differentiates us from that ideal of an infinite spirit for which all that exists and all truth lies open in a single moment's vision." Gadamer, *Truth and Method*, 543.

102. Ibid., 197–98.

103. Ibid., 344–45.

Second, the finitude of human existence places limitations on human knowledge and contradicts Hegel's concept of absolute spirit.[104] Hegel was caught in the contradiction between open progress in history and a "conclusive apprehension of its meaning."[105]

At the same time, Gadamer acknowledges that an essential aspect of our temporal existence is the need for some form of universal history. Both Christians and non-Christians have this need. Even in our finitude, we are constantly moved to questions that are beyond us.[106] However, our concept of universal history must be provisional and open to constant revision since it is a concept that we project from within our historical horizon. Just as every mediation between past and present occurs within an historical horizon, so also our projections of universal history emerge from our horizon. Thus, any conception we have of universal history is circumscribed by human finitude. "Each projection of universal history has a validity that does not last much longer than the appearance of a flash momentarily cutting across the darkness of the future as well as of the past as it gets lost in the ensuing twilight."[107] Universal history has the quality of a "bad infinite" in "which the end keeps delaying its arrival" in the ceaseless dialogue that we have with tradition.[108] "Gadamer attempted to do justice to our urge for unity, and also our frustration of never achieving it. There is in the bad infinite at once infinite hope and infinite deferral."[109]

In Defense of Universal History

Wolfhart Pannenberg, however, believed that the logical conclusion of Gadamer's view should lead to a form of universal history. "I myself, induced by H. G. Gadamer's hermeneutic, have tried to show that the task of interpretation as an attempt to fuse the horizons of the author and the interpreter presupposes the totality of history as its ultimate frame

104. Ibid., 356–57.

105. Gadamer, "The Heritage of Hegel," in *Reason in the Age of Science*, 40; Hodgson, "Hegel," 110.

106. Gadamer, "The Heritage of Hegel," in *Reason in the Age of Science*, 51.

107. Ibid., 61.

108. Ibid., 40.

109. Weinsheimer, *Gadamer's Hermeneutic*, 37.

of reference."[110] Since the essence and structure of all knowledge is historical. It only makes sense that the fusion of horizons should take place in the same context, in history.[111] This continuity does not stop with the present, for the present is only understood in light of the future.

Hermeneutical understanding shares the same basic structure of all human understanding. Just as a person understands his/her life only in relation to the whole of their family or community, we also need to have a provisional understanding of history as a whole in order to understand the particulars of history.[112] "Only a conception of the actual course of history linking the past with the present situation and its horizon of the future can form the comprehensive horizon within which the interpreter's limited horizon of the present and the historical horizon of the text fuse together."[113]

While Gadamer was correct to reject Hegel's concept of the future because it ignored the finitude of human existence, he was wrong to dismiss the idea of universal history just because Hegel formulated it incorrectly.[114] According to Pannenberg, we are justified to hold to a concept of universal history as long as it is provisional and anticipatory in nature.[115] However, this raises the theological question of how we can keep the future open while at the same time affirming the ultimate revelation of God in Jesus' life, death, and resurrection? Pannenberg's answer to this question lies in the proleptic nature of the Christ event.

> [T]he Hegelian conception of history is not in fact the only possible one, because the end of history can also be understood as

---

110. Pannenberg, *Theology and the Philosophy of Science*, 284; Pannenberg, "Hermeneutics and Universal History," 115 ff.

111. Pannenberg, "Hermeneutics and Universal History," 130–31.

112. Ibid., 120.

113. Ibid., 130.

114. Ibid., 134–35.

115. Pannenberg, "What is Truth?" 25. Hegel's concept of truth is complicated, but what Pannenberg is referring to is the relation between the particular and the concept to which it is related. For example, a true work of art is something which conforms to what the concept of art is. Since each particular art work is historically conditioned it cannot be a perfect or complete representation of the concept of art. The complete concept is only realized in the absolute idea according to Hegel. Hegel, *Hegel's Logic*, § 24a.2; Inwood, "Truth, Falsity, and Correctness," in *A Hegel Dictionary*, 299. Heidegger picks up this same point in his discussion of the nature of the work of art in *Poetry, Language, Thought*, 17–18.

something which is itself only provisionally known, and in reflecting upon this provisional character of our knowledge of the end of history, the horizon of the future could be held open and the finitude of human experience preserved. It is precisely this understanding of history as something whose totality is given by the fact that its end has become accessible in a provisional and anticipatory way that is to be gathered today from the history of Jesus in its relationship to the Israelite-Jewish tradition. Hegel was unable to see this because the eschatological character of the message of Jesus remained hidden to him, as was the case with New Testament exegesis of his time.[116]

The statue of the American Marines planting the American flag on the beach of Iwo Jima during World War II can serve as an analogy to help us grasp Pannenberg's point here. When the soldiers planted that flag they were claiming the island as American territory. In reality though, all they controlled at that historical moment was a few hundred yards of beach. Still, by planting the flag they were anticipating and declaring the ensuing consequent and control of the entire island. In a similar manner the death and resurrection was an eschatological event that occurred in the middle of time. Unlike the planting of the flag on a Pacific island, Jesus resurrection truly was an eschatological event, not just an act anticipating the final victory. The end of history occurred in a proleptic manner in the resurrection of Jesus. His resurrection opened the possibility for us to participate in his resurrection someday based on our relationship with Jesus. In the resurrection, we see the historically conditioned nature of truth and also an anticipatory, proleptic, understanding of universal history, which is still open.[117]

Gadamer felt that Pannenberg's discussion on this point was very useful and admitted that every act of interpretation requires some reference to the future, "and a universal-historical conception is unavoidably one of the dimensions of today's historical consciousness."[118] He did not perceive any basic difference between his position and Pannenberg's

---

116. Pannenberg, "Hermeneutics and Universal History," 135.

117. Pannenberg, "What is Truth?" 24–25.

118. Gadamer, "On the Scope and Function of Hermeneutical Reflection," in *Philosophical Hermeneutics*, 36–37. "There is indeed no disputing that the Christian and non-Christian histories of salvation . . . are a legitimate need of the human reason explicitly conscious of its historical character." Gadamer, "The Heritage of Hegel," in *Reason in the Age of Science*, 60.

except that "for the Christian theologian the 'practical purpose' of all universal historical conceptions has its fixed point in the absolute history of the Incarnation."[119] However, Pannenberg's point is much stronger than this. Pannenberg attempts to synthesize two apparently contradictory ideas: universal truth and historically contingent knowledge. Hermeneutical understanding requires a provisional universal history to function and the Christ event is the best formulation of universal history available.[120] The incarnation is not just a "practical purpose" for the theologian. Pannenberg attempted to establish a convergence of philosophical and theological hermeneutics in the concept of universal history that is best fulfilled in the Christ event.

> This solution satisfactorily meets the legitimate objections against Hegel, since it protects the openness of the future and the contingency of events, and still holds fast to the ultimacy of what appeared in Jesus, which makes possible the unity of truth. That it alone founds the unity of truth means, however, the demonstration of the truth of the Christian message itself. This is the sole possible proof of its truth.[121]

The difference between Gadamer and Pannenberg is more than just a matter of degree of emphasis. If Pannenberg's argument is correct, it means that any hermeneutical theory must consider three horizons: the past, the present, and the future.[122] This is especially important for biblical hermeneutics. "Interpretation in the New Testament, however, clearly includes, perhaps even stresses, the horizon of the future and its influence upon interpretation."[123] Yet this idea is not just limited to theological hermeneutics as Pannenberg claims, "the whole of reality can be understood more deeply and more convincingly through Jesus than without him."[124] The corollary to this conception of universal history means that Christianity should not be considered in isolation from wider questions but must be understood in relation to the whole of

---

119. Gadamer, "On the Scope and Function of Hermeneutical Reflection," in *Philosophical Hermeneutics*, 37.

120. Pannenberg, "What is Truth?" 24–26.

121. Ibid., 26.

122. Thiselton, *New Horizons in Hermeneutics*, 337.

123. McHann, "The Three Horizons," 14.

124. Pannenberg, "Focal Essay," 133.

history.[125] The revelation of God in Jesus Christ also gives us a historical perspective from which we can make better projections, though still provisional, about the universal horizon. "However, if Jesus rose from the dead, and if he is in fact the self-revelation of God, then we will be looking through the right prism, our interpretations will have a focus, and the hermeneutical circle we experience will truly be 'already' a spiral toward that definitive meaning and truth which has 'not yet' arrived."[126]

In conclusion, Gadamer appropriates Hegel's dialectical approach and the I/Thou relationship to explain our living and active relationship to the past. At the same time, he rejects Hegel's absolute spirit and universal history in favor of the bad infinite. Theologically, this position does not do justice to the incarnation. Jesus' resurrection gives us a foretaste of what the end of history will be like. This provides us with a provisional understanding of history that is more stable than Gadamer's bad infinite, which only grants us a momentary flash that cuts across the darkness of the future.[127] Pannenberg's appeal to the life, death and resurrection of Jesus Christ as a proleptic eschatological event resolved the difficulties concerning universal history and serves as a needed modification to Gadamer's hermeneutic.

In the next chapter we shall continue this discussion, but our attention shall turn to the contribution that R. G. Collingwood's logic of question and answer makes to how we encounter and understand the past. This then leads to the question of what form of knowledge does a hermeneutical model like Gadamer's entail?

125. Pannenberg, *Theology and the Philosophy of Science*, 296.

126. McHann, "The Three Horizons," 392.

127. Gadamer, "The Heritage of Hegel," in *Reason in the Age of Science*, 61.

2

Tradition and Hermeneutical Understanding

The Expansion of Collingwood's Logic of Question and Answer

HEGEL'S PHILOSOPHY PROVIDES ONE OF THE STARTING POINTS FOR Gadamer's hermeneutic. However, it soon becomes apparent that his hermeneutical approach differs from Hegel's in several significant aspects. In the previous chapter, I tried to demonstrate how Gadamer abandoned Hegel's concepts of universal history in favor of his "bad infinite," and how this was not incompatible with Pannenberg's concept of a provisional view of universal history constructed on the eschatological character of Jesus's life, death, and resurrection. Prior to that, I surveyed Gadamer's adoption of Hegel's dialectical approach and the I/Thou relationship. What I propose to investigate in the present section is how Gadamer appropriates R. G. Collingwood's logic of question and answer to explain the interrogative nature of our encounter with tradition. Because Collingwood's approach plays a central role in Gadamer's hermeneutic and is one of the leading elements in Jauss's formulation of reception theory, it is essential that we have an accurate understanding of the logic of question and answer.

The Return of the Question in Experience

We build up generalizations of our knowledge of the world through our experiences. However, this process tends to produce false generalizations that are continually being negated by new experiences. Hegel explained this through the dialectical process that consciousness performs.[1] "According to Hegel, experience has the structure of a reversal of consciousness and hence, it is a dialectical movement."[2] Experience is characterized by negation. Our original fore-conceptions of what the object or the subject matter of a text will be are negated through our experiences, and our understanding is transformed. It is no longer possible for us to undergo that experience in the same manner ever again. We cannot experience the same thing twice; we never undergo that same experience of negation. As a result, we say that we know better after the experience and that in the process both our knowledge and its object were transformed.[3] The mistake Hegel made was to argue that conscious experience of what was different should eventually lead to universal knowledge in which nothing is experienced as alien.[4]

> In the pressing forward to its true existence, consciousness will arrive at a point at which it gets rid of its semblance of being burdened with something alien, with what is only for it, and some sort of "other," at a point where appearance becomes identical with essence, so that its exposition will coincide at just this point with the authentic Science of Spirit. And finally, when consciousness itself grasps this its own essence, it will signify the nature of absolute knowledge itself.[5]

In German there are two words that can convey the English term for "experience": *Erlebnis* and *Erfahrung*. Dilthey attempted to overcome the weakness in Hegel's concept of universal history in order to defend against what he perceived as the threat of historical relativism. His hermeneutic was built on the term *Erlebnis*, which referred to lived, personal experiences that we organize our lives around. These types of experiences serve to either define or transform how we understand the whole of our lives, and they revise the way we understand our past and how we anticipate the future. However, Dilthey encountered a problem when he tried to base how we understand the experiences of other people in history on an analogy to personal experience, *Erlebnis*. He contended that the manner in which we understand ourselves through experiences

1. Hegel, *Phenomenology of the Spirit*, 49–57.
2. Gadamer, *Truth and Method,* 354.
3. Ibid., 354, 356; Warnke, *Gadamer*, 26.
4. Bernstein, "From Hermeneutics to Praxis," 97.
5. Hegel, *Phenomenology of the Spirit*, 56–57.

is related to and parallel to historical understanding.[6] However, can we move from the coherence of understanding that *Erlebnis* can give to an individual life to historical coherence that is not experienced on an individual level? Can a historian start from smaller units of historical events and build up to knowledge of universal history? These are questions that Dilthey never successfully solved.[7]

In contrast to Dilthey, Gadamer uses the term *Erlebnis* in a negative manner in his criticism of aesthetic experience.[8] The term he prefers to describe our encounter with tradition is *Erfahrung*, as Hegel did. *Erfahrung* can be understood in one of two ways. First, it can refer to the scientific meaning of the term, an experience that is repeatable. This is the way that many nineteenth-century thinkers such as Schleiermacher, Ranke, and Droysen understood the term.[9] For them, history was an empirical discipline because it could be repeated through the reconstruction of the original context. By contrast, Gadamer is interested in the second meaning of the term *Erfahrung* as a learning experience that negates and reverses our previous understanding. This should result in a person who is more open to other experiences and capable of learning from them. As a result, we can say that not every experience is an experience (*Erfahrung*) in the manner in which Gadamer uses the term. Negation, the "reversal of consciousness," and expansion of our horizon are some of the crucial elements that characterize genuine experiences, *Erfahrung*. Another crucial difference between the two terms is that *Erlebnis* is a first-hand, personal experience while *Erfahrung* can refer to either personal or vicarious experiences.[10] Weinsheimer and Marshall provide an excellent summary of Gadamer's use of the term *Erfahrung*.

> This kind of 'experience' is not the residue of isolated moments, but an ongoing integrative process in which what we encounter widens our horizons but only by overturning an existing perspective, which we can then perceive was erroneous or at least narrow. Its effect, therefore, is not simply to make us "knowing," to add to our stock of information, but to give us that

6. Warnke, *Gadamer*, 30–31.

7. Gadamer, *Truth and Method*, 224–42.

8. Ibid., 55–80.

9. Warnke, 27.

10. Weinsheimer, *Gadamer's Hermeneutic*, 87.

implicit sense of broad perspectives, of the range of human life and culture, and of our own limits, that constitutes a non-dogmatic wisdom.[11]

Genuine experiences, as Gadamer described them, do not yield or culminate in a complete understanding of universal history, as Hegel claimed, or even a full apprehension of the person, thing, event, or text we encounter. Every experience, and the knowledge we gain from it, is bounded by the temporality and finitude of human existence. Whenever we experience something, we experience it as either this or that. Thus, if experiences teach us anything it is that we should be open to what we can learn from new experiences.[12] It is because we do not know what our experience will be that we need to ask questions. "We cannot have experiences without asking questions."[13]

There are three aspects to the questioning nature of experience that are crucial for Gadamer's hermeneutic. The first is that we must recognize our finitude and ignorance in order to ask a question that discloses something about the object. There must be an openness to the questions we ask because the answer has not yet been settled. In contrast to assertions and propositions, which flatten and reduce meaning, questions allow meaning to emerge through our dialogical experience in a conversation with a partner or text.[14]

Second, an open question contains both positive and negative judgments. This is similar to Hegel's thesis and antithesis. However, instead of the sublation of both the positive and negative judgments (thesis and antithesis) into a higher synthesis, Gadamer argues that the conclusions we reach from a question are not the result of two propositions being sublated into a higher synthesis. Instead, we will retain some elements

11. Weinsheimer, "Translator's Preface," xiii.

12. For Gadamer "experience finds its fulfillment not in knowledge per se, but in a knowledge that opens onto ever new experiences. Hence Gadamer replaces the Hegelian conception of absolute knowledge with the phenomenological conception of experience which is finite through and through, whereby philosophy becomes an unending hermeneutical exposition rather than the drive toward a consummated system" Kisiel, "Ideology Critique and Phenomenology," 159.

13. Gadamer, *Truth and Method*, 362.

14. Ibid., 469. "Thus Gadamer concludes: 'In the assertion, the horizon of meaning of what actually wants to be said is concealed with methodical exactitude,'—precisely by its abstraction from the background of what is unsaid." Pannenberg, "Hermeneutics and Universal History," 124.

of what we learned from the question as correct and exclude others as inappropriate.[15] "What decides a question is the preponderance of reasons for the one and against the other possibility."[16] The process of gaining knowledge in this way requires that we are able to consider and project possibilities for the subject-matter, of its "being like this and being like that," which results in the exclusion of other possibilities.[17] What counts as something "being like this" or "being like that" depends on decisions that we render as human agents who are shaped by the limits of our historical horizon. At the same time, our horizon circumscribes the possibilities of the questions that we can ask.[18]

The third aspect to the questioning nature of experience concerns two elements or areas from which questions arise. The first area from which questions arise is the subject-matter, *die Sache*. "To conduct a conversation means to allow oneself to be conducted by the subject-matter to which the partners in the dialogue are oriented."[19] Genuine questioning requires openness for the claims of the other to be considered. This creates the hermeneutical space for all the other possibilities of meaning to come into play. It does not mean that we leave the subject-matter undecided, but that we ask questions about it until the truth emerges. A question must be directed at the subject-matter.[20] The advantage to the logic of question and answer is that it is directed toward what we can learn from the subject-matter of a text.

There is a double hermeneutic to the structure of question and answer. On the one hand, we have an object or text that is the product of a historical situation, and on the other hand we have a questioner who is situated in a different historical horizon. Gadamer is taking a very balanced approach here. While he argues that our historical horizon definitely determines the perspective from which we question the text, and as a result reveals certain aspects of the subject-matter that other horizons may not, he also maintains that we are truly concerned with the subject matter of the text.

---

15. Sullivan, 85.

16. Gadamer, *Truth and Method*, 365.

17. Ibid.

18. Weinsheimer, *Gadamer's Hermeneutic*, 207.

19. Ibid., 367.

20. Gadamer, "The Problem of Historical Consciousness," 159.

The important point about effective-historical consciousness, then, is not only that inquiry is always oriented by our concerns; although Gadamer makes this point, his argument is also that inquiry is always inquiry into a subject-matter and that the consensus reached about this subject-matter can reveal something 'true' about it.[21]

Collingwood's Logic of Question and Answer

In order to fully explicate the value of the logic of question and answer for history and hermeneutics, Gadamer turned to the person he called the "English Hegelian," R. G. Collingwood.[22] While Collingwood did not use the term "hermeneutics," his program of history as an imaginative reconstruction of the past is thoroughly hermeneutical. Historical understanding is achieved by considering the evidence we possess in the present and a re-enactment of past thoughts. The goal is not just to know the past as the past, but also to learn more about oneself.

As Collingwood passed by the Alfred Memorial as he walked through London's Kensington Garden day after day on his way to work during World War I, he began to ask himself what the architect had been attempting to accomplish when he designed this memorial. "What relation was there, I began to ask myself, between what he had done and what he had tried to do? Had he tried to produce a beautiful thing; a thing, I meant, which we should have thought beautiful? If so, he had of course failed."[23] His daily encounters with the Alfred Memorial were the stimulus from which he formulated the premise that historical understanding arose through asking the right questions. Statements and judgments about the past do not constitute historical knowledge by themselves. They must be understood in relation to the questions that they originally sought to answer.

---

21. Warnke, *Gadamer*, 146. The mistake that Richard Rorty makes in his appropriation of Gadamer is that he reduces the double hermeneutic to a single hermeneutic. He ignores Gadamer's concern for the subject-matter and, as a result, "All descriptions rather reflect 'ways of coping' that refer simply to the purpose of those who forge them." Ibid., 145; Bernstein, 97. See Rorty's arguments on this point in *Philosophy and the Mirror of Nature*, 357–59; Rorty, *Contingency, Irony, and Solidarity*, 4–9.

22. Hogan, "Hermeneutics and the Logic of Question and Answer," 264.

23. Collingwood, *Autobiography*, 29.

> I began by observing that you cannot find out what a man
> means by simply studying his spoken or written statements,
> even though he has spoken or written with perfect command
> of language and perfectly truthful intention. In order to find out
> his meaning you must know what the question was . . . to which
> the thing he has said or written was meant as an answer.[24]

The logic of question and answer is tripartite in structure. First, each question and answer must be relevant and appropriate to the context in which it occurs.[25] The second and third elements of the logic of question and answer concern the "rightness" of the relationship between the question and the answer.[26] The idea that each question and answer must be relevant and appropriate to the context in which it occurs follows the hermeneutical circle between the part and the whole. As a "part," the question or answer belongs to a broader context. From a hermeneutical perspective, questions and answers are inextricably entangled with one another in the hermeneutical spiral between the part and the whole. "The logic of question and answer proved itself a dialectic of question and answer in which question and answer are constantly exchanged and are dissolved in the movement of understanding."[27] As such, both the question and the answer must be appropriate for the subject matter of the text and the historical context in which it was written. The interpreter's problem is that the original question, to which the text is an answer, is often left unstated in the text and is forgotten over time. Recovering what the original question might have been requires the use of historical methods since it is a historical problem.[28]

Collingwood recognized that the interpreter's understanding of the question that the text originally sought to answer always arose within the horizon of the interpreter and would never be identical to the original question.[29]

> It is not a passive surrender to the spell of another's mind; it is
> a labour of active and therefore critical thinking. The historian

24. Ibid., 31.

25. Ibid., 37.

26. See the following section, "The Rightness of the Question," for a discussion of these elements to the logic of question and answer.

27. Gadamer, "The Heritage of Hegel," 47.

28. Ibid., 39.

29. Jauss, *Towards an Aesthetic of Reception*, 29.

> not only re-enacts past thought, he re-enacts it in the context of
> his own knowledge and therefore, in re-enacting it, criticizes it,
> forms his own judgment of its value, corrects whatever errors
> he can discern in it.[30]

Collingwood refers to the reenactment of the past in the context of the historian's historical horizon as the past being incapsulated in the present. "Historical knowledge is the re-enactment of past thought incapsulated in a context of present thoughts which, by contradicting it, confine it to a plane different from theirs."[31] At this point, there is a sublte difference between Collingwood and Gadamer's positions. Gadamer criticized Collingwood for attempting to reconstruct the original question according to the intentions of the author or agent.[32] Instead, Gadamer argues that just as the meaning of the text goes beyond what the author intended, the interpreter's understanding of the text should be concerned with the subject matter of the text itself and not be constrained to a reconstruction of the author's original intentions.[33]

Substantive versus Genetic Understanding

In order to appreciate Gadamer's discomfort with Collingwood's position in regard to the re-enactment of the past in the present we need to grasp a distinction Gadamer made between two forms of understanding: substantive and genetic. Substantive knowledge occurs when we understand the "truth" of something; we understand *die Sache* of the text. When we understand the "truth" of Euclid's theorem that the sum of the square of the sides of a right triangle is equal to the square of the hypotenuse, and how to apply this mathematical formula in a practical situation, we have achieved a form of substantive understanding. Genetic understanding is needed when we cannot attain substantive understanding, "when one cannot see the point of what someone else is saying or doing that one is forced to explore the conditions under which that person says or does it."[34] Unfortunately, Gadamer stressed

---

30. Collingwood, *The Idea of History*, 215.
31. Collingwood, *Autobiography*, 114.
32. Gadamer, *Truth and Method*, 371–73.
33. Ibid., 350.
34. Warnke, *Gadamer*, 8; Gadamer, *Truth and Method*, 180–81.

substantive understanding and subordinated genetic understanding to a supporting role. Georgia Warnke remarks:

> Gadamer fails adequately to distinguish these two senses of agreement, one of which entails a concrete unity of judgment and the other reflective and critical integration. In reducing the second sense of agreement to the first, moreover, he slips from investigation of the conditions of understanding to the basically conservative thesis according to which we are not only members of a tradition but also its ideological supporters.[35]

Along with others, she correctly observed that an interpreter may be interested in genetic questions (background and context) even if she has already reached a substantive understanding of the text's subject matter. For example, it is perfectly legitimate to ask questions about how the Greeks came to discover geometry even after we understand Euclidean theorems. "To this extent Gadamer seems to have overstated his case in claiming that genetic questions arise only when understanding in its strongest sense has failed."[36]

Gadamer's preference for substantive understanding appears to lie at the root of his discontent with how Collingwood formulated his notion of the re-enactment of the past. If this critique of Gadamer is correct, then we must maintain that both substantive and genetic forms of understanding play different yet essential roles in hermeneutic understanding. This is one area in which the work of Hans Robert Jauss advanced the hermeneutical tradition he inherited from Gadamer. For Jauss, both forms of understanding are crucial; we not only need to pay careful attention to the subject-matter of the text, but we must also investigate the conditions in which the text was produced and first received if were are to have an adequate understanding of it.[37]

MATTHEW 28: SUBSTANTIVE AND GENETIC UNDERSTANDING

Barth's, Bultmann's, and Jeremias's comments on Matthew 28:18–20 provide an illustration into the differences, problems, and significance of substantive and genetic forms of understanding for biblical

35. Warnke, *Gadamer*, 106.

36. Ibid., 9.

37. See my discussion of this point in chapter 3, theses 2–4.

interpretation.[38] Barth's article "An Exegetical Study of Mt. 28:18–20," provides an excellent example of a substantive approach of the Great Commission. As a general rule, Barth's exegetical interests were "not limited to a detailed historical and exegetical study of the words, sentences or concepts. Rather he aimed at bringing to light the subject-matter of the text."[39] According to Barth, the closing verses to Matthew's gospel must be understood in light of the death and resurrection of Christ. The resurrection and affirmation of Jesus's authority in 28:1–17 was the basis for the commission Jesus issued in verses 18–20. Those who submit to this commission in Matthew fall under Jesus's authority in a more intimate manner. "Go therefore and make disciples" not only founded the apostolic church, but it is a commission that was designed to be renewed by each and every successive generation of the church.[40]

> In the same manner Jesus "made" apostles from the first disciples (Mark 3:14–15), the apostles are called to make apostolic Christians of all others . . . It is constantly renewed as listeners themselves become "apostolic" and, as new disciples, begin to proclaim the good news.[41]

Barth defined the scope of the commission, "to all nations," according to two principles. First, it referred to people from every nation who were "received into discipleship." These disciples then bring their respective nations within the reach of Jesus's teachings.[42] Second, it was a reference to both the Gentiles and those from the house of Israel. Jesus's grace was offered to the Gentiles after Israel had rejected it. This resulted in the recapitulation of the old Israel and the birth of the new

38. The contrast between Barth's and Bultmann's hermeneutics was brought to my attention by Jeanrond in *Theological Hermeneutics*, 129–45.

39. Ibid., 130. The goal of exegesis for Barth was that God might reveal himself through the words of the scriptures. "God's revelation in the human word of Holy Scripture not only wants but can make itself said and heard." Barth, *Church Dogmatics* I/2, 502.

40. Barth, "An Exegetical Study of Mt. 28:18–20," 57, 61.

41. Ibid., 63. "To be a disciple is to be called to make new disciples. This is the evident implication of the Great Commission in Matthew 28:19. The disciples are told to make new disciples. The concept of 'discipleship' is a dynamic concept. It implies multiplication. . . . All nations are invited to this new fellowship. And therefore all disciples are called to this mission." Kvalbein, "Go Therefore and Make Disciples," 52.

42. Barth, "An Exegetical Study," 64.

eschatological community that was constituted of Jews and Gentiles.[43] "Baptizing" and "teaching" described the manner in which disciples were to be made. Baptism was "the priestly function of objectively introducing others into the realm of God's reign."[44] This "messianic power" was originally exercised by Jesus but has now been delegated to his disciples. The baptism phrase was not a liturgical formula but spoke of the cleansing that proclaimed someone's inclusion into the family of God. "Teaching" was the transferal of Jesus's prophetic office to his disciples so they might nurture and guide others. They were to teach without omission the entirety of what Christ had commissioned them. Therefore, teaching in the church could "only be repetitive of apostolic teaching."[45] In this manner, Barth explicates Matthew 28:18–20 in a substantive manner by focusing on the subject-matter of the text and the claims that he believed this pericope placed upon contemporary readers.

In order to illustrate what a genetic approach to interpretation looks like and hopefully illuminate why Warnke's criticism of Gadamer is correct, Bultmann's and Jeremias's interpretations of the same passage will be assessed. Bultmann approached Matthew 28:18–20 by means of the historical-critical method and form criticism.[46] In his opinion, the primary purpose of this passage was to give the early church assurance that there was life after death. As such, it fell within the category of "Passion" stories, which arose within the primitive church to teach that Jesus was victorious over death.[47]

> To this class most particularly belong the Easter stories. It was only natural for belief in the resurrection of Jesus to find immediate expression in such stories; and doubtless such stories were already in circulation in the Palestinian Church. They then grew rapidly and were developed in various ways, and the Easter stories which we now read in the Synoptics have all received their form in the Hellenistic Church.[48]

43. Ibid., 64, 67.
44. Ibid., 67.
45. Ibid., 69.
46. Bultmann, "Is Exegesis without Presuppositions Possible?" 291.
47. Bultmann, *History of the Synoptic Tradition*, 288.
48. Ibid., 305.

Matthew 28:18–20 also served a second role within the early church to lend support to the sacrament of baptism. As the rite of baptism became more significant, the early church developed "legends" about this ritual. According to Bultmann, Matthew's record of the last appearance of Jesus was a legend that provided an authoritative basis for the ritual of baptism and was appended to the story of the empty tomb in the second century.[49]

If we compare Bultmann with Barth on this passage, we see that Bultmann's genetic approach undermined the claim of the text, as opposed to Barth's interpretation. As such, Bultmann's comments on this passage appear to support Gadamer's criticism that the historical-critical method can constrain the possibilities of the text. In this instance, the claim of the Great Commission is muted because of the way in which Bultmann employed the historical-critical method to close off that possibility in advance.

Joachim Jeremias provides us with the second instance of a genetic approach to the text when he compares Matthew 28:18–20 with coronation rituals that were common in the ancient near east. These rituals consisted of three actions: (1) the elevation of the heir to the throne, (2) the presentation or proclamation of the new monarch's authority, and (3) the enthronement of the new king. Jeremias attempted to demonstrate how Matthew used a coronation ritual as a literary device to communicate the idea that the Kingdom of God had been inaugurated as a result of Jesus's death and resurrection. All three elements of a coronation are present in verses 18–20. First, we have the elevation of Jesus as heir, "all authority has been given to me" (18b). Then we have the proclamation of his authority, "go therefore and make disciples . . ." (19–20a). Finally, the enthronement of Jesus as the messianic king is conveyed in the promise that he gives, "and lo, I will be with you always" (20b).[50]

While Jeremias's conclusions are similar to Barth's, he arrived at them by means of a genetic study investigating the historical context

---

49. "We have indicated how the story of Baptism quickly became a cult legend in the Hellenistic Church. We must in the same way also recognize the command to baptize in Matt. 28:16–20 as a cult legend." Ibid., 306.

50. Jeremias, *Jesus' Promise to the Nations*, 39. Another example of the New Testament's use of this coronation motif is found in 1 Timothy 3:16 according to Jeremias. Ibid., 38.

in which the text was written. In this example, substantive and genetic understandings complement one another. Not only that, but Jeremias's results supplement Barth's interpretation by helping the modern reader to grasp the expression of the claim to royal authority that the original audience would have perceived based on their cultural preunderstanding. However, as the example from Bultmann demonstrates, we must be careful which methods we employ in genetic studies because of the manner in which a method has the possibility of closing off our openness to the claims of the text. The questions we ask should be appropriate for the subject matter of the text.

The Rightness of the Question and the Answer

In the last section we considered how, according to the logic of question and answer, questions must be relevant and appropriate to the subject matter of the text. In this section we will explore what Collingwood meant by the "rightness" of a question in regard to the subject-matter under study. A question must be related to and appropriate for the subject-matter of the text if we are going to judge it to be "right." If this dimension of the question is absent, then we would classify it as an inappropriate question and possibly refuse to answer it. To a large extent we judge a question "right" by means of common sense or intelligence.[51]

In a similar manner, the answer must be the "right" answer for the question. Collingwood is very careful in his choice of the term "right" to describe the relation between question and answer. By "right" he does not mean "true." "The "right" answer to a question is the answer which enables us to get ahead with the process of questioning and answering."[52] Collingwood uses the example of a question that Socrates asked "would you rather play draughts with a just person or a person who knows how to play the game?" The true answer, based on logic, would be the just person, since it assumes that justice and playing a game of draughts are compatible. However, the right answer is the second person, since it forms a link in the chain of questioning. Replying to Socrates with "a person who knows how to play" moves the dialogue forward.[53]

51. A question that is appropriate for the subject matter "is what we ordinarily call a sensible or intelligent question, not a silly one, or in my terminology it 'arises.'" Collingwood, *Autobiography*, 37–38.

52. Ibid., 38.

53. Ibid., 37–38.

Collingwood's logic of question and answer helps us define how we view terms such as "truth" or "meaning." "Whether a given proposition is true or false, significant or meaningless, depends on what question it was meant to answer; and anyone who wishes to know whether a given proposition is true or false, significant or meaningless, must find out what question it was meant to answer."[54]

The basis for this is found in Collingwood's criticism of propositional logic. Many forms of propositional logic contain an internal conceptual problem when they equate truth and meaning with grammatical construction. Instead, Collingwood argues that every proposition is an answer to a question, and one cannot understand the truth value or meaning of a proposition unless one knows the question that it answered.[55] "It seemed to me that truth, if that meant the kind of thing which I was accustomed to pursue in my ordinary work as a philosopher or historian . . . something that belonged not to any single proposition, nor even, as the coherence theorists maintained, to a complex of propositions taken together; but to a complex consisting of questions and answers."[56] Collingwood gave the following two statements by way of example: "The contents of this box are one thing" and "The contents of this box are many things." According to propositional theories of truth and logic, these statements appear to be contradictory. However, if we look at them from the logic of question and answer, the contradiction disappears because they may have been the answer to the following questions: "Does the box contain one chess set or several?" or "Is there one chess piece or more than one in the box?" The contradiction that a critic may have accused someone of making in their answer was never part of that individual's thought or answers. Rather, the contradiction was "foisted upon it by the critic."[57]

This is a significant point for the history of a text's interpretation. The logic of question and answer helps to explain how we may have different interpretations of the same passage of Scripture over time without viewing them as contradictory or being forced to accept all interpretations as equally valid. If interpretations are judged on the basis

54. Ibid., 39.
55. Ibid., 33–37.
56. Ibid., 37.
57. Ibid., 40–41.

of their rightness, then there can be more than one "right" interpretation according to the logic of question and answer. This stands in opposition to the traditional view that the interpretation should be "true," implying that there is only one correct interpretation. However, just because there can be more than one right interpretation does not mean that we cannot conclude that a particular interpretation is inappropriate.

While Collingwood does not explicitly define his view of history as hermeneutical, his logic of question and answer is very hermeneutical. For Collingwood, the past has no value until someone interprets it in the present. "The questioning process, under the influence of history, goes on, forming a spiral gradually replacing error with truth, but remaining essentially open."[58] This is very compatible with Gadamer's concept of the process of the transmission of a tradition and our interpretations of the texts within that tradition. In this process, our prejudices undergo a filtering process as inappropriate prejudices or questions are replaced with ones that are more appropriate. Questioning possesses the characteristics of Gadamer's "bad infinite" also. "Each generation and each individual raises new questions and gains a different perspective on history. For that reason the questioning process goes on, and history must be re-written by each generation."[59]

The Dialogue of Question and Answer

Like Heidegger and Hegel, Collingwood's influence on Gadamer is difficult to overstate. In fact, Gadamer considered Collingwood's *Autobiography* so significant he was responsible for its translation and publication in German. "Gadamer's enthusiasm for Collingwood's logic of question and answer is almost total."[60] However, Gadamer moved beyond Collingwood in two particular lines of thought. The first concerns the dialogical nature of understanding, and the second concerns the expansion of horizons that the logic of question and answer enables.

The Devaluation of Answers

Gadamer attempted to find a balance between the subject-matter of the text and the interpreter. This involved a double hermeneutic, the

---

58. Hogan, "Hermeneutics and the Logic of Question and Answer," 269.

59. Collingwood, *Autobiography*, 86.

60. Hogan, 270; see also Gadamer, "The Heritage of Hegel," 64–65 n. 14.

first adaptation Gadamer makes to Collingwood's logic of question and answer. Gadamer agreed with Collingwood's axiom that we can only understand a text or statement once we have understood it as a question. However, Gadamer viewed the logic of question and answer as a two-way street. He adopted Collingwood's argument that we must understand the question to which the text was a response. But then he goes beyond Collingwood—to understand a text as a question we must recognize it as an authentic question addressed us as well.[61] Not only does the historian ask questions about the text but at the same time he or she is questioned by the subject-matter of the text.[62]

According to Collingwood, the reader initiated the questioning process. Questions arose from within the 'real' life situations of an interpreter.[63] At the same time one can argue that the seeds of Gadamer's dialogical approach lie dormant in Collingwood. A question that arises from the practical life situations of an interpreter may lead to questions that the text originally sought to answer or may raise new questions that the interpreter must answer. As the interpreter asks questions of the text, new questions arise in response to the answers he receives. In order to illustrate this facet of historical questioning Collingwood uses an example from the life of Lord Nelson. During the battle of Trafalgar, Lord Nelson pondering whether he should remove his military decorations. This is not the type of question that arises naturally for the contemporary reader. The type of questions that naturally arise for us are along the lines of "how much longer shall I read this book," or "is the book giving me accurate information about Admiral Nelson?" There is a disparity between the questions Nelson was asking and the ones that we as interpreters ask. "No question that arises in this primary series, the series constituting my 'real' life, ever requires the answer 'in honour I won them, in honour I will die with them.'" However, a question from the "real" life situation of the interpreter may lead to questions of another dimension in which we imaginatively and sympathetically try to contemplate why Lord Nelson would have asked such a question,

61. Warnke, "Hermeneutics and the Social Sciences," 349.

62. Gadamer, "Reflections on My Philosophical Journey," 43.

63. "Every historical problem ultimately arises out of 'real' life." Collingwood, *Autobiography*, 114.

"and there live a life in which I not merely think about Nelson but am Nelson, and thus in thinking about Nelson think about myself."[64]

Secondary questions along these lines are 'incapsulated' according to Collingwood. By incapsulation, he means that such questions or thoughts are "perfectly alive" but are not part of the real life of the interpreter. There is a distance between the interpreter and the text or historical event of the past, a distance that the interpreter remains conscious. In a parallel manner, the processes and elements of our tradition that are passed down to us are incapsulated in the present.[65] This is summarized in one of Collingwood's famous axioms about history, "Historical knowledge is the re-enactment of past thought incapsulated in a context of present thoughts which, by contradicting it, confine it to a plane different from theirs."[66] Incapsulation can be seen as the means by which the text of the past contradicts, negates, challenges, or questions the horizon of the interpreter in a certain sense. Collingwood's conception of incapsulation shares certain traits with Hegel's use of sublation in that history is constituted by processes that are constantly being transformed and re-configured into new processes. In this way, the 'traces' of the past are incapsulated in the contemporary world. One of the most important roles the historian or interpreter plays in a community is to raise to consciousness how the past is incapsulated in the present.

> But suppose the past lives on in the present; though incapsulated in it, and at first sight it is hidden beneath the present's contradictory and more prominent features, it is still alive and active; then the historian may very well be related to the non-historian as the trained woodsman is to the ignorant traveller. "Nothing here but trees and grass," thinks the traveller, and marches on. "Look," says the woodsman, "there is a tiger in the grass." The historian's business is to reveal the less obvious features hidden

---

64. Ibid., 112–13.

65. Ibid., 113, 141–42. Collingwood makes an analogy to a person who stops smoking, but the desire to smoke remains incapsulated in him. The same phenomenon happens within cultures. Even if a nation renounces something like warfare, the residue of such thoughts will not disappear in a generation or two. While the first generation may abandon a certain practice or value, it is still incapsulated in what is passed down to future generations in the shape of stories about heroism or the glories of a just war. Ibid., 142.

66. Ibid., 114.

from a careless eye in the present situation. What history can bring to moral and political life is a trained eye for the situation in which one has to act.[67]

Once the guide has pointed out the tiger in the grass, the way in which the traveler looks upon their surrounding is transformed. Even though the hiker was appreciating the beauty of their surroundings they did not see the tiger hiding in the grass until the trained guide pointed it out to them. Their previous understanding is negated and this situation will never appear the same way to them again. In a similar manner, one of the tasks of the historian is to "point out" to the untrained observer how the past is truly incapsulated, but "hidden beneath the present's contradictory and more prominent features," in the present.

Is Gadamer's idea that the logic of question and answer is a two-way dialogue by nature—not only does the interpreter ask questions of the text but the text asks questions of the interpreter—valid? Pannenberg thinks that while Gadamer is basically correct in his thought on this point his argument needs to be modified slightly. He argues that Gadamer has underestimated the value and role which assertions play in any act of communication, especially those involving the study of texts from the past. Gadamer denies the value of assertions because they disguise the fact that, as statements, they are an answer to a question and in doing so it "conceals the priority of the question and so also its past, the process of conversation by which it arose."[68] Assertions also sever what one is attempting to communicate from the totality of its unexpressed horizon of meaning. "Thus Gadamer concludes: 'In the assertion, the horizon of meaning of what actually wants to be said is concealed with methodical exactitude,'—precisely by its abstraction from the background of what is unsaid."[69] The problem with assertions concerns how they are employed in a "method" to give the impression of having arrived exactness. Giving a statement while under interrogation is an example. "In a statement the horizon of meaning of what is to be said is concealed by methodical exactness; what remains is the 'pure' sense of the statements."[70] Hours

67. Ibid., 100.

68. Weinsheimer, *Gadamer's Hermeneutic*, 206.

69. Pannenberg, "Hermeneutics and Universal History," 124.

70. Gadamer, 469; "It is not by giving something a definite character that we first discover that which shows itself—the hammer—as such; but when we give it such a character, our seeing gets *restricted* to it in the first instance, so that by this explicit

of interrogation that the suspect has undergone are discarded and all
that is retained as evidence a few salient statements the suspect gave
during that time. These statements may be all that is presented to prove
the innocence or guilt of the defendant. This always results in a flatten-
ing and reduction of meaning. In response to this, Gadamer privileges
the quest and question over the supposed precision in knowledge that
methodological approaches champion.[71]

Drawing on Heidegger's phenomenological approach which
viewed assertions as a mode of Being-in-the-world, Gadamer maintained that propositional statements were a double-edged sword. For
Heidegger, assertions simplified or reduced the possible disclosure of
meaning that occurs during an act of understanding. An assertion reveals or highlights a particular aspect of something. For example, we
may state that the older son in the parable of the Prodigal Son (Luke
15:11–32) represents those from Israel who rejected Jesus's message,
while the younger son allegorically stands for the Gentiles.[72] While such
a reading of the parable communicates an aspect of how the meaning
of the parable is disclosed, it also restricts other possible readings. In
regard to the Prodigal Son, our interpretive vision is restricted once we
make or accept assertions like this and we miss how the older son may
be disclosing an aspect about a more mature believer whose life of faith
is based on obedience or possibly the resentfulness that someone may
harbor about the idea of the father having received the younger son
back into the family unconditionally.[73]

Pannenberg, by contrast, is much more positive about the role of
assertions and argues that communication would not be possible with-

---

restriction of our view, that which is already manifest may be made *explicitly* manifest
in its definite character. In giving something a definite character, we must, in the first
instance, take a step back when confronted with that which is already manifest—the
hammer is too heavy. In 'setting down the subject', we dim entities down to focus on
'that hammer there', so that by thus dimming them down we may let that which is
manifest be seen *in* its own definite character as a character that can be determined."
Heidegger, *Being and Time*, 197–99.

71. Gadamer, *Truth and Method*, 362.

72. This reading was advanced by both Jerome and Augustine and became the primary lens through which the parable was read throughout the Middle Ages. Wailes,
Medieval Allegories of Jesus' Parables, 238–42.

73. Views along this line were put forward by Jerome's contemporary, Ambrose, and
then advanced by John Calvin during the Reformation. Ibid., 243.

out assertions.[74] In fact, according to Pannenberg, Gadamer's hermeneutic requires the use of assertions if there is to be a fusion of horizons.
Coming to an understanding about a subject-matter of a conversation
(or fusion of horizons) involves the predicative sense of language. In order to restore a text to its original context requires the use of assertions
to explicate what was written and its background. Yet the predicative
character of language is always proportional: it always involves a degree
of objectivity and subjectivity.[75] This is not the same type of positivistic
or methodological use of statements that restrict language propositional
statements that Gadamer objected to.[76] Thus, Pannenberg's defense of
the role of assertions seems to be a valid criticism and correction which
helps to modify Gadamer's hermeneutic and restore a balance between
questions and answers from Gadamer's polemical argument in favor of
the question.

QUESTIONS AND HORIZONS

The second manner in which Gadamer developed Collingwood's
logic of question and answer concerns the potential of questions to
expand the horizon of the interpreter. While this concept is incipient
in Collingwood's work (for example, in his illustration of the guide
and the tiger in the grass), Gadamer elaborated how this expansion
of horizons occurrs.[77] In order to understand how questions function
in this manner, we need to understand how Gadamer interpreted the
Socratic dialogues. Socrates based his philosophical method on the art
of asking questions. In order for two people to have conversation that
has the possibility of reaching a mutual understanding, both partners
in the dialogue must realize that they do not possess all the answers

74. "Accordingly, the personal dimension of language (as communication) is only
accessible in its concrete substantiveness (with which, at any rate, its predicative character is connected)." Pannenberg, "Hermeneutics and Universal History," 125.

75. "The question of the given 'proportions' of the objectification and objectifiability
. . . avoid the false alternative between, on the one hand, the scientific ideal of absolute
objectivity (a complete disregard of everything subjective), which has not once proven
attainable in the natural sciences or in mathematics, and, on the other hand, the illusion
of a totally non-objectifying discourse, which is probably equally unattainable." Ibid.,
127.

76. Sullivan, *Political Hermeneutics*, 20–52.

77. Collingwood, *Autobiography*, 100.

but are concerned with finding the answers.[78] If assertions flatten and reduce the content of meaning, they also have the possibility to close off further conversation and questioning.[79] Whereas a question keeps open the possibility for further disclosures of truth. The openness of the question comes from the fact that the answer is not yet settled. Good questions open the door for new possibilities in understanding a text.[80]

Questions, by nature, are restricted and at the same time uncontrolled. They are restricted in the sense that they arise from within the horizon of the interpreter, from our preconceptions and prejudices. "They [questions] are bounded by a horizon. Within this horizon, openness consists in the possibility of the thing's being this way or that; but each of these possibilities must have been determined beforehand, and their determinacy marks the limits of a question's horizon."[81] A question is also restricted by the subject-matter of the text. According to the logic of question and answer, it must be appropriate to the subject-matter. At the same time, questions are not governed by the reader who questions the text. Questions come upon us like a sudden idea, *ein Einfall*. It is the sudden revelation of a question that advances the openness and possibilities of understanding and makes an answer possible. Gadamer describes the way a question falls upon us in the following manner:

> The real nature of the sudden idea is perhaps less that a solution occurs to us like an answer to a riddle than that a question occurs to us that breaks through into the open and thereby makes an answer possible. Every sudden idea has the structure of a question. But the sudden occurrence of the question is already a breach in the smooth front of popular opinion. Hence we say that a question too "occurs" to us, that it "arises" or "presents itself" more than that we raise it or present it.[82]

---

78. Socrates would question his opponents to reveal that their arguments were not as secure or sound as they assumed. In this way he placed them on equal footing with him so that they could engage in an open discussion starting from a position of ignorance. Sullivan, *Political Hermeneutics*, 80–83, 104–7. However, one of the problems with Plato's record of Socrates' dialogues is that they are to a certain extent contrived (depending how one sees the relation between Plato's writings and Socrates' teaching). This raises the question as to how 'open' they really were as dialogues.

79. Ibid., 80–84.

80. Gadamer, *Truth and Method*, 375.

81. Weinsheimer, *Gadamer's Hermeneutic*, 207.

82. Gadamer, *Truth and Method*, 366.

The interpreter is struck by questions from three directions: they come upon him like a sudden idea, they arise from to the subject-matter of the text, and they emerge from the historical horizon of the interpreter.

However, Gadamer wants to avoid any dichotomy between subject and object and therefore argues that questions merge with one another in the "play" of interpretation.[83] In the play of understanding, the interpreter questions the text and the text poses questions to the interpreter for which he/she does not already possess an answer. The questions that the text addresses to us are related to the question which the text originally answered in such a way that we cannot understand the one without the other. This merging or mediation of questions raised by the text and the interpreter is part of what Gadamer terms the fusion of horizons. It is important to remember, that for Gadamer, the fusion of horizons involves a double hermeneutic; both the text and the interpreter contribute to the fusion of horizons. In this process, not only are new possibilities for understanding the subject-matter of the text disclosed but at the same time the prejudices of the interpreter's horizon are put at risk by questions raised by the subject-matter of the text. "Thus disclosing new possibilities for questions and extending his own horizon by fusing it with that of the text. . . . being cognizant of his finitude, and realizing that he does not have the first word or the last, the interpreter holds himself open to history—that is, to the continuing event of truth."[84]

Hermeneutical Knowledge and Tradition

Bildung

The theme for the next chapter will focus on how the interaction between an interpreter and a text is characterized by play, performance and provocation. Before we jump to discuss those topics, there is one final area that needs to be addressed. What type of knowledge does hermeneutical understanding consist of or produce?

83. Ibid., 374.

84. Weinsheimer, *Gadamer's Hermeneutic*, 211.

The German term that Gadamer used to refer to hermeneutical knowledge is "*Bildung.*" Richard Rorty translated this as "edification."[85] By this, Rorty refers to the way in which we redescribe our world and thus "remake" ourselves in the process of interpreting the past. He believed Gadamer initiated a shift from "knowledge as the goal of thinking" to that of edification. In doing so, Rorty makes a strong distinction between two forms of thought: that of knowledge of things (or the real world) and how we use language to continually re-describe our world.[86] Is this a fair reading of Gadamer? Jeff Mitscherling claims that Rorty took a very superficial reading of Gadamer's work, especially concerning the term "*Bildung.*"

The term *Bildung* has a very rich heritage in the German philosophical tradition that Gadamer specifically attempted to engage and to advance.[87] The importance Gadamer attributed to the concept of *Bildung* can be clearly seen in how he devotes the opening argument of *Truth and Method* to a discussion of its history and relevance.[88] Prior to 1800, *Bildung* was primarily a theological term that referred to in the transformation of the human soul. "Being formation is here the pure property and possession of God, the birth of the Son in the soul, a transcendental process without means."[89] After the introduction of Lord Shaftesbury's work into German, *Bildung* adopted a much more humanistic tone. It referred to the formation and development of the human potential within the new and open society developing in Germany during that time. The works of Herder, Hegel, Humboldt, and Heidegger are characterized by this aspect of the term's meaning.[90]

For Hegel, the classical texts of antiquity played a crucial role in this formation of the individual. As we saw in his dialectic, there is a

85. "Since 'education' sounds a bit too flat, and *Bildung* a bit too foreign, I shall use 'edification' to stand for this project of finding new, better, more interesting, more fruitful ways of speaking." Rorty, *Philosophy and the Mirror of Nature*, 360.

86. Rorty's choice of the term "edification" is in line with his larger program that the goal of philosophy was primarily linguistic; the redescription of philosophical concepts and categories. Ibid., 358–60; Warnke, *Gadamer*, 157–59.

87. Mitscherling, "Resuming the Dialogue," 132; Warnke, *Gadamer*, 159.

88. See Gadamer, *Truth and Method*, 3–41.

89. Ritter, *Historisches Wortbuch der Philosophie*, 1:922, my translation.

90. "'The first, true, moral law is' according to Humbodlt: 'develop/form yourself and then the second: work on the other through that which you are.'" Ibid., 1:926. This idea is echoed in Heidegger's axiom, "Become what you are." *Being and Time*, 186.

movement from the self to self-alienation and finally a return to the self that characterizes the process of *Bildung*.[91] In the formation of self-consciousness, a person must raise his consciousness above his own historical particularity to a higher level of awareness. In raising above our individuality, we encounter our culture or tradition. In this encounter the individual experiences alienation (foreign aspects of their history or culture), which leaves them more mature and cultured than previous to this encounter with tradition. The higher that person's culture has matured, the more power it possesses to transform its members in their encounters with tradition, "the measure of culture is the measure of its actuality and power."[92] Hegel believed the classical texts of Greece and Rome were especially suited for this purpose since they were "remote and alien enough to effect the necessary separation" and they possessed "actuality and power."[93] Gadamer summed up the significance of Hegel's view of *Bildung* when he wrote:

> Every single individual who raises himself out of his natural being to the spiritual finds in the language, customs, and institutions of his people a pre-given body of material which, as in learning to speak, he has to make his own. . . . Historically, *Bildung* is not to be understood only as the process of raising the mind to the universal; it is at the same time the element within which the educated man (*Gebildete*) moves.[94]

While historical and philological methods may help us to study the past, they are derivative or specialized forms of understanding. *Bildung* is the universal form of understanding or knowledge which underlies all other forms of understanding, especially in history and the humanities (*Geisteswissenschaften*). *Bildung* is the cultivation of consciousness to be open or receptive to wider points of view, especially those preserved within tradition. It is a cognitive ability that enables the interpreter to perceive in concrete situations the possibilities open to him or her.

Bildung does not refer to the type of education that involves factual knowledge or technical expertise. For Collingwood, the application

91. See the discussion of Hegel's slave/master relationship above. Paul Ricœur also brings out how our understanding "the other" results in the growth of the interpreter's "own understanding of himself." Ricoeur, *The Conflict of Interpretations*, 17.

92. Ibid., 298.

93. Gadamer, *Truth and Method*, 14.

94. Ibid.

of historical methods (no matter how carefully they were followed) did not constitute true historical knowledge. Historical methods inherently have a "low potential because they involve a certain blindness to the realities of the situation." What is required is that the historian possess insight or intuition so that they may grasp the uniqueness of the historical situation or text and be able to apply it to their situation. [95]

Instead *Bildung* refers to the type of intellectual development that teaches a person to think for him or herself, to make judgments and to realize the possibilities and limitations in a situation. It is not just an awareness that there are different ways of understanding something or seeing the world, but it also involves the ability to discriminate and make judgments. In this sense, it is a universal and common sense that arises within specific historical contexts. Mitscherling condensed Gadamer's use of *Bildung* in the following manner: "*Bildung* is that process whereby the individual becomes critically self-conscious both of the role played by these 'handed-down' prejudices in his or her thought and of the practical value of these prejudices in the preservation or the attainment of the well-being of the individual and society as a whole." [96]

Vico and Sensus Communis

Because of the manner in which Hegel's dialectic led to absolute knowledge, Gadamer turned to other thinkers to define this term more clearly. [97] Continuing in his archaeology of the concept of *Bildung*, Gadamer drew upon Vico for his notion of *sensus communis* in order to show the relation between the individual and culture. *Sensus communis* is not an abstract form of universal reason but is instantiated in particular communities or nations at particular times. It allows one to judge what is right or wrong and gives the "human will its direction." As a result, it is also what founds a community or culture. Not only is the individual developed within his or her community's *sensus communis*, but as the individual is formed, the wider community's *sensus communis* is also reshaped and developed. [98]

---

95. Collingwood, *Autobiography*, 101, 106.

96. Mitscherling, "Philosophical Hermeneutics and 'The Tradition,'" 249.

97. Gadamer, *Truth and Method*, 15.

98. Ibid., 21–23.

During the nineteenth century, the German philosophical tradition evacuated the richness of meaning which was previously contained in the concept of *sensus communis*.[99] Instead of following Vico, Hegel, and Shaftesbury, who incorporated *sensus communis* into their philosophical systems, the German philosophical tradition pursued the direction set by Kant and Goethe. The philosophical consequences of this can be seen in the manner by which Kant reduced *sensus communis* to taste. What remained was an impoverished form of *sensus communis* that referred to individual, subjective taste and was denied many of the traditional roles it played in imparting knowledge.[100] This is one of the main reasons why Gadamer devoted so much attention to these concepts, he was swimming against the current of his philosophical tradition.

The primary work of Vico's that Gadamer cited was *On the Study Methods of our Time* in which Vico attacked the Cartesian method and attempted to reinstate the role and primacy of *sensus communis*.[101] Vico claimed that Descartes pursued a single method for truth and in doing so rejected all other forms of truth. The danger that Vico correctly perceived in the Cartesian method was that the 'old truths' of tradition would be lost. He argued that the classical ideals of *sapientia*, *eloquentia*, and *prudentia* were required for social life and these, in turn, presupposed some form of *sensus communis*. These traditional forms of knowledge play an important role in the development of not only the individual, but also the continuing formation of the community in which they live. One of the weaknesses of the scientific method was that common sense, tact, and practical judgment were excluded, or suffered from a greatly reduced status. But these forms of understanding are essential if we are to "discriminate between good and bad, right and wrong, important and unimportant and so on. In other words, they reflect a capacity for recognizing truth which perhaps cannot be reduced to method and for which there are no clear rules but which remains a form of knowledge equal to modern science itself."[102] A person schooled under the Cartesian method could become an expert or scholar in a particular subject, but someone trained in *sensus communis*

99. The exception to this was the Pietist movement which maintained the concept of *sensus communis*, especially in the works of Christoph Oetinger. Ibid., 27–30.

100. Ibid., 26, 33–34, 42–44.

101. Ibid., 19 n. 25; Verene, "Gadamer and Vico on *Sensus Communis*," 139.

102. Warnke, *Gadamer*, 159.

could attain wisdom and, according to Vico, the scholar will always be dependent on the person with wisdom. "Thinking well, speaking well, and acting well are crucial to life in the civil world."[103] As such, Vico offered a corrective to the methodological approach of the humanities of which Gadamer was so skeptical.

The Hermeneutical Relevance of Aristotle's Phronesis

The reduction of *sensus communis* and *Bildung* in the German tradition played a formative role in Gadamer's early work, a role which continued throughout his entire career. During the nineteenth century a struggle erupted in the *Geisteswissenschaften* (humanities) in German universities. The concept of *Bildung* as the cultivation of great ideas, was exchanged for the methodological approach of the *Altertumwissenschaft* (classics or study of antiquity), the accumulation of facts from history based on method. The idea of the formation of the soul in German education was decimated with the rise of *Altertumwissenschaft*.[104] As a result, Gadamer felt the universities of his day were populated with experts in their disciplines rather than gifted thinkers.[105] One of his earliest works, "Aristotle's *Protrepticos*" was in part an attempt to address this problem in German higher education.

Bildung and *sensus communis* are the central concepts that Gadamer used to outline how an individual applied what they learned from their encounter with culture or tradition. This brings us to the question of application, which is one of the central problem of hermeneutics. As such, it is characterized by a hermeneutical circle between the part/whole and individual/other that we have covered in the other aspects of Gadamer's thought.[106] In order to explain how universal forms of knowledge (such as rules, goals, or values) are related to the particular situations or problems in the movement of application, Gadamer incorporated Aristotle's teachings on *phronesis*. According to Aristotle, *phronesis* is the capacity that enables someone to think on-the-spot.[107] Practical knowledge,

---

103. Verene, 140.

104. Sullivan, *Political Hermeneutics*, 20–24, 165. Gadamer is not the first to react against this trend but stands in the line of Hegel, Nietzsche, and Heidegger.

105. Ibid., 112.

106. Gadamer, *Truth and Method*, 315.

107. Gadamer, "*Praktisches Wissen*," 230–48; Gadamer, "Reflections," 9.

phronesis, is a historical form of knowledge since it is always employed in concrete historical situations.[108] Through it "one can accumulate life experience and thus gain a sense of how to act in a unique situation."[109]

In the *Nicomachean Ethics*, Aristotle differentiated between three different forms of knowledge: *episteme, techne,* and *phronesis.*[110] *Episteme* is an exact form of knowledge concerned with unchanging truths. Philosophical systems or theoretical mathematics are examples of what would be considered *episteme*. This form of knowledge is arrived at through the use of reason and tested by coherence or correspondence. By contrast, *techne* and *phronesis* are both concerned with the application of knowledge to the flux of the historical world. *Techne,* like *episteme*, is an exact form of knowledge but it differs from *episteme* in that its *telos* is the application of knowledge to a concrete situation. The mastery of a craft or skill, such as carpentry, is an illustration of the type of knowledge one would consider *techne*. The skills and types of knowledge required to become a carpenter are learned through instruction and experience. However, unlike *episteme* it is always practiced in concrete situations (such as making cabinetry for a client's house).

The distinction between *techne* and *phronesis* is not as clear cut. While they are similar in that both are concerned with the application of knowledge to concrete situations, there are several significant differences between them. First, while we can learn *techne*, we can also forget it. If we don't practice a craft like carpentry for a few years, we can forget those woodworking skills. By contrast, *phronesis* is not a form of knowledge that we possess in advance (like the plans a craftsman may have for building a cabinet in a house). Nor is it something we can leave behind or forget since we are always involved in applying it to the concrete situation in which we find ourselves.[111] Second, *techne* is teleological in nature, it is oriented towards the finished product or goal. *Phronesis* is not teleological in that one cannot know the right means or ends in advance of the situation, primarily because we are never sure that the course of action we decide upon will achieve what we hope

108. Gadamer, "*Praktisches Wissen*," 241.

109. Sullivan, *Political Hermeneutics*, 132; Gadamer, "*Praktisches Wissen*," 239, 241–42.

110. Sullivan, *Biblical Hermeneutics*, 122–35; Schuchman, "Aristotle's Phronēsis," 44–48; Gadamer, *Truth and Method*, 314–24.

111. Gadamer, *Truth and Method*, 313.

it will. Making an ethical decision is one example of an application of *phronesis*. When we are confronted with a situation in which we should tell the truth there is no guarantee as to how the other party will receive what we say. In situations like these *phronesis* involves the deliberation of finding the right means to the end of 'well being.'[112] Finally, *phronesis* involves self-knowledge; it is determined by and determines the moral well-being of man or woman. It is bound to *arete* (virtue or excellence) and oriented toward it.[113] "All of these examples throw into relief the final point of divergence between *phronēsis* and *technē*: technical knowledge has no intrinsic, existential relationship to the being of the craftsman; one can have *technē* and yet deliberately do a bad job, but if a man deliberately and habitually does what is wrong, he does not possess *phronēsis*."[114] Following Aristotle's lead, Gadamer argued that hermeneutical understanding and knowledge is not a theoretical or abstract form of knowledge (*episteme*) or the result of the application of technical rules and methods (*techne*). Hermeneutical understanding is tied to the concrete situations we find ourselves in and is bound up with the virtue and character of the interpreter, a form of *phronesis*.

While I agree with most of Gadamer's points about *phronesis*, his distinction between *techne* and *phronesis* is too strong and needs to be softened. *Techne* and *phronesis* are not competing forms of knowledge; rather *techne* is often part and parcel of *phronesis*. While *techne* provides the type of knowledge that a craftsman may need to decide which methods to employ to reach a certain end, *phronesis* allows the interpreter to decide what approach they will take to a particular situation. In Collingwood's words, it involves the insight that allows the reader to grasp what is unique in this text and make the appropriate decision as to how to proceed. As such, *phronesis* not only functions after methods come to an end, but it also functions before one has decided how one is going to proceed in the situation, before the application of a method. *Techne* and *phronesis* should be seen as forms of knowledge that are in constant dialogue with and inform one another. In any practice, such as music, professionals must develop their skills, *techne*, through instruction, and rehearse the score to be performed. Pianists need to

---

112. Aristotle, *Nicomachean Ethics*, II.2.

113. Gadamer, "*Praktisches Wissen*," 241–42.

114. Schuchman, "Aristotle's Phronēsis," 46.

practice scales. Singers need voice coaches. The orchestra adheres to the conductor. In sports, the more professional one becomes, the more one must submit to regulations. In short, the 'objective' and *techne* are inextricably intertwined in the performance. At the same time, the athlete in the game or the musician in the performance will confront situations where the rules that they have learned break down, or come to an end. The ability to improvise is a highly valued ability in both music and sports and is a form of *phronesis*, to go beyond where the rules leave off. This involves the ability to make judgments about what is the best way to proceed in the present situation. It is not so much an objective judgment, but what is right in a practical and intersubjective frame of reference.

The exercise of *phronesis* is not solipsistic, but is related to social institutions that determine the standards of excellence appropriate to the practice of biblical interpretation. Both the athlete and the musician took lessons, practiced with others, belong to organizations, and perform before others. All of these levels of involvement entail different standards that the athlete or musician must follow. These standards appear to operate in a manner similar to Wittgenstein's shared forms of life in the exercise of judgment.[115] In a similar vein, reading and interpretation are communal forms of activity, even for the supposed scholar sequestered away in an ivory tower. There is a criss-crossing and overlapping between institutions, traditions, and cultures that allow others to examine someone else's work and say, "That is truly exceptional work," or "They applied the wrong exegetical method in this instance."

In summary, the relevance of *phronesis* for Gadamer's hermeneutic is grounded in the problem of application. The heart of the problem is how the same tradition is understood in different ways in different horizons. It involves the application of the universal (tradition or a text from that tradition) to the particular (the historical context of the interpreter).[116] The strength of Aristotle's concept of *phronesis* is that it incorporates all the elements involved in the movement of application. "The knowledge of which Aristotle speaks is characterised by the fact that it includes perfect application and employs its knowledge in the

---

115. Wittgenstein, *Philosophical Investigations,* § 241.
116. Gadamer, *Truth and Method,* 312.

immediacy of a given situation."[117] As a form of knowledge, *phronesis* incorporates both the personal and the corporate (what the reader inherits from their tradition and their participation in a community) experiences of the interpreter. Unlike *techne*, we cannot divorce ethical considerations from the practices we are engaged in. "In fact we shall see that this is perhaps the fundamental form of experience."[118] *Phronesis* also includes *synesis*, a sympathetic understanding of the other which is required if we are going to be truly open to the other.[119] "Once again we discover that the person who is understanding does not know and judge as one who stands apart and unaffected but rather he thinks along with the other from the perspective of a specific bond of belonging, as if he too were affected."[120]

Phonesis spotlights the fact that training someone in biblical interpretation, or any other area of theology for that matter, is not a matter of teaching them technical or professional skills but involves the cultivation and development (*Bildung*) of the individual. The biblical interpreter's *habitus* must be formed through serious dialogue with the Christian tradition and their community. This occurs through the fusion of horizons in the practice of biblical interpretation that results in the enlarging of their horizon—not just individually, but collectively as well.

Conclusion

In his defense of tradition, Gadamer provides an epistemological basis for the importance that tradition plays in our understanding of the world, and in particular of texts. He wants to raise to consciousness not just the fact that tradition plays a role in historical research, but also explore its productive role in hermeneutical understanding. Hegel's concept of sublation, Collingwood's logic of question and answer, and the Socratic dialogues are resources that Gadamer drew upon to illustrate how we should approach tradition and the texts handed down to us through tradition. Sublation and the logic of question and answer explain how there can be both continuity and discontinuity

117. Ibid., 322.

118. Ibid.

119. This is related to our need for openness to the other in a dialogue.

120. Ibid., 323.

within a tradition of interpretation. Every act of interpretation involves the sublation of previous readings and in the process transforms how we understand the text. Not only is our understanding of the text reconfigured, but our view of previous interpretations have changed as well. The logic of question and answer demonstrates that the manner in which we interpret a text is tied to the horizon in which our questions arise and also to the subject-matter of the text. Therefore, on the one hand, we should not expect the history of a text's interpretation to exemplify a gradual linear accumulation of knowledge about that text. Rather, we should expect it to take a twisted route, with unexpected twists and turns, new starts, and possible backtracking at points. On the other hand, since the subject-matter of the text is one of the partners in his double hermeneutic, the history of a text's interpretation will be characterized by elements of convolution and continuity.

Perhaps one of the more significant points in this chapter is that what we learn through our encounter with tradition is greater than our individuality. When someone interprets a text, what is gained is not just an incremental increase in his or her personal knowledge. Rather, the interpreter has participated in a process of tradition. This can best characterized under the concept of *Bildung*. This is not a solipsistic form of knowledge, but through his encounter with the text, the reader has been educated or formed (*gebildete*). At the same time, the *sensus communis* of that tradition or community is reshaped and developed because of that individual's encounter with the text. In other words, for Gadamer the biblical interpreter is a corporately rational being who cannot be separated from humanity's past, present, or future.

Knowledge that is passed down within a tradition is not cumulative, as Hegel believed. Instead it is dynamic and constantly on the move. Through the processes of sublation, question and answer, and the movement of application, the elements of tradition and our knowledge of texts such as the Bible are ceaselessly being translated, transformed, and expanded. This is not to say, as Richard Rorty does, that interpretation (and other disciplines) boils down to an endless redescription of a text. "Still, if others have used the insight into historicity to jettison the idea of reason itself, Gadamer does not. Our historical situatedness does not only limit what we can know with certainty; it can also teach us how to remember and integrate what we must not forget."[121] Gadamer argues, by means of his double hermeneutic, that we are truly concerned with understanding the subject-matter of the text, but that this always occurs from within the historical horizon in which we stand. The possibility for diversity in understanding through time and across cultures is not evidence that we are never arriving at better understandings of the subject-matter, or that our interpretations are not appropriate or correct. Instead, Gadamer's point is that when we understand, we will always understand differently, and this new understanding will contribute to the formation of future horizons of understanding. In this manner, Gadamer is able to find a middle position that explains the diversity in interpretations which can be true to the text and stand in a relationship to each other (in their tradition) without being reduced to an anarchy of competing views.

121. Warnke, *Gadamer*, 174.

3

Play, Performance, and Provocation

PRIOR TO THIS CHAPTER, I EXAMINED WHAT COULD BE CONSIDERED
the epistemological side to Gadamer's hermeneutic: the role experience
plays in understanding, the logic of question and answer, and what type
of knowledge best characterizes hermeneutical understanding. This
chapter will concentrate on a different, yet complementary, aspect of
his hermeneutic: the eventful character of understanding. In this respect, this chapter will revolve around two metaphors that perform a
central role in Gadamer's hermeneutic: play and performance. Play is
perhaps second only to the concept of the fusion of horizons in *Truth
and Method*. Gadamer uses this concept not only to overcome some of
the conceptual weaknesses in other hermeneutical theories but also as
an apologetic for the universality of hermeneutics and to keep the role
of method in its proper place.[1][2]

Pushing Play off the Playing Field

Over the past couple hundred years reading has shifted from a communal to a private activity. This is as much a result of the rise of the
printing press and the ready availability of reading material for the vast
majority of the population as it is the implications of the philosophical
and hermeneutical theories about reading and interpretation. The idea
of an individual reading an isolated text alone in a room is an illusion
that has its origins in the Enlightenment and is an idea that Gadamer
rejects. This solipsistic approach to reading is symptomatic of deeper
hermeneutical problems.

1. Gadamer, *Truth and Method*, xxxiv.
2. Ibid.

> At once Gadamer is involved in an argument against a view of aesthetic experience which has haunted us for nearly two hundred years: the isolated self reading the isolated text: the isolated self looking at the isolated painting. But there is no such thing as the text apart from its interpretation, and no reading or seeing self which does not bring its interpretative schematism to the text or painting.[3]

Some of difficulties that Gadamer identifies that lay behind an individualistic approach to reading involve how the concepts of play, presentation, and re-presentation function in every act of understanding.

One of the most important metaphors that Gadamer employs in his investigations and argumentation is "play." In Part I of *Truth and Method*, he devotes much of his effort in an attempt to develop a concept of play that moves beyond subjectivity, but at the same time recognizes the finitude of human existence in order to explain the mode of being of a work of art.[4] In Part II, he shows how play is the "in-between," or middle ground, between the text and the interpreter that is the locus of hermeneutics.[5] In the final Part, he explores how the play that characterizes language games is related to the play of interpretation.[6]

In order to understand the relevance of Gadamer's concept of play we need to see it in light of the reception history. This is not just an exercise in historical background, but the form of my argument follows one of the central themes of Gadamer's hermeneutic: our understanding is conditioned by what has been handed down to us in our tradition. Therefore, it is essential that we raise to consciousness, as much as possible, those elements of our tradition that have shaped our present understanding. This is why Gadamer retraces the conceptual development of play in philosophical thought. Not only does he want to show how this concept developed but also to reveal the points of resistance to his conception of play.

3. MacIntyre, "Contexts of Interpretation," 43.

4. Gadamer, 101–29.

5. Ibid., 295.

6. "The question, then, is how the playing of the language-game, which is for each person also the playing of the world-game, goes together with playing the artwork-game." Gadamer, "Reflections on My Philosophical Journey," 43.

Determinative and Reflective Judgment

Immanuel Kant is the person whom Gadamer views as leading us astray in regard to a individualistic and subjective view of play.[7] The fork in the road, in respect to the concept of play, occurred when Kant differentiated determinate judgment from reflective judgment. Determinate judgment concerns those instances in which we can subsume a particular under a universal. If we already possess the universal then such a judgment is considered determinate. If we have a particular but the universal must be found, then that judgment is reflective.[8] Determinate judgments involve empirical phenomena, while reflective judgments do not. "Determinate judgement possesses its concept and faces the difficulty of applying it properly to the multiplicity of spatio-temporal appearances, while reflective judgement is in search of its concept through its multiplicity. It obeys a peculiar principle—related to the feeling of pleasure and displeasure . . ."[9] The result of this distinction and separation in the forms of judgment was that real knowledge was restricted to those areas in which we can exercise rational and empirical assessments (determinate judgment) and the sensuous or aesthetic (reflective judgment) became autonomous.[10] Just as the creative mind of the artist is not subject to the application of rules, so also the tastes (reflective

7. The background to Kant's thought is found in Rousseau who argued that human existence was characterized by a "disenchantment of the world." The starting point for human development was located in the state of nature. Property, government, division of labor, and tradition have "alienated mankind in the modern from its true nature." He developed three means of reform in *Emile, The Social Contract,* and *Nouvell Heloise,* but his views were inconsistent. It was not until Kant "thought Rousseau's thoughts through to their end" in the dialectical opposition of nature and civilization, reason and feeling that a more systematic solution was offered. Jauss, "The Literary Process of Modernism from Rousseau to Adorno," 39–41.

8. Kant, *Critique of Judgment,* § IV.

9. Caygill, *A Kant Dictionary,* 54. See also Makkreel, *Imagination and Interpretation in Kant,* 3.

10. "In der 'Kritik der reinen Vernunft' unterstreicht Kant die Unzulänglichkeit des bloßen Spiel mit Vorstellungen im Gegensatz zur Erkenntnis: Das 'Spiel der Einbildung ist ohne die mindeste Beziehung auf Wahrheit.' Ohne die 'data der möglichen Erfahrung' sind die Begriffe für Kant 'ein bloße Spiel, sei es der Einbildungskraft oder des Verstandes.'" (In his Criticism the Pure Reason Kant underlines the insufficiency mere play in contrast to the the ideas of knowledge: The "play of imagination is without the least relationship to truth." Without it "the data of the possible experience," according to Kant "is mere play, be it the imagination or understanding/reason.") Corbineau-Hoffmann, "Spiel," 9:1384.

judgments) of the patron are set free from the same constraints. "What we experience in beauty—in nature as well as in art—is the total animation and free interplay of all our spiritual powers. The judgment of taste is not knowledge, yet it is not arbitrary."[11] Because aesthetic judgments are not governed by the application of rules or concepts they cannot be compared to or held at the same level as determinate forms of understanding.

> If we now examine the importance of Kant's *Critique of Judgement* for the history of the human species, we must say that his giving aesthetics a transcendental philosophical basis had major consequences and constituted a turning point. It was the end of a tradition but also the beginning of a new development. It restricted the idea of taste to an area in which, as a special principle of judgement, it could claim independent validity—and, by so doing, limited the concept of knowledge to the theoretical and practical use of reason. The limited phenomenon of judgement, restricted to the beautiful (and sublime), was sufficient for his transcendental purpose; but it shifted the more general concept of the experience of taste, and the activity of aesthetic judgement in law and morality, out of the center of philosophy.[12]

Knowledge that proceeds from aesthetic judgments is different from that which comes through empirical studies or from the exercise of practical reason and at the same time it is characterized by its ability to make universal claims that are able to be communicated to others. An example of this is when someone says, "Psalm 23 is not only very moving but it speaks to the needs of the human soul." This is a claim with universal scope and is clearly communicable, but it does not arise from determinate judgment.

When we declare that something is beautiful we employ a form of taste that is non-conceptual. We do not appeal to an ideal form of art or literature in our judgment of a particular work of art. How then are we able to make a judgment concerning the value of a work of art or a text? Kant's answer is that the work of art facilitates the free play of imagination and understanding. "Kant claims that this free play of cognitive faculties, this animation of our feeling for life occasioned by the sight of

---

11. Gadamer, *Philosophical Hermeneutics*, 219.

12. Gadamer, *Truth and Method*, 40–41.

the beautiful, implies no conceptual grasp of an objective content and intends no ideal of an object."[13] While reflective judgment is solipsistic and not rule-governed, it does possess an intersubjective dimension in that we should be able to communicate our judgments to others.[14] Or as Richard Bernstein says, "Taste is communal, not idiosyncratic."[15] The nature of reflective judgments does not mean that others will agree with our conclusions, but they should be able to understand the reasoning behind our judgments and confirm our reasoning or not.[16]

This presents a dilemma for Gadamer. On the one hand, he argues that we cannot approach history or texts as instances of a universal but must see them as particulars, "to understand this man, this people, or this state."[17] We must use a reflective form of judgment in which the particular is not subsumed under a universal. On the other hand, if we accept Kant's reduction of reflective or aesthetic judgment as a model for hermeneutical knowledge, we run into the problem that there are no objective rules for determining what is beautiful. For Kant, the feeling of the subject, not the concept of the object, was what was important. As a result, historical knowledge based on Kant's idea of reflective judgment reduces to idiosyncratic preferences.[18] Aesthetic judgments were best experienced by a detached spectator. To illustrate his point he claimed that, when Germans observed the French Revolution, it was their feelings as spectators, their reflective judgments, that were significant. As spectators, the Germans had a speculative sympathy with the French, a sentimental attitude of "well-wishing participation."[19]

Kant's ideas in this area resulted in a paradigm shift for the humanities. On the one hand, the humanities were no longer subjected to the method of the natural sciences in order to exercise determinate forms of judgment in their field. On the other hand, the autonomy and

13. Gadamer, *The Relevance of the Beautiful*, 96.

14. Kant, *Critique of Judgement*, 52.

15. Bernstein, *Beyond Objectivsm and Relativism*, 119.

16. Jauss, *Aesthetic Experience and Literary Hermeneutics*, xxxix, 1151–56.

17. Ibid., 5.

18. Weinsheimer, *Philosophical Hermeneutics and Literary Theory*, 48.

19. Kant, *Conflict of Faculties*, 153. This sympathetic response which the French Revolution evoked in the German observers revealed the hope for moral progress according to Kant. It demonstrated that a vicarious participation in the Good can inspire revolutions. Makkreel, *Imagination and Interpretation in Kant*, 1485–1.

free play of reflective judgment justified the use of empathy, genius, and feeling as "subsidiary elements" to the humanities.[20]

The French Revolution also demonstrates a major difference between Kant and Hegel. The French Revolution, with its concept of freedom for all, was an underlying theme in Hegel's work.[21] Because the Spirit was objectified in social institutions, according to Hegel, he argued that we cannot hold to a form of inner morality that is detached from the "objective structures of life that hold human beings together."[22] In contrast to Kant, who claimed that morality was independent from contextual conditions, Hegel asserted that there was a "common and normative reality that surpasses the awareness of the individual" that was the basis for our social reality.[23] Therefore, the significance of the French Revolution did not lie in the sympathetic feelings of the observers, but in the fact that the Spirit was objectified in and through human institutions in history. In this way, Hegel was able to reconcile the two forms of knowledge that Kant had separated. For Hegel, the *Geisteswissenschaften* possess a form of knowledge that is similar to that found in the natural sciences. "That in history a reasonableness should perdue and make itself manifest similar to that in nature was the bold thesis."[24]

Schiller: Free-Play and Aesthetic Differentiation

Friedrich Schiller embraced Kant's dichotomy between determinative and reflective judgment and widened the gap between them. In doing so, he made art independent from the realm of reality and linked it to beautiful appearances. At the same time, he changed Kant's concepts of taste and morality to an aesthetic imperative. For Kant, taste was the transitional bridge from sensual pleasure to moral feelings. But for Schiller, the autonomy of reflective judgment and taste was the basis for the freedom of play.[25] Unlike Kant, play was not animated from

20. Ibid., 41; Paslick, "The Ontological Context of Gadamer's 'Fusion,'" 406–8.

21. See the section, "I/Thou and Slave/Master," in chapter 1.

22. Gadamer, *Reason in the Age of Science*, 30.

23. Ibid., 31.

24. Ibid., 36.

25. "*Da das Spiel weder unterworfen ist, gilt es als frei: 'Die Erkenntnißkräfte, die durch diese Vorstellung ins Spiel gesetzt werden, sind herbei in einem freien Spiele, weil kein*

our experience of an artwork but was a human impulse. This impulse was not restricted to external realities but arose from the semblance of reality that was freely constituted within the individual. Play was not only an instinct or impulse that characterized human nature, but it was also what educated and enhanced our humanity. The goal of the play impulse, according to Schiller, was the formation of "a cultured society (*Bildungsgesellschaft*) that takes an interest in art."[26]

Under this concept of play, art was now understood in terms of its contrast and separation from the real world. Nature was no longer a comprehensive domain because art constituted an autonomous realm above or beyond nature. The implications of this were two fold. First, determinate knowledge and the universality of the scientific method of approaching the thing-in-itself was undermined. Second, the experience of an artwork took place in the free play of an aesthetic state which did not possess a direct relationship to reality. Play was understood only in terms of subjective categories.[27] The play involved in understanding an artwork or text consists in the double abstraction of both the individual and the text or artwork from their world or any contextual relationships outside of them.[28]

> What we call a work of art and experience (*erleben*) aesthetically depends on a process of abstraction. By disregarding everything in which a work is rooted (its original context of life, and the religious or secular function that gave it significance), it becomes visible as the "pure work of art." In performing this abstraction, aesthetic consciousness performs a task that is positive in itself. It shows what a pure work of art is, and allows it to exist in its own right.[29]

There were two consequences to this line of thought. First, aesthetic consciousness attained the level of universality since it was capable of viewing everything aesthetically. And second, there was a simultaneity

---

bestimmter Begriff sie auf besondere Erkenntnißregel einschränkt." (Since the game is not subjected, it counts freely: "The power of knowledge, which is set through this idea in play, is hereby in free play, because there is no certain idea which limit it to a particular rule of knowledge.") Corbineau-Hoffmann, "Spiel," 9:1385.

26. Ibid., 83; Detsch, "A Non-Subjectivist Concept of Play," 157.

27. Gadamer, *Philosophical Hermeneutics*, 66.

28. Gadamer, *Truth and Method*, 82–85.

29. Ibid., 85.

to aesthetic consciousness in that works from the past were cut free from their contextual relationships and were able to be experienced directly by a contemporary viewer. This simultaneity was not based on a monolithic concept of aesthetic taste but recognized that taste varies. Thus, there can be "a hundred different treatments of the same subject, to find a thousand different forms of expression for the thoughts and feelings common to all men."[30]

The impact of aesthetic differentiation can also be seen in the manner in which museums changed during this period. Before Schiller, museums reflected a particular taste or school. However, the impact of aesthetic simultaneity and universality resulted in museums attempting to expand or rearrange their exhibitions in order to appear as comprehensive as possible.[31]

Schiller is mistaken, according to Gadamer, because aesthetic judgment and taste depend on what is preferred by a society at any point in time; it is part of our social fabric. "Even its artistic interests are not arbitrary or in principle universal, but what artists create and what the society values belong together in the unity of a style of life and an ideal of taste."[32] Thus, play is never unbounded and free as Schiller claimed. If Gadamer is correct, then the concept of play, which determines how we perceive art, and more importantly, how we approach a text, needs to be reworked.

Nietzsche and the Play of an Absurd World

While Gadamer does not discuss Nietzsche's concept of play, he is significant to my discussion for three reasons. First, Nietzsche applied the concept of play to tradition and history. Second, he is often used by Heidegger as the foil for Heidegger's ideas. Third, Nietzsche reflects the logical conclusion to Kant and Schiller's arguments and, as such, he plays an important role in the development of modern literary theory and hermeneutics.

Nietzsche, however, did not approach this position from the avenue of aesthetics, as Schiller did, but from history. In *The Use and Abuse of History* Nietzsche attacked the nineteenth century's historical-critical

---

30. Schiller, *On the Aesthetic Education of Man*, cxxxi.

31. Gadamer, *Truth and Method*, 87.

32. Ibid., 84–85.

approach to history. Instead of proposing an alternative model of history, he pushed their conclusions to their logical end. "History must solve the problem of history, science must turn its sting against itself."[33] In doing so he reduced the world and all that can be known to history, but not a Hegelian form of history which possesses a higher order of Spirit or rationality behind it. For Nietzsche, the reason why things were the way they were was because of sheer chance and the principle of correlation.[34] "Even after suprahistorical essences or necessities are forgotten, things cohere, q follows p and is as it is partly because p was as it was. 'History' is simply this temporal coherence, this connectedness of things from one moment to the next."[35] While his argument denies the possibility for metaphysics (based on what occurs in history), it also asserts the continuity of history.[36] This connectedness is both a curse and a blessing. History and tradition are the unbearable weight of an unwilled past pressing down us.[37] In *The Gay Science*, he describes this as the 'Greatest Weight':

> What, if some day or night a demon were to steal after you into your loneliest loneliness and say to you: "This life as you live it and have lived it, you will have to live once more and innumerable times more; and there will be nothing new in it, but every pain and every joy and every thought and sigh and everything unutterably small or great in your life will have to return to you, all in the same succession and sequence—even this spider and this moonlight between the trees, and even this moment and I myself. The eternal hourglass of existence is turned upside down again and again, and you with it, speck of dust!"[38]

Eternal Recurrence precludes any form of freedom or variation from what has happened or will happen again.[39] Once we come to terms

33. Nietzsche, *The Use and Abuse of History*, 50.

34. The principle of correlation is not unique to Nietzsche, but is a widely recognized principle of historiography. It emphasizes the continuous web of cause and effect that governs the natural world. "Since we discern . . . the various historical cycles of human life influencing and intersecting one another, we gain at length the idea of continuity." Troeltsch, "Historiography," 6:718.

35. Roberts, *Nothing but History*, 65.

36. Heller, "Multiplicity and Unity in Nietzsche's Works," 322.

37. Nietzsche, *The Use and Abuse of History*, 5–6.

38. Nietzsche, *The Gay Science*, 273.

39. Copleston, *Friedrich Nietzsche*, 16; Kaufmann, "Translator's Introduction," in Nietzsche, *The Gay Science*, 17; Heller, "Multiplicity and Unity," 325.

with the idea of Eternal Recurrence, we realize that history is a closed system in which each moment affects those that follow it. History has no goal or God. Human beings are forever confined to the particular horizon of world history in which they find themselves. Redemption from this burden comes from how we embrace this unwilled past. "Or have you once experienced a tremendous moment when you would have answered him [the demon of Eternal Recurrence]: 'You are a god and never have I heard anything more divine.' If this thought gained possession of you, it would change you as you are or perhaps crush you."[40] Eternal Recurrence is a weight that presses down and threatens to crush us unless we embrace it, in which case it is liberating.

Because this is a large topic I will restrict the discussion to Nietzsche's ideas regarding play and Eternal Recurrence to those points that are relevant to reception theory. Play enters Nietzsche's philosophical system in two ways. First, Eternal Recurrence suggests that there is no purpose to history. Therefore, all human actions should not be seen as meaningful, but as meaningless play. Once we realize this the values we inherit from the past are no longer true but are only the trace or symptom of someone else's exercise of the Will to Power.[41] Second, in Nietzsche's program of deconstruction human creativity is freed from any constraints that historical contingency or suprahistorical movements may have placed upon how we understand the past.[42] By embracing Eternal Recurrence we are able to deconstruct and reassemble the absurdity of the past, and in this way give it meaning through our exercise of the Will to Power. Play arises from the conflict between the meaninglessness of the world and the subject who exercises Will to Power to give value to what is otherwise absurd.[43] "The will to power operates in a vacuum, so to speak. It creates its own values and sustains

---

40. Nietzsche, *The Gay Science*, 273–74; Corbineau-Hoffmann, "Spiel," 9:1386. This raises a possible conceptual inconsistency in Nietzsche's thought. How is it possible to hold to both the closed continuum of Eternal Recurrence and the creative freedom of the Will to Power?

41. If we accept Nietzsche's argument, we are pushed to an extreme form of nihilism. His thought in this area also foreshadows Richard Rorty's contention that philosophical inquiry is nothing more than a process of endless redescription.

42. Roberts, *Nothing but History*, 69.

43. Detsch, "A Non-Subjectivist Concept of Play," 169.

them in a world without a logical basis."[44] In this way, play functions as a hermeneutical tool to undermine and destabilize the cultural ideologies and morality that Nietzsche opposed. In a powerful way Nietzsche raised to consciousness how truth claims may be more about the use of power than describing reality. The danger is that his views are often employed to create a culture of suspicion rather than a critique of ideology. "Play as transgressive unreason and absurdity serves to correct the imbalance in culture and thought, and art, like play, standing apart from privileged modes of reason in culture, works to promote the spirit of unrest and misrule, challenging and directing its audience to new conceptions of reality."[45] Nietzsche's influence can be seen in the work of Derrida, Foucault, Barthes, and Lyotard who, in their own ways, attempt to undermine all systems of reason and expose them as systems of persuasion. The stakes for Nietzsche's ideas are especially high for biblical and theological studies; as Anthony Thiselton noted, "Theology serves to establish critically informed trust whereas the postmodern perspective rests on suspicion."[46]

The split that opened between determinative and reflective judgment not only reached its zenith in Nietzsche, but it was completely reversed. "If Kant and Schiller redefined play in such a way as to make it a useful concept for moderns, it was Friedrich Nietzsche who freed it from the constraints of reason."[47] The objective world of history is utterly meaningless and oblivious to human agency according to Nietzsche. We are ignorant of the play of the world and history until we grasp the true nature and significance of the world through Eternal Recurrence and by an act of the will enter into play with it. "Human nature stands, in other words, outside the totality of the world and must seek admittance to it."[48] In this way his concepts of the Superman and Eternal Recurrence are brought together. "Man must practice a heroic yea-saying to life, must live so that he will desire and affirm the eternal repetition of his actions."[49] On both sides, the concept of play is central

44. Ibid., 165; Vanhoozer, "A Lamp in the Labyrinth," 40.

45. Slethaug, "Play/freeplay, theories of," 146.

46. Thiselton, *Interpreting God*, 16.

47. Slethaug, "Play/freeplay, theories of," 145; see also Heller, "Multiplicity and Unity," 330–31; Corbineau-Hoffmann, "Spiel," 9:1386.

48. Ibid., 168

49. Copleston, *Friedrich Nietzsche*, 19. "It is the 'final, cheerfullist, exuberantly mad-and-merriest Yea to life." Ibid., 61.

to understanding Nietzsche's arguments. The absurdity of the world is compared to a child who endlessly builds and demolishes sand piles on a deserted, desolate beach.[50] When we enter the play of history we are not creating any transcendental values, we are merely entering into the unending play of the world.[51] As historical beings we find ourselves in the unending play of history which is utterly meaningless except for those values we ascribe to it. Because the play of human understanding corresponds to the play of the world every interpretation we arrive at will prove meaningless and washed away with the passage of time.[52] In this way, Nietzsche carried the Romantic tradition's concept of play through to its most extreme conclusion.

Heidegger: The Play of Truth

Heidegger views Nietzsche as the conclusion to the western philosophical tradition. The distinction and separation between the visible and the invisible is one of the main trajectories in which this tradition has developed according to Heidegger. In the development of this tradition, those things which were visible and transitory lost their value and were reduced to the status of mere objects. Until finally, the visible world was viewed as totally senseless and absurd by Nietzsche. Heidegger's concepts of truth as disclosure, thrownness, and play reverse many of the trajectories of thought concerning the topic of play that started with Kant. While 'play' is not a central thesis in Heidegger's thought, it and his conception of truth form the background to Gadamer's hermeneutic in this area.

Heidegger's clearest discussion of play is found in *The Principle of Reason*. Because human beings have a desire to control, we attempt to find a reason for everything. This desire is reflected in scientific methods that attempt (through objectivity) to detach the observer from the movement of play. However, this is an impossible ideal to achieve because there is an opposing movement of play which impoverishes our

50. Heller, "Multiplicity and Unity," 321. Nietzsche derived this from Heracleitus's 52nd fragment. Corbineau-Hoffmann, "Spiel," 9.1386–87.

51. "The Will to Power is expressed in temporal terms in the theorem of Eternal Recurrence which posits the endlessly self-creative, self-destructive play that is the cosmos, as one which must repeat itself endlessly throughout eternity." Nietzsche, *The Gay Science*, 324–25; also, 336.

52. Detsch, "A Non-Subjectivist Concept of Play," 167.

ability for "building and dwelling in the realm of what is essential. There is an enigmatic interconnection (*Wiederspiel*, counter-play) between the demand to render reasons (*Grund*) and the withdrawal of roots (*Bodens*, foundation, footing). It is important to see the form of the movement occurring in this lofty play (*Spieles*) between rendering and withdraw."[53] Play occupies the space between the opposing movements of giving or delivering reasons and the pulling back or withdrawing of the foundational answers of what is essential.

This concept of play can also be seen in Heidegger's concept of truth. According to Heidegger, ἀλήθεια means "unconcealment" or "disclosure." Truth as disclosure is related to its opposite: concealment or hiddenness.[54] Truth is an event of disclosure that takes place within the referential contexts in which we live.[55] Because truth as disclosure takes place in finite, temporal human existence, it is never final, comprehensive, or determinate. Every event of disclosure is characterized by concealment.[56] Concealment and revealment are ontologically related to each other. In every disclosure of truth not only does something come to light but something remains hidden.[57]

> Thanks to this clearing [between disclosure and concealment], beings are unconcealed in certain changing degrees. And yet a being can be concealed, too, only within the sphere of what is lighted. Each being we encounter and which encounters us

53. Heidegger, *The Principle of Reason*, 60. Alternate translations mine. While I agree with Lilly's translation most of the time, I feel that the metaphorical use of Heidegger's terms is often missed in his translation, so I have tried to incorporate that into the text.

54. Tugendhat, "Heidegger's Idea of Truth," 88; Heidegger, *Being and Time*, 57.

55. "Being-true as Being-uncovering, is in turn ontologically possible only on the basis of Being-in-the-world." Heidegger, *Being and Time*, 261; Tugendhat, "Heidegger's Idea of Truth," 91; DiCenso, *Hermeneutics and the Disclosure of Truth*, 62. One of the most important existential categories associated with the play of concealment and disclosure is Being-towards-death. Death presents us with a tension between Being and non-Being that is part of the play structure of the cosmos. Death presents being qua abyss (*Ab-Grund*), "which as the most radical possibility of existence is capable of bringing what is most elevated to the clearing and lightening of being and its truth." Heidegger, *Poetry, Language, Thought*, 112.

56. Heidegger, *Being and Truth*, 265. "Truth, in its nature, is un-truth." Heidegger, *Poetry, Language, Thought*, 54.

57. Gadamer, *Philosophical Hermeneutics*, 226.

> keeps to this curious opposition of presence in that it always withholds itself at the same time in a concealedness.[58]

Hiddenness is not the result of error or ignorance but belongs to Being itself. In fact, it is hiddenness that makes disclosure possible. Truth is characterized by the play between concealment and unconcealment, which means truth will always remain continual and provisional. "Truth, in Heidegger's understanding, will never establish itself irrevocably and definitively, with a plenitude of reality. It is a process which can never be completed because the hidden will never relinquish its hold on that which emerges from it."[59] We can never fully grasp a person, thing, or event in the totality of its Being, because this would mean that no further perspectives or referential contexts would remain which could evoke new possibilities of disclosure which are concealed from us in our interpretive horizon.[60]

However, this does not allow one to conclude that all disclosures are equally true or valid. False understanding or interpretations are not a disclosure but a covering up, according to Heidegger. This takes place when we uncover the entity in a way that it is not itself.[61] The truth of an interpretation is related to how the interpretation reveals or sheds light on that text or object. "To say that an assertion 'is true' signifies that it uncovers the entity as it is itself. Such an assertion asserts, points out, 'lets' the entity 'be seen' (ἀπόφανσις) in its uncoveredness. The Being-true (truth) of the assertion must be understood as Being-uncovering." To say that something is true means there is some degree of conformity of our knowledge with the facts that have been disclosed in the event of understanding.[62] In this respect, Heidegger takes a middle position concerning the meaning of a text.

58. Heidegger, *Poetry, Language, Thought*, 53.

59. Detsch, "A Non-Subjectivist Concept of Play," 169.

60. Ibid., 53. For a very clear discussion of referential contexts in Heidegger, see Mulhall, *Heidegger and Being and Time*, 99–104.

61. Tugendhat's article has an excellent critique of Heidegger's concept of truth as disclosure. He demonstrates how Heidegger adopts a very narrow definition of uncovering or disclosure as "pointing out." This raises two problems: (1) how do we differentiate truth from pointing out, and (2) false assertions are disclosive also (there is an element of unconcealment in their concealment). While Heidegger does not address these problems, they raise questions about how we are to judge between falsehood and truth in his system. "Heidegger's Idea of Truth," 86–92.

62. Heidegger, *Poetry, Language, Thought*, 51–55.

It is worth noting that "science is not an original happening of truth, but always the cultivation of a domain of truth already open, specifically by apprehending and confirming that which shows itself to be possibly and necessarily correct within that field."[63] This helps to explain Thomas Kuhn's theory of the history of science as paradigm shifts. The creative thought required to conceptualize the field of research in a new paradigm would be an original event of truth. The period of normal science that would follow once the new paradigm is adopted would not fall under the category of truth as play, but would be the "cultivation of the domain of truth already opened up."[64]

If we return to *Der Satz vom Grund*, we find that play is simply part of the fabric of existence and, as such, it needs no explanation. "The 'because' withers away in play. The play is without 'why.' It plays since it plays. It simply remains a play: the most elevated and the most profound."[65] Play is a to-and-fro movement of understanding without aim or purpose that constantly renews itself in repetition. On the one hand, the nature of play is determined by the thrownness of Being. As such, the field of play has no boundaries, "of rules, of rules of play, of calculus."[66] On the other hand, play is characterized by freedom. Rules may restrict play, but at the same time play is erratic and open to new possibilities of disclosure.[67]

Therefore, the transmission of a tradition will not be a smooth process but will often appear broken or erratic because of the playful manner in which the new or unexpected breaks forth in a tradition.[68] Kisiel sums up Heidegger's position when he states that Heidegger "insists that there is a final leap through the normal conversation with the tradition to the creative event, which does not abide by previously established laws, but creates its own norms that bestow a unique

63. Heidegger, *Was heisst Denken?*, 62.

64. See Kuhn, *The Structure of Scientific Revolutions.*

65. Heidegger, *The Principle of Reason*, 113; Heidegger, *Der Satz vom Grund*, 188.

66. Ibid., 112, 186.

67. Kisiel, "The Happening of Tradition," 372. For Heidegger, the danger of taking a conservative approach to tradition is that it erects restrictive rules that stifle play.

68. Heidegger, *The Principle of Reason*, 90–91; Heidegger, *Der Satz vom Grund*, 154. In this way, Heidegger's concept of play shares a common thread with Nietzsche's. Like Nietzsche, he cites Heracleitus's 52nd Fragment to demonstrate the playful nature of the cosmos. "Αἰών παῖς ἐστι παίζων, πεσσεύων ἡ παιδὸς ἡ βασιληίη." The ἀρχή that governs the nature of being is that of a "child that plays." Ibid., 113, 188.

bearing on the original thinker and changes the normal course of history fundamentally."[69]

Heidegger's notion of play, and the playful structure of truth as disclosure, reverses many of the ideas found in the trajectory from Kant to Nietzsche. Play is not separated from or differentiated from other forms of knowledge. All truth, whether it is scientific or aesthetic, is characterized by the play of concealment and disclosure. Truth, as an original occurrence, takes place in the space created in the play between disclosure and concealing and, in this sense, is a historical happening. Truth occurs in many different manners: from that found in a work of art, to the founding of a political state, a religious ceremony, or the questioning of a thinker.[70] This means that we cannot differentiate the aesthetic from everyday life because all disclosures of truth are constituted by *Dasein's* thrownness. In this way, Heidegger overcomes the subjectivity inherent in the previous conceptions of play.

Gadamer's Concept of Play

As I mentioned at the outset of this chapter, play is one of the fundamental concepts in *Truth and Method*. Gadamer criticizes both historicism and aesthetic consciousness for the same reason; they are both alienated forms of true historical being and, as a result, we cannot truly experience art or history through them. It is through his development of the concept of *Spiel* (play or game) that he seeks to solve the problems located in historicism and aesthetic consciousness. However, he must first correct the subjectivity inherent in previous conceptions of play.[71]

Gadamer does not want to evacuate subjectivity from the concept of play but to transcend it. "Play is more than the consciousness of the player, and so it is more than a subjective act."[72] The truth claim of a work of art raises a hermeneutical question that reveals the limits of method. We cannot provide an adequate explanation of art from a methodological perspective. In order to answer the question of how we

69. Kisiel, "The Happening of Tradition," 377.

70. Ibid., 62.

71. Gadamer, "Reflections," 27.

72. Gadamer, "Forward to the Second Edition," in *Truth and Method*, xxxvi.

understand an artwork Gadamer insists we must look at the "mode of being of the work of art itself."[73]

Play does not refer to the subjective state of mind of the observer or creator but, play refers to the mode of Being itself, and especially to the "mode of being of art itself."[74] Play is best understood as the medium through which understanding takes place and not in terms of subject/object, player/game, or psychological categories. Play is a primordial mode of Being characterized by a "to-and-fro movement" that is not oriented towards a telos, but renews itself with each and every movement.[75] Human existence is characterized by and experiences the playful nature of Being. Play exists independently of the consciousness of the players and, as such, play takes primacy "over the consciousness of the player."[76] Richard Detsch points out how both Heidegger and Gadamer share the same paradoxical assumption when it comes to play. "The both posit a dimension which, unlike modern existential philosophy, transcends human subjectivity; but unlike the older metaphysical-theological speculation, they both hold fast to human finiteness."[77]

There is one fundamental point at which Gadamer and Heidegger's concept of play differ. For Heidegger, tradition restricted the room for play and, as a result, he argued that we needed to include the freedom of poetic release in the concept of play. Gadamer, in contrast, takes a much more positive approach toward tradition. The playing field is the temporal room of tradition.[78] The playful event of understanding is possible only because of what is handed down to us in our tradi-

73. Gadamer, *Truth and Method*, 100. Gadamer's argument parallels the central thrust of Heidegger's essay, "The Origin of the Work of Art," in *Poetry, Language, Thought*.

74. Gadamer, *Truth and Method*, 101.

75. Ibid., 101–4. Gadamer follows Heidegger's definition of play at this and many other points. See Heidegger, *The Principle of Reason*, 112–13; Heidegger, *Der Satz vom Grund*, 186–88.

76. Gadamer, *Truth and Method*, 102. In German, the term for play (*spielen*) carries a semantic range of meaning that is not as clearly seen in the English. Gadamer cites this semantic range to show how one can play (*spielt*) a game, or to refer to that fact that something is happening (*sich abspielt* or *im Spiele ist*). His point is that in German *spielen* is not primarily something someone does, but conveys the idea that the subject of play is play itself. Ibid., 104; Gadamer, *Philosophical Hermeneutics*, 66.

77. Detsch, "A Non-Subjectivist Concept of Play," 160.

78. Kisiel, "The Happening of Tradition," 371–72.

tion and how what is handed down addresses and strikes us. In this way, tradition is constantly playing itself out in new possibilities.[79] This point becomes very clear if we contrast Gadamer's idea of play with Nietzsche's. For Nietzsche, because we dwell in an absurd world, play knows no bounds. However, for Gadamer, tradition is not absurd nor an oppressive weight pressing down on us, but it is the soil from which productive understanding arises. We all stand in a reciprocal relationship to a tradition. The one conditions the other, and vice versa, whether or not we are aware of it. It is the playing field in which we play out every act of understanding.[80]

According to Gadamer, while play is not teleological, it is purposeful. "Play fulfills its purpose only if the player loses himself in play."[81] By this, Gadamer means that there is a seriousness to play which gives it a purpose. This can be seen in the way we refer to a person who holds himself back and does not enter into the spirit of the game as a spoil sport.[82] The player must approach play seriously, not by approaching play in an objective manner (as if it were an object to by studied) but by becoming involved in the play of a game.[83] This is a significant aspect to play for Gadamer. To be seriously involved in play means that we are part of the game that is taking place. The distinction between subject and object (player and game) is not appropriate since there would be no game without the players. When a player distances herself from the play she was involved in (in order to critically reflect on it), play breaks down and she is no longer in the game.[84] When applied to textual interpretation, play as the hermeneutical medium for understanding reveals the weaknesses of approaching a text from the perspective of the subjectivity of the author (Schleiermacher) or the interpreter (Schiller).

Play as a fundamental hermeneutical category allows Gadamer to go beyond the dominance of method in the humanities, while at the same time not denying the validity of method at different points (the performing of the tasks in the game).

79. Detsch, A Non-Subjectivist Concept of Play," 162.

80. Ibid., 168.

81. Gadamer, *Truth and Method*, 102.

82. Linge, "Editor's Introduction," in Gadamer, *Philosophical Hermeneutics*, xxiii.

83. Gadamer, *Truth and Method*, 102.

84. Ibid., 117.

> The real subject of playing is the game itself. This observation
> does not contradict the fact that one must know the rules of
> the game and stick to them, or by the fact that the players un-
> dergo training and excel in the requisite physical methods of
> the game. All these things are valuable and "come into play" only
> for the one who enters the game and gives herself to it.[85]

As such, method falls under, or into, the medium of play. Play, as part of
the primordial nature of being, is the medium in which understanding
takes place. The application of method in interpretation is a derivative
form of understanding. In our quest for objectivity we employ methods so that we may obtain a degree of certitude in our interpretations.
However, the concept of play reveals that this is not only a false ideal,
but the concept of play also stands in active opposition to these ideals.
One of the significant aspects of art is that this is the area in which
we experience this opposition to method most clearly. How does one
objectively approach Van Gogh's painting of the peasant's shoes in a
manner which does justice to it as a work of art?

Play as the Being of Artwork

While play, as a fundamental aspect of Being, is non-teleological, it can
open the possibility for other forms of activity which do have structures
and purposes, such as games, artwork, and musical performances. For
Gadamer, the highest form by which play can be experienced is that
of art. "My thesis, then, is that the being of art . . . is part of the event
of being that occurs in presentation, and belongs essentially to play as
play."[86]

The fact that play requires someone to play seems obvious. But
in Gadamer's phenomenological examination of play, the players and
that which is played are essential. It is only when a player is seriously
involved in play that what is being played presents itself; it comes into
being. An artwork does not exist in and of itself, as a self-sufficient object. Rather, the artwork comes into being only in the playful interaction
between it and the viewer. This concept of art is based on Heidegger's
analysis found in his essay, "The Origin of the Work of Art."

---

85. Linge, "Editor's Introduction," xxiii; Gadamer, *Truth and Method*, xxix.
86. Ibid., 116.

In order to illustrate the nature of what an artwork is, Heidegger considers Van Gogh's painting, "A Pair of Shoes" (1885). As one looks at this picture he or she notices all sorts of things: "the toilsome tread of the worker . . . the dampness and richness of the soil . . . the quiet gift of grain . . . This equipment belongs to the earth, and is protected in the world of the peasant woman."[87] But how does one discover such things in a work of art? Certainly not by the application of a method, "but only by bringing ourselves before Van Gogh's painting. This painting spoke."[88] In the event of experiencing the picture a disclosure of truth takes place concerning this pair of peasant shoes. An unconcealment takes place. "If there occurs in the work a disclosure of a particular being, disclosing what and how it is, then there is here an occurring, a happening of truth at work."[89] The term "art-work" is illustrative of the being of art for Heidegger. In the interaction with the viewer, a "work" happens in the disclosure of the truth of the painting.

Gadamer describes this as the consummation of play. In viewing the painting, we are caught up into the play of understanding in which a world is projected by the work of art. Play as presentation is realized in the re-presentation that we experience in viewing the painting. There is a unity of truth (the subject/object split is transcended) that we experience in the work of art. To step back and ask questions about the origin or technical aspects of the painting severs us from the true experience of the work of art. We are no longer caught up in play and cannot grasp the truth claim of the work of art that comes into existence when we are involved in the play of the artwork.

This type of reflection also implies a form of aesthetic differentiation between "the work itself from its representation" for Gadamer. At the same time, he does not wish to "deny that here there is a starting point for aesthetic reflection."[90] The various presentations of a work are not exempt from all constraints but are restrained by the structure and contingencies that are part of the world of the artwork. This allows us to make judgments about the correctness of a representation. However, the danger that Gadamer takes great pains to avoid in this type of

87. Heidegger, *Poetry, Language, Thought*, 34.
88. Ibid., 35.
89. Ibid., 36.
90. Gadamer, *Truth and Method*, 118.

reflection is that we might fall back into Kant's two forms of judgment and an aesthetic concept of play. Therefore, Gadamer is highly critical of all attempts to reintroduce critical reflection back into hermeneutics. This is one of the major points over which Gadamer disagrees with Jauss. However, we shall have to wait until the next chapter to see if Jauss is successful in his attempt to include some form of reflection and methodology in his hermeneutic.

Presentation and the Transformation into Structure

The fact that play requires players reveals that human play always plays something. First, the player chooses to play this rather than that. This means that human play is not characterized by an unrestricted freedom, but it takes place in a space specifically marked out and reserved for the play in which we have chosen to engage. "Human play requires a play-ing field."[91] Second, play involves performing tasks (i.e., a child's game may involve the task of playing with a ball). Human involvement in play is possible only because it involves tasks. However, it is important to note that the purpose of play is not accomplished in the performance of the tasks involved in the game, but in "the ordering and shaping of the movement of the game itself."[92]

An essential trait of art as play is that "all play is potentially a representation for someone."[93] In performing the actions in a game, presentation takes place. As the players perform the tasks of the game they are also involved in a self-presentation. On the one hand, there is a degree of difference between a child playing and a musical performance in terms of presentation to others. On the other hand, all forms of play are characterized by an openness toward a potential audience which moves play beyond self-presentation to "representing for someone." The *Schauspiel*, or theatrical performance, is a clear illustration of this principle. As the actors (players) perform the play, a presentation oc-curs. This involves their self-presentation as they play themselves out in the tasks they perform. "Only because play is presentation, is human play able to make representation the task of a game."[94] The *Schauspiel*

91. Ibid., 107.
92. Ibid.
93. Ibid., 108.
94. Ibid.

takes its mode of existence in its performance in that this form of play (the drama) is written by an author for its performance by players to an audience. The potential nature of any presentation reaches its completion in the audience, spectators, viewers, or readers.[95] Play is realized not just in the players but also those who watch the play. "In fact, it is experienced properly by and presents itself (as it is 'meant') to, one who is not acting in the play but watching it. In him the game is raised, as it were, to its ideality."[96] Therefore, play is best defined as the "process that takes place 'in between' the player and the game."[97]

As we saw above, play cannot be approached objectively, by means of a neutral subject who employs methods in his reflecting on the origin of the play or aspects of its presentation. Critical reflection creates a distance between the player and play which drops the player out of play. Most of us are familiar with this type of experience when a critic's comment breaks the "spell" of the play (I have a drama or movie in mind) in which we are involved.

> In this 'world' of the film, we have been lowered into a lifeboat, and are battered by the roaring wind. Our stomachs turn as the boat rises high, then drops twenty feet into a trough between the waves. We hear the sound of the spray, and as lightning breaks across the sky we catch a glimpse of the ship we have just left . . . An awestruck voice whispers besides us "No one would ever think that the Director had used a two-foot model in a six-foot tank." The spell has been broken by the comment of a critic, who necessarily speaks on the basis of a critical approach.[98]

Nor can play be apprehended through the free-play of the viewers' aesthetic consciousness. Rather, play is the "in between" that involves the participation of the players and the audience in the presentation of the play.[99]

Because artistic presentation, as play, exists for an audience, play is transformed into structure. While play is without purpose or intention, it can lead to activities that possess purpose and structure. By transformation into structure, Gadamer "means that something is suddenly

95. Ibid., 108–9.
96. Ibid., 109.
97. Ibid., 109, 117.
98. Thiselton, *New Horizons*, 315–16.
99. Gadamer, *Truth and Method*, 117.

and as a whole something else, that this other transformed thing that it has become is its true being, in comparison with which its earlier being is nil."[100] The author of the drama, the script, and the players no longer exist in themselves. Play transforms the author's script and the player's performance into what they are playing.[101] The actors become the characters and the stage becomes the setting for the drama. "Thus transformation into structure means that what existed previously exists no longer. But also that what now exists, what represents itself in the play of art, is the lasting and true."[102] This same transformation takes place in reading literature. Just as the being of the work of art is play and must be viewed by the spectator in order for it to be actualized, "so also it is universally true of texts that only in the process of understanding them is the dead trace of meaning transformed back into living meaning."[103]

In respect to the audience, play transforms into a world (structure) in which the audience dwells. Gadamer's argument at this point rests on Heidegger's idea that a work of art projects a 'world.' Van Gogh's painting of the peasant shoes illuminates how we experience the world presented by an artwork. This projection does not occur through description or explanation "but only by bringing ourselves before Van Gogh's painting. This painting spoke. In the vicinity of the work we were suddenly somewhere else than we usually tend to be."[104] The world that is projected exists in a playful conflict with the 'earth.' Earth refers not only to the physical and historical environment in which we live, but it also consists in the intersubjective life-world from which all human understanding takes place. The truth of the work of art is that the work of art opens up a world. In the artwork, a world arises and as a result, there is a disclosure of truth. When we view Van Gogh's painting of the peasant's shoes something new is revealed or disclosed that "is not simply the manifestation of a truth, it is itself an event."[105] We actively participate in this disclosure of the world of the work of art through the "opening of oneself to the event of encounter and standing in it in

100. Ibid., 111.
101. Ibid., 112.
102. Ibid.
103. Ibid., 164.
104. Heidegger, *Poetry, Language, Thought*, 35.
105. Ibid., 224.

such a way that the being of the work of art shows itself, steps forth, appears."[106] In this way, Gadamer writes that play is a transformation into truth; "it produces and brings to light what is otherwise constantly hidden and withdrawn."[107] The split between subject and object is reconciled as both participate in the "in-between" of play.

What does this mean in relation to the history of a text's interpretation? When we apply Gadamer's concept of the transformation of play into structure to the history of a text's reception, we realize that there can be no "single meaning" for the text. Different acts of interpretation will never arrive at the same understanding of a text. While the task of interpreting a text can be repeated (we are performing the same text), it cannot be re-enacted in exactly the same manner because the conditions under which the performance is performed cannot be identical.

Rituals and festivals help us to grasp how there is both continuity and discontinuity in interpretation. A religious ritual, such as Lord's Supper, displays affinities with textual interpretation because it only exists in its celebration (or performance) just as the meaning of a text is also a performance.[108]

The celebration of a ritual, such as the Lord's Supper, possesses two distinct but related forms of temporality. First, it is historically temporal. Originally this meal was celebrated by Jesus with his disciples. After his ascension it came to be celebrated by his disciples in light of his death and resurrection. And our contemporary observances of the Eucharist, while celebrating the same ritual, would most likely be completely unrecognizable to the early church. The ritual changes from one week, or celebration, to the next because the historical horizon it is celebrated in changes. A ritual like the Lord's Supper is not one and the same, but it is historical in that "it exists by always being something different.[109] Like a text, a festival displays this curious temporality of celebration, disap-

---

106. The experience of art is not something that we do, but is something we are absorbed into; it is the "work" of art. Palmer, "Ritual, Rightness, and Truth," 540.

107. Gadamer, *Truth and Method*, 112.

108. While textual interpretation and the celebration of a festival are similar, it is important to note that they are not identical for Gadamer. Palmer, "Ritual, Rightness, and Truth," 534.

109. Gadamer, *Truth and Method*, 123–24 n. 225. Gadamer is arguing against the Platonic idea that a festival could be an "ideal" which remains unchanged while its manifestation in history will always be different. For Gadamer, there is no Platonic ideal behind the festival, just as there is no ideal 'meaning' behind the text.

pearance, and then returning in the next celebration. No two celebrations are replicated in the same manner, but the Eucharist is open to an unlimited number of re-enactments. At the same time, our celebration must be appropriate to what is being observed. The "rightness" of the celebration is related to both the ritual being observed (similar to the manner in which a musical performance is related to the score being performed) and to the customs and tradition of those who are observing it.[110]

The second form of a festival's temporality is that it is contemporaneous. This occurs in the same manner that a musical piece only exists in its performance and involves the participation of the audience.[111] "'Contemporaneity' means that in its presentation this particular thing that presents itself to us achieves full presence, however remote its origin may be."[112] When we remember Christ's sacrifice in the communion meal we do not compare this celebration with previous celebrations, or even the original one, but we fully participate in the present celebration.[113] This is not the same thing as simultaneity, which sees every point in time as equally present and is based on the free-play of aesthetic consciousness by which texts, or festivals, from the past are cut off from their contextual relationships so that we are able to experience them directly.[114] Contemporaneity, by contrast, involves the recognition that there is a historical distance between what is being celebrated and the present celebration: between Jesus' last meal with his disciples and our remembrance of that meal. The distance between the past horizon and the present is not ignored but is what makes participation in the ritual possible. We recognize the alterity of what is being celebrated and in doing so we return to the present. "The past must be made manifest to the present because its presence and immediacy are not given."[115] This is a hermeneutical movement that must be performed.

110. Palmer, "Ritual, Rightness, and Truth," 531–33.

111. "A festival only exists in being celebrated." Gadamer, *Truth and Method*, 124.

112. Ibid., 127. Gadamer gleaned contemporaneity from Kierkegaard, who claimed that in the preaching of the word a mediation between our present and the life, death and resurrection of Jesus took place, so that we experience the latter as a present reality.

113. Ibid., 128.

114. See the above section, "Schiller: Free-Play and Aesthetic Differentiation."

115. Weinsheimer, *Gadamer's Hermeneutics*, 115.

Presentation, Imitation, and Recognition

Whereas Heidegger speaks of the conflict between world and earth, or disclosure and concealment to explain the event of truth in the work of art, Gadamer employs the concepts of imitation (or mimesis) and recognition.[116] Mimesis, or imitation, is what holds textual interpretation from falling into an unending play of signs to be interpreted.

Imitation plays an important cognitive role in that it is related to preunderstanding. When we imitate someone we are not trying to hide ourselves behind a disguise but to represent that person.[117] As such, imitation is related to our fore-knowledge of the person and our audience's pre-understanding of them as well. Even if we or our audience are completely ignorant of the person being imitated, our prejudices about human life and the world still allows mimesis to function. As Robert Alter argues good literature presupposes and makes use of the vehicle of mimesis in order to present to us "lives that might seem like our lives, minds like our minds, and desires like our own desires."[118]

The cognitive function of recognition allows us to make judgments about the correctness of the representation. Umberto Eco writes that recognition transpires when some event, thing, or person is "viewed by an addressee as the expression of a given content, *either through a pre-existing and coded correlation or through the positing of a possible correlation by its addressee.*"[119] There must be some form of agreement or conformity between what we already know of the thing and what is

---

116. Once again, Gadamer is attempting to defend concepts which have fallen into disrepute. Mimesis, or imitation, used to serve as one of the underlying hermeneutical and literary concepts. However, since the early 1960s, it has come under increasing criticism, especially from French theorists such as Barthes, Genette, Derrida, and Foucault. For an excellent discussion of concerning the fall of mimesis, see Alter, "Mimesis and the Motive for Fiction," 228–32.

117. Gadamer, *Truth and Method*, 113. This concept is difficult to grasp in English because of our use of two related hermeneutical terms: imitation and mimesis. While both convey the idea of correspondence and resemblance, imitation denotes the idea that it is a static or exact copy, whereas mimesis leans more to the side that there is a dynamic and active relationship between the representation and the thing represented. Gadamer's concepts at this point are much more in line with the term mimesis. Mayaryk, *Encyclopedia of Contemporary Literary Theory*, s.v. "Mimesis," by John Baxter. For an excellent discussion of the history of mimesis, see Gebauer and Wulf, *Mimesis*.

118. Alter, "Mimesis and the Motive for Fiction," 248.

119. Eco, *A Theory of Semiotics*, 221.

presented in the artwork.[120] This is what allows us to say, "Yes, that's the way it really is."[121]

As Aristotle realized, the cognitive value of recognition in mimesis does not end once the reader or hearer has realized this correspondence. For example, when a child imitates her parents she does so in a manner that highlights certain traits, characteristics or mannerisms (often to the amusement of one parent and to the consternation of the other). Our ability to recognize these traits or characteristics is a pleasurable activity because it involves our cognitive capacities.[122] "This is the reason why people take delight in seeing images; what happens is that as they view them they come to understand and work out what each thing is (e.g. 'This is so-and-so')."[123] This is a significant contribution made by Aristotle. Mimesis is not the wooden replication of what is already known but *every* act of mimesis is a creative event or action that is disclosive in nature. Every mimetic representation has the potential to bring forth new understanding and insight into the subject matter.

Gadamer concurs with Aristotle; "The joy of recognition is rather the joy of knowing *more* than is already familiar."[124] In its representation there is a "bringing forth" of the thing represented. This may involve isolating the subject matter of the text from its original context, or highlighting certain facets of it while passing over others.[125]

> All true imitation is a transformation that does not simply present again something that is already there. It is a kind of transformed reality in which the transformation points back to what has been transformed in and through it. It is a transformed reality because it brings before us intensified possibilities never seen before.[126]

120. Ibid., 51–52.

121. For Gadamer, the expression, "It is so," is related to the experience of "it comes forth." "*So ist es'—so ist es 'richtig'*" (It is so—it is 'right' so!). The way we sense the rightness of something is related to disclosure. Palmer, "Ritual, Rightness, and Truth," 108.

122. Aristotle, *Nicomachean Ethics*, 1174.b14; Aristotle, *Poetics*, 8.2.

123. Aristotle, *Poetics*, 3.1.

124. Gadamer, *Truth and Method*, 114; Alter, "Mimesis and the Motive for Fiction," 245–46.

125. Aristotle, *Poetics*, 5.5, 8.2. The four gospels illustrate this idea. Each one is a mimetic representation of the life of Jesus that differs from the other three by the way they highlight certain aspects of his ministry and teaching, and ignore other elements.

126. Gadamer, *The Relevance of the Beautiful*, 64.

Every encounter with a text is part of the still unfinished happening of the work itself because of the way we recognize 'more' than we knew previously.

The interpretation of Jesus' parables are illustrative of the functions of mimesis and recognition. At the level of preunderstanding, the fictional characters and narrative situations represented in the parables would have been easily recognized by Jesus' audience in relation to the people and situations of their daily lives. Many of the themes contained in the parable would have been recognized in relation to their theology and overall understanding of the scriptures.[127] The intersubjective world that Jesus' audience shared with the parable drew them into the parable's projected narrative world and allowed them to make judgments concerning its correctness.[128] While hearers were caught up in the play of the presentation of the parable, they were confronted by its truth claim. By the time Jesus reached the conclusion to his parable it has questioned, challenged, or reversed the preunderstanding of his audience's theological framework.[129] In the parable of the Good Samaritan, the hearer is challenged to reconsider his definition not only of who his neighbor is but also what it means to obey the greatest commandment. The intersubjective world shared by the hearer and the parable evokes the hearer's expectations, which are then revised or expanded in relation to the truth claim presented in the parable. This is not a one time revision. If this were so, then once the parable was understood for the first time we would end up with a fixed or determinate meaning: a code that would determine the meaning of the parable for every successive encounter with it. We would no longer recognize correspondences between our world and that projected by the parable, but between the parable and this established meaning. Imitation would be reduced to copying, we would no longer recognize 'more.'

127. Baird presents a very strong case that Jesus actually adapted his parables to match the particular background of the specific audience he was addressing at that time. *Audience Criticism and the Historical Jesus*, 103. Via extends the shared world of the parables beyond the original audience to generations of future readers, including the present one. For example, the parable of the Prodigal Son would relate to anyone who has experienced family life. *The Parables*, 126.

128. Funk, *Language, Hermeneutics and Word of God*, 138–40, 179; Alter, "Mimesis and the Motive for Fiction," 234–35.

129. Thiselton, "The Parables as Language-Event," 440–2; Linnemann, *Parables of Jesus*, 18–23.

Jauss develops Gadamer's idea of mimesis farther by showing how this is an important aspect in the formation of an interpretive tradition. With the recognition of 'more' that mimesis allows, a trajectory of interpretation begins to take shape. In the first reading of a text, recognition is based on the relation of the text to the intersubjective world of the original readers. However, future readers will incorporate what previous readers recognized in the text. Thus, the 'more' that is recognized contributes to the expansion and transformation of successive horizons or reader's expectations.

> Only as the horizon changes and expands with each subsequent historical materialization, do responses to the work legitimize particular possibilities of understanding, imitation, transformation, and continuation—in short, structures of exemplary character that condition the process of the formation of literary tradition.[130]

Let me attempt to illustrate the role of recognition in the formation of the tradition of biblical interpretation. John 11:33 records that when Jesus came to the tomb of Lazarus he was ἐνεβριμήσατο in his spirit. The German and English commentators follow two different historical trajectories of thought on how this verb should be interpreted. The English commentators prefer to translate this verb as referring to Jesus being "deeply moved" or "groaning" in his spirit, while the Germans prefer the more active meaning of Jesus becoming "angry." On the English side, this tradition of interpretation dates back to the King James translation and is reflected in many recent translations.[131] Beasley-Murray mentions these traditions of interpretation in his commentary on John.

> This understanding of ἐμβριμάομαι has controlled the expositions of Bernard, Temple, Strachan, Sanders, Morris, Marsh, Lindars, Bruce, as also of Lagrange and F. M. Braun. By contrast Luther's rendering, "*Er ergrimmte im Geist und empörte sich*," i.e., "He was angry in the spirit and distressed," has controlled German interpretations to the present day, which gen-

130. Jauss, *Towards an Aesthetic*, 64. See also Paul de Man's comments on mimesis in the introduction, xxii.

131. The following are just two examples. The recently revised (1995) New American Standard Bible translates this as, "he was deeply moved in spirit," and the New Revised Standard Version has, "he was greatly disturbed in spirit."

> erally departs from it only by way of stronger expression . . .
> Such is the interpretation followed by Bultmann, Büchsel,
> Strathmann, Schnackenburg, Schulz, Haenchen, and Becker in
> their commentaries.[132]

This example illustrates the manner in which what previous readers or interpreters recognize in the text contributes to the horizon of expectations of future readers. In this way, the correctness of what is recognized as being represented in the text is partially determined by what the previous readers recognized.

Internal and External Representation

Alasdair MacIntyre offers a helpful clarification of Gadamer's concept of representation and recognition. MacIntyre differentiates between external and internal representations that an image may possess.[133] External representation is the type of representation that we would classify as occurring in a copy. It is the type of representation that occurs in a passport photograph. You can compare the picture and the person and inquire about the degree of resemblance between the two. By contrast, internal representation discloses or reveals features that can only be grasped in the representation itself. Rembrandt's portraits reveal to us aspects or features of the subject's personality or position in life that we may have not recognized in the face of the person being depicted if we had personally known them.[134] Certain key features or traits of the person represented can only be discerned in the representation and it is through the representation that "we learn to see what is represented." It is not a copy of the thing in the world, but it is a disclosure of its

---

132. Beasley-Murray, *John*, 192. There are a few exceptions; in the English, Westcott, Hoskyns, Barrett, Brown interpret this verb as being angry. Ibid., 193.

133. Alter makes a parallel argument when he claims that we can categorize literature along the following two poles. At one end are the more poetical and literary texts which systematically project "the illusion of reality and shatters it." At the other end is "the realist novel" which tries to maintain a close affinity with reality. Alter, "Mimesis and the Motive for Fiction," 238–39.

134. "It turns out that we are not, in asserting truth or falsity, asserting or denying some relationship between part of language and a non-linguistic feature of the world; we are always comparing one linguistic characterisation with another. Truth is a property of internal as much or more than of external representation, elsewhere just as in art." MacIntyre, "Contexts of Interpretation," 44–45.

heightened being.[135] This is in agreement with Aristotle's view on mimesis. Both the reflective and projective movements transpire at the level of mimesis. They are a result of how the viewer participates in and configures the mimetic representation.

Internal and external representation are related to different literary genres. Umberto Eco realizes that there is a wide spectrum to the nature of texts. At the one end of the spectrum are closed texts that are designed to arouse "a precise response on the part" of the reader. At the other end are open texts that function primarily by generating meaning through the play which the reader enters into with the text, or as Roland Barthes writes, the "*jouissance du texte.*"[136] St. Paul's request to Timothy to bring him his cloak, books (βιβλία), and parchments (μεμβράνας) in 2 Timothy 4:13 is an example of a closed text, while Jesus' parables are good examples of open texts designed to project a world into which the reader enters.[137] "Different genres within scripture will call forth different kinds of correlation, because of their different types of mimêsis."[138]

However, there is no such thing as a pure closed or open text. Even the most closed texts "are in fact open to any possible 'aberrant' decoding" when readers from different horizons read the text.[139] The most open text is also not open to any interpretation. In writing an open text, the author has structured it in such a manner that it is not open to accidental interpretations, but it outlines or projects a "closed project" for the reader to realize.[140] "A text can succeed in being more or less open or

135. Ibid., 44.

136. Eco, *The Role of the Reader*, 3–10. Eco appears to have developed these concepts from Lotman's theory of grammar-oriented and text-oriented cultures. Eco, *A Theory of Semiotics*, 136–38.

137. However, even the parables are characterized by a high degree of external representation, or as Via would term, "low mimetic." While the parables are fictional they remind us of everyday people and situation; there is nothing mythical or romantic about them. Via, *The Parables*, 96–100.

138. Young, *The Art of Performance*, 154.

139. Searle shows that even a simple statement such as "the cat is on the mat" is open to numerous interpretations. These depend on the kinds of assumptions we make about the presence of gravity, the possibility of there being wires suspending the cat over the mat, or that the mat is stiffened and propped up at an angle. Searle, *Intentionality*, 121–24.

140. Eco, *The Role of the Reader*, 8–9. Gadamer takes a parallel argument when he argues that "The aesthetic object is not constituted by the aesthetic experience of grasping it, but the work of art itself is experienced in its aesthetic quality through the process of its concretization and creation." Gadamer, *Truth and Method*, 118 n. 219.

closed."[141] Therefore, play will characterize, to a certain extent, the act of understanding a closed text. At the same time, the playing field opened up by a particular text will vary according to the nature of that text.[142]

When we appropriate Gadamer's and Jauss's hermeneutics to biblical studies we must keep in mind that Gadamer used literary texts as an example of the ideal form of play and Jauss was primarily interested in the study of Medieval literary texts that we would classify as being more externally representative.[143] However, the Bible contains a wide range of literary genres with a wide diversity when it comes to whether they are internally or externally representative. The danger lies in thinking that we can apply one concept of representation to all texts. This is especially true if we were to follow Gadamer and Jauss in adopting literary texts as the primary example since some the biblical texts, such as the gospels, are characterized by a higher degree of internal representation. "The implied reader of these texts understands them not as an enclosed fictional world but as an imaginative rendering of prior reality."[144]

In summary, Gadamer's ideas on play, imitation, and recognition overcome the problems associated with play which date back to Kant's separation of determinate from reflective judgment, which eliminated the classical role mimesis played and attributed genuine knowledge to the sciences only. In recognizing what is already known, but in a deeper or more authentic manner, the representation of play reinstates the position of cognitive knowledge in the arts.[145] It also presents a resolution to the problems that we inherited from Kant. On the one hand, there are those who argue for the determinate meaning of a text. E. D. Hirsch is perhaps the best known contemporary literary theorist who claims that through the application of method one can "achieve 'true' or 'highly

141. Ibid., 5.

142. Thiselton points out the danger of not making this distinction between different types of texts and the space for play that they open up. If all texts are subsumed under the model of the open text, then texts can no longer function as a basis for rational action. We cannot limit interpretation to one single model; to do so traps us within one interpretive model. Biblical texts transcend one category of texts and must have a theory broad enough to encompass the variety of functions that they perform. Thiselton, *New Horizons*, 129–32.

143. See Gadamer's "The Eminent Text and Its Truth," 3–10, for his view of literary, and especially poetical, texts.

144. Watson, *Text and Truth*, 34.

145. Gadamer, *Truth and Method*, 115.

probable' interpretations."[146] In order to accomplish this, Hirsch bases his hermeneutic on a concept of meaning which is distinct from significance and relies on a split between the subject and the object.[147] The result of taking such a positivistic approach toward biblical interpretation is that the productive possibilities for play are restricted from the start. On the opposing side are those that follow Schiller and Nietzsche's concept of the unending freedom of play. Derrida argues that deconstruction is a never-ending mode of play of the text. The idea that there is a fixed textual meaning is only an illusion.

> Every meaning which is presumed to stand by the commentator is shown to be no more than a play between simulation and dissimulation. The true nature of every text therefore is to be in a state of flux as long as it is engaged by the reader and is reduced to a mere trace when the engagement is over because the text has no determinate essence.[148]

Weinsheimer warns us that both extremes, that a text has only one meaning and that a text possesses an unlimited number of equally valid readings, kill any intellectual interest for interpreting a text. "For understanding lives in the play of equivalence and difference."[149] Gadamer's concept of play avoids the problems of the anarchy of unrestricted heterogeneous interpretations and the intellectual confinement of determinate meaning, which kills the possibility for play. However, if the truth of a work of art arises or is instantiated in its performance or representation, then how do we differentiate between the different truth claims realized in different performances?

Playful Truth

What is truth in relation to the play of interpretation? This is a difficult question to answer because Gadamer does not explicate his theory of truth at any one point, but rather it is one of the main themes that he weaves throughout *Truth and Method*.[150] However, I believe it is possible

146. Arthur, "Gadamer and Hirsch," 183.

147. Ibid., 184, 194. See DiCenso, *Hermeneutics and the Disclosure of Truth*, 85–90, for an incisive analysis of Hirsch's hermeneutic on this point.

148. Valdés, *Identity of the Literary Text*, 303.

149. Weinsheimer, *Philosophical Hermeneutics*, xiii, emphasis added.

150. Or as Bernstein says, truth is "one of the most elusive concepts in Gadamer." "From Hermeneutics to Praxis," 96; Riser, "The Remembrance of Truth," 123.

to pull together several of the strands which Gadamer uses in weaving his tapestry so that we can arrive at a fairly clear picture of what truth involves in regard to play and interpretation.

First, truth occurs in the meaningful happening of play. It is something in which we participate, like a player in a game. The truth of an artwork is something which strikes us as meaningful.[151] For Heidegger, this happening of truth takes place in the disclosure of Being. Gadamer provides a greater historical grounding to his mentor's concept in that he is primarily concerned with explicating how the event of truth occurs in our conversation with tradition; through the works of art and texts that are handed down to us in it.[152] The disclosive character of the happening of truth means that it will always be provisional. There will always be some degree of un-truth with the truth. Or to put it negatively, our finitude and historical thrownness means "that there are many things that are true that we are not capable of recognizing because we are, without being cognizant of it, limited by prejudices."[153]

Secondly, truth is related to the subject matter of the text. It involves our ability to recognize some degree of conformity or correctness between what is represented and the representation. This is not based on a correspondence theory of truth, in which the work of art or the text are mainly descriptive of the subject matter they are portraying. Rather, truth is more in line with a coherence model, in which our interpretive context and preunderstanding inform our experience of the text or work of art. As such, to ask questions about truth involves asking questions "about the structures that inform our modes of being-in-the-world."[154] Perhaps the most important element which comes into play here is the language which we inherit from our tradition. We judge an interpretation to be "true" when what it discloses about the text is in harmony with what we perceive in the subject matter of the text (*die Sache*). Both sides of this equation occur through language. "The veracity of an interpretation is determined by the appropriateness of what is

151. Gadamer, *Truth and Method*, 490. "It is worth emphasizing that for Gadamer truth appears neither at the beginning nor at the end but in the interim, in the process of representation." Weinsheimer, *Gadamer's Hermeneutics*, 119.

152. Gadamer, "What is Truth?" 36, 45–46; Lammi, "Hans-Georg Gadamer's 'Correction' of Heidegger," 496.

153. Gadamer, "What is Truth?" 40.

154. DiCenso, *Hermeneutics and the Disclosure of Truth*, 147.

said (and how it is said) to the text. As the aphorism states '*adaequatio intellectus ad rem*.'"[155]

However, truth in interpretation does not stop there. Truth also includes the disclosive potential involved in mimesis and play. Truth is not limited to repeating what is already known; it also includes the possibility for aspects of the subject matter to be understood in ways never seen before. "The joy of recognition is rather the joy of knowing more than is already familiar."[156] Once again, this brings out the provisional aspect of truth. Future horizons of understanding will always contain the possibility for the "joy of knowing more." Truth is provisional because the conditions from which it arises—language, history, and tradition—are never a universal whole that allows for all that is possible in the text to be recognized. Because there will never be any last word concerning the meaning of a text, each and every generation has the responsibility to interpret the text for themselves.

Finally, truth is not only characterized by its eventfulness, but it is also a process which takes place over time in our dialogue with tradition. There are two aspects to this which were covered in the previous chapter that should be kept in mind. The manner by which we enter into dialogue with our tradition is the logic of question and answer which involves a double hermeneutic. Not only does the interpreter need to ask questions that are appropriate for the text, but at the same time he or she is questioned by the text.[157] This dialogue with tradition is also characterized by the I/Thou relationship. We must allow tradition to truly say something to us, to exercise its truth claim on our lives. We must be open to tradition in such a way that it can say something to us.[158] Truth is realized through dialogue. In the process of a conversation our ideas are questioned and tested, which results in the revision and correction of our previous understanding.[159] "Gadamer seeks to show that there is a truth that is revealed in the process of experience (*Erfahrung*) and that emerges in the dialogical encounter with the very tradition that has

155. Gadamer, "What is Truth?" 36.

156. Gadamer, *Truth and Method*, 116.

157. Gadamer, "Reflections on My Philosophical Journey," 43.

158. Gadamer, *Truth and Method*, 452–53; Weinsheimer, *Gadamer's Hermeneutics*, 205.

159. Grondin, "Gadamer on Humanism," 56.

shaped us."[160] The question now becomes, how does this actually take place in respect to the practice of interpreting texts?

Performance and Tradition Formation

Play provides a hermeneutical path that navigates a channel between the Charybdis of only one correct interpretation for a text and the Scylla of every reading being equally valid. "The work can be multiply interpreted, multiply true, without disintegrating into fragments or denigrating into empty form."[161] This takes place not only synchronically, but even more significant for Gadamer, diachronically in the formation of a tradition.

Certain forms of play are capable of repetition. A game, such as England vs. Germany in the 1998 EuroCup semifinal, was a one-time form of play; it can never be repeated. However, other forms of play, such as music, drama, literature, and artworks, are all repeatable forms of play. This is part of what transformation into structure (*Gebilde*) involves. A dramatic play (*Schauspiel*) is characterized by the fact that it is a form of play that has been transformed into structure that is capable of being presented more than one time. In successive performances of a play, such as Hamlet, a tradition of performances or interpretations begins to take shape.[162] Structure allows play to be repeated and its significance to be understood; yet play is transformed into structure only when it is played.[163]

A musical performance helps elucidate Gadamer's idea. Every performance of a musical composition is the same because of the structure of the score, yet the music's full being is realized only in the presentation. Since play is structure, there must be a "meaningful whole" to that form or instance of play that allows for repeated performances of the work. The score of the music, the text of a book, or the painting by Van Gogh are examples of structure. At the same time, the play's full being, and structure, are only realized in each presentation.

---

160. Bernstein, "From Hermeneutics to Praxis," 97.

161. Weinsheimer, *Gadamer's Hermeneutics*, 100.

162. "For instance, whether we are familiar with the literature on Shakespeare's work or not we approach his work in a way influenced by a tradition of Shakespeare interpretation so that we assume its excellence, importance and so on." Warnke, *Gadamer, Hermeneutics, Tradition and Reason*, 96.

163. Gadamer, *Truth and Method*, 117.

The playing field that mimesis opens up creates the potential for an endless possibility of performances, but at the same time it is not an unbounded playing field. While a musical score or text may have more than one right interpretation, it does not mean that there are no wrong interpretations.[164] This is a point that Jauss, as we shall see in the next chapter, is in full agreement with: "the text itself is thus able to limit the arbitrariness of interpretation, guaranteeing the continuity of its experience beyond the present act of reception."[165] A performance must be faithful to the structure, or score, just as a reading must be faithful to the subject matter of the text.[166]

> This constitutes the obligation of every presentation: that it contain a relation to the structure itself and submit itself to the criterion of correctness that derives from it. Even the extreme of a completely distortive presentation confirms this. It is known as a distortion inasmuch as the presentation is intended and judged to be the presentation of the structure.[167]

The interpretation of texts shares this same structure of play and presentation. As a work of art only comes into being when someone views it, "so also it is universally true of texts that only in the process of understanding them is the dead trace of meaning transformed back into living meaning."[168] Differences in the historical horizon in which the music is performed or the text read will bring out different aspects in their respective presentation.[169] This is one reason why the meaning of

164. For Gadamer, "the mimetic field, although endless by its practical performances, is not a house of mirrors without referent, an endless play of copy copying a copy. Rather, to be caught with the mimetic field is to be caught in a play of truth." This is one of the differences between Gadamer and Derrida. Riser, "The Remembrance of Truth," 131.

165. Jauss, "The Theory of Reception," 60.

166. "The important point about effective-historical consciousness, then, is not only that inquiry is always oriented by our concerns; although Gadamer makes this point, his argument is also that inquiry is always inquiry into a subject-matter and that the consensus reached about this subject-matter can reveal something 'true' about it." Warnke, *Gadamer*, 146.

167. Gadamer, *Truth and Method*, 122.

168. Ibid., 164.

169. Ibid., 117, 126, 140, 148. "This occurrence means the coming into play, the playing out, of the content of tradition in its constantly widening possibilities of significance and resonance, extended by the different people receiving it. Inasmuch as the tradition is newly expressed in language, something comes into being that had not

a text will exceed the best intentions of its author. Understanding is not just an act of reproduction but is productive also.[170] With each presentation there is an overflow or emanation of being.

The reception history of Matthew's story of the magi is a dramatic demonstration of this point. Within the first four centuries, magi were interpreted as representing the three ages of human development (youth, middle age, and the elderly), pagan magicians, kings, and people for the continents of Africa, Asia, and Europe. Visual depictions of this story focused on the devotional elements of the story (coming, seeing, and worshipping Christ). In his commentary on Matthew, Ulrich Luz noted that the discrepancy between the text and its artistic representation was "thought provoking." Martin O'Kane notes that this overflow of meaning from the text was appropriated by the artists to communicate the significance of this story to contemporary viewers, to show that this baby was relevant to men and women in every age.[171] While the interpretations and representations of the story of the magi exceeded what Matthew may have intended, by and large, they were still played out within an appropriate field of interpretive play.

The ontological nature of play is not an either-or situation but a both-and, involving identification and difference. Anthony Thiselton believes the metaphor of musical performance helps us to grasp the relationship between the poles of continuity and variability in interpretations as well.

> The Bible may be compared to a musical score. What 'controls' or sets limits to the scope of the present performance is the notation of this composition as it was composed at some time in the past. If it is not based on the score, the present performance is not a performance of this composition. Nevertheless, what the current audience experiences in the present is the actual

existed before, and that exists from now on. We can illustrate this with any historical example. Whether a given traditionary text is a poem or tells us of a great event, in each case what is transmitted re-emerges into existence just as it presents itself. There is no being-in-itself that is increasingly revealed when Homer's Iliad or Alexander's Indian Campaign speaks to us in the new appropriations of tradition; but, as in genuine dialogue, something emerges that is contained in neither of the partners by himself." Ibid., 462.

170. Ibid., 296.

171. O'Kane, *Painting the Text*, 44–45; Powell, *Chasing the Eastern Star*, 131–71; Trexler, *The Journey of the Magi*.

performance, and no two performances will be quite the same. Wooden repetition may turn out to be less faithful to the score than the use of creative imagination. Yet the creativity of the performer still takes place within clear limits. For without faithfulness to the score, the performance would not be a faithful interpretation of that work.[172]

Successive performances form a tradition with which later performances must come to terms. Both the audience and the performers will be affected by past performances which serve as either conscious models to be followed or constitute part of the audience's background understanding.[173] These previous performances not only serve as a model for future performances but they also "become so fused with the work that concern with this model stimulates an artist's creative interpretative powers no less than does concern with the work itself."[174] This is tied in with the cognitive importance of recognition. Classic performances or interpretations are incorporated into the history of the text's influence and become part of the future readers' horizons of expectations. In this way, previous interpretations serve as markers that determine the field of play by which future readers will judge the correctness of their readings. Thus, we have two regulative norms to determine the validity of any interpretation according to Gadamer: the subject matter of the text and those interpretations that are recognized within a tradition (consciously and/or part of our pre-understanding) as authoritative.

> The text that is handed down to us is a fusion of previous opinions about it, a harmony of voices, as Gadamer often puts it, to which we add our own. But this means that the object of hermeneutic understanding is already a fusion of the interpretations of a tradition and our encounter with it is an encounter with the tradition.[175]

While some performances and interpretations are more influential than others, none should reach the point where they are recognized as being definitive or canonical. The mimetic nature of play means that previous performances cannot be blindly imitated. As part of our tradition, pre-

---

172. Thiselton, "Knowledge, Myth and Corporate Memory," 74.
173. Ibid., 61.
174. Gadamer, *Truth and Method*, 119; Warnke, *Gadamer*, 90.
175. Warnke, *Gadamer*, 90.

vious reading or performances constitute the playing field for our understanding the musical piece, drama, or text. Instead of the two poles
usually associated with interpretation, the interpreter and the text, we
now have three poles: the text, its *Wirkungsgeschichte* or tradition of
interpretation, and the interpreter located within his or her historical
horizon.

Putting Our Prejudices at Risk: The Play of Interpretation

Familiar and Foreign

The claims of the text primarily strike us in two ways. The first involves
the hermeneutical circle of part to whole. We begin every act of reading for understanding by projecting an anticipation of completeness
(*Vorgriff der Vollkommenheit*) by which we try to grasp the unity of the
text's meaning.[176] In the process of reading, our projected meaning is
open to correction; it is constantly placed at risk while we read the text.
This gives the reading process direction and is constantly revised as we
move through the parts of the text.[177] The second is the presupposition
that what the author says in the text is true, which is based on a hermeneutic of charity—that the author knows the subject matter better than
we do.[178] Hermeneutically, this requires that we are conscious of the
otherness of the text and are responsive to the truth claims that it makes
against our fore-conceptions.[179]

The hermeneutical principles of the anticipation of completeness
and openness to the truth claims of the text rest on the assumption that
we are related to the subject matter of the text in some manner.[180] We

176. Gadamer, "*Vom Zirkel des Verstehens,*" 28.

177. Ibid., 31.

178. This point is identical to his epistemological defense of tradition. We must
realize that our knowledge is finite and that others know more than we do about some
topics. Gadamer, *Truth and Method,* 280.

179. See chapter 1 for my discussion of the I/Thou relationship; Gadamer, "*Vom
Zirkel des Verstehens,*" 29.

180. Gadamer, "The Problem of Historical Consciousness," 147. "Just as the recipient of a letter understands the news that it contains and first sees things with the eyes
of the person who wrote the letter—i.e., considers what he writes as true, and is not
trying to understand the writer's peculiar opinions as such—so also do we understand
traditionary texts on the basis of expectations of meaning drawn from our own prior

could never hope to comprehend a text that is totally foreign to us. Or as Wittgenstein so cleverly writes, "If a lion could talk, we could not understand him."[181] At the same time, our relationship with a text or tradition is never complete. There is always an element of brokenness in the transmission of a tradition.[182] There is a polarity between the familiarity we have with a text and its foreignness, which is not psychological in nature, but is part of the ontological nature of tradition.[183]

Forgetfulness is a fundamental reason why traditions are not comprehensive repositories of the past. It is worth reminding ourselves that we have finite minds that are capable of retaining only so much.[184] According to Nietzsche, since we selectively appropriate the past, most of what is handed down to us in tradition is forgotten. We are primarily interested in those achievements or failures in the past that can provide a model or an example that we can apply to our present situation. As a result, much of the past is passed over and forgotten in Nietzsche's monumental approach to history. Forgetfulness plays a more complex role for Heidegger. Historical existence is characterized by an element of forgetfulness in which the truths we currently possess are leveled down and covered over by tradition.[185] This is one of the reasons why he pursued etymological studies; he sought to remove the encrusted the layers of meaning that had leveled down the original connotations of terms like like *aletheia*, *logos*, and *physis* through history and recover the pristine meaning of these words.[186]

---

relation to the subject matter." *Truth and Method*, 294.

181. Wittgenstein, *Philosophical Investigations*, 223e.

182. This concept is not new, but played a central role in Petrarch's rhetorical theories. For him, "what tradition preserves or rather entails, is not a deposit of familiar meanings but something strange and refractory to interpretation, resistant to the present, uncontainable in the given world in which we find ourselves at home." Bruns, "What is Tradition?" 8.

183. Gadamer, *Truth and Method*, 295.

184. Nietzsche, *The Use and Abuse of History*, 6–7.

185. One of the central problems that Heidegger addresses in *Being and Time* concerns how philosophy has forgotten the question of Being (*das Sein*) and shifted to beings (*das Seiende*). The result is that western philosophy is dominated by a technical objectifying use of language and has lost its understanding of Being. Heidegger, *Being and Time*, 21, 46–48. For a fuller discussion, see Heidegger, "*Die Zelt des Weltbildes*" in *Holzwege*, 69–105.

186. Roberts, *Nothing but History*, 129.

This reveals an important aspect to our historical reality; the past is not simply part of our present horizon because we remember it, but also because it has been forgotten. In fact, one of the reasons why understanding is possible at all is because tradition and language are forgetful. "The transitory sinks into a forgetting and it is this forgetting which makes it possible to hold fast and to preserve those things which have faded and fallen into forgottenness."[187] The past would present itself to us as a complete totality with which we would be totally familiar if we didn't forget. If we experienced tradition in a comprehensive manner it would not only be beyond our comprehension but it would also be meaningless.[188] As time progresses we filter the past by forgetting the ephemeral and mundane while retaining what stood out as significant. The forgetful nature of tradition allows certain ideas, events, and texts to stand out as more significant or meaningful. This also implies that tradition is not a homogeneous whole, but is characterized by diverse and possibly conflicting ideas. As such, tradition is subversive of any form of totalization.

Alongside forgetting, Gadamer places remembering or recollection. In recollection, there is a halting of the passing away and being covered over processes by which ideas become part of our pre-understanding.

> Recollection is always what comes to one, and comes over one, so that something that is again made present to us offers, for the space of a moment, a halt to all passing away and forgetting. But recollection of being is not a recollection of something previously known and now present once again; rather, it is recollection of something previously asked, the reclaiming of a lost question. And a question which is asked again is no longer recollected; it becomes a question again and is now asked anew. It is no longer a recollection of something that was once asked—it is posed anew.[189]

As such, recollection is built on the ideas of the logic of question and answer, sublation, and recognition. When we remember the past, we

187. Gadamer, "The Continuity of History," 239–40.

188. The example Danto uses to illustrate this point is a supercomputer that can record every event as it occurs. While this computer would only be able to chronicle the past, it would not be able to bring out its significance or meaning of the past events. *Analytic Philosophy of History*, 112–42. See also Nietzsche, *The Use and Abuse of History*, 6–7.

189. Gadamer, "Reflections on My Philosophical Journey," 35.

do not turn the past into a historical object, but re-collect it so that it becomes a living reality for us.

We must continually reappropriate and renew tradition because it is characterized by forgetting and remembering. This is not a passive process but is an aspect of historical existence that we must actively engage. This is perhaps the core of Gadamer's project: how do we engage tradition in this conversation? Therefore the task of hermeneutics is concerned with "the art of bringing what is said or written to speech again."[190]

The Productive Function of Temporal Distance

This brings temporal distance into the center of hermeneutics. The temporal distance between text and interpreter was perceived as a hurdle to understanding that must be overcome by historicism because it created a separation between the historian and her object. By contrast, temporal distance plays a productive and positive role in understanding, according to Gadamer. Temporal distance stands at the center of contemporary hermeneutical theories because of the manner in which it functions as the medium through which understanding takes place.[191] The breadth of this temporal distance is not an empty chasm between us and the text, nor is it a abyss filled with erroneous views that we have progressed beyond, rather it is filled with the conventions of tradition. "Our historical consciousness is always filled with a variety of voices in which the echo of the past is heard. It is present only in the multifariousness of

---

190. Lammi, "Hans-Georg Gadamer's Correction of Heidegger," 501, 506; Gadamer, *Reason in the Age of Science*, 119.

191. *"Aus dieser Zwischenstellung, in der sie ihren Stand nimmt, folgt, daß ihr Zentrum bildet, was in der bisherigen Hermeneutik ganz am Rande blieb: der Zeitenabstand und seine Bedeutung für das Verstehen. Die Zeit ist nicht primär ein Abgrund, der überbrückt werden muß, weil er trennt und fernhält, sondern sie ist in Wahrheit der tragende Grund des Geschehens, in dem das gegenwärtige Verstehen wurzelt. Der Zeitenabstand ist daher nicht etwas, was überwunden werden muß."* (The significance of temporal distance of time for understanding forms (stands at) the centre of contemporary hermeneutics, while in the past it remained entirely on the fringe. Time is not primarily an abyss which must be bridged, because it separates and keeps us distant. Rather, it is in truth, the ground in which bears the event/happening in which present understanding is rooted. Temporal distance is not something that must be overcome.) Gadamer, *"Vom Zirkel des Verstehens,"* 32. Gadamer, *Truth and Method*, 297.

such voices: this constitutes the nature of tradition in which we want to share and have a part."[192]

Not only does temporal distance play a productive role in understanding but it also serves a critical purpose. As a tradition progresses we are constantly remembering and forgetting various elements of our tradition. Not everything that we possess at any point in time is productive, helpful, or beneficial. Therefore, the prejudices which we inherit from our tradition are not a nice neat package, but they contain elements that have been forgotten or leveled down but may still be operating subconsciously in our background network of beliefs. A tradition is constituted with prejudices that have the potential to distort communication and prejudices that have the possibility to allow for a better understanding of the text or subject at hand.

Gadamer affirms the need to distinguish appropriate prejudices that lead to understanding from false prejudices that produce misunderstanding. In order to make this distinction our prejudices must be raised to consciousness. However, as long as our prejudices continue to operate unnoticed, we cannot foreground (*abheben*) or make ourselves aware of them. This would be easy to accomplish if prejudices were something of which we were consciously aware. The problem is that most of our tradition is invisible to us. It operates prereflectively as the background, *Vorhabe*, which enables understanding.[193] We are so at home in our tradition that we are often totally unaware of how our decisions and actions are influenced by it.

As long as our prejudices continue to operate unnoticed we cannot foreground them. Once we bring a prejudice up to reflection it loses some of its hold on us. "Reflection on a given preunderstanding brings before me something that otherwise happens behind my back."[194] In order for this to happen, something about this particular element of tradition must strike us as odd, out of place, or foreign; or as Gadamer says, "it must be provoked."[195] When a favorite tool is broken or misplaced our pre-reflective assumptions about that tool are provoked ac-

192. Gadamer, *Truth and Method*, 284.

193. "History is always invisible to the participants in it; and for this reason methodological prophylactics, however necessary, always ultimately fail." Weinsheimer, *Philosophical Hermeneutics*, 38.

194. Gadamer, *Philosophical Hermeneutics*, 38.

195. Gadamer, "The Problem of Historical Consciousness," 157.

cording to Heidegger. We do not take much notice of a tool as long as it is working properly and is in the proper place. But when this referential context is violated, we not only take greater notice of the tool but also what it was related to and the purposes it served. "The more urgently we need what is missing, and the more authentically it is encountered in its un-readiness-to-hand," the more it stands out.[196] For Gadamer, temporal distance, or the otherness of that element of tradition, violates the pre-reflective referential contexts of our prejudices and causes us to not only take notice about that object, but also to ask questions about it. The distance between the past and present creates a tension that is needed for that element of our tradition to be raised to consciousness before we are able to critically reflect on it.

There are two primary ways in which our prejudices are placed at risk when we interpret a text. First, we always construct an anticipated completeness or unity for the text we are reading. This anticipated completeness is projected off our preunderstanding of the text, or if we know very little about the text, from our experience of other texts which may be related to it by genre, historical period, or subject matter. Hirsch illuminates the significance of this point when he argues that even if a person does not read the classical texts of their tradition they will still meet them through second or third-hand sources. The foundational texts of our tradition and the literary canon are not self-contained books sitting on the shelf, but help shape and form the tradition to which we belong.[197] Therefore, we are familiar with these texts before we read them. This is one reason why someone may presumptuously believe that they are familiar with a traditional text like the Bible even though they have never read it.[198] However, when this person reads these texts their preunderstanding is negated and their prejudices are provoked. This negative experience opens our prejudices to questioning. Weinsheimer describes this movement in understanding as implying "that we are willing to integrate the meaning of the text

196. Heidegger, *Being and Time*, 103–5. A parallel concept developed in literary theory, particularly Russian Formalism; the power of literature to break our habituated, referential contexts by presenting things in new and unexpected ways is known as "defamiliarization." Holub, "Reception Theory and Russian Formalism," 277–78. This is a concept which Jauss will integrate into Gadamer's hermeneutic.

197. Hirsch, *Cultural Literacy*, xiv.

198. Weinsheimer, *Gadamer's Hermeneutic*, 166.

with our previous preconceptions by making them conscious, bringing them into view, and assimilating them to what the text reveals."[199] In this sense, reading the classic biblical commentaries and theological works introduces us to what we already have with us, our pre-understanding. It brings our prejudices and preunderstanding to the forefront and makes them open to reflection and revision.[200]

The second way in which our prejudices are provoked is through the logic of question and answer and keeping ourselves open to the truth claims of the text. Because our understanding of the world is constantly changing, some of the truth claims of a historically or culturally distant text may confront us as being partially or blatantly untrue. "We also realise that sometimes a work that grips us when it confronts us in historical distance would seem untruthful to us if it were a contemporary creation."[201] Bultmann's confidence that our technological progress had rendered the worldview of the New Testament obsolete is one illustration of how the truth claims of the biblical text was confronting his modern prejudices.[202] However, if we read the Bible, or any other text, in a manner in which we try to find answers that agree with our assumptions, then we are not truly engaging in dialogue with that text and genuine understanding is foreclosed according to Gadamer. We must approach the text with questions that are appropriate and at the same time remain open to the questions which the text may ask us.[203] In both instances, temporal distance is what creates the space or tension for the otherness of the text to provoke our prejudices.

Historically Effective Consciousness

Our belonging to and conversing with tradition is what Gadamer terms historically effected consciousness (*wirkungsgeschichtliches Bewußtsein*). On the one hand, this term expresses the idea that our consciousness is effected by and brought into being by our tradition. On the other hand,

199. Ibid., 167.

200. "In either case, teaching the classics functions to acquaint students for the first time with what they have always known, to bring that foreknowledge to explicit consciousness and thus make it available for denial and affirmation." Weinsheimer, *Philosophical Hermeneutics*, 142.

201. Gadamer, "The Eminent Text and Its Truth," 9.

202. Bultmann, *Kerygma and Myth*, 5.

203. Gadamer, "*Vom Zirkel des Verstehens,*" 30.

our being conscious of belonging to and being conditioned by history is also contained in the term. [204] "This ambiguity is that it is used to mean at once the consciousness effected in the course of history and determined by history, and the very consciousness of being thus effected and determined."[205] The recognition and adoption of historically effected consciousness as a universal element in understanding which should be elevated to the center of our hermeneutic is the main thesis in *Truth and Method*.[206]

Historically effected consciousness is characterized by the hermeneutical elements that I have developed in the first half of this book. It functions in a manner similar to self-understanding by which we come to understand ourselves when we recognize ourselves in the other. This involves a reconciliation between the outward and returning movements of the hermeneutical circle. In studying a text from our tradition, such as the Bible, we learn how to make ourselves at home in the historically distant world of the text. But then we must reconcile this alienated self in a returning movement when we make the questions of the Bible our questions and apply it to our horizon, allowing the Bible to say something to us.[207]

The hermeneutical experience of tradition is also characterized by the negation of our expectations, which then leads to a more appropriate understanding of the subject matter. As opposed to the certainty which a methodological approach toward the Bible may promise us, the negative nature of experience does not destroy this security so much as it develops and cultivates our openness to the other and our ability to learn from experience. "The hermeneutical consciousness culminates

204. For Gadamer this involves the realization of the limits of our self-understanding in relation to the throwness and finitude of our existence, "that is, as the 'historically effected consciousness' which is 'more being than consciousness'—*mehr Sein als Bewußtsein*." Gadamer, "Reflections on My Philosophical Journey," 27. This can be seen in Gadamer's choice of the words to express the idea. *Sein* is part of consciousness, *Bewußtsein*. "The emphasis should be on the '*sein*' that contains historically conditioned structures and not on an empty, flickering awareness." Ibid., 60 n. 30. See also *Philosophical Hermeneutics*, 38.

205. He continues, "Obviously the burden of my argument is that effective history still determines modern historical and scientific consciousness; and it does so beyond any possible knowledge of this domination." Gadamer, *Truth and Method*, xxxiv.

206. Ibid., xxxiii.

207. Ibid., 346, 361.

not in methodological sureness of itself, but in the same readiness for experience that distinguishes the experienced man from the man captivated by dogma."[208]

Biblical interpreters who are experienced in this sense have gained not only objectifiable knowledge but, even more significantly, they have undergone a development (*gebildet*) which has enabled them to grow in *phronesis*.[209] *Bildung* or *phronesis* gives readers the ability to not only apply the text to their situation but also enables them to perceive their bond to tradition. It not only raises the interpreter's mind to an awareness of his or her tradition but also enables the "educated man (*Gebildete*)" to move in it.[210] This overcomes the division between reason and authority which the Enlightenment raised.[211] Through historically effected consciousness, Gadamer is able reconcile the study of history with its effects (*Wirkungen*) in such a manner that there is a unity between them. This is not a new element that Gadamer thinks should be included in hermeneutical theory, but as I pointed out above, it is something that has always been the part of the nature of our historical existence and which needs to be elevated to the center of our hermeneutic.[212]

Tradition, and the texts that it passes down, is not a closed book. The playful nature of understanding and the disclosive character of imitation/mimesis which allows us to recognize more than we knew before means that tradition is an open book which is still being written. The history of the interpretation of the Bible also presents us with a partially constructed historical map of abuses of the text which should be avoided, as well as legitimate insights and responses which disclose new possibilities for the life of the church.[213] "What hermeneutical reflection dictates is that we be aware of this self-critical moment present in all such criticism, for only in such awareness will we be able to recognize those moments of the past that we wish to creatively move beyond."[214] It is also a transformative form of learning in that our prejudices are

208. Ibid., 362.

209. Palmer, *Hermeneutics*, 193.

210. Gadamer, *Truth and Method*, 14; Warnke, *Gadamer*, 174.

211. Warnke, *Gadamer*, 166; Thiselton, *New Horizons*, 327; Brown, *Boundaries of Our Habitation*, 34.

212. Gadamer, *Truth and Method*, 282–83.

213. Thiselton, "Knowledge, Myth, and Corporate Memory," 73; Jauss, *Towards an Aesthetic*, 59.

214. Mitscherling, "The Historical Consciousness of Man," 738.

brought into play when we enter into dialogue with our tradition. Thus, Gadamer's hermeneutic, and *wirkungsgeschichtliche Bewußtsein* in particular, not only presents the philosophical hermeneutical grounds and rational for a *Wirkungsgeschichte* approach to biblical interpretation, it also provides an apologetic for this approach.

Conclusion: What Do We Do with Gadamer?

Having arrived at the conclusion to my discussion of Gadamer's hermeneutic, I am left with the question, "How do we put this into practice?" The absence of any form of methodological direction or guidance is one of the most frequent criticisms leveled at Gadamer.[215] However, we must remember that Gadamer's project was descriptive, not prescriptive, as he stated in the introduction to *Truth and Method*. "My real concern was and is philosophic: not what we do or what we ought to do, but what happens to us over and above our wanting and doing."[216] In one sense then, it would not be appropriate to criticize him for failing to answer a question which he never intended to answer, one which he felt was not only outside the bounds of his hermeneutic but was also antithetical to it in his opinion.

Gadamer's reluctance to even hint at some form of method or criteria is based on his criticism of the historical-critical method that we inherited from the nineteenth century and the imposition of the methodology of the natural sciences into the human sciences. Behind this stands his argument that method is something that someone throws

215. For one of the most incisive critiques of Gadamer's hermeneutic concerning the question of criteria for determining legitimate interpretations, see Hinman, "*Quid Facti* or *Quid Juris?*" 512–35. His criticism of Gadamer centers around what he perceives as internal contradiction concerning truth in Gadamer's thought. If truth is identified as part of the hermeneutical process itself, then we are reduced to a position in which we cannot critique the truthfulness of any interpretation. If on the other hand, we can make some form of judgment concerning the truth of an interpretation then truth cannot be identified as part of the hermeneutical process. Hinman thinks that Gadamer never succeeds in solving the apparent contradiction in his work. However, I think that Hinman misses several of the points which Gadamer raises concerning the rightness of the question, phronesis, and intersubjective elements that are involved in hermeneutical understanding and allow us to make judgments concerning the truth of an interpretation.

216. Gadamer, *Truth and Method*, xxviii.

over an object in order to determine a specified result.[217] This restricts the disclosive possibilities that one could learn from the text. In the humanities, this restriction is even more severe, for it reduces the possible communication between the interpreter and tradition to a one-way dialogue. The subject ends up asserting him or herself as a master over his or her tradition. As a result, history is reduced to facts and tradition is no longer our conversation partner and teacher.

However, Apel claims that Gadamer's negation of the role of method in hermeneutics is based on an outmoded and mistaken view of method. In Apel's opinion, Gadamer relinquished the human sciences' claim to methodology and objectivity to the natural sciences too quickly.[218] On the one hand, Apel agrees with Gadamer that the methodological approach of the natural sciences cannot be hermeneutically defended because it misses the intersubjective dimension of human knowledge and the role which language plays in understanding. On the other hand, he argues that rules and methods play an important role in hermeneutical understanding. It is not an "either-or" but a "both-and" situation according to Apel.[219] His position is very similar to the argument that was made earlier in regard to the relationship between *techne* and *phronesis*.[220] One form of knowledge does not exclude the other, but actually requires it for its proper functioning.[221] In the same manner, method can play an important role in understanding.

At the same time, Gadamer does give some partial recognition to the role and need for method in the humanities.[222] However, the only point at which I have found Gadamer advocating the use of method concerns the need to employ genetic research when substantial understanding is not possible.[223] More than this is needed if we are going to successively apply Gadamer's hermeneutic to biblical interpretation. We

217. Holub, *Reception Theory*, 36.

218. Warnke, "Translator's Introduction," in Apel, *Understanding and Explanation*, xvi.

219. Apel, "The A Priori of Communication"; "Types of Rationality," 307–50; *Understanding and Explanation*, 50–68.

220. See the section, "The Hermeneutical Relevance of Aristotle's *Phronesis*," in chapter 2.

221. See the section, "Hermeneutical Knowledge and Tradition," in chapter 2.

222. "Therefore I did not remotely intend to deny the necessity of methodical work within the human science (*Geisteswissenschaften*)." Gadamer, *Truth and Method*, xxix.

223. See the section, "Substantive and Genetic Understanding," in chapter 2.

really need some form of methodological framework to incorporate all the different interpretive approaches to the Bible that have developed over the years and are in practice today.

In *Theology and the Philosophy of Science* Pannenberg contends that some form of criteria is needed if theology is not going to be reduced to mere emotive statements.[224] Methods and theories do not operate primarily by describing reality (a Cartesian form of positivism which Gadamer correctly opposes) but are provisional explanatory devices that are revised in light of the object to which they are applied. They are often retrospective by nature which is why the lessons learned from tradition point forward to new insights and discoveries.[225] The question becomes, "Is it possible to find some model which can fit within or complement Gadamer's hermeneutic that we can apply to the practice of biblical interpretation?" In order to answer this, I will turn to one of the most logical places, Gadamer's student, Hans Robert Jauss.

224. Pannenberg, *Theology and the Philosophy of Science*, 34–35; Thiselton, *New Horizons*, 334–35.

225. Pannenberg, *Theology and the Philosophy of Science*, 138–39, 156–57.

4

Jauss and His Challenge to Literary History

Introduction

EVER SINCE HANS ROBERT JAUSS DELIVERED HIS LECTURE "LITERARY History as a Challenge to Literary Theory" at Konstanz, Germany in 1967 he has been the leading figure in what has come to be known as reception theory. However, reception theory is not as widely known in the Anglo-American culture as it is in Germany. As Jauss has noted, "to the foreign ear questions of 'reception' may seem more appropriate to hotel management than to literature."[1]

Why has reception theory not been more widely read and studied in the Anglo-American tradition? Robert Holub thinks that the primary reason for this is that we have tended to be more heavily influenced by French schools of thought than German. The works of Roland Barthes, Paul de Man, and Paul Ricœur have been very influential in our hermeneutics. Among the many German scholars who work in reception theory, only Wolfgang Iser's works are widely read in English.[2] However, Iser's work does not serve as an adequate introduction to reception theory for the Anglo-American reader for two reasons. First, Iser makes very few references to Jauss in his work, thus giving the false impression that these two colleagues at Konstanz University do not work that closely together.[3] And secondly, he does not fully develop the

1. Holub, *Reception Theory,* ix.

2. In particular, Wolfgang Iser's two books, *The Implied Readers* and *The Act of Reading.*

3. For example, in *The Act of Reading,* Iser only mentions Jauss briefly in a few footnotes.

role of history as Jauss does.[4] As a result, his work is often associated with reader response theorists, such as Stanley Fish, in hermeneutical discussions.[5]

This situation improved slightly in the late 1980s with the publication of three of Jauss's books from the University of Minnesota Press, and the journal New Literary History printing several articles on reception theory. However, while his work is now more familiar to the English reader, it is still viewed as a peripheral hermeneutical or literary theory. "Although most major theorists and many coming into the field are now familiar with the general precepts of reception theory, to my knowledge there are no endeavours to extend or refine a position based on these precepts; nor are there any major studies in English—again outside of American Germanistik—which put this theory into practice."[6]

One of the primary purposes of this book is to help to resolve this deficiency, at least in the field of biblical hermeneutics. The goal of the next three chapters can briefly be outlined along the following lines. First, this chapter will concentrate on the basic hermeneutic that Jauss develops for reception theory. There are two reasons for this: first, to introduce the English reader to Jauss's work, and second, to critically examine those points which are significant for biblical studies. Second, the following chapter will probe some of the wider hermeneutical concepts that both Jauss and Gadamer share. Is Jauss's hermeneutic a deviation from or a logical extension and development of Gadamer's hermeneutic? And third, chapter 6 shall be devoted to exploring several of the more significant points of reception theory for this thesis, such as the role of the classic text and the question of plurality and continuity in a tradition of interpretation.

One final point needs to be mentioned before we turn to discuss Jauss's work, and that concerns the fact that the use of the title "reception theory" immediately runs into problems because of a complex of German terms and concepts which are related to this idea. These concepts include *Wirkungsgeschichte* (the history of the impact of a text),

---

4. In his book, *Die Appellstruktur der Texte*, Iser developed a preliminary idea of literary history. He followed this concept in *The Implied Reader*, but by the time he wrote *The Act of Reading* the history of reading had almost been entirely replaced by an ahistorical phenomenology of reading. Holub, "Trends in Literary Theory," 89.

5. Holub, "Trends in Literary Theory," 80–96.

6. Holub, *Crossing Borders*, 22–23.

Rezeptionsgeschichte (the history of reception), *Wirkungsästhetik* (the aesthetics of effect or response), and *Rezeptionsästhetik* (aesthetics of reception). Robert Holub offers the following strategy in order to help us navigate amongst this complex of German hermeneutical terms. "I have adopted the following policy: 'reception theory' refers throughout to a general shift in concern from the author and the work to the text and the reader. It is used, therefore, as an umbrella term and encompasses both Jauss's and Iser's projects as well as empirical research and the traditional occupation with influences."[7]

Background to Jauss's Thought

There were several major shifts that took place in Germany prior to and during the 1960s that help explain the rise of reception theory, and in particular Jauss's theories. Alongside a public discontent with economic problems, there was a growing discontentment in the academic realm. The "Memorandum for the Reform of the Study of Linguistics and Literature," which Jauss, Wolfgang Iser, and others penned arguing for methodological and institutional change is evidence of his concerns in this area early in his career. Specifically, there were growing doubts within the German academic community about the methods and values for teaching literary studies.[8] German literary studies had come to a point of crisis within the current paradigms by which it was being practiced.[9] One of the their main complaints with the historical-critical and formalist approaches was that they suppressed and concealed the role of the reader. While readers are an indispensable element to any act of interpretation, the function of readers was rarely discussed. It is only through the experiences of those who read, interpret, and apply the message of the texts that literary traditions are formed. As a result, Jauss sought to find theory which did justice to the "dynamic process of production and reception from author, work, and public" and would

---

7. Holub, *Reception Theory*, xi–xii.

8. Ibid., 7–12; For evidence of Jauss's continued concern over educational reform, see Segers, "An Interview with Hans Robert Jauss," 90–95.

9. Jauss's adoption of Kuhn's concept of paradigm shifts will be covered in the next chapter.

hopefully liberate literary studies from the dry and dusty methodological approaches.[10]

On the practical side, Jauss's interest in these issues arose from his study of medieval literature. His study of these texts raised questions for him concerning the possibility of direct aesthetic understanding of the text, the role which the original horizon of the text played in understanding, and the possibility of historical mediation through background information.[11] His address, "Literary History as a Challenge to Literary Theory," was an attempt to not only address the prevailing views of his day but also define a solution.

> I tried to imagine a new literary history, one that opened the closed circuit of author and work in the direction of the receiver, and was meant to make of this receiver, whether a reader or the public, the intermediary between the past and the present, the work and its effects. Such a history would have to stand up against the ideal of objectivity espoused by the old, discredited literary history, and also the demands for exactness laid down by those sociologists and structuralists who scoffed at historical understanding.[12]

The Fall of Literary History

Jauss's main area of concern is the relationship between literature and history. One of the greatest challenges he faced was to reformulate and revive the concept of literary history since it had fallen from the position it once enjoyed 150 years ago. Prior to the 1960s literary history was seen as an outdated form of knowledge that was too historically oriented and did not approach literature aesthetically. This was a valid criticism that had to be overcome if reception theory was going to succeed.

This crisis in literary history can be traced to the nineteenth century when literary studies appropriated the positivistic approaches of scientific methodology. The result was that literary history was swallowed up by general history. This approach did not do justice to the history of literature in two ways. First, it did not consider the categori-

10. Jauss, "Der Leser als Instanz einer neuen Geschichte der Literatur," 325–26.

11. Ibid., 218; Jauss, "The Alterity and Modernity of Medieval Literature," 184ff.

12. Jauss, *Question and Answer,* 224.

cal distinction between literary effects and what positivistic history can study. In literature, there is a connection between the author who creates the meaning and readers who realize it over and over. Positivistic approaches to history missed this connection because they compared one work with others and one author with other authors. And second, the communication process between author, text, and receiver was severed.[13] This follows the same criticism that Gadamer raised concerning methodological approaches to history: by objectifying the text you have emasculated it and do not allow it to confront you.[14] As a result, the text is detached from the creative act and you are only left with the traces or relics of a creative mind. "The individual text has no value in itself but only serves as a source—i.e., only as material conveying knowledge of the past historical context, just like other silent relics of the past."[15]

The two traditional solutions were put forward to meet the invasion of positivistic history in literary studies. The first solution approaches literary history by arranging the material according to general patterns, such as genre, in order to consider the individual works within the framework of a chronological series. The significance of the author, or the interpretation of his or her work is reduced to an occasional aside. In the end, literary history is swallowed up by a history of culture. The second solution arranged literary history according to the history of great authors and evaluated different literary texts according to a rubric of "life and work" essays. In this approach less known authors and works were ignored and the development of elements such as literary genres was overlooked. Both suffered the loss of the aesthetic dimension of qualitative judgments and considered the results of such studies as antiquarian knowledge.[16] There are good reasons to hesitate before including any form of judgments about the quality and significance of past works within literary theory. "For the quality and rank of a literary work result neither from the biographical or historical conditions of its origin, nor from its place in the sequence of the development of a genre

---

13. Jauss, "History of Art and Pragmatic History," in *Towards an Aesthetic,* 51–52.

14. See the section, "The Rehabilitation of Prejudice and Tradition," in chapter 1.

15. Gadamer, *Truth and Method,* 198, also 275.

16. Jauss, "Literary History," in *Towards an Aesthetic,* 4; Holub, *Reception Theory,* 55–56.

alone, but rather *from the criteria of influence, reception, and posthumous fame, criteria that are more difficult to grasp.*"[17]

Marxism

In Jauss's mind, the two most promising schools of thought to offer solutions to this crisis in literary history in this century are Marxism and Formalism. The strength of Marxism lay in its emphasis on the idea that art and literature are not independent activities but are part of life-processes, and only when this is considered does history cease to be a collection of lifeless facts. Marxism sees literature as part of the human appropriation of the world.[18] A second strength of Marxism is that it does not have a relativistic or an uncritical attitude towards tradition as many theories do.[19]

There are several areas of Marxist thought that were unacceptable to Jauss. The main point of contention between Jauss and Marxist critical theorists concerned the role that production played.[20] Production was the fundamental starting-point and the main factor for Marxist approaches to literary criticism.[21] How the text was received by readers and its literary effects, while important, remained secondary in Marxist literary theory.[22] Because literature was reduced to mankind's appropriation of nature and the control of economic processes it could only reflect what was already known within that social and historical horizon.[23] Mimesis and the play of interpretation were restricted to what was already known, you could not recognize more in the text or work of art.[24] Jauss also questioned how literature could serve a revolutionary function if one could only recognize "the stabilized images and

17. Jauss, "Literary History," in *Towards an Aesthetic,* 5, emphasis added.

18. Jauss, "Literary History," 11.

19. Holub, *Reception Theory,* 123.

20. Ibid., 126; Jauss, "The Idealist Embarrassment," 202; Segers, "An Interview with Hans Robert Jauss," 88; see also Naumann, "Literary production and reception," 107–15.

21. Holub, *Reception Theory,* 126.

22. Jauss, "The Idealist Embarrassment," 195–97.

23. Jauss, "Literary History," 14; Jauss, "The Idealist Embarrassment," 193, 206–7.

24. See the section, "Play as the Being of Artwork," in chapter 3.

prejudices of their historical situation" and not allow for the disclosure of more which can create new perspectives on the world.[25]

In order to overcome the weaknesses inherent in Marxist literary theory, one must recognize the double character of literature; it not only expresses reality but it also creates reality.[26] The influence of Heidegger's concept of the work of art, through Gadamer, on Jauss is evident here. In the act of reading a text, a disclosure of truth takes place, much like Heidegger's illustration concerning Van Gogh's painting of the peasant's shoes. This disclosure is not prior to, or alongside the text, but occurs in the act of reading. There is an essential unity to the text between its expression of reality and the reality that it forms. Literature not only is a product of social influences and serves as a repository of culture, it also performs a socially formative function. Literature is not only a product of social conditions but it is also an agent of social change.[27]

This socially formative or norm-building function of literature is very significant for the history of biblical interpretation. The interpretation of the Bible has resulted in practices that have had profound consequences, both positive and negative. Ulrich Luz argues that because texts possess a socially formative power, and in particular theological texts, we must have a 'hermeneutic of consequences.' "For this kind of hermeneutic, the study of the history of effects is essential, because it shows what the consequences of biblical texts in history were."[28]

Formalism

The turn toward literary theory in biblical studies is one of the most significant developments in biblical hermeneutics in the past thirty years. Formalism was a phase which both biblical and literary studies passed through, but the time lag in biblical studies has been much greater than in literary studies. As a movement, Formalism was primarily a Russian linguistic and literary movement that originated with Roman Jakobson's work, *Sborniki po teorii poeticheskogo iazyka* (*Studies on the Theory of Poetic Language,* 1916). As a school, it died out by the end of the 1920s

25. Jauss, "Literary History," 14.

26. Ibid., 14–15.

27. Holub, *Reception Theory*, 122.

28. Luz, *Matthew in History*, 92–93; Räisänen, "The Effective 'History' of the Bible," 309.

when many of the formalists were forced to abandon their views due to constant criticism from Marxist critics. Formalism's influence was much longer lived though. It exercised a considerable impact on the Prague School, largely due to the fact that Roman Jakobson moved there in 1921. In the West, Formalism had little direct impact except on French structuralism, particularly in the works of Roland Barthes and Gérard Genette. It was not until the publication of Viktor Elrich's book, *Russian Formalism: History and Doctrine,* in 1955 and the republication and translation of some of the original Formalist works that it became widely known in German and Anglo-American literary studies.[29] Dan O. Via, and Daniel Patte applied this approach to biblical interpretation in the 1980s.[30] One of Jauss's objectives was to retrieve the useful concepts of Formalism, which were lost when literary studies rejected Formalism, and reincorporate them into literary theory. In this sense, Jauss's use of Formalism and his moving beyond it presents a promising avenue of research for biblical hermeneutics.

Dissatisfaction with literary studies that were dominated by the historical-positivistic approach of the nineteenth century was the seedbed from which Formalism arose. Jakobson criticized the tendency he saw in literary studies to exchange the study of literature for something else, namely the examination of the historical conditions external to the text in order to gain an understanding of the intentions of the author and aid in the interpretation of the text, which the historical-positivist paradigm practiced. Two strands that bound the various Formalists together were: (1) their attempt to redefine the study of literature and place it on equal footing with other 'scientific' methods, and (2) the idea that a text was an aesthetic entity which reflected reality through its own internal structures. Formalists employed the following tools to achieve these goals: the difference between poetic and practical language in texts, defamiliarization, the relationship between story and plot, and literary evolution.[31] As such, Formalism represents a turning from the external conditions of historical and causal explanation to the strategic priority of the internal organization of the literary text and its aesthetic

29. Kolesnikoff, "Formalism, Russian," in Makaryk, *Encyclopedia of Contemporary Literary Theory,* 53–60.

30. Thiselton, *New Horizons in Hermeneutics,* 486–94.

31. Tynjianov, "On Literary Evolution," 68–78.

effects.[32] This was both the strength and weakness of Formalism. Its focus on aesthetic perception and the relationships between the text and its recipients were its strong points. However, its focus on the sum total of literary devices in the text to the exclusion of historical and social factors was its weakness.[33]

The ability of literature to break open everyday language and understanding through the devices of defamiliarization and the difference between poetic and practical (or everyday) language is one aspect of Formalism that Jauss wanted to retain. Practical language was concerned with clear communication through reference to objects or accepted concepts while the goal of poetical language was the experience of the sounds or textures of the text.[34] Paul Ricœur agrees with this assessment of the distinction between poetical and practical language. "What binds poetic discourse, then, is the need to bring to language modes of being that ordinary vision obscures or even represses."[35] According to Formalism, one of the primary goals of literature is to present something in an unexpected or novel manner and thus, disrupt our habitual patterns of recognition.[36] Literary texts achieve this by 'defamiliarizing' our understanding of the world by presenting it in new and unexpected ways. This opposition between the world presented in the text (poetical language) and reality (practical language) gives the reader a basis for

32. For more on this shift in literary paradigms see the next chapter.

33. Jauss, "Literary History," 16; Holub, *Reception Theory*, 30–31, Kolesnikoff, "Formalism, Russian," 58–59. Jauss mainly considers the works of Roman Ingarden, Jan Mukarovsky, and Felix Vodicka.

34. Since Jakobson and some of his early colleagues were linguists, it is easy to understand why they were attracted to the question of the difference between poetical and practical language use. Kolesnikoff, "Formalism, Russian," 53–54. This distinction appears to have been inherited from positivism which viewed the explicit meaning of a text as cognitive and the implicit meaning as a form of emotive language. Practical language is cognitive, of the semantic order, because it refers to the actual world. Poetical is extra-semantic in that it consists of the weaving together of emotive evocations that lack cognitive value. Cf. Ricœur, *Interpretation Theory*, 46. Vanhoozer is mistaken in his argument that Jauss picked up this dualism between poetic and practical language from Romanticism, and misses the more direct and significant influence of Formalism. Vanhoozer, "A Lamp in the Labyrinth," 34.

35. Ricœur, *Interpretation Theory*, 60.

36. Defamiliarization takes place at three levels. At the linguistic level, it makes language difficult through the use of difficult sounds and words. It disrupts at the content level by challenging accepted ideas. And at the literary level, it deviates from the accepted literary norms and genres.

comparing the claims or perspectives of the text with their horizon of expectations.[37]

These ideas concerning defamiliarization parallel Heidegger's concepts about the power of everyday language and conventional norms to conceal our understanding of things. As long as a hammer is in its proper contextual relationships, the manner in which we understand the hammer as a hammer and its significance is "inconspicuous" to us because it lies hidden in the common language we share.[38] But when the contextual relationships that govern our use and expectations of the hammer are disrupted it is defamiliarized to us.[39] Heidegger and Gadamer develop this line of thought to show that the power or effect of art involves a push (*Stoß*) that disrupts or breaks "complacent meaning expectations."[40] Reading always involves how the text strikes the reader and how the meaning of the text is then related back to the reader's preunderstanding.[41] For Jauss, the processes of defamiliarization and the tension between poetical and practical language allow the text to strike (push) the reader and disclose new perspectives to view the world by disrupting the reader's expectations and everyday understanding.

While the opposition between poetical and practical language may serve as a helpful tool for the study of particular genres, poetical or literary texts, its applicability to other forms of literature is limited. For instance, in the Bible, this opposition may prove fruitful in the investigation of poetical texts such as Psalms or Ecclesiastes but its value for a text which is more historical is questionable. We cannot restrict the manner in which we experience art or texts to reflective aesthetic pleasure, which is built upon the differentiation between poetic and practical language.[42] By contrast, Gadamer's concepts of play, presentation, and the transformation into structure (see the previous chapter) present a much broader hermeneutical model that is able to incorporate all the different genres and literary devices employed in such a diverse collection of books as found in the Bible. The concept of poetical versus

---

37. Jan Mukarovsky, "Standard Language and Poetic Language," 1050–57; Holub, *Crossing Borders*, 16.

38. Heidegger, *Being and Time*, 199.

39. Ibid., 105.

40. Dallmayr, "Prelude: Hermeneutics and Deconstruction," 85.

41. Gadamer, "Reflections on My Philosophical Journey," 55.

42. Gadamer, *Truth and Method*, xxxi.

practical language, and especially its use of defamiliarization, can be preserved as long as it is seen within a larger hermeneutical framework of play that allows for a much wider range of literature than poetical or literary texts.

The introduction of the diachronic perspective into literary studies through the concept of the evolution of literary forms, functions, and genres is one of the most significant contributions made by Formalism. This offers a needed correction to the positivistic approaches that viewed literary works as a closed system that was connected at best by a general sketch of history, the works of an author, a style, or a particular genre. Formalism sought to relate one text to others in order to discover their evolutionary relationships. An author has a certain amount of genres and linguistic styles from which to select when composing her text. It is through the creativity of the author and her use of the literary conventions that genres are modified and new ones are created. However, once a text is written it becomes a literary fact and is incorporated into the literary tradition that then shapes the possibilities for future authors. The elements of defamiliarization that were new and unexpected for the original audience have been "leveled down" and become part of the horizon of expectations for successive generations of readers and no longer function to disrupt their expectations.[43] The decisive feature of a work's evolutionary significance is its innovative character that was perceived against the background of other works of literature.[44] As opposed to Darwinianism, literary evolution is not a linear process but is punctuated by struggles and breaks.[45] Formalism's contribution of the idea of change and development in literature, with its focus on innovation that allows for a combination of history and artistic significance, plays a central role in reception theory.

If Marxism failed because it did not consider the aesthetic dimension of reception, Formalism suffered from a lack of historical perspective.[46] Jauss criticized Formalism for viewing the text as autono-

43. Mukarovsky, "Standard Language and Poetic Language," 1052–53.

44. Jauss, "Literary History," 33. The sole criterion of this evolution, according to Formalism, is the appearance of new literary forms and "not the self-reproduction of worn-out forms, artistic devices, and genres, which pass into the background until at a moment in the evolution they are made 'perceptible' once again." Ibid., 16–17.

45. Jauss, *Towards an Aesthetic,* 105.

46. Kolesnikoff, "Formalism, Russian," 58–59.

mous and only examining what is internal to the text and intertextual systems.[47] Formalism's program of explaining a work's place in history by examining its change in literary forms was not an adequate basis from which to construct literary history. According to Jauss, Formalism must be opened up so that the relation of the text to the questions left by preceding works (the text as an answer to those questions) and the questions that the text in turn leaves behind, are considered.[48] Like Marxism, Formalism missed how literature informs culture and the progress of history.[49] In order to solve this shortcoming, Jauss proposed that Formalism should be modified to include considerations concerning the original horizon of expectations in which the text first appeared, the horizon of the reader, as well as those elements which are internal to the text.

Jauss's solution to the crisis in literary history is to combine Marxism's demand for historical mediation and Formalism's advances in the realm of aesthetic perception with Gadamer's concept of the horizon of expectation of the reader to construct a new model of literary history.[50] One of the main issues that must be corrected in both Marxism and Formalism is the limited role they assign to the reader.[51] Because readers are not just passive agents but play a formative role in shaping literary history they must play an active role in literary theory.

> The historical life of a literary work is unthinkable without the active participation of its addressees. For it is only through the process of its mediation that the work enters into the changing horizon-of-experience of a continuity in which the perpetual inversion occurs from simple reception to critical understand-

47. Holub, *Reception Theory*, 30–31.

48. Ibid., 64.

49. Jauss, "Literary History," 40.

50. "The task for a new literary history, therefore, becomes to merge successfully the best qualities of Marxism and Formalism." Holub, *Reception Theory*, 57.

51. "Reader, listener, and spectator—in short, the factor of the audience—play and extremely limited role in both literary theories. Orthodox Marxist aesthetics treats the reader—if at all—no differently from the author; it inquires about his social position or seeks to recognize him in the structure of a represented society. The Formalist school needs the reader only as a perceiving subject who follows the directions in the text in order to distinguish the [literary] form or discover the [literary] procedure." Jauss, "Literary History," 18–19.

ing, from passive to active reception, from recognized aesthetic norms to a new production that surpasses them.[52]

Jauss's Provocation: "Literary History as a Challenge to Literary Theory"

The most logical point to start any discussion of Jauss's works is his essay, "Literary History as a Challenge to Literary Theory," for which he is best known and which has been one of the most widely discussed papers on literary theory in Germany.[53]

This essay was provocative by nature and presented not only a challenge to the inadequacy of the literary theories at that time but also offered a solution in the form of a proposal for a new paradigm in literary studies. His appeal to Friedrich Schiller's inaugural lecture of 1789, "What Is and Toward What End Does One Study Universal History," is a clear indication of this. Schiller called for a new approach to history and literature because the answers to the questions which the classical-humanist paradigm asked were no longer satisfactory. This paradigm developed during the Renaissance and derived guidelines from classical texts which served as norms to evaluate all other works of literature.[54] Schiller realized that, with the rise of historicism, classical literature could no longer be held as embodying atemporal norms and thus, this approach was in crisis. Schiller was not only able to explain why his generation was facing a crisis in literary studies at that time but he also established the expectations of nineteenth-century literary history.[55] Jauss prepared his readers to receive his work in a similar manner by referring to Schiller's essay in the introduction to his lecture.

Jauss's essay is divided into two sections. In the first section, he covered a lot of the same material I discussed in the previous section in order to set the stage for his proposal. His proposal is laid out in seven theses that constitute the second half of his essay. Since this is such a significant work for understanding Jauss's thought the rest of this chapter will be devoted to these theses.

52. Ibid., 19.

53. Holub, *Reception Theory*, 69.

54. See the section on "Paradigm Shifts" in the next chapter for a discussion of how the concept of paradigms functions heuristically and apologetically in Jauss's work.

55. Jauss, "Literary History," 6.

Thesis 1: *Literary history must move from historical objectivism which is based on the aesthetics of production and representation to an aesthetics of reception and influence.*

Collingwood's axiom that "History is nothing but the reenactment of past thought in the historian's mind" plays perhaps an even more significant role in the history of literature.[56] Literary history is not based primarily on facts but on the experience of texts by readers. In this respect, Jauss develops Gadamer's metaphor of a musical score and its repeated performances to define literary history. "A literary work is not an object that stands by itself and offers the same view to each reader in each period. . . . It is much more like an orchestration that strikes ever new resonances among its readers and that frees the text from the material of the words and brings it to a contemporary existence."[57] Literary history is a continual process of aesthetic reception. The endless collection of objective facts that some literary histories produce misses the eventful character of the text as well as the manner in which the concretization of the meaning of the text can play a historically constitutive role. Texts are not like historical events. On the one hand, they only become an event when a reader reads them in light of other works which in turn shapes his reception of future works. On the other hand, they lack effect or influence if they are not appropriated by a reader.[58] It is only through reception, through the interrelationship between the literary work and the reading public, that a work of literature reveals its structure and meaning.[59]

56. Collingwood, *The Idea of History,* 228; Jauss, "Literary History," 21.

57. Jauss, "Literary History," 21.

58. Ibid., 20–22.

59. Jauss, *Towards an Aesthetic,* 73.

Thesis 2: The aesthetic of reception can avoid psychologizing by looking at the influence of work in the period of its appearance, from pre-understanding of genres, and from themes already familiar in other works.

A text does not appear in a vacuum but makes use of signals, genres, and other traits familiar to the readers. This means that the event of aesthetic experience is not an arbitrary subjective experience, "but rather the carrying out of specific instructions in a process of directed perception, which can be comprehended according to its constitutive motivations and triggering signals, and which can also be described by a textual linguistics."[60] There is an intersubjective horizon that determines the effects or influences of a text. Because texts employ conventions that the reader inherits from other texts and which become part of the forms of life or the reader's language game(s), the effect of the text is not an event that is purely private, but it is intersubjective in character.[61] Jauss's point is not to reduce literary history to a sociology of knowledge but he is arguing that there is historical data available to the literary historian in this area.[62]

In order for a reader to comprehend a text he must possess the foreknowledge to make that text understandable. The expectations that the reader brings to the text are inherited from his tradition and the rules that he has learned from reading other texts. These expectations are "then varied, corrected, altered, or even just reproduced" as he reads the text.[63] This results in a semiotic expansion and correction of the reader's system. The various horizons of expectations (that in which the work first appeared and the successive horizons in which it is read)

60. Jauss, "Literary History," 23.

61. Jauss's thought offers parallels with the later Wittgenstein here, in as far as an utterance or text gains its currency from the intersubjective world of shared co-operation and training. For Wittgenstein, this intersubjective world is primarily discussed in terms of training, while Jauss prefers to discuss it in terms of tradition. Wittgenstein, *Philosophical Investigations*, §240–44, and esp. 293.

The same holds true for works of art. In order to appreciate a work of art the view must understand the conventions the artist employs in their depiction, know something of the artistic tradition this work stands in, and know what stories or events the artist is depicting. O'Kane, *Painting the Text*, 61.

62. Jauss, "Literary History," 22–24.

63. Ibid., 23.

are by nature intersubjective and therefore open to investigation. One could determine if the author was writing in a manner with which the original readers would have been familiar or if the author was being innovative in the manner she was structuring the text by studying the genres familiar to the author and the original readers.

The intersubjective dimension for studying the horizon of expectations also includes the intertextual relationships between texts. Umberto Eco and Jonathan Culler help delineate the role that intertextuality plays in hermeneutics. According to Eco, the process by which the characters on a page become a "sign-function" involves the production of the sign (word or meaning) that arises in the act of recognition.[64] A code must pre-exist to enable the person to see the relation between the action and the content in order for a human action to be recognized as an expression of some content.[65] Culler develops these ideas in relation to the practice of reading texts and the inter-subjectivity of understanding. "When a speaker of a language hears a phonetic sequence, he is able to give it meaning because he brings to the act of communication an amazing repertoire of conscious and unconscious knowledge." Reading is no exception to this rule. "To read a text as literature is not to make one's mind a *tabula rasa* and approach it without preconceptions; one must bring to it an implicit understanding of the operations of literary discourse which tells one what to look for."[66]

Anyone who lacks this knowledge will be baffled when presented with a text such as a parable. "He would be unable to read it as literature . . . because he lacks the complex 'literary competence' which enables him and others to proceed. He has not internalised the 'grammar' of literature which would permit him to convert linguistic sequences into literary structures and meanings."[67] In a manner similar to Wittgenstein, Culler argues that we must be trained in the rules, conventions, and

64. "Recognition occurs when a given object or event, produced by nature or human action (intentionally or unintentionally), and existing in a world of facts among facts, comes to be viewed by an addressee as the expression of a given content, either through a pre-existing and coded correlation or through the positing of a possible correlation by its addressee." Eco, *A Theory of Semiotics,* 221.

65. "I am speaking to you; you understand me because my messages are emitted following rules of a communally shared code." Eco, "Social Life as a Sign System," 61.

66. Culler, *Structuralist Poetics,* 113–14.

67. Ibid., 114.

forms of literature in order to understand literature. A general experience of the world and society is not enough to make a reader competent
to understand literary works.[68]

> But it is clear that the study of one poem or novel facilitates the
> study of the next: one gains not only points of comparison but
> a sense of how to read. One develops a set of questions which
> experience shows to be appropriate and productive and criteria
> for determining whether they are in a given case, production;
> one acquires a sense of the possibilities of literature and how
> these possibilities may be distinguished. We may speak, if we
> like, of extrapolating from one work to another, so long as we do
> not thereby obscure the fact that the process of extrapolation is
> precisely what requires explanation.[69]

In the interpretive or reading process, Culler is interested in how
conventions and intertextuality enable, but also limit, the possible readings of a text. He is not concerned with, nor does he believe that there
is, one correct interpretation of a text. Just as the linguistic categories of
langue and *parole* are dialectically related to each other, so are texts and
intertextual systems. Culler defines intertextuality this way:

> "Intertextuality" thus has a double focus. On the one hand, it
> calls our attention to the importance of prior texts, insisting that
> the autonomy of texts is a misleading notion and that a work
> has the meaning it does only because certain things have previ-
> ously been written. Yet in so far as it focuses on intelligibility,
> on meaning, "intertextuality" leads us to consider prior texts as
> contributions to a code which makes possible the various effects
> of signification. Intertextuality thus becomes less a name for a
> work's relation to particular prior texts than a designation of
> its participation in the discursive space of a culture: the rela-
> tionship between a text and the various languages or signify-
> ing practices of a culture and its relation to those texts which
> articulate for it the possibilities of that culture. The study of in-
> tertextuality is thus not the investigation of sources and influ-
> ences as traditionally conceived; it casts its net wider to include
> anonymous discursive practices, codes whose origins are lost,
> that make possible the signifying practices of later texts.[70]

68. Culler, *Structuralist Poetics,* 114–20.
69. Ibid., 121.
70. Ibid., 104.

Jauss emphasizes both the diachronic and synchronic aspects to intertextuality. For example, when we read a detective story we understand it in a synchronic relationship to other detective stories we have read. At the same time, a detective story may be a reworking of a previous novel, or it may be picking up themes and ideas from classical literature. The reader's pleasure and interest in the text arises from the manner in which our expectations are generated between works. Intertextuality functions like a "well-known game with familiar rules but unknown surprises."[71]

And finally, the intersubjective dimension of the horizon of expectations may be seen in the opposition between poetic and practical functions of language. What may have been a new and innovative literary style or manner of communicating an idea when the text was first written becomes part of the literary competence of successive generations of readers. As a result, later readers do not experience the same tension between poetical and practical language or the disruptive power of the text that the original readers did.[72]

The relevance of this for biblical studies can seen in the history of parable studies. Christian Bugge and Paul Fiebig criticized Adolf Jülicher's work, *Die Gleichnisreden Jesu*, for interpreting Jesus' parables from the perspective of classical Greek literature and ignoring the Jewish and rabbinical genre of *mashal* which serves as a better model for understanding the form and content of Jesus' parables. The result is that Jülicher perceived Jesus as a nineteenth-century German who was versed in the Greek classics.[73] The meaning of a parable was reduced to expressing one clear moral point that should be explicated by the exegete in as general a term as possible.

71. Jauss, "Theses on the Transition," 144.

72. Jauss, "Literary History," 16, 24; Jauss, "Thesis on the Transition," 141.

73. Kissinger, *The Parables of Jesus*, 72–74, 77–83; Jülicher, *Die Gleichnisreden Jesu*, 6–118.

Thesis 3: The artistic character of a work can be determined by the influence or effect of a text on its audience. The change in horizons that the text brings about through the negation of the familiar or opening up of new perspectives is a result of the aesthetic distance between the text and its audience, which can be objectified through the audiences' reactions and the critics' judgments.

If a work is closely aligned with the audience's horizon of expectations then no horizontal change is produced. Jauss classifies this as "culinary art."[74] For Gadamer, the point Jauss is making concerning "culinary art" is vitally important. If we experience no provocation, negation, or push (*Stoß*) from the work of art, then we have not had an experience (*Erfahrung*). Without this provocation, we will never learn to recognize what we do not know, learn to ask questions, or mature and develop (*Bildung*) as individuals, communities, and traditions.[75]

At the same time, tradition has a leveling, or homogenizing power on even the most innovative and provocative works. The aesthetic distance between the text and the original audience diminishes for later readers "to the extent that the original negativity of the work has become self evident and has itself entered into the horizon of future aesthetic experience, as a henceforth familiar-expectation."[76] Classical texts and great artworks suffer from this form of horizontal change. To protect and/or rescue great literary works from being reduced to culinary art "requires a special effort to read them 'against the grain' of the accustomed experience to catch sight of their artistic character

---

74. He appears to have adopted this term from Heidegger who complained that modern art had been reduced to a "matter for pastry cooks" because it had been deprived of it ability to make a truth disclosure. Heidegger continues, "It makes no essential difference whether the enjoyment of art serves to satisfy the sensibilities of the connoisseur and esthete or to provide moral edification.... On the strength of a re-captured, pristine, relation to being we must provide the word 'art' with a new content." Heidegger, *An Introduction to Metaphysics,* 131–32. Heidegger makes this point in his argument against the reduction of thinking to calculation, language being pressed into the service of trivia, and art to aesthetics. Thiselton, *The Two Horizons,* 330–35.

75. Gadamer, *Truth and Method,* 354–56; Weinsheimer and Marshall, "Translator's Preface," in *Truth and Method,* xiii; Kisiel, "Ideology Critique and Phenomenology," 159.

76. Jauss, "Literary History," 25; Jauss, *Question and Answer,* 16.

once again."[77] In biblical hermeneutics, the classical example of this is the removal of the negation or subversive character of the parables. The negation in the parable of the Good Samaritan is no longer recognized in our horizon of expectations. Even the title we apply to this parable (the "good" Samaritan) betrays this fact. The shock, which the original audience experienced as the parable, reversed their expectations as to who the hero of the story was is almost the exact opposite of our horizon of expectations.[78]

There is a dialectical relationship between texts and horizons of expectations. Some works violate or break the audiences' expectations to such an extent that the audience is only able to gradually appreciate the text with the passage of time. This takes place as the horizon of expectations develops or alters so that the aspects of the literary work in question can be appreciated. The reception of the novels *Fanny* and *Madame Bovary* in the nineteenth century illustrates this. Both books were written at the same time, on a similar subject matter (adultery), and to the same audience. *Fanny* was immediately received and enjoyed several reprintings while *Madame Bovary*, which violated many of the literary expectations and norms of the original audience, gained acceptance gradually.[79] As the horizon of expectations shifted the fortune of the two books was reversed.

> As *Madame Bovary*, however, became a world-wide success, when at first it was understood and appreciated as a turning-point in the history of the novel by only a small circle of connoisseurs, the audience of novel-readers that was formed by it came to sanction the new cannon of expectations; this canon made Feydeau's weaknesses—his flowery style, his modish effects, his lyrical-confessional clichés—unbearable, and allowed *Fanny* to fade into yesterday's bestseller.[80]

77. Jauss, "Literary History," 26. Umberto Eco makes an important contribution to this discussion by showing that even classical or provocative texts can be consumed by the naive reader in a manner which is equivalent to Jauss's argument about 'culinary art.' A naive reader will not appreciate or enjoy the text in the manner that a critical reader will. This is not just the result of being a poor reader but involves the relationship between the structures or strategies in the text and the competence of the reader. Eco, *The Role of the Reader*, 9–10, 204–16.

78. Jauss, "Literary History," 25–28.

79. Jauss, "Die beiden Fassungen von Flauberts Education sentimentale."

80. Jauss, "Literary History," 28. The reception of Moby Dick is another excellent example of this phenomena. "Moby Dick received mixed reviews when it was pub-

The reception of a particular text, in turn, shapes and alters the aes-thetic norms of that tradition and, as a result, those works which were formerly accepted as successful books are now seen as outmoded; our appreciation of them has been withdrawn.

This same phenomena occurs in biblical studies. A prime exam-ple of this is, once again, Jülicher's *Die Gleichnisreden Jesu*. While the historical-critical method was recognized for determining the original meaning of the gospels during the nineteenth century it was not until the publication of Jülicher's book that this method was applied to the parables in a thoroughgoing manner. Until Jülicher, the parables were interpreted allegorically and classified as allegories. Jülicher's work dis-pelled both of these ideas: the parables are not allegories nor should they be interpreted allegorically despite the fact that this had been the accepted practice since the earliest days of the church. Based on Cicero's classifications, Jülicher argued that a parable was an extended simile and that an allegory was composed of multiple metaphors. Jesus' parables were not allegories but extended similes.[81] As such, the parables were reduced to moral stories which contained one point of correspondence with the world and conveyed one central teaching.

The impact of Jülicher's work is such that if a modern scholar wishes to introduce an allegorical dimension into his or her reading of the parables they must fight against what has been accepted as exegeti-cal convention since Jülicher.[82] His work represents a definitive turn in the interpretation of the parables from allegorical to other categories. "So thoroughly did Jülicher do his work that for a time it almost seemed

lished, and proved to be a popular disaster. Not until Raymond Weaver began reviving Melville some seventy years later did the book attract much attention. For a few years, critics debated its value and eventually advocates won, and the great ungainly book was enshrined in the hall of fame: it was tacitly deemed canonical by something approach-ing a general consensus. Since then, it has been treated as scripture by most people working in American literature: that is to say, its genre has been examined like the bibli-cal midrashim; numerous hypotheses of its overall meaning have been constructed; exegeses of individual chapters or symbols have been performed; the book has become required reading in thousands of schools; most educated people claim to be conversant with it. Only rarely does one see a negative evaluation of it any more; it has passed beyond that stage." Arthur, "Gadamer and Hirsch," 186.

81. Cicero *Orator ad M. Brutus* xxvii 94; Jülicher, *Die Gleichnissreden Jesu,* 1:51.

82. For example, Craig Blomberg devotes the first fifth of his book on the parables to rehabilitating the concept of allegory. Blomberg, *Interpreting the Parables,* 30–38. See also Barr, *Old and New in Interpretation,* 103–4; Louth, *Discerning the Mystery,* 96–97.

as if he had spoken the last word on the parables."[83] It is interesting to note that Jülicher credits Alexander Bruce as the person who broke the allegorical method of interpretation. However, Bruce's use of the historical-critical method to the parables resulted in his being severely criticized, and almost given a formal censure, by the Free Church of Scotland.[84] In this sense, while Bruce's work was not well received it helped to shift the horizon of expectations and in this way prepared the way for the reception of Jülicher's work.

In Jauss's earlier work, the most important criteria for determining the influence of a text concerned the manner by which the text negated the preunderstanding of its audience. In his later work, Jauss softened this position dramatically.[85] Negation was no longer the primary means by which a work provoked its reader, and the reception value of a text was not limited to its provocation. The reception of a text may take a wide spectrum of reactions in different horizons of readers, including the manner in which a text may affirm the accepted norms and conventions of the readers. This is one area in which Jauss corrected Gadamer's thought. For Gadamer, the provocation of our prejudices by a text is achieved primarily through the concept of negation.[86] Jauss gives two primary reasons for this modification in his hermeneutic. First, if tradition levels-down the provocative power of a text, then how do we explain a text's continued reception and significance within a tradition? The exemplary and normative character of classic texts clearly demonstrates the limited role that negation can play in the transmission of a tradition of literature.[87] Second, you cannot reduce the historical reception of a text to one factor such as negation. Rather we must also include other communicative functions of literature such as role

---

83. Hunter, *Interpreting the Parables,* 38. See ch. 1 of Jones, *The Art and Truth of the Parables.* Little acknowledges the significance of Jülicher's work but prefers to see Jeremias as the figure around whom the past century of parable research has revolved. See Little's three articles on "Parable Research in the Twentieth Century."

84. Hunter, *Interpreting the Parables,* 37–38. Jülicher at the same time criticized Bruce's work for developing a three-story model of parables which weakened his ability to define what a parable was. Jülicher, *Die Gleichnisreden Jesu,* 1:300.

85. Jauss, *Aesthetic Experience,* 12–15; Jauss, "Der Leser," 331.

86. For one example of this, see Gadamer, "The Problem of Historical Consciousness," 156.

87. Jauss, *Towards an Aesthetic,* 64.

identification, the extension of ideas, and literature's socially formative and affirming function.[88]

Literature fulfills both an anticipatory and archaeological function. In the latter, texts do not merely negate existing norms and prejudices but mediate norms and values from the past by allowing the reader to rediscover them, and thus, literature serves the purpose of mediating such norms with various spheres of life within the horizon of the reader. This dual function is theologically significant. Not only does the Bible speak to us most sharply when it "addresses us as adversary, to correct and to change our prior wishes and expectations," as Calvin and Luther claimed.[89] It also fulfills an archaeological role in that through the reading of the Bible we are called upon to remember and preserve what has been handed down to us. There is a third reason why this shift is important in relation to the third thesis. If the concept of negation stands at the center of reception theory, then we will end up with a view of tradition that is characterized by novelty, rupture, and discontinuity. If reception theory is broadened to include other elements, along with negation, then it takes a *via media* that is able to attend to both continuity and diversity within a tradition.

If we return to the example of the parable of the Good Samaritan, the widening of reception theory to other communicative functions beside negation become obvious. While we may not experience the negation of the parable that the original Jewish audience would have identified with the Samaritan, the socially-formative function of the parable is still experienced to this day. We are to show mercy and compassion as the Samaritan did.

88. This is especially true if we consider the role which question and answer plays in Jauss's thought. "The coherence of question and answer in this history of an interpretation is primarily determined by categories of the enrichment of understanding (be they supplementation or development, a reaccenting or a new elucidation), and only secondarily by the logic of falsifiability." Ibid., 185; Jauss, *Aesthetic Experience*, 15; Jauss, *Question and Answer*, 148, 224–25; Holub, *Reception Theory*, 79.

89. Thiselton, *New Horizons*, 9.

Thesis 4: The reconstruction of the original horizon of expecta-
tions allows us to compare past and present understanding and
forces us to become aware of the text's history of reception which
mediates the two horizons.

Jauss, like Gadamer, follows Collingwood's axiom that, "We can understand a text only when we have understood the question to which it is
an answer," in regard to reconstructing the original horizon of expectations.[90] The reconstructed question is never identical with the original
question the text sought to answer because any reconstruction of a past
horizon is always enveloped in the present horizon of the interpreter.

> The reconstruction of the horizon of expectations, in the face of
> which a work was created and received in the past, enables one
> on the other hand to pose questions that the text gave an answer
> to, and thereby to discover how the contemporary reader could
> have viewed and understood the work . . . It brings to view the
> hermeneutic difference between the former and the current un-
> derstanding of a work; it raises to consciousness the history of
> its reception . . .[91]

This means that the history of a text's reception results from the unfolding of the potential meaning of the text. Meaning does not solely reside
in the original horizon but to an "equal degree" comes from the interpreter's horizon.[92] One of the traits of a text is that, in the words of Paul
Ricœur, it possess a "surplus of meaning."[93] There is no "timelessly true"
meaning for a text that is available to the reader. This would require that
the reader could step outside history and the errors of his predecessors.
Meaning does not solely reside in the original horizon but arises from
the text's interaction with successive generations of readers.

> Since such folds [possible meaning unnoticed by author or
> original audience] can first be discovered only through the in-
> terpreter's later horizon, and can be expounded on only by as-
> similating them in a new interpretation, this horizon ought not
> simply be erased by aligning it with the earlier horizon when an
> anticipatory assumption proves unfounded. Instead, the content

90. Gadamer, *Truth and Method,* 370; Jauss, "Literary History," 29.

91. Ibid., 28.

92. Gadamer, "The Alterity and Modernity of Medieval Literature," 184.

93. Ricœur, *Interpretation Theory,* 29–36.

of the horizon of one's own expectation must be brought into
play, and mediated through the alien horizon in order to arrive
at the new horizon of another interpretation.[94]

The two horizons must be brought into play, which results in an ongoing process of constituting the meaning of a text. In order for the fusion
of horizons to take place, the interpreter must pose the question that
draws the text "back out of its seclusion" so that the text can answer
and "say something" to us. "This also means that 'while a right elucidation never understands the text better than the author understood it,' it
does surely understand differently. Yet this difference must be of such
a kind as to touch upon the Same toward which the elucidated text is
thinking.'"[95]

The idea that there may be more than one right interpretation
does not, in this case, imply that there are no wrong interpretations.
The 'score' of the text, the tradition of the text's interpretation, and the
reconstruction of the horizon in which the text appeared are all intersubjective elements that separate Jauss's hermeneutic from the more
subjective approaches of Richard Rorty or Stanley Fish.[96] As a result, it
follows that our interpretations of classical texts, such as the Bible, are
always provisional by nature and open to review while at the same time
must faithfully address the text and its subject matter. If we slide off to
one side or the other of this position, the writing of new commentaries
is a futile exercise.

Thesis 5: A text must be seen in its position in its "literary series" in order to recognize its historical significance.

"Put in another way, the next work can solve formal and moral problems left behind by the last work, and present new problems in turn."[97]
Formalism's concept of literary evolution was a step in this direction.
However, its criterion of innovation in the process of literary evolution was one-sided and could not adequately explain the growth and

94. Jauss, *Question and Answer,* 206–7.

95. Ibid., 207.

96. Paul de Man notes that Jauss has always viewed such subjective hermeneutical
models "with a measure of suspicion." "Introduction," in Jauss, *Towards an Aesthetic,*
xix.

97. Jauss, "Literary History," 32.

development of literature. One must also consider the horizon of the reader and the aesthetics of reception. Literary history is not just concerned with a chronological series of literary facts. It must seek the questions left behind by the text and the solutions the text offered to the questions that were posed to the author. In order to recognize these questions, the interpreter must bring their experiences into play, "since the past horizon of old and new forms, problems and solutions is only recognizable in its further mediation, within the present horizon of the received work."[98]

Literary works offer possible solutions to the questions that were posed by previous texts and also present new questions. This means that the 'new' is not merely literary innovation but is a historical category. This takes place when an author willfully reappropriates the past in her work or provides an unexpected or new perspective on past literature, "allowing something to be found that one previously could not have sought in it."[99]

> The new also becomes a historical category when the diachron-ic analysis of literature is pushed further to ask which historical moments are really the ones that first make new that which is new in a literary phenomenon; to what degree this new element is already perceptible in the historical instant of its emergence; which distance, path or detour of understanding were required for its realization in content, and whether the moment of its full actualization was so influential that it could alter the perspective on the old, and thereby the canonization of the literary past.[100]

The implications for this thesis upon biblical studies are immediately apparent. Questions about the historical and intertextual relationships between the synoptic gospels is one example of how this thesis relates to New Testament studies. Which gospel came first, how did the

98. Ibid., 34. "Its [historical knowledge] object is therefore not a mere object, something outside the mind which knows it; it is an activity of thought, which can be known only in so far as the knowing mind re-enacts it and knows itself as so doing. To the historian, the activities whose history he is studying are not spectacles to be watched, but experiences to be lived through in his mind; they are objective, or known to him, only because they are also subjective, or activities of his own." Collingwood, *The Idea of History*, 218.

99. Jauss, "Literary History," 35. This is one of the main theses in his essay, "The Dialogical and the Dialectical *Neveu de Rameau.*"

100. Jauss, "Literary History," 35.

subsequent authors edit or expand upon the previous text's rendition of one of the events in Jesus' life, and so on?[101] At the same time, our considerations in regard to this thesis cannot end with questions about the biblical texts. We also need to consider the position that different commentaries hold within the "literary series" of biblical interpretation. Commentaries and interpretations are not just answers to questions about the meaning of the text, but also present questions for future commentators. This means that the tradition of biblical interpretation is constituted by the logic of question and answer in which the meaning of the biblical texts unfold through time. "The two poles of the past 'givenness' of the Bible and its present interpretation do not (or at least should not) stand in opposition to each other. In this respect, the history of biblical interpretation . . . is the history of both false trails to be avoided and of insights to be developed further." [102] The reception history of the Bible presents us with a history of legitimate responses to the text that have shaped the formation of the Christian tradition because of their exemplary character and illegitimate responses that hopefully will be avoided by future interpreters. The Holy Spirit guides the Church by clarifying the truth through the communal life of the Church. As the church finds itself instantiated in ever changing historical and cultural horizons new and richer insights into the Bible are realized.[103] If this corporate, tradition-constituted form of knowledge constitutes our understanding of the Bible in such a dynamic fashion, then Jauss's hermeneutic offers a very important resource to not only interpret the Bible but also to cultivate and correct this corporate form of knowledge.

Thesis 6: Advances in the field of linguistics allow us to overcome the dominance of diachronic methods in literary history.

One of the presuppositions behind Hegel's philosophy of history was that every event that occurred at a similar point in time was equally informed by the significance of what led up to that moment. However,

101. The most significant text in this field, even though it is now dated, is Bultmann, *The History of the Synoptic Tradition.*

102. Thiselton, "Knowledge, Myth and Corporate Memory," 73; Jauss, *Towards an Aesthetic,* 59.

103. Himes, "The Ecclesiological Significance of the Reception of Doctrine," 152.

different contemporaneous events are conditioned by their own particular history or time curves. Any moment in history is therefore a collection of historically heterogeneous events. The significance of this for literary history is that texts that appear contemporaneously are, in reality, a heterogeneous collection of texts, each shaped and informed by different time curves. Therefore, the literary historian needs to incorporate synchronic, "cross-section" studies into her work in order to be able to grasp the differences between texts that are written during the same time period, especially if there is cultural proximity between the texts. Synchronic studies allow us to see how the competing values and structures are realized in different texts which appear contemporary with each other during such changes. This enables us to formulate some form of heuristic framework to examine and explain the questions asked, the answers received, and the significance of the changes in the "system of relationships in the literature of a historical moment."[104] The significance of a work often comes to light as the results from diachronic and synchronic studies overlap.

The heterogeneous mixture of texts in a tradition or literary horizon is also subject to the leveling power of tradition just as masterworks are. What may appear to be a body of diverse and competing texts in the horizon of the original readers coalesces into a collective body of works that shape the literary expectations, values, and prejudices of succeeding generations.[105] This is especially important when one considers works that were written during epochal changes, or what Kuhn would call "paradigm shifts." Synchronic studies helps us to grasp which texts played a more significant role in shaping our tradition. Successive synchronic cross sections should produce points of intersection with diachronic studies. As the literary scholar finds these points of intersec-

104. Jauss, "Literary History," 36–37. Jauss's work corrects Hegel's idea that differences between beliefs and ideas occurred between different historical epochs, not within them. An idea which is still found in the work of Gadamer. Larmore, "Tradition, Objectivity, and Hermeneutics," 269–70.

105. Jauss, "Literary History," 38. The leveling power of tradition is also seen in Kuhn's work. Text books that are written after a scientific revolution has taken place level out scientific history by presenting it as the steady accumulation of facts and gradual development of theories until the reader arrives at current research paradigm. In this way, the competing values prior to the paradigm shift are domesticated into the prejudices of the paradigm that prevailed. Kuhn, *The Structure of Scientific Revolutions,* 136–43.

tion, they will reveal the "literary evolution in its moments formative of history as well as its caesurae between periods."[106] The contours of a literary tradition can be established through the changes in the different horizons of expectation.

This raises an interesting question concerning the plurality and continuity in biblical interpretation. On the one hand, it affirms the possibility of different interpretations of a passage based on the idea of different "time curves" which shape those interpretations or approaches to the Bible. On the other hand, it would seem to indicate that the continuity we see in the history of biblical interpretation is the result of the leveling power of tradition. What were considered heterogeneous readings of the biblical text when they appeared are often perceived by future readers as homogeneous elements of their tradition. A tradition does not preserve all the questions that contributed to its formation: some are forgotten, some erased by a definitive answer, and others renewed.[107] The leveling power of tradition is both a selective process filtering which literary expectations will constitute future expectations and, at the same time, it is a forgetful process. As Heidegger claimed, tradition enables us not only to recover the past by making the foreign familiar, but it also "blocks our access to those primordial sources" by making us forget their significance.[108] Forgetting is as much a part of historically effective consciousness as is remembering.

One of the critical contributions that this sixth thesis makes to biblical studies is that it provides us with a method to recover some of the questions and answers that have been forgotten within our tradition. We gain invaluable resources that provide us with a wider field of play to approach a text as we recover the questions and answers that constituted different periods of the tradition of biblical interpretation. At the same time, this mode of study should contribute to the development of our phronetic knowledge, what Gadamer termed *Bildung*. We should become more sensitive to wider perspectives on a text's possible

106. Jauss, "Literary History," 36–39.

107. Jauss, *Question and Answer*, 70, 219.

108. Heidegger, *Being and Time*, 43. Heidegger's philosophy served as a corrective to Hegel's program of absolute knowledge of history and at the same time the cumulative or evolutionary approach to historical knowledge. There is always an element of concealment or forgetfulness in every act of disclosure or remembering. Gadamer, "Hegel and Heidegger," 107; Gadamer, *Philosophical Hermeneutics*, 226–27.

interpretations and wiser in determining which of these are most appropriate for the present horizon. From an ecumenical perspective, the recovery of lost questions and answers reveal the diversity of questions that our tradition has homogenized and allows us to not only see the validity of other traditions of interpretation but also enables us to better engage them in dialogue. "Reception entails the respectful hearing of the other's statement of faith and the discernment that the statement is coherent with the apostolic tradition and perhaps further illuminates one's own experience of the Christian life."[109]

Thesis 7: Literary history is a special history with a unique relationship to general history.

Jauss is concerned with the relationship between literary history and general history in this essay. In particular, he wants to overcome the model in which the interpretation of a text is accomplished by placing the text in its proper historical context. This misses the fact that the history of a text's interpretation is an essential element for our ability to understand it. Therefore, he had to rethink the relationship between literary and general history. Marxism, Formalism, and Structuralism failed to see how literature informed society and shaped history. The social function of literature occurs when "the literary experience of the reader enters into the horizon of expectations of his lived praxis, performs his understanding of the world, and thereby also has an effect on his social behavior."[110]

Jauss expands the role of negative experience found in Gadamer's hermeneutic by incorporating Karl Popper's thought on the productive role of negative experience from the sciences. According to Popper, each hypothesis and observation presupposes a horizon of expectations. The disappointment or falsification of an expectation is what enables a researcher to make contact with reality. While Jauss does not fully agree with Popper's theory, it does illustrate the "productive meaning of negative experience."[111] However, unlike real life, the reader does not bump into reality when his or her expectations are negated. The experience of reading creates a freedom from the constraints of daily life and has the

---

109. Himes, "The Ecclesiological Significance," 155.

110. Jauss, "Literary History," 39.

111. Ibid, 41.

possibility to disclose new perspectives to the reader. "Thus a literary work with an unfamiliar aesthetic form can break through the expectations of its readers and at the same time confront them with a question, the solution to which remains lacking for them in the religiously or officially sanctioned morals."[112]

Literary history must synchronically study the social conditions and background that affect the expectations of the author and audience.[113] However, we must take care that we do not reduce literary hermeneutics to a theory of production like Marxism. As we saw above, the surplus of meaning inherent in a text allows it to extend beyond the original horizon and play a socially formative function in the life of successive readers.[114]

> The gap between literature and history, between aesthetic and historical knowledge, can be bridged if literary history does not simply describe the process of general history in the reflection of its works one more time, but rather when it discovers in the course of "literary evolution" that properly socially formative function that belongs to literature as it competes with other arts and social forces in the emancipation of mankind from its natural, religious, and social bonds.[115]

Jauss concluded is that literary history had to include the "eventful nature of the literary work as well as its constitutive historical role."[116] Reception history is a process that occurs in the experiences and interpretations of those who "absorb their message, enjoy or judge them, acknowledge or refute them, select and forget them, and to such an extent form traditions, and those who finally assume an active role by answering a tradition and producing new works."[117]

This last thesis parallels and reinforces the argument Ebeling and Froehlich made concerning the need to integrate biblical exegesis and church history. According to Jauss, the reception history of a biblical

112. Ibid., 44.

113. Ibid., 41.

114. Jauss, "Der Leser," 338–39; Jauss, *Towards an Aesthetic,* 91; see also Ricœur, *Interpretation Theory,* 25–44.

115. Jauss, "Literary History," 45.

116. Holub, "German Theory in the United States," in *Colloquy of the Center for Hermeneutical Studies,* 43.

117. Jauss, "Der Leser," 325.

text is related to church history through the socially formative function that literature performs. In particular, Jauss would emphasize that in the reception of a biblical passage new perspectives and possibilities for living in the world are disclosed and thus, emancipate the church from traditional, cultural, or religious bonds. Martin Luther's interpretation of Romans 1:17 is the paradigmatic example of this in the Protestant tradition. However, Luz stresses that the socially formative function is not always emancipatory. The history the interpretation of Matthew 27:25, "His blood be on us and our children," demonstrates the manner in which a text may be abused or misinterpreted. The interpretation of this verse has been used in the past to support the persecution of the Jewish believers. "The history of effects shows that texts have power and therefore cannot be separated from their consequences. Interpreting a text is not simply playing with words but an act with historical consequences."[118] While both Jauss and Gadamer would have most likely agreed that this is not a genuine example of dialogue with the text, it is nevertheless an effect produced by the reception of the text which has shaped the history of the Christian tradition and needs to be included in its *Wirkungsgeschichte*.

118. Luz, *Matthew in History,* 33.

5

Horizons, Levels of Reading, and Aesthetic Experience

THE INFLUENCE OF GADAMER ON THE FIELD OF HERMENEUTICS CAN-
not be overstated, and this is particularly true for Jauss who was a student of Gadamer's. While Jauss built on Gadamer's foundation, he also
makes distinctive contributions of his own. These include the horizon
of expectations, the three levels of reading, and aesthetic experience.
What I propose to accomplish in this chapter is to consider several of
the broader hermeneutical aspects of Jauss's work in which he modified
or extended Gadamer's hermeneutic.

The Horizon of Expectations

The concept of the horizon of expectations stands at the centre of Jauss's
theory.[1] Traditional historical-critical approaches recognize that every
interpreter is bound to his historical horizon but at the same time try
to overcome this restriction by bracketing the interpreter's horizon.[2]
The only a priori this model recognizes is logic and facts, or empirical data, which exist independent of observation and can be objectively
and intersubjectively validated.[3] By objectively observing the facts of
history, like a biologist objectively observing the specimen under the

---

1. Jauss, *Question and Answer*, 224.

2. Apel, *Towards a Transformation of Philosophy*, 43–55. The naiveté of the historicism consists in its trust in methodology which it mistakenly believed allowed it to
escape the need for reflection and forget its own historical relevance. Gadamer, "*Vom
Zirkel des Verstehens*," 34.

3. This corresponds to Leibniz's two principles: the truths of reason and the truths
of facts. Apel, "The A Priori of Communication," 5.

microscope, their goal was to escape the influence of their historical horizon.[4]

The result was that in their attempt to objectively reconstruct the past, they were still unwitting captives of their own horizon. "Whoever believes that it is possible to arrive at the other horizon, that of some prior time, by simply disregarding one's own inevitably introduces subjective criteria concerning selection, perspective, and evaluation into his supposedly objective reconstruction of the past."[5] Albert Schweitzer is known for his comment about the results of such a naive historical practice in the nineteenth century's quest for the historical Jesus. This quest only succeeded in producing "a figure designed by rationalism, endowed with life by liberalism, and clothed by modern theology in an historical garb."[6] It is naive to think that it is possible to understand another horizon by disregarding one's own horizon. The pervasiveness of the ideal of historical objectivity is still felt today in biblical studies. Some of the most highly respected commentary series continue to approach the Bible as an ancient text, a relic from the past which is subjected to objective technical analysis.[7]

As a response to this paradigm of historiography, Gadamer developed Heidegger and Husserl's concept of the horizon which moves with the interpreter as they move and live.

> Every experience has its horizon of expectation: all consciousness exists as a consciousness of something, and thus, always also exists within the horizon of already formulated and still forthcoming experiences . . . Experience is formed in the functional swing from anticipation (preconception) to the fulfillment or disappointment of the anticipation. Even the new that is unexpected is "new in the context of a certain knowledge"; within the horizon of disappointed expectation, it becomes something that can be experienced, something that opens a new horizon, and thus demonstrates that "every actual horizon . . . [has] within it a system of potential horizons."[8]

4. Jauss, "The Identity of the Poetic Text," 146–47.

5. Jauss, *Question and Answer*, 198.

6. Schweitzer, *The Quest of the Historical Jesus*, 62.

7. Bockmuehl, "A Commentator's Approach," 57.

8. Jauss, *Question and Answer*, 203–4.

The implication of this concept for hermeneutics involves a shift from understanding as the interpretation of a text as an historical artifact to understanding as a probing of possible meaning that arises from the fusion of horizons: from meaning as a static concept to a dynamic one.[9] Understanding was taken for granted by historical-positivism, historical distance did not alienate. What was required for an interpreter to understand a text was historical, grammatical, and philological interpretation. Thus, understanding was reduced to a form of translation.

Understanding is no longer guaranteed for Gadamer or Jauss. Historical distance between the horizons alienates the reader from the text and creates a need for reflective mediation between the horizons of the text and the reader. In opposition to the historical-positivist school which sought to overcome or bracket historical distance between the two horizons through the objectivity promised by a methodological approach, Gadamer bases the fusion of horizons on the realities of historical distance. The possibility for productive understanding lies in the temporal distance between the horizons, which is not to be overcome, but which allows the interpreter to see the foreignness of the text before the two horizons are fused. This allows the otherness of the text to appraise the interpreter's prejudices and for interpretation to be an experience that changes the interpreter.[10]

One of the essential characteristics of the concept of horizon for Jauss is the relationship between experience and expectation. "Whereas experience can organize the past into a spatial and perspectival whole, expectation is directed at the open horizon of individual, not yet realised possibilities."[11] Expectations allow for, and are directed at, new experiences that can break open our horizon of expectations based on previous experiences. The hermeneutical spiral continues as new horizons of expectations arise that will allow for different perspectives and will be corrected and modified in turn. Jauss is building on Heidegger's hermeneutical circle between the projection of "Being-towards-possibilities" and "potential-for-Being" which is disclosed in the projective act, and Gadamer's appropriation of Hegel's dialectic of experience, negation,

---

9. Ibid., 200.

10. Ibid.; Gadamer, *Truth and Method*, 300–7; Jauss, *Question and Answer*, 205.

11. Jauss, *Question and Answer*, 202.

and sublation.[12] According to Jauss, "experience and expectation are so entwined in one another as a conceptual pair—both in the apprehension of history and in the horizon of aesthetic experience—that 'no expectation [can exist] without experience, and no experience without expectation.'"[13] Everything, even the innovative, is understood from the perspective of what we inherit from the past.

History and aesthetics are integrated by Jauss in the concept of *Erwartungshorizont*, or horizon of expectations. As I mentioned previously, Jauss developed this notion from Gadamer's concept of the horizon which refers primarily to the historical world in which we live and is constituted by the prejudices which we inherit from our tradition. What is surprising to note is that Jauss does not rely primarily on Gadamer for the definition of this concept but rather turned to the art historian, E. H. Gombrich. For Gombrich, the "horizon of expectations" is the "mental set, which registers deviations and modifications with exaggerated sensitivity" and which allows the viewer to decipher a work of art.[14] Robert Holub provides a helpful definition for Jauss's use of this term. "'Horizon of expectations' would appear to refer to an intersubjective system or structure of expectations, a 'system of references' or a mind-set that a hypothetical individual might bring to any text."[15] *Erwartungshorizont* refers primarily, but not exclusively, to the expectations a reader brings to a text, or as Gombrich would say, "We come to their work with our receivers already attuned."[16] One example of this is the manner by which our (direct or indirect) exposure to a certain type of genre will shape how we approach other texts we consider part of that genre.

Jauss's interest in the productive role which the original horizon of expectations plays in understanding arose while he was working on medieval texts.[17] His work in this area revealed to him the problems inherent in direct aesthetic understanding through the text alone or historical mediation through background information. In order to remedy

---

12. Jauss, *Question and Answer*, 203–5.

13. Ibid, 202–3.

14. Gombrich, *Art and Illusion*, 53; see also Eco, *A Theory of Semiotics*, 204–8.

15. Holub, *Reception Theory*, 59.

16. Gombrich, *Art and Illusion*, 53.

17. Jauss, *Question and Answer*, 218.

the shortcomings of other literary methods, he argued that it is possible to partially reconstruct the original horizon of expectations of the original audience through historical study. The goal of this reconstruction is not an empathetic understanding of the original readers' experience but to examine the expectations and preconceptions of the original addressees.[18] This allows the critic to gain some degree of appreciation for how the text either appealed to, affirmed, or negated the expectations of the reader. There are two benefits from this type of study. First, it allows the critic to determine the literary merit of the work as it appeared in its first horizon based on how the text affirmed or negated the norms of that horizon, and how the reception of the text shifted over time. Second, it also allows the reader to experience the "alterity" of the text, its historical distance from their horizon of expectations.[19]

Gadamer and the Passive Fusion of Horizons?

Some have criticized Gadamer because his concept of the fusion of horizons can be perceived as a passive merging of two image fields into one field of vision. Jauss felt that this negated Gadamer's thrust, which was to discover the historical difference and alienation created by temporal distance and to bring the text into the present through conversation.[20] The tension between the two horizons not only allows us to recognize what is foreign in the text, it also challenges or questions our prejudices. We are struck or provoked by the text which results in either an affirmation or denial of our prejudices.[21] For this reason, Jauss prefers to speak of a mediation of horizons, which implies a more active and reflective participation on the reader's part than Gadamer's fusion

18. Ibid., 222.

19. Alterity is defined as "the recognition of the contrast with modern experience." Jauss, "The Alterity and Modernity of Medieval Literature," 187.

20. See Gadamer, *Truth and Method*, 363–77, for his discussion on conversation and the logic of question and answer.

21. Jauss, "*Der Leser*," 339; Jauss, *Question and Answer*, 202–3. The background for these ideas can be found in Heidegger's work. "In interpreting, we do not, so to speak, throw a 'signification' over some naked thing which is present-at-hand, we do not stick a value on it; but when something within-the-world is encountered as such, the thing in question already has an involvement which is disclosed in our understanding of the world and this involvement is one which gets laid out by the interpretation." *Being and Time*, 190–91.

of horizons, which connotes a more passive stance, in that "Gadamer sometimes does not give an active role to interpreters."[22]

> For me, it is an active synthesis, which maintains the tension between the text of the past and my present experience. All hermeneutical reflection must consciously develop this tension ... Only in this mediating of two different horizons, you arrive at a new experience, which changes the interpreter him/herself.[23]

According to Jauss, the mediation between the horizons of expectations takes place in two different movements which are interrelated. It must mediate between the original inception and present experiences or understandings of the text. At the same time, it must also mediate between "the horizon of expectations, which a work of art evokes, confirms or even transcends, and the horizon of experience which the recipient brings to bear."[24]

Since he is concerned primarily with literary texts these two movements involved in the mediation of horizons appear to be fairly comprehensive. However, for some biblical texts there appears to be a third horizon which should also be brought into play. This third horizon is that of horizon of the audience implied in the text. J. Arthur Baird demonstrated that the audience Jesus addressed in the gospel accounts plays a significant role when interpreting one of those stories. In contrast to Jeremias, who claimed that the narrated audience is one of the least stable elements in the gospels, Baird's careful analysis revealed that it is one of the most consistent elements, especially when the evangelists were narrating Jesus' parables.[25]

> It would seem highly probable that the audience was of great importance to those who recorded the tradition because they believed the message of the *logia* was audience-centered. They believed the Jesus of the *logia* taught selectively, accommodating his message to his audience to such a degree that the nature of the audience became an important part of the message of the logion itself. This was then preserved with unique fidelity,

22. Merriman, "Minutes of the Colloquy," 60.

23. Ibid., 52–53.

24. Ibid., 52. In his essay, "Literary History," Jauss focused primarily on the first form of this mediation of horizons. In his later work, the second movement came to play an equal role. Jauss, "*Der Leser*," 338.

25. Baird, *Audience Criticism*, 61–62.

for anyone knowing about Jesus would have realized that the audience was needed for correct and meaningful reproduction of his teaching. This means to us that the audience has become a hermeneutic factor of first importance.[26]

It would seem, then, that for certain biblical texts we need to incorporate a third movement into the mediation of the horizon of expectations, between the horizon of the audience addressed within the text and our present horizon of expectations.

Jauss's Mediation of Horizons

If Gadamer has been criticized for presenting a passive fusion of horizons, others have attacked Jauss for introducing a new form of authoritarianism to hermeneutics. Instead of claiming that there is only one correct meaning for a text, Jauss introduced "a grain of relativism by making 'correct interpretation' dialogically depend on the relation between the text and the reader's changing situations."[27] They perceive as being too exact the language which Jauss used when he described his efforts to historically reconstruct the original questions which the text sought to answer. They think that he claims to have uncovered 'the' question to which the literary work was a response.[28]

When asked if he thought that there were 'true' questions that need to be asked or if there was one true meaning to a text, Jauss responded, "Your question poses, in my sense a false alternative: it is just the new question which permits me to uncover something which, till now, had not yet been seen in the text. Were it not as an implied meaning in the text, my question would not find a new answer and would have to be abandoned."[29] Jauss's answer illustrates his adoption of Collingwood's position concerning the "rightness" of the question. New questions uncover something new in the text only when they are answered by the text; they must be appropriate to the text. Question and answer stand in a dialogical relationship to each other, and cannot be divided or set in opposition. Thus, even our understanding of past horizons and genres are the result of questions which we ask within our horizon and

---

26. Ibid., 134.

27. Gumbrecht, "Dialectics or Authoritative Monologue," 35; Smith, "Response," 46.

28. Gumbrecht, "Dialectics," 34–35.

29. Jauss, "The Dialogical and the Dialectical *Neveu de Rameau*," 55.

which will be different from the questions asked in other horizons of interpretation.

These criticisms appear to flow primarily from the manner in which they perceive Jauss's appropriation of history to reconstruct the horizons of expectations. Jauss's attempt to introduce the reconstruction of the original horizon of expectations is seen as a return to either a positivistic approach to literary history based on objective facts or as an essentialist view of the text. However, these criticisms do not give due weight to Jauss's agreement with Gadamer on this point. All understanding, even historical reconstruction, takes place within a horizon of expectations. Even the reconstruction of the original audience's horizon will be perceived differently at different times. Jauss's hermeneutic is historical, not in the sense that it refers to the employment of the historical-critical methods to determine the original meaning of the text, but rather in the much wider sense of the term. His hermeneutic is historical (*wirkungsgeschichtlich*) in that it includes not only the original horizon in which the text appeared, but also the tradition of interpretation of the text from that time until the present, and the present readers' horizon of expectations.

While Jauss holds to the possibility of a partial reconstruction the original horizon of expectations from historical data and literary genres, he does not hold to an essentialist view of the text or its meaning. There is no timeless, correct interpretation for a text. Rather, he follows Heidegger's concept of the work of art and Gadamer's play as presentation and the transformation into structure. In this way, Jauss follows Gadamer's middle road between the unlimited play of meaning and an authoritarian, or essentialist, view of meaning. In every act of interpretation there is some degree of identity which arises from what is given in the text, and at the same time "the non-identity which is arrived at by interpretation."[30] It is similar to the manner in which each performance of a musical score is different (non-identical), but at the same time a performance of the same score (element of identity). The act of interpretation involves the mediation of the different horizons, which results in the meaning of the text being concretized.

The interpretation of any given text, and especially, significant texts like the Bible, must be performed by each and every generation since

---

30. Ibid., 60; Heidegger, *Holzwege*, 197.

every act of understanding takes place in a historical horizon. "This is not a defect of the theory but its most liberating feature, for it ensures that no fixed view ever prevails and that each generation must read the texts anew and interrogate them from its own perspective and find itself concerned, in its own fashion, by the work's question."[31] A decade before Jauss wrote his inaugural address, Bultmann realized almost the same conclusion in this area. "Since the exegete exists historically and must hear the word of Scripture as spoken in his special historical situation, he will always understand the old word anew."[32]

Three Levels of Reading and the Logic of Question and Answer

The goal of Gadamer's hermeneutic is for the interpreter to consciously enter into the living process of transmitting a tradition. The basic thrust of his hermeneutic is that understanding is historical and dialogical in nature. The alienation created by our temporal distance from the past allows us to enter into a conversation with the past through the logic of question and answer. At the same time we must realize that we dwell within the effects of history (*Wirkungsgeschichte*), which place limits on our consciousness beyond which we can never completely get. However, Jauss asks if there is not an internal conceptual contradiction in Gadamer's hermeneutic. While he agrees with most of Gadamer's thought, he questions whether his concepts of historical distance and the fusion of horizons implies a contradiction between active and passive forms of understanding.[33] This is why Jauss prefers to speak of a "mediation" rather than a "fusion" of horizons since it implies that understanding is an active process in both movements of understanding.

The area of Gadamer's hermeneutic in which Jauss shifts from "fusion" to "mediation" pertains primarily to the logic of question and answer. Following Collingwood and Gadamer, Jauss bases the dialogical interaction between text and reader in the dialogue of question and

31. Godzich, "Introduction," in Jauss, *Aesthetic Experience*, xii–xiii.

32. Bultmann, "Is Exegesis without Presuppositions Possible?" 296. Ebeling also commented on this, "This peculiarity of historical interpretation enables us to understand the essential unfinished nature of historical research and the necessity of constant renewal . . ." *The Word of God and Tradition*, 18.

33. Jauss, *Question and Answer*, 205.

answer. For Gadamer, the capacity of the question "to open up and hold open possibilities" serves as the grounds for the hermeneutic priority of the question.[34] "To understand something therefore means to understand something as an answer, and more precisely, to test one's own view against that of the other, through question and answer."[35]

Jauss is more specific than Gadamer in his use of the metaphor of a "conversation" with the text through question and answer. In order for the fusion of horizons to take place, the interpreter must pose a question that draws the text "back out of its seclusion" so that the text can answer and "say something." This is very similar to Pannenberg's criticism of Gadamer's metaphor of a conversation. Pannenberg argued that a text cannot protect itself from premature agreement (misunderstanding) as a conversation partner can, therefore a text must be empowered by the interpreter to assert itself. The priority that Gadamer gave to the question, which strikes the reader, must be balanced to include the role of assertions, or answers.[36] Not only did Jauss agree with Pannenberg's critique but he also thought that Gadamer's mediation of the past and the present in a tradition sells understanding short since it did not include a critique of the tradition as well.[37]

Gadamer's idea that "to understand meaning is to understand it as the answer to a question"[38] is limited in its application according to Jauss. Poetical texts exemplify this limitation. A poem yields a mode of perception that stands in contrast to everyday perceptions and creates the possibility to discern new perspectives on the world. The logic of question and answer is temporarily suspended during this primary perceptual understanding or aesthetic experience in which the reader experiences the linguistic power or artistry of the text, and "thereby, the world in its fullness of significance."[39] When we read a poem our first reading of the poem becomes the horizon for our second reading. What the reader perceived in the movement of aesthetic experience can

34. See Sullivan, *Political Hermeneutics*; Gadamer, *Truth and Method*, 362–68.

35. Jauss, *Question and Answer*, 213.

36. Jauss, "Limits and Tasks," 108; Pannenberg, "Hermeneutics and Universal History," 121–24, 177.

37. Jauss, "Literary History," 28–32; Jauss, *Question and Answer*, 66, 226.

38. Gadamer, *Truth and Method*, 375.

39. Jauss, *Towards an Aesthetic*, 142.

be articulated and reflected upon in subsequent readings and levels or interpretation.

This shifting of question and answer to the second level of reading resulted from the criticism he received from his inaugural essay, *"Literaturgeschichte als Provokation."* Marxist literary critics in East Germany considered Jauss's essay a defense of the traditional status quo, while in West Germany it was seen as subverting the literary tradition. Jauss's work following this essay can be seen in large part as a response to these criticisms, especially in regards to the important role which negativity played in his earlier hermeneutical theory. In his second book, *Aesthetic Experience and Literary Hermeneutics*, Jauss clarified and corrected his position in response to these criticisms.[40] He attempted to achieve this by modifying his position in three different ways. First, as we saw in the discussion of his third thesis, he reduced the role which negativity plays in his hermeneutic. Second, in its place he elevated the role of aesthetic experience. And third, he developed the three different levels of reading as a heuristic device to explain the overall structure of his hermeneutic. The first reading is an aesthetically perceptive reading, the second is an exegetical reading, and the third is a historical reading. The three successive readings of a text are compared with the movements of comprehension, interpretation and application. "The steps might be described phenomenologically as three successive readings."[41] While these three movements cannot be separated from each other in practice, we can make distinctions between them that help us examine them.

First Reading—Aesthetic Perception

In his essay, "The Poetic Text within the Changes of Horizons of Reading," Jauss questioned the viability of Gadamer's assertion that understanding, interpretation, and application form a unity which is to be realized in practice. Jauss agrees with Gadamer that these three movements form a triadic unity and that any division between them is artificial to a certain degree. At the same time, he maintains that we can and should examine and explicate each of these movements. It is

---

40. Godzich, "Introduction," in *Aesthetic Experience*, xiv–xv. See also the discussion on Jauss's third thesis above.

41. Jauss, *Towards an Aesthetic*, 140.

by examining each movement that Jauss attempts to "demonstrate what kind of understanding, interpretation, and application might be proper to a text of aesthetic character."[42]

In *Aesthetic Experience* Jauss explains the difference between understanding and interpretation according to pre-reflective and reflective aesthetic experience. Pre-reflective aesthetic experience is directed toward something which is constituted by the reader in the process of performing the text, it points beyond everyday experience. In reflective aesthetic experience, the reader adopts the role of an observer. However, this does not mean that she ceases to enjoy the text but rather that she recognizes the real-life situations that concern them in the aesthetic object. For Thiselton the relationship between "pre-critical" reading and interpretation is analogous to the relation between the reader and the critic. "As readers we allow ourselves to be mastered by the text. The text has its way with us. Our expectations are aroused and even at times manipulated. We feel what we are meant to feel; we live out the story. But the role of the critic reverses the relationship. The critic scrutinizes the text as his or her object of enquiry."[43] Pre-reflective, aesthetic reading is very similar to what Gadamer claims should be the experience of the audience (or anyone who participates in play). Our attention does not extend beyond the boundary of what is presented in the play, poem or performance. To reflect upon what is being presented results in our dropping out of the presentation of play. According to Jauss, this occurs in the first level of reading in which understanding takes place through the reader's aesthetic perception or experience of the text. Aesthetic perception occurs through the process of reading in which the text "like a 'score' indicates for the reader" its significance.[44]

Murray Krieger's metaphor of window–mirror–window helps to explain the manner in which the reader's aesthetic perception of the text is related to the real world and how this aesthetic perception serves as the basis for reflective interpretation, or the second level of reading. First, the text is like a window through which we look. This window looks into a room of mirrors which reflect internally within the various elements and relationships in the narrative world of the text. At this

42. Ibid.
43. Thiselton, *New Horizons*, 316
44. Ibid., 141.

level, the familiar and the previously unrecognized characters, events, and characters in the narrative and are organized into new patterns of relationships which create new existential possibilities for understanding. Finally, the mirrors transform back into a window once again through which we now perceive new perspectives on the world.[45] Thus, reflective aesthetic experience permits the reader to see anew, to explore other worlds of the imagination, and realize possible future actions.[46]

This first perceptual reading can also be described as an experience of collecting evidence about the text. As the reader moves through the text in the first reading she builds up a comprehension of the text's whole from the parts. This then serves as the presupposed horizon for the second movement, interpretive reading. "The interpretation of a poetic text always presupposes aesthetic perception as its pre-understanding; it may only concretize significances that appeared or could have appeared possible to the interpreter within the horizon of his preceding reading."[47] As such, it both "opens up and delimits the space for possible concretizations."[48] The differentiation between the first and second levels of reading is not an artificial distinction. It is analogous to rereading a poem; the first reading forms the horizon for the second reading.

Second Reading—Interpretation and the Logic of Question and Answer

Each reading is incorporated into the preliminary understanding of the next reading. What the reader grasps in the first aesthetically perceptive reading is reflected upon in the second reading. In this way, Jauss moves Gadamer's logic of question and answer from the first to the second movement of reading and grounds the primary or logically first form of understanding on aesthetic pleasure.[49] Thus, Gadamer's idea that to

45. Krieger, *A Window to Criticism*, 30–36, 59–65.

46. Jauss, *Aesthetic Experience*, 5–10.

47. Jauss, *Towards an Aesthetic*, 142–43.

48. Gadamer's axiom "To understand means to understand something as an answer" is restricted by Jauss to this secondary movement of interpretation and not to the primary act of perceptual understanding which produces the aesthetic experience. Jauss, *Towards an Aesthetic*, 145.

49. If we extend Jauss's metaphor of the three successive readings to Gadamer's hermeneutic we see that the logic of question and answer would fall within the first reading. "Thus the dialectic of question and answer always precedes the dialectic of

understand something is to understand it as an answer is limited to the second, interpretative, reading. The reader's aesthetic experience of the text constitutes the primary act of understanding or perception. This then allows them to employ the logic of question of answer from which a particular understanding is concretized as an answer to a question.[50] In the second reading, this conversation with a text must consciously mediate between the two horizons in order to avoid the dominance of the interpreter's horizon in the process interpretation. It is through the hermeneutics of question and answer that allows the interpreter attempts to re-engage the text in dialogue.[51] To put it another way, in the first reading a "fusion" of horizons takes place in the reader's aesthetic experience of the text. In the second reading, a "mediation" of the horizons of the text and the interpreter occurs through the logic of question and answer.

The second reading is a movement from the whole, which is inherited from the first reading, to an examination of the parts of the work.[52] Perceptual understanding becomes the horizon for reflective interpretation.

> The explicit interpretation in the second and in each further reading also remains related to the horizon of expectation of the first, i.e., perceptual reading—as long as the interpreter claims to make concrete a specific coherence of significance from out of the horizon of meaning of this text, and would not for example, exercise the license of allegories to translate the meaning of the text into a foreign context, that is to give it a significance transcending the horizon of meaning and thereby the intentionality of the text.[53]

The meaning of a text is not a pre-given timeless commodity. Instead, the meaning of a text is defined according to the performance of the text by a reader at both the first and second levels of reading. The

---

interpretation. It is what determines understanding as an event.' Gadamer, *Truth and Method*, 472.

50. Jauss, "Limits and Tasks," 112–13.

51. Jauss, *Aesthetic Experience*, 217.

52. In this way, the hermeneutical circle of part/whole is incorporated in Jauss's theory. Jauss, "Limits and Tasks," 115–16.

53. Jauss, *Towards an Aesthetic*, 142.

reader concretizes one among many possibilities of significance in the second interpretative reading.

> When one recognizes the hermeneutical premise that the whole meaning of a lyrical work must be understood not as a substance, as a timeless predetermined meaning, but as a proposal of a meaning, one can expect from the reader enough discernment to see that in the act of interpretive comprehension he can concretize only one of the poem's meanings, and that its pertinence for himself must not exclude its debatability for others.[54]

It is a fundamental hermeneutical principle that the questions asked arise from the horizon of the interpreter and, as a result, not every question can be posed in each horizon. Rather, the text under investigation should correct and determine which questions are to be asked and in what order.[55] But this does not mean that the relevance of other concretizations of the meaning of the text are excluded from consideration in the process of interpretation. Every interpretation falls under the hermeneutic of partiality since understanding and interpretation are not achieved through objective means of description but are characterized by the selective taking of perspectives from within an interpreter's horizon of expectations.

Third Reading—Historical Distance, "What Did the Text Say?"

The third level is the one most familiar to traditional historical-grammatical hermeneutics, but is usually practiced as the first level.[56] This is because the historical method overlooks the fact that aesthetic perceptual understanding constitutes a provisional understanding of the text that allows us to call other hermeneutical principles into play. Jauss's transposing of the traditional exegetical questions and methods (i.e., historical, cultural, and word studies) to the third level of reading is one of the defining traits of his model of reception theory.

> Literary hermeneutics has remained for the longest time under the influence of the paradigms of history and of the interpretation immanent in the text; and that explains its present

---

54. Jauss, "Limits and Tasks," 115–16.

55. Jauss, *Towards an Aesthetic*, 113, 139.

56. Jauss, "Limits and Tasks," 116.

laggardness. The scholars limited their work to exegesis, left their concept of comprehension inarticulate, and neglected the problem of application so completely that the turn to reception aesthetics, which in the sixties began to close the development gap, reached an unexpected success as a 'change of paradigms.'[57]

This third level of reading involves the historical-reconstructive reading of the text.[58] Just as the second interpretive reading is related to the first aesthetically perceptive reading, so also the third historical reading is related to the other two levels. The aesthetic character of a text serves as the means to bridge the historical distance between the text and the present. At the same time, aesthetic comprehension is also dependent on the reconstruction of the original horizon of expectations which guards against the text being naively read in light of the "prejudices of the present and its expectations and therefore renders possible through the definite separation of the past and present horizons, the demonstration of the text's otherness."[59] The historical-reconstructive methods serve a controlling function by protecting the temporal distance of the text from the reader's horizon and thereby allowing the text to be seen in its alterity.[60] Every bit of detail that can be found should be questioned as a possible source. There are two things such a quest should look for: (1) the text's response to expectations of a formal kind, such as those raised by its literary tradition, and (2) the text's response to questions concerning meaning raised in the life-world horizon in which the text was produced.

One of the hermeneutical implications of the logic of question and answer is that the recipient of a text is now actively involved as a mediator of the text. This places the text and the reader on almost equal footing. The reader must adopt a posture which is open and oriented to the concerns of the text and address the questions the text originally sought to answer and those it left behind. The questions we ask should be directed to discovering the questions the author sought to answer, but we must keep in mind that the questions we ask are conditioned by our contemporary interests. If we employ the logic of question and

57. Ibid., 96.
58. Jauss, *Towards an Aesthetic*, 146.
59. Jauss, "Limits and Tasks," 116–17; Merriman, "Minutes of the Colloquy," 53.
60. Jauss, *Towards an Aesthetic*, 146.

answer in an appropriate manner we should be able to judge if we understand the text in the same manner as the original audience did, if we understand it differently, or if we have misunderstood the text.[61] It is only when we bring our experiences and horizon into play and the horizons are mediated, that we will able to make determinations along these lines.[62]

Historical investigation is also required because the transmission of literature down through a tradition may have been restrained through domination or distortion. Jauss considers "the ideological-critical suspicion that literary transmission may not unfold in absolute freedom; it may be pseudocommunicatively constrained," a critical insight which requires vigilance on the part of the interpreter. In this case, literary communication between the horizons is not transparent but must be retrieved from the power of tradition to incorporate what is heterogeneous into it.[63] In this way, Jauss overcomes one of the major criticisms that has been persistently made against Gadamer, the need for some form of critique of ideology within hermeneutics. The inclusion of a critique of ideology, or 'hermeneutics of consequences,' is an extremely important aspect of reception theory's possible contribution to the fields of biblical interpretation and church history. "Biblical texts whose consequences have been hatred, exclusiveness, and injustice call for critical questioning, even if they correspond superficially to the history of Jesus or even if they are his own words."[64]

Third Reading—Application, "What Does the Text Say to Me?"

This transforms the questioning stance of the reader from "What did the text say?" to "What does the text say to me, and what do I say to it?"[65]

61. Jauss, *Question and Answer*, 62. Stephen Fowl strongly opposes this approach. For him, the literary approach to the scriptures does not require historical research. *Engaging Scripture*, 1–61. However, in the last two chapters of his book Fowl seems to negate the argument in the first half of the book when he engages in historical and philological studies in the book of Ephesians.

62. Jauss, "Literary History," 34.

63. Jauss, *Question and Answer*, 226; Kisiel, "Ideology Critique and Phenomenology," 155–58; Misgeld, "Modernity and Hermeneutics," 164–75.

64. Luz, *Matthew in History*, 92.

65. Jauss, *Towards an Aesthetic*, 146.

The interpreter must remain open to the truth claims of the text and "allow the self to be cross-examined by the text while examining it."[66] The move from understanding through interpretation to application is needed, lest the attempt to reconstruct the original question of the text slides back into the lifeless facts of historicism.

The transformation of the question "What did the text say?" to "What does the text say to me, and what do I say to it?" demonstrates that hermeneutics is concerned with the entire process, from understanding, through interpretation, to application.[67] This is not to say that application is limited to some form of practical action, but that it is equally, if not more so, the broadening "of the horizon of one's own experience vis-à-vis the experience of the other."[68]

In an interview with Rien Segers, Jauss summarized these three movements and their relationship to each other:

> Interpretation as the concretization of a specific significance (among other possible significances which earlier interpreters have concretized or later interpreters can still concretize) always remains bound to the horizon of the first reading, perceiving aesthetically and understanding with pleasure; it next has the task of illuminating the verbal and poetic conditions which, from the construction of the text, orient the primary act of understanding. Application includes both acts of understanding and interpretation insofar as it represents the interest in transporting the text out of its past or foreignness and into the interpreter's present, in finding the question to which the text has an answer ready for the interpreter, in forming the aesthetic judgement of the text which could also persuade other interpreters.[69]

66. Jauss, *Question and Answer*, 65.

67. Jauss does not see the unity of these three movements as something new to him or Gadamer, but rather has always been an integral part of every hermeneutical theory (whether this was recognized or not). "I only wish to emphasize the fact that an implicit understanding of the unity of comprehension, interpretation and application has formed the basis of hermeneutics not only since the period of the Enlightenment, but since the very ancient practice of the *ars interpretandi*, and that the new pattern of various methods of interpretation did not simply substitute the old paradigm of various meanings of the text, but refined and developed its forms." Ibid., 97–98.

68. Jauss, *Towards an Aesthetic*, 147.

69. Segers, "An Interview with Hans Robert Jauss," 85.

These three movements are rooted in the priority of the horizon of the first aesthetic reading. This is part of Jauss's desire to make the aesthetic reading and the aesthetic character of the text the "definite and provable premise of its interpretation."[70] However, the three levels of reading are not a based on a temporal priority, nor is it necessary to perform these steps in the same order. "The priority of aesthetic perception in the triad of literary hermeneutics requires the horizon, but not the temporary priority of the first reading; this horizon of perceptive comprehension can also only be acquired by repeated reading or by means of a historical comprehension."[71] An example of this is Jauss's case study on the "Myth of the Fall" (Genesis 3). In this study, his first step is to examine the horizon of the first reading, then the original horizon, and finally he turns to the history of reception.[72] Thus, while it is possible to speak of the distinctions between understanding, interpretation, and application one must keep in mind the fundamental unity of these three movements.

The Hermeneutic Validity of Aesthetic Experience

Gadamer is very suspicious of Jauss's attempt to introduce aesthetic experience as one of the foundations for hermeneutics, and for good reason. Aesthetic experience involves a double differentiation according to Gadamer.[73] It involves an abstraction of the text from the world in which it originated and the reader from his horizon. As a result, aesthetic experience is not a very stable platform from which to seek a text's truth claims. It is strictly aesthetic pleasure. "Pure seeing and pure hearing are dogmatic abstractions that artificially reduce phenomena. Perception always includes meaning."[74] If Gadamer had been directing his criticism toward Jan Mukarovsky or Paul Valéry, then his criticism would have been exactly on target. For Mukarovsky, questions about truthfulness do not apply to the enjoyment of poetic texts.

---

70. Jauss, "Limits and Tasks," 112.

71. Ibid., 119.

72. Jauss, *Question and Answer*, 95–100.

73. Weinsheimer, *Gadamer's Hermeneutic*, 93.

74. This criticism is related also to the problems inherent in the concepts of unlimited play and poetical versus practical language that were covered in previous chapters. Gadamer, *Truth and Method*, 92.

Paul Valéry provides a clear illustration of aesthetic differentiation of which Gadamer is critical.

> Walking, like prose has a definite aim. It is an act directed at something we wish to reach . . . The dance is another matter. It is of course a system of actions; but of actions whose end is in themselves. It goes nowhere. If it pursues an object, it is only an ideal object, a state, an enchantment, the phantom of a flower, an extreme life, a smile—which forms on the face of the one who summoned it from empty space.[75]

If aesthetic experience is pure perception, as Mukarovsky, Valéry, and others claim, then every reading of a text is a new creation. There is no correct reading, meaning, or criteria to determine what would count as a correct reading. This leads to a form of hermeneutical nihilism.[76] We end up with a radical discontinuity, a collection of unrelated, individual experiences that shatters any possible identity for the text or the possibility for a tradition of a text's transmission to form.[77]

Gadamer correctly argues, in my opinion, that our experience of any text must allow for knowledge and truth claims. As the art historian Gombrich noted, "If art were only, or mainly, an expression of personal vision, there could be no history of art."[78] Every aesthetic perception involves relationships. We understand something as something.[79] It is only when we understand these relationships that we can appreciate the artistic qualities of the text.[80] This experience of a text is best understood if we compare it with the phenomena of self-understanding. In order to understand ourselves we must experience others. Continuity among all our different experiences comes from the manner in which we compress what appear to be a discontinuity of experiences into the continuity and identity of our self-understanding. In the same manner, Gadamer argues, we sublate these experiences of art and literature into our human existence, and this corresponds to the historical nature

75. Valéry, "Poetry and Abstract Thought," 921–22.

76. Gadamer, *Truth and Method*, 94–95.

77. Ibid.

78. Gombrich, *Art and Illusion*, 3.

79. Heidegger, *Being and Time*, 19.

80. "Only if we 'recognize' what is represented are we able to 'read' a picture; in fact, that is what ultimately makes it a picture. Seeing means articulating." Gadamer, *Truth and Method*, 91.

of human life.[81] A tradition of interpretation comes into being in this way; through the continual encounters with the text, which by nature never exhaust the potential of the text but are unfinished events, and are incorporated into the prejudices, phronesis, and communal knowledge within that tradition.

Jauss was well aware of Gadamer's criticism, but remained adamant that "The primary experience of a work of art takes place in the orientation to its aesthetic effect, in an understanding that is pleasure, and a pleasure that is cognitive."[82] He agrees with Gadamer's criticism, but only to the degree that aesthetic experience is related to abstract aesthetic pleasure. The problem with Gadamer's criticism, while valid, is that it is directed at the abstraction of aesthetic consciousness that emerged in the nineteenth century.[83] By contrast, Jauss has attempted to rehabilitate the hermeneutical role of aesthetic experience.[84]

There are three classical functions or modes of aesthetic experience which Jauss considers important for understanding the nature of aesthetic experience. *Poiesis* involves the active participation of the reader in constructing the aesthetic object, or as Heidegger would say, the "work" of art. *Aesthesis* is the pleasure that comes from seeing and recognizing. It is the knowledge we learn from the possibilities that we realize in reading the text. In this way, *aesthesis* is similar to the recognition of mimesis. The way in which the disclosure and the recognition of these possibilities transforms the reader's self-understanding, changes her beliefs, and liberates her mind to consider new perspectives on the world is the function of *catharsis*. These three functions are not arranged hierarchically, but form "a nexus of independent functions."[85]

Aesthetic experience is pre-reflective in that it is directed at the reference, or world projected by the text and extends beyond everyday

81. Ibid., 96–100.

82. Jauss, *Aesthetic Experience*, xxiv.

83. Ibid., 26–28, 91–92.

84. Jauss attempts this rehabilitation in order to overcome the problems that he saw in the role that negativity played in his (and Gadamer's) hermeneutic. Roland Barthes also attempted a similar rehabilitation of aesthetic pleasure. However, he still fell prey to Gadamer's criticism since he denied the possibilities of any form of dialogue between the reader and the text. Reading is a passive act of experiencing the pleasure of the language in the text. Barthes, *The Pleasure of the Text*.

85. Jauss, *Aesthetic Experience*, 35, 46–95.

experience. At the same time, aesthetic experience is reflective since the reader is able to adopt the role of an observer who recognizes the relationships between the elements in the text and his situation.[86] As such, aesthetic experience is not pure perception or abstracted pleasure, but it requires that the reader understand the original horizon of the text in order to protect the otherness of the text from being naively assimilated into his horizon.[87] It also requires a certain level of literary competence on the part of the reader which comes from his familiarity with the genre of the text and previous interpretations or understandings of the text. Instead of a discontinuity of individual experiences which results from abstracted aesthetic pleasure, Jauss's model of aesthetic experience contributes to, and takes place, within the continuity of a tradition of interpretation.[88]

Aesthetic experience includes cognitive knowledge and the truth claims of the text as Gadamer argued. One of the strengths of Jauss's position is that the interpretation of a text is not restricted to experts but is open to the average, educated reader. Reception theory is not based on an ideal form of reader, but rather a contemporary reader who has an average level of education. Alongside the average reader, Jauss placed the "commentator with scholarly competence, who deepens the aesthetic impressions of the reader" through historical, philological, literary and other forms of research and criticism.[89] Reception theory protects a text such as the Bible from being taken captive by the trained scholars and opens its interpretation and the history of its effects to a much wider community than a theory such as the historical-critical method does. "Interpretation that bypasses this primary aesthetic experience is the arrogance of a philologist who subscribes to the error that the text was not created for readers but for him, to be interpreted by such as he."[90]

---

86. Ibid., 5–10.

87. Jauss, "The Alterity and Modernity of Medieval Literature," 185.

88. "Significance which is unlocked through aesthetic experience, arises from the convergence of effect [*Wirkung*] and reception. It is not an atemporal, basic element which is already given; rather, it is the never-completed result of a process of progressive and enriching interpretation, which concretizes—in an ever new and different manner—the textually immanent potential for meaning in the change of horizons of historical life-worlds." Ibid., 183.

89. Jauss, *Towards an Aesthetic*, 144. For an excellent article that demonstrates how to apply these ideas to a teaching situation, see Eckert, "Hermeneutics in the Classroom," 5–16.

90. Jauss, *Aesthetic Experience*, xxix.

6

Macro and Micro Shifts in a Tradition

Introduction: The Historical Character of Textual Interpretation

ONE OF THE PERENNIAL QUESTIONS CONFRONTING CONTEMPORARY hermeneutics is how to resolve the tension between the plurality and continuity of interpretations. Under the historical-critical model, the truth or meaning of a text is sought through historical reconstruction, philological, grammatical, and sociological studies and is grounded in the relationship between the author and the text. The possibility for determining a definitive interpretation is based on a methodological approach toward the text. The assumption is that just as we can repeat a scientific experiment to achieve the same results, so we can discover the author's meaning through the correct application of the methods of interpretation. Thus, it is thought that the nature of the text and the proper use of methods should guarantee a high degree of continuity in interpretation since the goal is to move closer to the original meaning intended by the author. Divergent interpretations are the result of misunderstanding or the application of the wrong method.

Another related strategy, which has been employed in contemporary biblical interpretation to provide a rationale for the historical diversity of interpretations of a particular text, is to make a distinction between the *meaning* of the text as intended by the author and the *significance* of the text as it realized by different interpreters at different points in history. The name associated with this view it that of E. D. Hirsch, who defined meaning as "what the author meant by his use of a particular sign sequence," in contrast to significance, which "names a relationship between that meaning and a person, or a conception, or a situation, or indeed anything imaginable."[1]

There are two problems with this view. First, understanding is reduced to a subjective process that takes place between the creative mind of the author and reproductive mind of the interpreter. This stands in distinction to the meaning of the text that is objective and historically fixed. Second, the distinction between meaning and significance is not that straightforward.

> The distinction between meaning and significance is at best difficult to apply to the history of interpretation, for it is indisputably the case that interpreters of Plato, Aristotle, or Scripture in different historical eras differed in what they thought they saw in the text and not just in their views of the significance of the 'same' textual meaning for themselves. Interpreters of Paul, for instance, have not been arguing all these centuries only over what Paul 'means' *pro nobis*, but also over the claim Paul makes regarding the subject matter.[2]

If Jauss and Gadamer are correct in arguing that this approach overlooks or downplays the significance of the horizon of the interpreter and the alienation created by historical distance, then correct understanding can no longer be guaranteed and the challenge of historical distance presents the need for some other form of mediation than the historical-critical method offers.

For Jauss, the truth of the meaning of a text can "be recovered only when it is sought in the change in the horizon of historical experience—and comprehended as an on moving, and always partial concretization of meaning."[3] Each and every act of understanding involves a fusion of horizons that results in a concretization of the meaning of the text. The meaning of a historically distant text does not solely reside in its original horizon, but takes place in the constant fusion between the two horizons. The meaning of a text is performed in the "unfolding" of the

---

1. Hirsch, *Validity in Interpretation*, 8, see also 49–57. While Hirsch attempts to ground the meaning of a text in the author's intention, his argument is more nuanced than many of his critics recognize, he is not arguing that we will arrive at the author's intentions, but that there is nothing to prohibit a valid understanding of the text. Ibid., 17, 31.

2. Linge, "Editor's Introduction," in Gadamer, *Philosophical Hermeneutics*, xxiv.

3. Jauss, *Question and Answer*, 201.

text's potential through the concretization of actual readings in history. "The meaning of a work of art as well is extracted only during the progressive process of its reception; it is not a mystic whole that can reveal itself totally on its first showing."[4] Subsequent concretizations of the text change and expand the horizon of expectations as history progresses. In this process, various interpretations of a text serve to create structures or trajectories of interpretation that serve to legitimize future "possibilities of understanding, imitation, transformation, and continuation—in short, structures of exemplary character that condition the process of the formation of literary tradition."[5]

The transmission of a literary or interpretive tradition cannot be reduced to the sum total of the prejudices that a tradition passes on. It requires a receiving consciousness without whose participation this process cannot take place. This receiving mind is required to ask a question of the text so that it may give an answer. The questions that the reader asks of the text are "decided first and foremost by an interest that arises out of the present situation, critically opposes it, or maintains it."[6] The fulfillment or disappointment of these questions contribute to the transformation of the horizon for subsequent readers. The dynamic of change that takes place from one horizon to the next is seen in the fact that an interpretation that satisfied the expectations of one horizon are no longer acceptable to the next generation of readers. There is a continual testing and evaluating of questions and answers within a tradition. The historical character of a text's tradition of interpretation is not constituted by atemporal questions or answers which the text supplies that are valid in every historical horizon. Rather it is characterized

---

4. Jauss, *Towards an Aesthetic*, 59.

5. Ibid., 64, emphasis mine; Jauss, *Question and Answer*, 201–4. Even the interpretation of the most open-structured fictional or lyrical text, which is designed to stimulate the imagination of the reader, displays a continuity which shows how new responses to a text are related to the reader's expectations. The second *Poetic und Hermeutik* colloquium examined different interpretations of Apollinaire's poem *L'Arbre*. While they recognized the validity of different interpretations of this work by the people who attended the colloquium they also realized that these different interpretations did not contradict each other. The conclusion they reached was that even with a highly poetic text the first reading can give a "unifying aesthetical orientation." Jauss, "Limits and Tasks of Literary Hermeneutics," 118–19.

6. Ibid., 65.

by a living and dynamic dialogue between the text and its interpreters shaped by question and answer.

> In the historical tradition of art, a past work survives not through eternal questions, nor through permanent answers, but through the more or less dynamic interrelationship between question and answer, between problem and solution, which can stimulate new understanding and can allow the resumption of the dialogue between the past and present.[7]

In order to understand the phenomena of a text and the history of its reception we need both tradition and innovation, continuity and plurality. These are not opposing poles in Jauss' theory, but are related to each other. Perhaps the clearest indication of this comes in the way these elements interact with each other in the history of a tradition. The history of biblical interpretation consists of both tradition and innovation, archaeology and anticipation, and we need to preserve both sides of the coin. Commentaries or interpretations that follow the norms of past works are only imitative. An interpretation that attempts to express only what is new or innovative is, as Jauss writes, merely an expression of "dilettantism (or the tedium of science fiction)."[8] "In the realm of the arts tradition realizes itself neither in epic continuity nor in a *creatio perpetua*, but in a process of mutual production and reception, determining and re-determining canons, selecting the old and integrating the new."[9]

In this chapter we will consider two aspects of reception theory that address the issues of continuity and plurality within a tradition of biblical interpretation. The first is an appraisal of Jauss' adoption of Thomas Kuhn's model of paradigm shifts. While a great deal has been written on Kuhn's concept of paradigm shifts, his work deserves some attention in this text as well for the following two reasons. First, because Kuhn's work is explicitly appropriated by Hans-Robert Jauss, Kuhn's ideas serve as important background by which we can not only understand Jauss' work but modify it if needed. Second, the concept of paradigm shifts and its related concepts provide useful heuristic tools for considering not only macro but micro shifts within a tradition.

7. Ibid., 70, 34.

8. Jauss, "Tradition, Innovation and Aesthetic Experience," 376.

9. Ibid.

The second half of this chapter will focus on these micro, or semiotic, shifts that occur in an interpretive tradition. In particular, I will examine the interpretive history of how the condition that the boy suffers from in Matthew 17:14–20 has been understood. In the following chapter I will examine the question of macro, or paradigmatic, shifts in regard to the interpretation of parables. These two aspects, paradigm and semiotic transformations, touch on several of the most important questions concerning plurality and continuity within a tradition of interpretation.

Jauss's Appropriation of Thomas Kuhn's Paradigm Shifts

The name most widely associated with the concept of paradigm shifts is that of Thomas Kuhn.[10] While his work, *The Structure of Scientific Revolutions*, sparked a paradigm shift in academic circles, the ideas that Kuhn exposed were not radically new. Kuhn admitted that he borrowed the idea that the progression of knowledge occurred through "succession of tradition-bound periods punctuated by non-cumulative breaks" from other fields.[11] Art and literary and political history have long employed similar concepts to describe their fields. Rather it appears that it was the way in which he employed these concepts to the history of science, the strongest domain for logical, positivistic approaches to the history of the development of knowledge, and his liberal use of examples to illustrate the relation between tradition and innovation, which attracted so much attention to his work. This is rather ironic since *The Structure of Scientific Revolutions* was originally published as part of *The International Encyclopedia of Unified Science*, which has been described as "the summa of logical positivism, the movement that viewed the nature of science as the most strictly synonymous with its logic."[12]

---

10. *The Structure of Scientific Revolutions* was translated into over sixteen languages and sold over one million copies. In his obituary in the New York Times, Kuhn's work is described as a "profoundly influential landmark of 20-century intellectual history." Van Gelder, "Thomas Kuhn, 73: Devised Science of Paradigm," *The New York Times*, June 19, 1996. Gary Gutting makes the bold claim that Kuhn's book "has had a wider academic influence than any other single book of the last twenty years." "Preface," in *Paradigms and Revolutions*, v.

11. Kuhn, *The Structure of Scientific Revolutions*, 208.

12. Hollinger, "Kuhn's Theory," in Gutting, *Paradigms and Revolutions*, 214, 195–99.

The shift from a linear, evolutionary or cumulative model to explain the history and development of knowledge to a model that incorporates paradigm shifts is one of the most important conceptual shifts in historical methodology in the past fifty years. Until recently, the evolutionary or cumulative model was the dominant model used to explain the history and development of knowledge. Knowledge progressed in a more or less linear accumulation of discoveries and insights. This linear or cumulative model of tradition or knowledge is also widely accepted either implicitly or explicitly in biblical interpretation and other theological disciplines. Nicholas Lash comments, "Almost all theories of doctrinal development tend to assume that the history of Christian doctrine is a more or less unified process of continual, if erratic, growth and expansion."[13] While Kuhn accepted that the linear model could explain the growth of knowledge during certain periods of history, it was not appropriate for explaining long term development of knowledge, changes in theories, or shifts in research paradigms.[14]

With the shift to theories of history that take the situatedness of the historians and their subject more into account, questions concerning historical discontinuity have come to the foreground. The foregrounding of change and discontinuity in the revolutionary or paradigm-shift model enables us to pay greater attention to the historical situatedness of the historian and his/her subject, and to examine problems of historical discontinuity in thought. However, this in turn raises a whole new set of questions and problems. "The immediate difficulty facing someone who decides to write on the problem of change and continuity is that there is

13. Lash, *Change in Focus*, 145. To cite another example, John Baker speaks of doctrinal development taking place according to two principles. The first is an organic growth or unfolding of what is logically implicit in the origins of the Christian faith accompanied by a second principle of rational correction and criticism. "In short, doctrinal development may be described as the community working out a fuller understanding of its inheritance of faith and submitting this to the test of time, that is, of the life and thought of the Christian people in future generations." Baker, "Carried about by Every Wind?: The Development of Doctrine," in Thiselton, *Believing in the Church*, 265–66.

14. Kuhn, *The Structure of Scientific Revolutions*, 10. "This important book is a sustained attack on the prevailing image of scientific change as a linear process of ever-increasing knowledge, and an attempt to make us see that process of change in a different and, Kuhn suggests, more enlightening way." Shapere, "The Structure of Scientific Revolutions," in Gutting, *Paradigms and Revolutions*, 27.

no aspect of Christian belief, doctrine and activity which does not form part of, and is not increasingly felt to form part of, the problem."[15]

While Kuhn attempted to distance his concepts for the history of science from the humanities, his work is important for biblical interpretation for the following reasons. First, similar twists, turns, and changes in the direction of research and the worldview of the community occur in biblical studies as well. Even though these paradigm shifts are not as sharply defined as they are in the natural sciences, they are still very significant in biblical studies. Second, if the paradigm shifts are as dramatic in the sciences as Kuhn argues, then the questions he raises present an exaggerated form of what we should expect to see in the humanities. Thus, if the problems and questions that arise in relation to paradigm shifts in the sciences can be resolved, we are in a stronger position to claim that they can be resolved in biblical studies as well.

Perhaps more directly, Kuhn's model of the history of science serves two purposes in Jauss's hermeneutic. On the one hand, Kuhn's work serves as a complement to the concept of punctuated evolution that Jauss adapted from Formalism. On the other hand, Jauss argued that literary studies are currently experiencing a state of crisis for which the solution required a paradigm shift, namely to a literary theory that incorporates the history of the text's reception. Thus, Kuhn's concept of paradigm shifts serves an apologetic function in Jauss's hermeneutic. As such, Kuhn's concept of paradigm shifts provides a useful heuristic device to understand certain aspects of reception theory. [16]

Continuity and Discontinuity in Paradigm Shifts

The Structure of Scientific Revolutions generated a great deal of discussion and debate over the manner in which knowledge is accumulated and passed down within a tradition of inquiry. Some, such as Richard Rorty and Israel Scheffler, read Kuhn as supporting the view that the shift from an old paradigm to a new one preserves very little if any continuity between the two paradigms. Communication between

15. Lash, *Change in Focus,* vii.

16. Because Thomas Kuhn's work is so well known and influential, I shall limit my discussion to those works that are explicitly appropriated by Jauss. This is not to argue that Kuhn's theories are the best or most refined. In that regard, I think the work of Imre Lakatos in the sciences, Alasdair MacIntyre in the humanities, and especially Wolfhart Pannenberg's *Theology and the Philosophy of Science*, present advances on Kuhn's work.

researchers operating in the two different paradigms is incommensurable and for a researcher to switch paradigms amounts to an irrational act of conversion.[17] Others, including Kuhn himself, claim that his earlier work suffered from rhetorical exaggeration that he softened and corrected in his later works. According to this view, Kuhn holds to a soft position on incommensurability. Communication between paradigms, or the lack of it, is a matter of degree, not total incommensurability.[18] In order for paradigms to serve a legitimate function in reception theory we must resolve the question of whether Kuhn supports a strong or weak view of incommensurability between paradigms.

The history of science revolves around two concepts: normal science and paradigm shifts, or revolutions. During periods of normal science, research takes place within a paradigm that is shared by the members of a research community or scientific field.[19] Paradigms provide a communally shared body of "intertwined theoretical and methodological belief" which allows for selection and evaluation in scientific

17. Rorty, *Contingency, Irony, and Solidarity*; also Barbour, "Paradigms in Science and Religion," 223–45.

18. Blaug, "Kuhn versus Lakatos," in Gutting, *Paradigms and Revolutions,* 141–42; Doppelt, "Kuhn's Epistemological Relativism," 34–36. Kuhn's corrections of his earlier views can be seen in the revisions which he made to the 1962 edition of *Scientific Revolutions*, the "Postscript" he included in the second edition, and his essays in *Essential Tension*. In this respect, it is worth noting that Rorty seems to cite primarily from the 1962 edition of *Scientific Revolutions* and does not explicitly engage Kuhn's second edition or later works.

19. One of the sources for conceptual confusion and misunderstanding in *Scientific Revolutions* is the wide manner of ways in which he uses the term "paradigm." In the "Postscript" Kuhn attempts to address the potential for misunderstanding in his use of this term. He claims that he primarily uses the term in two ways. "On the one hand, it stands for the entire constellation of beliefs, values, techniques, and so on shared by the members of a given community. On the other, it denotes one sort of element in that constellation, the concrete puzzle-solutions which, employed as models or examples, can replace explicit rules as a basis for the solution of the remaining puzzles of normal science." The first use is sociological understanding of the term, the second is to understand it in terms of exemplary past achievements which govern present research. Kuhn, *Scientific Revolutions*, 175; Kuhn, *The Essential Tension*, 294. Margret Masterman lists twenty-one different ways in which Kuhn uses this term in his book. "The Nature of a Paradigm," in Lakatos and Musgrave, *Criticism and the Growth of Knowledge*, 59–89. Shapere argues that Kuhn's lack of clarification and qualification of 'paradigm' results in a theory that is too vague and ambiguous to be useful. Shapere, "The Structure of Scientific Revolutions," 38.

research.[20] If paradigms are primarily understood in terms of the theories, it is hard to explain the dominance of a paradigm within a research community. Paradigms represent much more than theories; they also include the constellation of a group's commitments and beliefs according to Kuhn. This involves symbolic generalizations that are employed by the group (such as $f=ma$), models that provide metaphors and analogies for explanations, and exemplars of concrete problems and solutions that are often used to teach students.[21] Exemplars provide ways of seeing problems and solutions that form the basis for "tacit knowledge" that does not follow rules or techniques. In this sense, exemplars serve a pedagogical function. One of the ways members of a particular group or discipline "learn to see the same things when confronted with the same stimuli is by being shown examples of situations that their predecessors in the group have already learned to see as like each other and as different from other sorts of situations."[22] The role of shared examples cannot be understated. They are part of the educational process by which the members of a research community learn to see things in a certain way "naturally" and provide the context in which researchers learn the rules of their discipline and how to apply them.

At the same time, a paradigm restricts the questions that can be asked and the range of answers that the community will accept.[23] This is an essential dimension to any form of knowledge. "In order for us to understand anything, we have to fail to perceive a great deal that is there. Knowledge is always purchased at the expense of what might have been seen and learned but was not."[24] The range and scope of the questions that can be asked within any paradigm will always be a small percentage of what conceivably could be asked.[25] As one paradigm succeeds its predecessor new insights into the subject matter are disclosed or discovered. At the same time, some aspects of understanding are lost

20. Kuhn, *The Structure of Scientific Revolutions*, 10–17.

21. Musgrave, "Kuhn's Second Thoughts," in Gutting, *Paradigms and Revolutions*, 39.

22. Kuhn, *The Structure of Scientific Revolutions*, 193–94, 43–48, 181–91.

23. "Paradigm procedures and applications are as necessary to science as paradigm laws and theories, and they have the same effects. Inevitably they restrict the phenomenological field accessible for scientific investigation at any given time." Ibid., 60.

24. Oppenheimer, "Tradition and Discovery," 15.

25. Kuhn, *The Structure of Scientific Revolutions*, 35.

since the questions that promoted those insights are no longer asked, or the answers may no longer be considered valid in the new paradigm.

While the centrality of an authoritative text, such as the Bible, is one of the elements that constitutes the continuity of the Christian tradition, the function it serves in this tradition has changed over time. As the tradition changes the questions put to the text will also change. The questions which Martin Luther and the Reformers asked of the Bible are very different from those asked by Origin and Augustine. These questions were embedded in their stage in the narrative of the Christian tradition. The answers they received from the text in turn contributed to the growth of the tradition and how the authoritative role of the Bible was understood at that stage.

It is at this point that parallel ideas in Heidegger's conception of preunderstanding can help us to explicate some aspects of Kuhn's notion of paradigms. By way of review, Heidegger uses three German terms to explain how preunderstanding operates. *Vorhabe* is what we possess in advance, the network of our cultural background which makes us who we are and is translated as fore-having. *Vorsicht* is something we see in advance, our conceptual vocabulary and schemes, or fore-sight. And *Vorgriff* is something we grasp in advance or the fore-conception of the object. Heidegger's "point is that even before I begin consciously to interpret a text or grasp the meaning of an object, I have already placed it within a certain context (*Vorhabe*), approached it from a certain perspective (*Vorsicht*) and conceived of it in a certain way (*Vorgriff*)."[26] These fore-structures or fore-projections are necessary for our being able to understand anything. They enable us to place the text, event, person, or thing within a familiar context, giving us a point of access or relationship by which to understand it.

Kuhn's concept of paradigms is related to all three aspects of preunderstanding.[27] *Vorhabe* corresponds to Kuhn's sociological use of the term paradigm to describe the disciplinary matrix-skill and tacit knowledge that scientists or interpreters acquire in order to enable them to perform their research. *Vorsicht* parallels Kuhn's use of exemplars and

26. Warnke, *Gadamer*, 77.

27. Kuhn, *The Structure of Scientific Revolutions*, 10, 41–42; Shapere, "The Structure of Scientific Revolutions," 29. This reading of Kuhn can also be reinforced by noticing the similarities between his thought and Wittgenstein's later philosophy. Thiselton, "Knowledge, Myth and Corporate Memory," 58.

past achievements to define what counts as a problem and a solution, and in particular how they "project" their research. And Heidegger's concept of *Vorgriff* corresponds to the anticipations, hypotheses, and theories which can be confirmed.[28] The activity of forming and confirming interpretations makes use of assumptions and a web of background practices. While this background often goes unstated in the presuppositions of a theory, it determines what we will count as a valid result or theory.[29]

Those who read Kuhn's text as presenting a strong case for the incommensurability between paradigms claim that there is no data in itself, since all data is theory laden. As Rorty writes, "In verifying a theory we move in a circle from hypothesis to data, and data to hypothesis, without ever encountering any bare facts which could call our whole theory into question."[30] Stanley Fish is perhaps one of the better known exponents of this view in literary theory. According to him, there are no determinate components in literary theory; every component is the product of interpretation. Thus, there can be no "'given' [in reference to the text] if by given one means what is there before interpretation begins."[31] If Fish, Rorty and others are correct in pressing Kuhn for incommensurability and relativism, then all we are left with is a plurality of interpretative communities or strategies.[32] On a synchronic axis, communication between paradigms is achieved only through the rhetoric of persuasion, not through rational argumentation. On a diachronic axis, tradition is fractured into distinct epochs. We are shut off from our past since their world was constituted by paradigms that are incommensurable to the ones we hold today. However, if Kuhn's paradigms are not this strong, then we can learn from other views. There is the possibility for continuity in the midst of diversity and progress in what we learn from the past.

28. Dreyfus, "Holism and Hermeneutics," 8–10.

29. Ibid., 10. "But the important point for the natural sciences is that natural science is successful precisely to the extent that these background practices which make science possible can be taken for granted and ignored by the science." Ibid., 16.

30. Ibid., 4, 11. Rorty, *Contingency*; Barbour, "Paradigms in Science and Religion," 223–45; Scheffler, *Science and Subjectivity*, 84.

31. Fish, "Why No One's Afraid of Wolfgang Iser," 7–8.

32. Feyerabend, *Farewell to Reason*, 34, 69; Stegmüller, "Accidental Theory of Change," in Gutting, *Paradigms and Revolutions*, 86–87.

The manner in which Kuhn sees anomalies function in paradigm shifts demonstrates that he does not support a strong form of relativism and incommensurability. According to Heidegger, when something violates our preunderstanding—an anomaly—it opens the possibility for a new disclosure of understanding for that object. It is only when the contextual relationships of these conventional norms are disrupted that our understanding of something, such as the hammer, becomes explicit. When a hammer is missing, or broken, we realize what the hammer was "ready-to-hand *with*, and *what* it was ready-to-hand *for*."[33] The possibility to understand the hammer in new ways or grasp particular aspects of the hammer that had gone unnoticed in the past is disclosed.

This same idea is picked up by Kuhn, but employed at the level of a system or paradigm. The domination of a paradigm is disrupted only when a paradigm enters into a period of epistemological crisis. This occurs when a persistent anomaly becomes generally recognized and is given more attention because it is seen to be in explicit conflict with some of the core beliefs of the scientific community. During this phase, the solutions proposed for resolving the anomaly will move from those that are closely aligned with the presuppositions of the research community to those that diverge from, or even challenge, the accepted conceptual scheme. The result of trying to resolve the questions an anomaly raises is that "it conceptualizes its phenomena in ways that automatically bring new and previously unnoticed (or uninteresting) dimensions of these phenomena into the center of scientific attention and inquiry."[34] In this process, the rules for normal science begin to get blurred. Copernicus provided an illustration of this when he complained about the blurring of rules which resulted in astronomers being so "inconsistent in these [astronomical] investigations . . . that they cannot even explain or observe the constant length of the seasonal year."[35]

There are three ways to resolve an epistemological crisis in Kuhn's opinion. In some instances, the paradigm may eventually provide a solution. The anomaly may be labeled as unsolvable and set aside with

33. Heidegger, *Being and Time*, 105, 195, 199–200, 411–12.

34. Doppelt, "Kuhn's Epistemological Relativism," 45–46.

35. "With them it is as though an artist were to gather the hands, feet, head and other members for his images from diverse models, each part excellently drawn, but not related to a single body, and since they in no way match each other, the result would be monster rather than man." Kuhn, *The Copernican Revolution*, 138.

the hope that later developments may provide a solution to it. Or in the final instance, a new paradigm that proposes a solution may emerge from the crisis.[36] In any case a paradigm is not rejected just because it has bumped into nature in some manner that challenges its views. The rejection of a theory always involves more than just the comparison of a theory with its object of inquiry. A paradigm is only rejected when there is a rival to take its place.[37]

When adjudicating between competing theories, scientists place the highest value on the ability of a theory to raise and solve puzzles. In this way Newton's mechanics surpassed Aristotle's, and Einstein's improved upon Newton's "as instruments of puzzle-solving."[38] This implies that in Kuhn's system there are theory-independent values and standards by which to judge the progress of a new theory over an older one. "The decision to reject one paradigm is always simultaneously the decision to accept another, and the judgment leading to that decision involves the comparison of both paradigms with nature and with each other."[39] In other words, even in the most revolutionary paradigm shifts there are trans-paradigmatic values which the members of a community can appeal to and apply to judge between the different competing conceptual schemes. From a historical point of view, while we may not agree with the paradigms of those who preceded us, we can still study, understand, and learn from those paradigms and the results they produced.

36. Kuhn, *The Structure of Scientific Revolutions*, 84.

37. Kuhn, *The Essential Tension*, 234. Kuhn is not arguing that the sudden emergence or recognition of an anomaly invalidates a paradigm. While Kuhn is in fundamental agreement with much of Popper's work, he disagrees with Popper's criteria of "falsification by direct comparison with nature." Kuhn claims that it is possible for anomalies to exist for some time without challenging a paradigm's theories because they could be considered either solved by ad hoc hypotheses or they could be considered irrelevant. Kuhn, *The Structure of Scientific Revolutions*, 67–78. Kuhn criticized Popper for overlooking periods of normal science and focusing on paradigm shifts, for applying the standards of evaluation found in logic to science, and as a result ignoring the social dimension to science. Kuhn, *The Essential Tension*, 266–92. To be fair, Kuhn overlooked what Popper terms the "principle of tenacity," or the way in which scientists protect a theory with ad hoc secondary hypotheses. Popper, *The Logic of Scientific Discovery*, 50, 82–83; Blaug, "Kuhn versus Lakatos," 139.

38. Ibid., 205–6.

39. Kuhn, *The Structure of Scientific Revolutions*, 77, emphasis added. To reject a paradigm while not embracing a competing one is tantamount to rejecting science itself in Kuhn's view. Ibid., 79.

While Kuhn denies that long-term progress in science proceeds by a steady linear accumulation of facts and revision of theories, he does not advocate the position which opponents like Scheffler attribute to him, namely that the acceptance or switching of paradigms is an irrational process. "In fact, however, Kuhn is trying to express a third alternative: an account of scientific authority in terms of the informed judgment of the community of trained scientists."[40]

The two movements of normal science and paradigm shifts which Kuhn employs to characterize science produce what he calls an "essential tension" in the researcher. Normal science is characterized by what he calls "convergent" thinking, whereas paradigm shifts are characterized by "divergent" thinking. In a similar manner, Paul Ricœur uses the terms "sedimentation" and "innovation" to describe these two poles which constitute a tradition.[41] During periods of normal science we would expect to see continuity in a discipline's research. Paradigm shifts, on the other hand, produce a plurality of methods and results until a new paradigm is accepted which is discontinuous from the previous paradigm to varying degrees.

The ability to support a tension between these two forms of thought is a prime requisite for scientific research. "Very often the successful scientist must simultaneously display the characteristics of the traditionalist and of the iconoclast."[42] However, this does not mean that most iconoclastic interpretations are accepted during periods of paradigm shifts, let alone periods of normal research. During the latter there will be a large number of areas of possible research for which the paradigm will not be asking questions. To wander off and investigate them from an open-minded perspective would be counter-productive and, in Kuhn's opinion, a move back to a pre-consensus stage of research. At the same time, during paradigm shifts, the new theories or novel discoveries that emerge always do so from the context of old theories and beliefs which determine what "the world does and does not contain."[43] "I hope to have made meaningful the view that the productive scientist must be a traditionalist who enjoys playing intricate games by preestablished

40. Gutting, "Introduction," in *Paradigms and Revolutions*, 8.

41. Ricœur, "The Text as Dynamic Identity," in Valdés and Miller, *Identity of the Literary Text*, 181–82.

42. Kuhn, *The Essential Tension*, 227.

43. Ibid., 232–37, especially 234.

rules in order to be a successful innovator who discovers new rules and new pieces with which to play them."[44] Kuhn's theory presents a model by which we can see a balance and role for both plurality and continuity, tradition and innovation.

Paradigms and Literary History

The concept of paradigm shifts plays a significant role in reception theory, and in Hans Robert Jauss's work in particular. The history of literary studies is not characterized by a steady, linear accumulation of understanding in which each successive generation of readers arrives at a closer and more accurate understanding of the text. As in the natural sciences, a paradigm serves to guide a community of literary scholars as long as it answers the questions which that community is asking. For Jauss, the central trans-paradigmatic question or value is the task of explicating the text to the present generation of readers. When a paradigm is no longer capable of explicating the text in a relevant manner then it is discarded in favor of one which is capable of answering these questions. Thus, literary studies are characterized by paradigm shifts which introduce "qualitative jumps, discontinuities, and original points of departure," not only in the theories and methods employed, but also in which texts are considered authoritative or canonical (in the literary, not the biblical sense). "In other words, a given paradigm creates both the techniques for interpretation and the objects to be interpreted."[45]

According to Jauss, four major paradigms characterize the history of modern literary theory. The first is what he terms the classical-humanist paradigm of literature. During the Reformation and the Renaissance, literary theory was based on classic texts that were seen as the norm and model for other works of literature. Not only were the classical texts accepted as canonical, but they functioned as the norm for literary studies. For example, Cicero's work on rhetoric not only served as a guideline for what constituted a good piece of literature but it was also considered a part of the literary canon. This paradigm entered into a period of crisis when history as a modern discipline began to develop. Initially, history was seen as a method that could help raise the standards of literary appreciation. However, the application of historical methods

44. Ibid., 237.
45. Holub, *Reception Theory*, 1–2.

to literary studies also revealed how classical texts were products of their own time. As a result, a distance was opened between the reader and the classical texts which had not been realized in such a dramatic fashion until that time. Until questions concerning the historicity of the texts were asked, classical texts could perform the roles they did within the classical-humanist paradigm because the readers did not perceive a high degree of temporal or cultural distance between themselves and the classical texts. When they began to realize this distance their ability to explicate and apply classical texts to their horizon in a straightforward manner fell apart. With the development of historical questioning during the Reformation and Renaissance, the classical-humanist paradigm entered into a period of epistemological and methodological crisis. The problem of historical distance not only became more acute, but moved to the center of the paradigm. It became one of the central problems for which the classical-humanist paradigm could not provide an answer. The classical-humanist paradigm collapsed when classical literature was no longer seen to be unique or incomparable, embodying atemporal norms by which to judge other works.

This brought about the shift to the historical-positivist paradigm which dominated literary studies in the nineteenth century. During this period, philological and source studies, critical editions, and the reconstruction of the pre-history of the text took center stage. To give their research a sense of direction, they often made use of national ideology. The highest aspirations of a nation were embodied in its canon of classical works which brought to speech what was latent in the nation's culture and history. The historical-critical method was both a strength and weakness for this paradigm. On the one hand, it clearly revealed the historical distance between the text and the reader, allowing the text to speak in its own terms and not be dominated by the preunderstanding of the reader to the extent it had under the classical-humanist paradigm. On the other hand, it raised questions about how a text from the distant past could speak to the present historical horizon. This is one of the problems that Hegel clearly realized in his concept of the "Spirit of Fate." For Hegel, one aspect of the epistemological crisis facing the historical-positivist paradigm was the alienation of the present from the past which historical methodology raised to consciousness. To dramatize his point he compared the classical texts, both secular and

Christian, to archeological ruins, "stones from which the living soul has flown."[46]

During the first half of the twentieth century (1900 to the 1950s), the aesthetic-formalist paradigm rose, in large part due to the dissatisfaction with the historical-positivist paradigm in its attempt to explain literature solely on the basis of historical methods. Russian Formalism, New Criticism in America, and the work of Oscar Walzels in Germany are all examples of this paradigm shift. In each one of these movements there is a theme of protest against the historical-critical method. In response to this, one of the central themes of the third paradigm is the elevating of the literary work to an autonomous, independent object of research. Russian Formalism is perhaps the most sophisticated of these schools and considers a text as the sum of all its elements. The problem for this paradigm lays in one of its original premises, the idea of "*L' Art pour l' Art.*" Formalism overcame this weakness by examining a text's relationship to the works that preceded it. This opened the door for asking questions about literary evolution and the dialectical relationship between texts which produced high points of literature and new genres. However, Jauss asserts their confidence in the inexhaustibility of a great work's possible aesthetic interpretation weakened during the 1950s, and that by the 1960s this paradigm had reached a point of exhaustion.[47]

Jauss believes that we are in the midst of a fourth paradigm. During the 1960s, the inadequacies of the different methods that attempted to reconstruct the past or to approach the text in itself resulted in the suppression of questions concerning application.[48] The renewed interest in hermeneutics, the rise of alternative methods, and problems concerning the teaching and content of the literary canon in a society permeated by mass media are all evidence for the need of a new paradigm. While the shape of the new paradigm has not yet been determined, it must integrate the three movements of understanding, interpretation, and application if it is to succeed. Thus, Jauss's adoption of Kuhn's theory of

---

46. Hegel, *Phenomenology of Spirit,* 455–56.

47. Jauss, "*Paradigmawechsel in der Literaturwissenschaft,*" 47–51; Jauss, "The Literary Process," 27–32, 54–57; Segers, "Readers, Text and Author," 16; Holub, *Reception Theory,* 1–3. Eagleton follows almost the same taxonomy as Jauss for these paradigm shifts. Eagleton, *Literary Theory,* 74.

48. Segers, "An Interview with Hans Robert Jauss," 84.

paradigm shifts in his literary theory also serves the apologetic function for the relevance of his ideas.[49]

Paradigms and the Logic of Question and Answer

While Kuhn's concept of paradigm shifts serves a fruitful function in Jauss's thought, Jauss does not blindly appropriate Kuhn's ideas. An important modification Jauss makes in Kuhn's theory concerns the question of what instigates a paradigm shift in literary theory. According to Kuhn, a research community begins to be open to change when a persistent anomaly penetrates to the core of its research paradigm.[50] Jauss asks what makes an anomaly become more significant at a certain time if it was there all along. For example, what led to the scientific breakthrough in the double helix structure of DNA? This discovery did not occur because of the development of X-ray photography, but it came about by asking the question, "What atoms like to lie next to each other?" Because Kuhn overlooked the logic of question and answer, he missed the function they performed in undermining the prevailing paradigm and the continuity they can hold across paradigms.[51]

The criteria by which a new paradigm is judged to be successful, and the degree to which it replaces the old paradigm, is based on its ability to answer questions that the old paradigm could not. A new paradigm "can only be accepted and developed in significance to the degree that it is able to solve, or promise to solve, a problem that is acutely felt in, or first intrudes on, the synchronic system of canonized questions and answers of a given life-world."[52] Questions from previous paradigms are part of the new paradigm's content and the new paradigm must show how it answers those questions. To do this it must "occupy all the positions, and all the 'empty spaces' in the former model."[53] In this way,

---

49. Holub, 12, 154. Others are sympathetic to Jauss's call for a new paradigm in literary studies. Rabinowitz, "Whirl without End," in Atkins and Morrow, *Encyclopedia of Contemporary Literary Theory*, 81–95, especially 82.

50. Kuhn, *The Structure of Scientific Revolutions*, 67, 52–76.

51. Jauss, *Question and Answer*, 69–70. Jauss does not take this example from Kuhn's work but from James Watson's work on the double helix structure of DNA.

52. Ibid., 70.

53. Ibid. The challenge of mass-media is an example of a question which Jauss feels needs to be addressed in order for a new paradigm to be successful. The influence of mass media has not been addressed in previous paradigms, but because of

Jauss synthesizes Collingwood's logic of question and answer with the concept of paradigm shifts. When applied to literary studies, this means that literary history should not be approached from the perspective of author and text, or events, but rather from the historical perspective of questions and answers that shape the texts which authors create and guide the interpretations of readers.[54]

It is at this point, I believe, that Alasdair MacIntyre's work offers a more constructive and useful model for reception theory than Jauss's appropriation of Kuhn's work. Like Jauss, MacIntyre emphasizes continuity between paradigm shifts in a tradition; not everything is thrown into question at one time. MacIntyre also develops the role of question and answer within paradigm shifts. This is seen in his concept that what helps to define a particular tradition is its 'core problematic.' When a tradition is no longer able to address the questions in its core problematic in a manner that satisfies its members that tradition is said to enter an epistemological crisis.

> Each tradition, to some significant degree, stands or falls as a mode of enquiry and has within itself at each stage a more or less well-defined problematic, that set of issues, difficulties, and problems which have emerged from its previous achievements in enquiry. Characteristically, therefore, such traditions possess measures to evaluate their own progress or lack of it, even if such measures necessarily are framed in terms of and presuppose the truth of those central theses to which the tradition gives it allegiance.[55]

According to Jauss, this is one area in which we see a difference between paradigm shifts as Kuhn envisioned them taking place in the natural sciences and how they occur in literary studies. The impulse for literary paradigm shifts is situated in the core problematic that confronts

---

its pervasiveness in contemporary society it must be included in any new literary theories. "... *diese Literatur tritt in der Lebenspraxis völlig hinter dem zurück, was der Fernsehapparat vor Augen stellt, was sich der Normalverbraucher am Kiosk kauft, was uns alle in den ästhetisch oft raffinierten Formen der Werbung überflutet. Davor schützt weder die Besinnung auf das antike Erbe noch der Appell an die Bildungsgüter der nationalen Vergangenheit."* "*Paradigmawechsel*," 55. The development of courses in film and culture at many seminaries during the past twenty years is one area in which this is felt in the field of theology.

54. Jauss, *Question and Answer*, 70.

55. MacIntyre, *Whose Justice? Which Rationality?*, 166.

every paradigm of literary studies: the challenge of snatching a work out of the past through new interpretations and translating it into the present, making the experience of it available again. A literary paradigm falls into crisis when it is no longer able to engage texts in a manner that allows them to speak to the present through new interpretations or to contemporary readers' translations. "Or to say it another way, each generation places new questions to the work of art from the past which is made to speak and to give us answers again."[56] Paradigms do not shift in literary studies because of the presence of persistent anomalies, since there is generally no comparable field of empirical observations like there is in the natural sciences. Rather, these shifts take place because the previous paradigm cannot bring the text to speech again in that horizon. The ability for any literary or biblical hermeneutical theory to rescue a text from the past and enable it to address the contemporary reader is an essential element of what MacIntyre would define as part of the core problematic for any hermeneutical theory.

It is at this point that the work of Alasdair MacIntyre compliments and offers some significant advantages to Kuhn's thought for reception theory. First, MacIntyre's use of epistemological crisis allows us to determine if a tradition is progressing, is static, or is deteriorating. How can we tell if a tradition is moving forward or has arrived at an epistemological crisis? In order to illustrate this concept MacIntyre uses the examples of the faithful employee who is suddenly sacked. Such instances reveal to us that the premises and inferences we held about others have broken and are thrown into question. In a similar manner, we inherit schemata from our tradition for interpreting authoritative texts. An epistemological crisis is reached when the agents within a tradition realize that their scheme of interpretation has broken down in specific ways. "An agent who is plunged into an epistemological crisis knows something very important: that a schema of interpretation which he has trusted so far has broken down irremediably in certain highly specific ways."[57] As a result skepticism, ambiguity, and the possibility of alternative interpretations become a central feature of that tradition at that

---

56. *"Oder anders gesagt: die von jeder Generation neu zu findende Frage zu stellen, auf welche die Kunst der Vergangenheit für uns wieder Antwort zu geben und zu sprechen vermag."* Jauss, *"Paradigmawechsel,"* 55, my translation.

57. MacIntyre, "Epistemological Crisis", 59.

point in its history.[58] The questions which historical studies introduced into literary studies at the end of the classical-humanist paradigm are a good example of a paradigm breaking down in specific ways.

Second, a successful resolution to an epistemological crisis will result in a new paradigm that will not only answer the question which it confronted, but also explain why the old paradigm could not solve it. It will possess retrospective justification by providing an answer the previous paradigm could not provide. Progress in a tradition is measured by standards internal to it which measure its success in overcoming various issues in its core problematic. Once again the similarity with Jauss's work is very clear. One of the theses Jauss advances is that "the new work can solve formal and moral problems left behind by the last work, and present new problems in return."[59] Or to put it another way, each interpretation of the Bible will present solutions to questions that previous interpretations raised, and at the same time they will present new questions "as the horizon of the 'solutions' which are possible after it, poses and leaves behind."[60] Thus we should not expect a final, definitive interpretation for a biblical passage, but should view each interpretation within its context in the narrative history of a tradition as a solution to questions and also as posing new questions.

The solution to an epistemological crisis must also have the ability to explain why the previous scheme could not solve the problem and stand in continuity with the tradition's history of inquiry up until that time. It requires the discovery and framing of new types of theories which meet three highly exact requirements. One, the new conceptual scheme must provide solutions to the problems confronting the tradition in a systematic and coherent way. Two, this new conceptual scheme must also be able to explain why the tradition's old scheme could not solve the epistemological crisis. Three, the first two steps must be carried out in continuity with the conceptual and theoretical structures that have previously defined that tradition. This new scheme is not totally derivable from the old; if this were the case then it would not have been an epistemological crisis. However, to find a solution the participants in the tradition must exercise their imagination. In this respect, an

---

58. MacIntyre, *Whose Justice? Which Rationality?*, 362.

59. Jauss, 32.

60. Ibid., 34.

epistemological crisis demonstrates the importance of the role of *phro-nesis* for the health of a tradition. The ability of members of a tradition to solve a problem for which the rules and procedures of their tradition could not provide a solution requires *phronetic* judgment.[61]

The concept of epistemological crisis gives a retrospective charac-ter to a tradition's truth claims. The fact that an epistemological crisis can only be recognized in retrospect may explain why the Catholic tradition did not recognize the questions Luther did; they did not go through the same epistemological crisis and paradigm shift, and thus did not recognize it. But for the Protestants the questions that Luther raised are a defining moment in the formation of the Protestant tra-dition. "To have passed through an epistemological crisis successfully enables the adherents of a tradition of enquiry to rewrite its history in a more insightful way."[62] This history allows us to see the continuity of a tradition and to explicate more clearly the structure of justification that supports the tradition's truth claims. Such truth claims are built on the idea that the later stages of a tradition presuppose the earlier findings of a tradition and explain them in a way earlier stages may not have realized and may have even rejected if they considered them. They must also be able to explain why the epistemological crisis arose and could not be solved by the earlier stage. The later stages must also be conceptually richer and provide more direction in the way the rational enquiry should proceed; it must have a better conception of the goal. This enriched conception must provide explanation and a *telos* for the tradition.[63]

Third, truth is defined as unsurpassability. For MacIntyre, the theory of truth which presupposes a sentence-to-fact correspondence "has been as conclusively refuted as any theory can be."[64] By making use of his concept of epistemological crisis and change in traditions MacIntyre develops a retrospective "form of a theory of falsity."[65] It is the discrepancies between the new formulations of beliefs and concepts and the network of beliefs previous to the crisis which allows one in hindsight to call the old beliefs false. After a paradigm shift, the world is

61. See chapter 2 for a fuller discussion of *phronesis* and hermeneutical knowl-edge.

62. MacIntryre, *Whose Justice? Which Rationality?*, 363.

63. Ibid., 80.

64. Ibid., 358.

65. Ibid., 356.

perceived in new ways. When this new understanding is retrospectively compared with the previous paradigm's presuppositions they are judged to be inadequate or false. The new paradigm presents its members with what they perceive as a better correspondence between its beliefs and practices and the world.[66]

To put it negatively, members at one stage in a tradition are able to look back on their predecessor's rational inadequacies and claim that these inadequacies or incoherencies "will never appear in any possible future situation, no matter how searching the enquiry, no matter how much evidence is provided, no matter what developments in rational enquiry may occur."[67] The criterion to check a tradition's truth claim is simple. The claims that have survived the strongest possible questions and objections can be justified as true.[68] Not only does this involve considering the debates and views internal to a tradition but also the arguments put forward in rival traditions. Thus, on the synchronic level, the belief, theory, or new interpretation must be viewed as unsurpassable and superior to the interpretations put forward by rival traditions at the stage it occurs in its tradition. It must also be justified diachronically in relation to previous schemata, and have retrospective justification according to the criteria needed to solve an epistemological crisis.

In contrast to Kuhn, who argues that there is not ontological truth in theories and that there is no way to say what is really there apart from theories, MacIntyre has a modified theory of ontological truth. For simple sentences, such as "the cat is on the mat," we can accept a correspondence theory which judges if the statement matches up with or represents an actual state of affairs. But at the level of a tradition a much more sophisticated theory is needed. "Rather, we are concerned with the whole system of concepts, epistemological and metaphysical theories—and even with 'local' theories of truth!"[69] For example, the

66. Ibid., 357.

67. Ibid., 358. "At this point we can see the wisdom of MacIntyre's definition of truth. The criterion (unsurpassed so far) provides the best possible evidence for truth (will remain unsurpassed), and, furthermore, the criterion has a reasonable (conceptual) connection with the meaning of truth. The criterion falls short of a necessary and sufficient condition for truth—truth claims are fallible, as are all other claims." Nancey Murphy, unpublished manuscript, "Philosophical Resources for Postmodern Evangelical Theology," 25.

68. Ibid.

69. Ibid., 32.

narrative history of science allows us to see that we can confidently say that some things are really "not there," such as humors or negative weights; concepts that once held considerable currency in scientific thought. However, other existence claims have survived a series of theories or epistemological crises. Examples of these include molecules, cells, and electrons. While our conception of them has been modified, this is not grounds for denying that they have excellent warrants. In much the same manner, we could make truth claims about particular textual interpretations. Those views that have demonstrated their appropriateness across paradigm shifts or in several different paradigms would seem to indicate that there are excellent warrants for asserting the validity of that interpretation. Thus, to borrow a phrase from E. D. Hirsch, "validity in interpretation" would appear to be something that is tradition-constituted just as it is grounded in the application of the hermeneutical methods appropriate to that paradigm.

Parables and Paradigms

As I mentioned in the introduction, some in biblical studies also feel the need for a new paradigm that includes the effective history of the Bible. Whereas Jauss organizes the history of literary theory under four paradigms, the same type of generalization cannot be made in biblical studies. Instead one must speak of paradigm shifts in localized terms. Even within New Testament studies different shifts have occurred at different times. The study of parables is an illustration of this. If the shift to the historical quest for Jesus took place between 1774, with Lessing's anonymous publication of Reimarus's *Fragments,* and Strauss's *Life of Jesus* in 1835, then we can see how the application of the historical-critical method to the parables lagged behind the study of other aspects Jesus' life.

It was not until the publication of Jülicher's book, *Die Gleichniss-reden Jesu,* in 1886, that this method was applied to the parables in a thoroughgoing manner. Until Jülicher, the parables were classified as allegories and interpreted accordingly. Jülicher dispelled this idea, arguing that the parables were not allegories nor should they be interpreted allegorically despite the fact that this had been the accepted practice since the earliest days of the church.[70] Based on Cicero's literary classifications, Jülicher argued that a parable was an extended simile, and as a result a contained only one point of comparison. An allegory, by contrast, was composed of multiple metaphors.[71] As such, the parables were reduced to moral stories that contained one point of correspondence with the world and conveyed one central teaching.

Since then many have criticized Jülicher for inappropriately employing concepts from classical rhetoric to define what constitutes a parable and have attempted to correct his classification of parables. However, one honor cannot be denied Jülicher. His work represents the most significant paradigm shift in the interpretation of the parables from allegorical to other categories.[72] "So thoroughly did Jülicher do his work that for a time it almost seemed that as if he had spoken the last word on the parables."[73] The impact of his work is such that, even after one hundred years, if modern scholars wish to introduce an allegorical strategy into their reading of the parables they must swim against the current of what has been accepted as exegetical convention since Jülicher.[74]

Jülicher presented us with a choice. Either the parables are allegories which require a shared code in order to interpret them, or they can be interpreted without the reader and the communicator possessing a

70. While A. B. Bruce's work preceded Jülicher's, it was not widely received and therefore did not serve as the stimulus for the paradigm shift as Jülicher's did. See also the discussion of Jauss's third thesis in chapter 3.

71. "*Aristoteles autem translationi et haec ipsa subiungit et abusionem nem, quam katachresin vocat, ut cum minutum dicimus animum pro parvo; et abutimur verbis propinquis, si opus est vel quod delectat vel quod decet. Iam cum fluxerunt continuo plures translationes, alia plane fit oratio; itaque genus hoc Graeci appellant allegorian: nomine recte, genere melius ille qui ista omnia translationes vocat. Haec frequentat Phalereus maxime suntque dulcissima; et quamquam translatio est apud eum multa, tamen immutationes nusquam crebriores.*" Cicero, *Orator ad M. Brutus* xxvii.94; Jülicher, *Die Gleichnissreden Jesu*, 1:51.

72. Little, "Parable Research in the Twentieth Century I," 356–57. "It was, however, Adolf Jülicher who imparted a definitively new direction in their study . . ." Jones, *The Art and Truth of the Parables*, 3. Jones organizes the history of parable interpretation according to pre- and post-Jülicher. Ibid., 3–40.

73. Hunter, *Interpreting the Parables*, 38.

74. Crossan, *In Parables*, 25. For example, Craig Blomberg devotes the first fifth of his book on the parables to rehabilitating the concept of allegory. Blomberg, *Interpreting the Parables*, 30–38. See also Barr, *Old and New in Interpretation*, 103–4; Louth, *Discerning the Mystery*, 96–97.

shared code. For Jülicher, the second choice was the only viable one. Ever since the publication of his work the majority of exegetes have mercilessly criticized allegorical approaches for interpreting the parables.

> It is Patristic allegorization that sticks in the gullet of modern theology . . . at all levels this allegorization is something deplored . . . Why is this? Basically, I think because we feel that there is something dishonest about allegory. If you interpret a text by allegorizing it, you seem to be saying that it means something which it patently does not. It is irrelevant, arbitrary: by allegory, it is said, you can make the text mean anything you like.[75]

Following Gadamer, Louth attributes the modern attitude towards allegory to the prejudices which theology has inherited from the Enlightenment. These prejudices include the search for an objective meaning in a text through the use of methods, the Romantic concept of meaning located in the reconstruction of the author's intentions, and the attempt to break free from tradition.[76]

The work of Christian Bugge and Paul Fiebig are early exceptions to this rule. They attempted to correct Jülicher's work by comparing the parables to similar passages in the Talmud and other Jewish literature. They concluded that Jülicher inappropriately applied Greek literary concepts to the parables when, in fact, Jewish texts contained better parallels to the parables. Significant for this study was their conclusion that Jesus' parables contained allegorical elements at various levels.[77] While they arrived at a different conclusion than Jülicher regarding the allegorical nature of the parables, I would argue that they were still operating within the same paradigm as Jülicher. This can be seen in two areas. First, the primary methodological consideration in their work was the historical-critical method. Second, the central question which they attempted to answer was the same as Jülicher's: "Are the parables allegories or not?"

Form-criticism introduced not only a new methodological approach to the study of the parables but also new questions. As a result, it represents a second paradigm shift.[78] The work of Rudolf Bultmann and

75. Louth, *Discerning the Mystery*, 96–97.

76. Ibid., 98–107.

77. Bugge, *Die Haupt-Parabeln Jesu*; Fiebig, *Die Gleichnisreden Jesu*.

78. For a discussion of Bultmann's contribution in this area, see Jones, *The Art and Truth*, 42–51.

Martin Diblelius typifies this school of thought which postulated that the allegorical elements found in the Synoptic gospels were the result of the theological reflection of the early church and did not reflect Jesus' original teaching.[79] C. H. Dodd tried to show that we must examine the parables in relation to how Jesus understood his ministry and the Old Testament motifs that Jesus employed in the parables.[80] Using a form-critical analysis of the parables Dodd and Jeremias differentiated several *Sitz im Leben* in which a parable operated. Jeremias' contribution came from the manner in which he attempted to find the earliest form and context of each parable by examining ten different means by which the parables were transmitted in the primitive church. When the parables were recontextualized to these different *Sitz im Leben* they were seen to generate new and different meanings.[81] Both Jeremias' and Dodd's work represent one of the definitive turning points in the study of the parables. "There can be no going back from this work of Jeremias. It is perhaps the greatest single contribution to the historical understanding of the parables."[82]

What separates the present, or fourth, paradigm from the third involves the manner in which one understands the message of the parable. For both Dodd and Jeremias understanding was primarily a reflective, conscious operation on the part of the interpreter. With the shift to the present paradigm, the reader's understanding is transformed at a deeper or pre-reflective level. This is partially based on concepts such as Heidegger's idea that a parable "projects a world" and Ricœur's work on how symbols "give rise to thought."[83] The shift to this paradigm was

---

79. Bultmann, *The History of the Synoptic Tradition*, 198.

80. Cadoux's work, while it preceded and prepared the way for Dodd and Jeremias, was not as influential as their work. Little, "Parable Research in the Twentieth Century I," 360.

81. According to Dodd, Jesus uttered the parables in the midst of a period of intense eschatological crisis. By the time the gospels were written the church had experienced a prolonged period of growth and the eschatological crisis was now understood to be a distant future event. This led to the church reinterpreting Jesus' parables in light of their situation. Dodd, *The Parables of the Kingdom*, 34–35, 102–5. These multiple meanings are not the result of a theory of meaning but arise from a theory of multiple settings.

82. Perrin, "The Parables of Jesus," 340. However, Hunter thinks that all Jeremias did was "dot the i's and stroke the t's of Dodd's exposition." Hunter, *Interpreting the Parables*, 39.

83. Walhout, Lundin, and Thiselton, *The Responsibility of Hermeneutics*, 98–102.

instigated by the New Hermeneutics' view that understanding was an existential event or process. Ernst Fuchs, for example, claimed that the parables were language-events in which Jesus communicated self-understanding of his relationship to the world and to God. The parables, as language-events, offer the possibility for the reader to share in this understanding. Readers are not detached observers who reflect on the parable but are active participants in the parable and find themselves being questioned in it.[84] The earlier work of Eta Linnemann is another example of the existential approach in this paradigm. The role of the parable is to get the hearer to make a decision which is in line with Jesus' view of the world; this brings the hearer into a new understanding of her situation. In order for the reader to make this decision, she must understand the ideas and images in the parable so that she can make a correspondence between the narrated world projected in the parable, Jesus historical situation, and her historical situation.[85] The stronger the opposition between the hearer and the narrator, or the narrated story world in the parable, the more significant will be the hearer's decision.

The question no longer concerns whether a parable contains one point or moral, as Jülicher argued, or is open to multiple meanings, which the allegorists tended to find. Rather, the core problematic now revolves around the manner by which a parable projects a 'narrative world.' Parables are now seen as aesthetic objects which possess an existential-theological dimension.[86] It is the manner by which a parable challenges or reverses the audience's expectations that is the distinguishing trait of a proper parable according to this approach.[87] Conversely, to approach a parable as an allegory reduces the parable to a collection of propositional truths contained in its multiple references and misses the function of the narrative whole which projects a world into which the reader or hearer is meant to enter. "Allegory . . . is not an apricot with a stone set in its centre and we in search of that stone, but an onion whose manifold layers constitute its totality and whose multiplicity is its

84. Thiselton, "The Parables as Language-Event," 440–42; Kissinger, *The Parables*, 182–84.

85. Linnemann, *Parables of Jesus*, 18–23.

86. Via, *The Parables*, 70–1.

87. Crossan, "Parable, Allegory, and Paradox," in Patte, *Semiology and Parables*, 253.

message. We have been taught, of course, to prefer apricots to onions."[88] Dan Otto Via, John Dominic Crossan, and Bernard Scott are some of the more prominent supporters of this position. This final paradigm is more heavily influenced by literary theories, in particular reader-response theories, than by other fields of thought in biblical studies. As such, it represents a unique turn or paradigm shift in relation to the rest of New Testament or biblical studies.

When we speak of paradigm shifts in biblical interpretation we must qualify it by specifying which particular aspect or area of biblical interpretation this paradigm shift took place in. The fact that it took almost one hundred years before the historical-critical method was applied to the parables demonstrates that paradigm shifts do not necessarily occur at the same time in every field of biblical studies. And the three paradigm shifts within the field of parable interpretation represent questions that are unique to the study of the parables, which in turn have shaped a history of interpretation for the parables.

Paradigms and Semiotic Shifts

If normal science represents a period in which knowledge grows in a cumulative or linear fashion, paradigm shifts, in large part, do not. In the change from one paradigm to the next, not only are theories replaced, but so are the shared rules and standards of research. At an even more fundamental level, these changes involve semiotic transformations in the use and definition of concepts.

One of the examples Thomas Kuhn cites to explain these semiotic transformations is the shift from a geocentric to a heliocentric theory of the solar system. Under the Ptolemaic system, the earth was the fixed body around which the planets and other heavenly bodies revolved. The term "earth" not only referred to the terrestrial body that we live on, but it also carried connotative references to "fixed," "firm," and "stable." These definitions and their connotative associations were not restricted to astronomical theory but were part of the much wider, everyday use of language. This is one reason why Copernicus was ridiculed when he claimed the earth revolved around the sun and not vice versa. The idea that the earth was constantly in motion not only contradicted Ptolemaic theory but also brought into question the use of these terms

88. Ibid., 277.

and their employment in common language use. The term 'earth' was a "paradigm-case of fixity," or stability.[89]

> Part of what they [Copernicus' Ptolemaic critics] meant by "earth" was fixed position. Their earth, at least, could not be moved. Correspondingly, Copernicus' innovation was not simply to move the earth. Rather, it was a whole new way of regarding the problems of physics and astronomy, one that necessarily changed the meaning of both 'earth' and 'motion.' Without those changes the concept of a moving earth was mad.[90]

Copernicus did not simply say the earth moved, but introduced a whole new set of problems in physics that required new meanings for "earth" and "motion." Since new paradigms arise from old ones and employ the previous paradigm's vocabulary, semiotic shifts in one semantic domain require other terms and concepts to fall into new relationships with each other. A ripple effect of semiotic transformations occurs. Depending on how closely the various terms are related to the primary concepts, undergoing redefinition will determine the extent to which these transformations impinge upon them also. In the Copernican paradigm shift, the term "planet" had to be redefined "so that it could continue to make useful distinctions in a world where all celestial bodies, not just the sun, were seen differently from the way they had been seen before."[91]

89. Thiselton, *The Two Horizons*, 405; Doppelt, "Kuhn's Epistemological Relativism," 46.

90. Kuhn, *The Structure of Scientific Revolutions*, 149–50; Kuhn, *The Copernican Revolution*, chaps. 3–7. Another excellent illustration which Kuhn provides is how, when Aristotle and Galileo looked at a heavy body swinging back and forth on a string, they saw different things. Aristotle taught that a body will move from a higher position to a lower position of natural rest by its very own nature. Therefore, "the swinging body was simply falling with difficulty," reaching its lower position of rest through the long process of oscillatory motions. By contrast Galileo saw new relationships between weight, height and velocity. This was made possible by the "late medieval paradigm" theory of impetus in which Galileo was trained. "When Aristotle and Galileo looked at swinging stones, the first saw constrained fall, the second a pendulum." Kuhn, *The Structure of Scientific Revolutions*, 121.

91. Kuhn, *The Structure of Scientific Revolutions*, 128–29, 149. Doppelt points out that many of those who claim that paradigms are incommensurable confuse the manner in which sense and reference function. They argue that in the shift from Ptolemaic to Copernican cosmology the reference of the term "planet" changed, not its sense which remained stable. In contrast, Kuhn is claiming that even though the connotation of the concept changed there is still a stability of reference which allows for commensurability. This is partly based on the manner in which rival paradigms share

It is on this basis that Kuhn makes one of his most famous statements: "when paradigms change, the world itself changes with them."[92] In his later work he modified the strength of this statement to a more balanced position: "though the world does not change with a change of paradigm, the scientist afterward works in a different world."[93] The changes in definitions and concepts from the previous paradigm to the new one transforms the "reactions, expectations, and beliefs" of those who share that paradigm. "The scientist who embraces a new paradigm is like a man wearing inverting lenses. Confronting the same constellation of objects as before and knowing that he does so, he nevertheless finds them transformed through and through in many of their details."[94]

While he does not cite Wittgenstein directly at this point, Kuhn does appear to allude to Wittgenstein's duck/rabbit illustration.[95] "What were ducks in the scientist's world before the revolution are rabbits afterwards."[96] As we saw above, at the level of *Vorsicht*, the paradigm that a person accepts shapes his beliefs and expectations—whether he sees

---

"their everyday and most of their scientific world and language." Competing paradigms are not isolated floating islands imprisoned by their own languages. Doppelt, "Kuhn's Epistemological Relativism," 37–38. "What we saw in the case of translation and the possibility of communication across the frontiers of our own languages is confirmed: the verbal world in which we live is not a barrier that prevents knowledge of being-in-itself but fundamentally embraces everything in which our insight can be enlarged and deepened. . . . As verbally constituted, every such world is of itself always open to every possible insight and hence to every expansion of its own world picture, and is accordingly available to others." Kuhn, *The Structure of Scientific Revolutions*, 201. See Gadamer's discussion of the relationship between language and world in *Truth and Method*, 383–491, esp. 447.

92. Kuhn, *The Structure of Scientific Revolutions*, 111.

93. Ibid., 121; Gutting, "Introduction," in *Paradigms and Revolutions*, 20. Those who hold to a strong view of incommensurability love to cite passages like this [the previous quote in the text above] from Kuhn to show that there is no neutral language to which one can appeal. Musgrave does not find this argument convincing. For example, a Copernican defines the earth as a planet while the Aristotelians did not. Musgrave fails to see why the two sides could not explain their respective positions to each other in a manner they could understand, without resorting to some form of a "theoretically neutral observation language." Musgrave, "Kuhn's Second Thoughts," in Gutting, *Paradigms and Revolutions*, 49, 52 n. 9.

94. Kuhn, *The Structure of Scientific Revolutions*, 121.

95. Wittgenstein, *Philosophical Investigations*, §114–15.

96. Kuhn, *The Structure of Scientific Revolutions*, 111.

a duck or rabbit when looking at the line drawing. "What a man sees depends both upon what he looks at and also upon what his previous visual-conceptual experience has taught him to see."[97] Wittgenstein's remarks concerning how the language and tradition in which we are trained frame the questions we ask and our perceptions provide further support for Kuhn's argument.

> One thinks that one is tracing the outline of the thing's nature over and over again, and one is merely tracing round the frame through which we look at it. A picture held us captive. And we could not get outside it, for it lay in our language and language seemed to repeat it to us inexorably.[98]

Alasdair MacIntyre's inquiry into two different names for the same city in North Ireland illustrates not only the importance for understanding the use of a term within a tradition, but also the strength by which these definitions and connotations influence the views of a community. The Irish refer to this city as *Doire Columcille*, which means St. Columba's oak grave. The English name for the same city is Londonderry, which stems from the merchants from London who immigrated there.[99] For a person from one of these respective communities to employ the other tradition's name for that city would call into question or deny the semiotic associations or network of beliefs behind his/her tradition.

There is a caveat that must be mentioned in relation to semiotic transformations and paradigm shifts. While a paradigm shift often involves transformations in the semiotic code and relationships, semiotic shifts are not dependent on paradigm shifts. Semiotic relationships are not stable, but are part of culture and tradition and shift through time. As a result, semiotic codes and relationships undergo change due to the linguistic innovations, and any number of other factors that impinge upon a culture's linguistic practices.

When we apply these insights to a tradition of interpretation, be it literary studies or biblical interpretation, we must realize that these traditions are embodied in languages. Not only are the principles of rationality embodied in a tradition, but language, ways of life, and understanding are all socially embodied. In order to learn about a tradition

97. Ibid., 113, 121.
98. Wittgenstein, *Philosophical Investigations*, §114–15.
99. MacIntyre, *Whose Justice? Which Rationality?*, 376–79.

one must learn its language, and in order to learn a language one must learn that language's tradition. Even something as simple as naming the 'earth' requires a familiarity with the tradition, for names always have referential and connotative content. The use of a name involves beliefs, such that if the belief (e.g., the fixity of the earth) were found to be false then the name could no longer be used in the same way.

The "Moon-struck" Boy (Matthew 17) and Semiotic Shifts within a Tradition

If semiotic transformations exercise such a profound affect on how we interpret the world in the natural sciences then these shifts in the semiotic code must have at least an equal if not greater authority in the process of interpreting a text. This is not because semiosis is primarily restricted to linguistic communication. Umberto Eco has demonstrated how natural signs carry semiotic signification. For example, the manner by which we can infer the presence of fire from the sign of smoke involves a semiotic act of signification.[100] But when we turn our attention to the interpretation of texts these semiotic processes become much more significant. In a sense, a text is doubly semiotically encoded. First, the author is able to employ a particular sign vehicle because it denotes a particular cultural unit (such as the definition for a word as found in a dictionary) and a sign is connotatively related to other words in different semantic fields. Second, readers are able to understand and read a text because the semiotic training they have received as part of their historical horizon allows them to recognize the relationships that a sign possesses (whether they are the same relationships the author possessed or not).

The interpretation of what the child is suffering from in Matthew 17:15, "Lord, have mercy on my boy for he is a *lunatic* (σεληνιάζαται) and suffers a great deal," is an example of how our understanding of a biblical text is linked with semiotic shifts in other domains of our tradition. The goal of this section is to explore how the semiotic relationships of the term σεληνιάζαται were employed in the horizon of the author and the original readers of Matthew's gospel and then how these relationships were transformed and reconfigured in the course of the history of the interpretation of this passage.

100. Eco, *A Theory of Semiotics*, 17.

THE ORIGINAL HORIZON OF MATTHEW'S GOSPEL

The Greek term Matthew uses is σεληνιάζαται, which literally means "struck by the moon." This condition would have been perceived in first-century Palestine in relation to a complex of ideas, including evil influences of the moon and/or parents having had intercourse under the moon. The idea that the moon could exert an evil influence on our lives is reflected in Psalm 121:6, "The sun will not strike you by day, nor the moon by night," where the power of the moon to affect one's health is compared with that of sunstroke. The notion that the moon beamed harmful influences was not limited to Israel but was widespread in ancient near east.[101]

A similar view was held in regard to the effects of naked exposure to lamp or candle light. There are several passages in the Babylonian Talmud which attribute the cause of epilepsy or lunacy to this. "And do not stand naked in front of a lamp,' for it was taught: He who stands naked in front of a lamp will be an epileptic, and he who cohabits by the light of a lamp will have epileptic children."[102] While the Talmud postdates Matthew's Gospel, it represents earlier traditions and views held within Judaism and as such helps us to understand the complex semiotic relationships which would have informed how Jesus' and Matthew's audiences would have perceived this affliction.

The consequences of being considered "moon-struck" in Jewish Palestine were more far reaching than a physical or mental illness. First, epilepsy was considered a bodily defect that disqualified a person from Temple service or filling certain roles in a synagogue.[103] This was based on the purity laws of the Hebrew Bible. Second, associated with this were concerns for preserving a pure and healthy family line. "A man should not marry into a family which has a recurrent history of epilepsy or

101. Dahood, *Psalms III: 101–150*, 218; Allen, *Psalms 101–150*, 152; Plutarch *Quaestiones Convivales* 659e–f.

102. *b. Pesahim* 112b, in Epstein, *Hebrew-English Edition of the Babylonian Talmud*. The Talmud preserves evidence of a fourth possible association with the concept of epilepsy. In *b. Ketubbot* 77a, the Hebrew word which is translated as "epileptic" is נכפשׁ. The translator's gloss at the bottom of the page notes that the Nif'al form of this verb, נכפשׁ, can be translated as, "to be overtaken by a demon." This is the only mention in the Babylonian Talmud to a demonic or spiritual cause to epilepsy, and represents a later interpretative gloss to the text.

103. *b. Berakhot* 44b.

from a family of lepers."[104] These eugenic concerns appear to have been originally applied to the priestly lineage but over time were extended to everyone of the Jewish faith. To be "moon-struck" or an "epileptic" in Jewish culture during the New Testament era involved a combination of values about purity and eugenics, along with the perception that epilepsy was both a lunar and a spiritual affliction.[105]

Without going into a detailed exegetical study, these semiotic networks help us to understand some of the nuances in Matthew's account of Jesus' healing of the boy. First, it helps us to understand why the author associated but also differentiated epilepsy from demoniacs and paralytics in Matthew 4:24.[106] On the one hand, epilepsy was mentioned in connection with bodily ailments such as paralysis. On the other hand, it was associated with demonization in other contexts. In Matthew 17 the issue becomes a bit more clouded. Matthew uses the specific term, σεληνιάζαται, to define the boy's illness. This is noteworthy if we consider that Matthew has redacted Mark's more generic description (ἔχοντα πνεῦμα ἄλαλον [he has a speechless spirit], Mark 9:17) with a much more specific term. By using this specific verb, Matthew is associating the boy's condition with cultural views that associated the effects of the moon upon a person's life.[107] However, when Matthew narrates the actual event of the healing of the boy he mixes these ideas even more. The two verbs "rebuked" (ἐπετίμησεν αὐτῷ) and "departed" (ἐξῆλθεν ἀπ' αὐτοῦ) in verse 17:18 are frequently used in association with demonic exorcisms in the Gospels. However, the

104. *b. Yebamot* 64b.

105. This can be seen not only in the perspectives just mentioned but also by the way in which epilepsy was believed to be cured by the use of amulets, in the same manner that amulets were used in association with physical other illnesses *b. Shabbat* 61a.

106. Contra Keir, who interprets Matthew 4:24 in the following manner: "The text here reads, δαιμονιζομένους καὶ σεληνιαζομένους καὶ παραλυτικούς. It seems most unlikely that there were enough epileptics in Galilee to warrant their being treated as a separate category and it is suggested that the phrase be translated, 'demon possessed, that is epileptics and paralytics,' (possibly sufferers from hysterical conversion symptoms)." Keir, "New Testament Exorcism," 109. Current estimates place the ratio of epileptics to the general population between 1:75 and 1:200. This would mean that there would have been a significant number of epileptics in Galilee, in contrast to Keir's assumption. "It is however, an extremely common condition, and is the commonest neurological illness of young people . . . The highest incidence rate occurs in the age group under 5 years." Seiden, "Epilepsy."

107. Pilch, *Healing in the New Testament*, 85.

third phrase, "the boy was cured" (ἐθεραπεύθη ὁ παῖς), seems to infer that the boy was healed from a physical infirmity. Was this boy demon possessed or physically disabled? Matthew does not answer this question but appears to mix the two categories.[108]

Perhaps it would be best to say that Matthew and the original audience to whom the gospel was written would have recognized a certain degree of differentiation between these conditions, but at the same time they would have been porous categories for them. In their worldview, the condition of epilepsy would involve questions about the child's conception, the effect of the moon, bodily defects, and demonization in a manner that one does not necessarily exclude others. As far as the condition from which the child would have been perceived to suffer, the baleful effects of the moon and/or demonization would have been foremost in their thoughts. Combined with this would have been the social stigmatization that would have been placed upon the child, and by extension his family, because of this sickness. These perceptions are very different from the ones we hold today about similar symptoms. The modern worldview tends to understand illnesses primarily as a condition that afflicts the health of one individual. In this particular case, epilepsy is viewed as being a neurological condition that can be controlled by the use of drugs or surgery. However, as John Pilch notes, in the ancient worldview illness was "a socially disvalued condition or state that involves and affects many others besides the stricken individual."[109]

Did the "Moon Strike" People in the Roman Empire?

As the readership of Matthew's gospel expanded from what was most likely a mixed church with Jewish and Gentile believers to churches composed primarily of Gentiles, the semiotic code behind epilepsy shifted in two respects. First, given the right circumstances epileptic seizures were perceived in the Greco-Roman culture as the ecstatic result

---

108. John Pilch suggest two possible explanations for what appears to be a mixing of categories to us. First, Matthew as an author may not present a clear taxonomy of illness. And second, in this particular miracle story, Matthew may have structured his story so that Jesus is presented as a healer who can "deal with the results of the broad area that includes effects of the environment as well as the activity known as witchcraft." Pilch, *Healing in the New Testament*, 81, 85.

109. Ibid., 76.

of a divine encounter.[110] According to Apuleius (second century AD) the unsophisticated soul of a child could be lulled into a subconscious state so that it lost contact with its body and returned to a primordial, spiritual nature.[111] Apuleius wrote that the boy must be "fair and unblemished in body, shrewd of wit and ready of speech, so that a worthy and fair shrine may be provided for the divine indwelling power" which will manifest itself in the divination that occurs.[112] This helps us to understand why Hippocrates used the term *hieron nosema* (the sacred disease) to refer to what we label as epilepsy.[113]

This divine encounter was not always viewed positively in the Greco-Roman culture. Epileptic seizures were frightening experiences that could also be viewed as an act of retribution by one of the gods or the result of demonic possession. During the New Testament period, the attribution of epilepsy to demonic possession was a popular belief. Even when epilepsy was understood as a form of possession, the god that had caused this malediction was seen to hold the key to healing the individual, often through some form of religious purification.

The medical works of Hippocrates and Galen preserve a counter-voice to the perception of epilepsy mentioned above. Both authors taught that this illness was the result of natural causes and could be cured through natural means. Hot, dry wind, diet, and the effects of the moon were all considered as possible causes of this affliction. As Galen noticed, the effects of epilepsy were weaker at half moon and much stronger during the full moon.[114] The following excerpt from Hippocrates is quoted at length because it not only illustrates a

110. "Epilepsy was regarded as *morbus sacer et divinus*, and sufferers were regarded as holy, divine messengers (perhaps because of the similarity of the fits to behavior during trances)." Sussman, "Sickness and Disease," in *Anchor Bible Dictionary* 6:12. See also Sorensen, *Possession and Exorcism*, 104–7.

111. Apuleius, *Apologia*, 43; Kee, *Medicine, Miracles, and Magic in New Testament Times*, 98.

112. Apuleius, *Apologia*, 43.

113. Even though the uses of the term "epilepsy" (*epilēpsia*) is attributed to Hippocrates, he never used this specific term in his works. Collier, "Epilepsy," in Bett, *A Short History of Some Common Diseases*, 120–21. Hippocrates records how healers in the Greek temples would attempt to discern which god had possessed an epileptic child based on the symptoms of their seizures. For example if the person suffered seizures on the right side of the body Athena was to be blamed. Hippocrates *The Sacred Disease* 147.2.4.

114. Temkin, *The Falling Sickness*, 26.

naturalistic perception of epilepsy but describes in detail the progress and recovery from an epileptic seizure.

> I hold that the *sacred disease* is caused in the following way. When much wind has combined throughout the body with all the blood, many barriers arise in many places in the veins. Whenever therefore much air weighs, and continues to weigh, upon the thick, blood-filled veins, the blood is prevented from passing on. So in one place it stops, in another it passes sluggishly, in another more quickly. The progress of the blood through the body proving irregular, all kinds of irregularities occur. The whole body is torn in all directions; the parts of the body are shaken in obedience to the troubling and disturbance of the blood; distortions of every kind occur in every manner. At this point the patients are unconscious of everything—deaf to what is spoken, blind to what is happening, and insensible to pain. So greatly does a disturbance of the air disturb and pollute the blood. Foam naturally rises through the mouth. For the air, passing through the veins, itself rises and brings up with it the thinnest part of the blood. The moisture, mixing with the air, becomes white, for the air being pure is seen through the membranes. For this reason the foam appears completely white. When then will the victims of this disease rid themselves of their disorder? When the body exercised by its exertions has warmed the blood, and the blood thoroughly warmed has warmed the breaths, and these thoroughly warmed are dispersed, breaking up the congestion of the blood. The disease finally ends when the foam has frothed itself away, the blood has re-established itself, and calm has arisen in the body.[115]

Like other illnesses, epilepsy resulted from an imbalance between the four humors that constituted the human body. In particular, a seizure resulted when the brain was melted into phlegm and instead of being discharged from the body by means of the eyes, mouth, or nose it descended into the body and cooled in the veins. Once cooled, this phlegm disrupted the normal flow of air (breath) or blood. A seizure ceased after

---

115. Hippocrates *Breaths* 2.14.1–64, 2.4.118, 126, 128, 130, 132; Hippocrates *Air, Water, Places*, 2.3.22–23. Jones, "Introduction to *The Sacred Disease*," in *Hippocrates*, 2:133. Galen's *Consilium de Puero Epileptico*, which is extant in tenth-century Arabic. "He followed the Hippocratic School of Cos in counseling hygienic measures, careful feeding and occupation in treatment, and states that he had often seen the disease arrested by the occurrence of an attack of quartan fever." Temkin, *The Falling Sickness*, 26.

the blood had warmed, the congestion dissipated (seen by the foam in the sufferer's mouth), and balance between the humors was once again restored.[116] In fact, the title of Hippocrates' text, *The Sacred Disease*, is misleading, since he not only attempted to explain the 'sacred disease' in terms of physiological explanations but also attacked the idea that this illness was due to supernatural influences. In the very first line of *The Sacred Disease* he argued that this disease is no more divine than any other, but like all other illnesses had natural causes. In fact, it was only due to ignorance that people perceived it as being divine in origin.[117]

Apuleius' work is instructive of how these different perspectives of epilepsy overlapped in the Greco-Roman world. When Apuleius was accused of causing a slave boy to have an epileptic seizure by means of a magical incantation he mounted a threefold argument in his defense. First, he put forward the possibility that the boy may suffer from the 'sacred disease'. Second, he raised the question that someone else may be responsible for casting a curse upon the child. And finally, he seems to rest most of his defense on a naturalistic view of the disease. The boy's affliction was caused by "the overflowing of ... pestilential humour into the head." Therefore he recommended that the boy "needs a doctor rather than a magician."[118] Apuleius seemed to have little trouble shifting back and forth between a naturalistic to supernatural (benign or malevolent) cause and view of this illness. With the exception of Hippocrates and Gallen, who argued for only one perspective, Apuleius' views are probably representative of the vast majority within the Roman Empire. "The disease might have been called sacred because a deity had sent it, or because a demon had been thought to enter the patient, or because it attacked those who had sinned against *Selene*, the goddess of the moon," or because, "its cure was not human but divine."[119]

---

116. Hippocrates *The Sacred Disease* 147.2.159–63.

117. Hippocrates *The Sacred Disease* 147.2.139–41; Levy, "Epilepsy," in Kiple, *Cambridge World History of Human Disease*, 717.

118. Apuleius also records for us the ostracism that epileptics suffered from in Greco-Roman society. "Nobody dares to eat with him [Thallus] from the same dish or to drink from the same cup, and it is even suspected that he has been sent away lest he contaminate the family." Apuleius, *Apologia,* 43; Kee, *Medicine, Miracle and Magic,* 98; Temkin, *The Falling Sickness*, 8–9.

119. Temkin, *The Falling Sickness*, 7.

As the church spread from its Palestinian roots to the broader Roman Empire, the semiotic correlations and network of beliefs in Greco-Roman culture became part of the semiotic framework by which the boy's affliction in Matthew 17 was read. Jewish concerns about eugenics, religious purity, and participation in the religious life of Israel faded to the background and questions about demon possession or the effects of the moon on the humors in the brain came to the forefront for Matthew's readers.

Origen's Debate about the Moon

Origen was one of the first great expositors of the Bible in the church. From around AD 200 until 254 he served as a leader of the church, theologian, biblical scholar, apologist, and preacher in Alexandria. His work on Matthew not only represents one of the earliest preserved commentaries but was seen as an authoritative work up to and during the Reformation.[120] "Both the quality and the quantity of Origen's critical scholarship were enormously in advance of his contemporaries."[121] In regard to the question of the boy's affliction in Matthew 17, Origen directly engaged the presuppositions that readers in the early church inherited from their culture and brought with them to their reading of the text. It is for these reasons that we now turn our attention to his work on Matthew 17.[122]

Origen's discussion centered on what he considered two very important misconceptions his contemporaries held when they read this Matthew 17. While he acknowledged that the Greek term σεληνιά–ζαται was etymologically derived from the σελήνη (moon) he warned that one must not make the mistake of associating the source of this ailment with the moon. Magicians and heretics, such as Celsus, erred in that they attributed divine characteristics to the heavenly bodies, some

120. Eusebius records that Origen wrote his commentary on Matthew when he was sixty years old. Eusebius *Ecclesiastical History* 253.

121. Wiles, "Origen as Biblical Scholar," 1:461.

122. In section five of his commentary on Matthew, Origen presents an allegorical interpretation of this passage and what it means to be 'moon-struck.' However, due to space constraints I am going to limit my questions to section six where he proceeds with a more literal interpretation of Matthew 17.

of which affect our lives in a malevolent manner, such as the moon, and others in a benevolent manner.[123]

Teachings along this line had to be completely rejected by the believer according to Origen. The sun, moon, and stars were created by God and subject to the same conditions as the rest of creation. At the same time, Origen cited several biblical passages that related how the moon, along with all the other heavenly bodies, participated with the rest of creation in giving praise to God. Therefore he concluded that, "No star formed by the God of the universe" could ever work evil. The physicians erred on the flip side of the coin. While they denied that the moon exercised any form of spiritual influence, it still afflicted the child through natural means; "the moist nature in the head being moved in sympathy with the light of the moon."[124] Both the magicians and the doctors slandered God's created order when they attributed the cause of this condition to the moon.[125]

Contrary to these views, Origen claimed that the true nature of the boy's sickness should be clear to anyone who believed in the gospel. The boy was possessed by an "unclean and dumb spirit."[126] However, he could not completely deny the role which the moon played in this condition. Therefore, Origen hypothesized that the impure spirit which caused the seizures carefully observed the phases of the moon in order to deceive those who observed the boy's suffering, so that they would attribute its cause to the moon.[127]

The influence of Origen's interpretation of this passage on his contemporaries and those who followed him is reflected in a homily on

123. Origen *Contra Celsus* 5.7. For an example of how the god of the moon or the sun may afflict someone, see Boudreaux, *Codicum Parisinorum*, 156.5–11.

124. Origen *In Mattheium* 13.6, in *Matthäuserklärung*, my translation; Origen *Contra Celsus* 5.13.

125. Origen's argument that this illness was not governed by the moon was based on his opposition to Gnostic teachings, especially Celsus, that taught that the planets influenced human life on earth and were connected with the soul's ascent in the next life. These ideas originated in Persian, Mithraic, and Stoic sources, not the Christian Scriptures. Origen *Contra Celsum* 6.19–23.

126. "ἀπὸ πνεύματος ἀκαθάρτου, ἀλάλου . . ." Origen appears to have harmonized Mark 9:17 and Luke 9:42 with Matthew 17 in his description of the spirit which was oppressing the boy. Origen, *In Mattheium*, 13.6.

127. Origen *In Mattheium* 13.6

Matthew 17 by John Chrysostom. His reading of this passage follows his predecessors almost point by point.

> For the evil spirit, to bring a reproach upon nature, both attacks them that are seized, and lets them go, according to the courses of the moon; not as though that were the worker of it;—away with the thought—but himself craftily doing this to bring a reproach on nature. And an erroneous opinion hath gotten ground among the simple, and by this name do they call such evil spirits, being deceived; for this is no means true.[128]

While not every interpreter followed Origen's exegesis, his interpretation set the pattern for how this boy's affliction would be read for over one thousand years, including many of the most influential theologians during that period.[129]

By the time of Calvin, Hippocrates and Galen's view, which attributed epilepsy to the lunar phases, had reemerged to become the dominant view in medieval medical practices. The explanation that the moon governed the boy's illness in Matthew 17 was a fact proven by experience for Calvin.[130]

> The term lunatic [*Lunatici*] is applied to those who, about the waning of the moon, are seized with epilepsy [*comitiali morbo*], or afflicted with giddiness. I do not admit the fanciful notion of Chrysostom, that the word lunatic was invented by a trick of Satan, in order to throw disgrace on the good creatures of God; for we learn from undoubted experience [*docet enim certa experientia*], that the course of the moon affects the increase or decline of these diseases. And yet this does not prevent Satan from mixing up his attacks with natural means. I am of opinion, therefore, that the man was not naturally deaf and dumb, but that Satan had taken possession of his tongue and ears; and

128. Chrysostom *Homilies on Matthew* 57.3.

129. This appears to have been a wide spread view among church officials and the populace as well during the Medieval period. Lennox, *Epilepsy*, 1038–39. One of the better known exceptions to a demonic interpretation of this passage is that of St. Basil, who believed that the phases of the moon exerted great influence upon all living things. Because the moon's light emitted moisture that penetrated everything on which it shone, it had a powerful effect on the brain. Evidence of this could be seen in how quickly fresh meat went rancid under a full moon. "Evidently the moon must be, as Scripture says, of enormous size and power to make all nature thus participate in her changes." St. Basil, *Hexaemeron*, Homily 6, "The Creation of Luminous Bodies."

130. Nutton, "From Galen to Alexander," 38.1–14; Temkin, *Galenism*.

> that, as the weakness of his brain and nerves made him liable
> to epilepsy [*cerebri et nervorum debilitas eum morbo comitiali
> obnoxium*], Satan availed himself of this for aggravating the
> disease.[131]

Chrysostom and Origen's argument that a demon was mimicking the phases of the moon was rejected in favor of the prevailing medical paradigm of his day.[132] This also allowed Calvin to synthesize a natural diagnosis with a spiritual one. Because it was believed that certain individuals were susceptible to the phases of the moon due to mental or nervous debilities Calvin postulated that a demon took advantage of this same constitutional weakness and aggravated the boy's condition by rendering him deaf and dumb.

A quick survey of commentators from the Reformation until 1900 reveals that most followed a trajectory of interpretation very similar to Calvin's reading of the boy's affliction. At the turn of the eighteenth century, Matthew Henry defined a lunatic as "one whose distemper lies in the brain, and returns with the changes in the moon."[133] Like Calvin he believed that a demon exacerbated the child's condition. One hundred years later Adam Clarke reflected the perseverance of this interpretation. The child's illness was the result of the phases of the moon upon those who were "more sensible to these variations."[134] This reading of the boy's infirmity was the norm until 1902 when William Alexander published his study on *Demon Possession in the New Testament*. While he takes a more nuanced approach to epilepsy as a disease (distinguishing between epilepsy and epileptic insanity) he still concluded that the

131. Calvin, *Commentary on a Harmony*, 2:322; Latin added from *In Harmoniam*, 2:124.

132. "Nor do I accept the imagination of Chrysostom that Satan invented this name (*lunaticus* or *comitiali morbo*) as a trick to spray (throw) disgrace on the good creation: for we are taught by the sureness of experience (*docet enim certa experientia*) that the course of the moon increases or decreases these diseases." Calvin, *In Harmoniam*, 2:124, 1:127, translation mine; see *Commentary on a Harmony*, 2:322, 1:245.

133. Henry, *An Exposition of the Old and New Testaments*, 5:197.

134. Clarke, *The Holy Bible . . . With a Commentary*, 3:178. Benson is another example who sees the illness stemming from the moon's influence being compounded by a demon taking advantage of this neurological weakness. Benson, *The New Testament . . . with . . . Notes*, 1:151.

"bright moonlight of the Orient . . . has an exciting effect on those afflicted with epileptic insanity."[135]

The diagnosis and treatment someone suffering from epileptic seizures would have received at the best hospitals in Europe and North America would have been very similar to that practiced by Hippocrates and Galen until the last quarter of the nineteenth century. It was not until Samuel Wilks (1824–1911) demonstrated that potassium bromide could be used to control seizures that Hipporcratic approaches for treating epilepsy were replaced with modern medical treatments. Shortly before World War I, Phenobarbital (invented in 1912) was proven by Alfred Hauptmann to be more effective at controlling the patient's seizures with less side effects than potassium bromide. Not until the invention of the electroencephalograph in 1929 did anyone understand the relationship between the cascading effect of neurological signals and epileptic seizures.[136] The result of these discoveries and other medical advances in the treatment of epilepsy has been nothing less than an entire paradigm shift in how we perceive this affliction today from those just over one hundred years ago.

What was clearly obvious to Calvin about this boy's condition strikes most modern readers as anything but that. I find it particularly insightful that William Pringle, a contemporary translator of Calvin's *Harmony of the Evangelists*, felt compelled to include a footnote when he translated Calvin's comments on the use of σεληνιάζαται in Matthew 4:24. Views such as those held by Calvin reflected superstitious beliefs that had been dispelled by advances in scientific knowledge. "The term *seléniazomenoi*, in this and similar passages, does not imply, that the sacred writers supported the common opinion, any more than the English word lunatic . . . countenances an exploded theory . . ."[137]

When a modern commentator discusses the Greek term σεληνιά—ζαται in Matthew 17:15, her understanding of what the boy is suffering from is almost unanimously in favor of our contemporary medical understanding of epilepsy.[138] John Wilkinson's article, "The Case of the

135. Alexander, *Demonic Possession*, 64; see also 81–88 for his discussion of Matthew 17.

136. Lennox, *Epilepsy*, 1:23–32.

137. In Calvin, *Commentary on a Harmony*, 1:245 n. 1. Others include Wilkinson, "The Case of the Epileptic Boy," 40–42.

138. Kee, *Medicine, Miracles, and Magic*, 50; Blomberg, *The Historical Reliability of the Gospels*, 88.

Epileptic Boy," typifies our contemporary understanding of this passage. Using a redactional approach to Matthew 17, Mark 9, and Luke 9 he constructs a medical history of the boy's condition (its onset, progress, and symptoms) that leads to a diagnosis of epilepsy.[139] Wilkinson reads every indictor of the boy's suffering mentioned by the evangelists in light of the modern medical paradigm for epilepsy. Matthew's use of σεληνιάζαται is dismissed because it implies "that the fits came every month, but we cannot be certain since the word probably embodies a superstition rather than accurate observation."[140]

However, the same manifestations of the boy's suffering recorded in the gospel accounts were not overlooked or ignored by Calvin or Origen, and they clearly arrived at very different appraisals of the situation than Wilkinson. The early church fathers clearly perceived this to be an instance that demonstrated either demonic possession or the baleful influence of the moon. Origen and Chrysostom countered that to attribute this to the moon was to blasphemy God's creation; therefore, it must be an instance of demonic oppression. By the time of Calvin, medical science had attributed this ailment to the influences of the moon on the weakness of the nervous system. Today we see a neurological condition that is not related to the lunar phases or demonic influence. Language determines, to a large extent, what we will actually see in the text.

This short study demonstrates three benefits from examining the history of a text's reception. First, in doing so, the twists and turns in the semiotic code provoke our prejudices (or linguistic background) which cause us to question the validity of our present understanding and semiotic code. Second, past interpretations present us with different perspectives on the text (new ways to look at the picture, as Wittgenstein would say). They present us with hermeneutical resources that allow us to grasp more possibilities for the disclosive potential of the text. To interpret the healing of the boy in Matthew 17 from a medical perspective negates many of the nuances in the passage concerning Jesus' authority, his work of redeeming a fallen race, and the story's relationship with the previous pericope concerning Jesus' transfiguration (for example, Matthew's record that Jesus face shone like the sun in 17:2 should most

139. Wilkinson, 39–41.
140. Ibid., 40.

likely be read in conjunction with the boy being struck by the moon). And finally, it demonstrates how reading the Bible involves a complex interaction between the text, the reader and his or her language, culture, and tradition. As such, it affords us a glimpse into how the questions, methods, practices, and criteria internal to the practice of biblical inter-pretation have undergone paradigm shifts in regard to Matthew 17:15 over the past two thousand years.

7

The Summit-Dialogue of Authors and the Reception of the Wedding Feast

ONE OF THE CONTRIBUTIONS THAT HANS ROBERT JAUSS MADE TO RECEP-
tion theory that has been overlooked in the theological appropriations
of his work has been his concept of the "summit-dialogue" of authors.
The conscious appropriation and reassessment of a predecessor's work
plays a significant role in the formation of a literary tradition since
this is the level at which an active and reflective conversation within a
tradition occurs. The goal of this chapter is to explore the appropriateness of the concept of a "summit-dialogue" of authors for biblical and
theological hermeneutics. The first section of this chapter will attempt
to summarize a few key points of Jauss's thought on this concept. The
second section will explore its relevance for biblical studies by way of a
case study on the reception history of the parable of the Wedding Feast
(Matthew 22:1–14).

Jauss's "summit-dialogue"

The English term "summit-dialogue" is translated from two German
terms Jauss uses almost interchangeably when referring to this concept.
The first is *der Gipfeldialog der Autoren,* or the summit or peak dialogue of authors. The second is *der Höhenkamm der Autoren*, and can
be translated as the mountain ridge, or highest ridge, or highest level
of authors.[1] Living in Colorado, I find the image of the rise and fall of
a mountain ridge helpful when trying to grasp his use of these terms.
The peaks that protrude above the rest form the distinctive backbone of
a range and correspond to the authors or readings that define or shape

---

1. See Jauss, *"Der Leser,"* 326–40.

the history of a text's reception. Jauss observed how certain authors represent "peaks" or significant points the reception history of Augustine's work.

> Pascal as a reader of Montaigne, Rousseau as a reader of Augustine, Lévi-Strauss as a reader of Rousseau are examples for the summit level of dialogue between authors. The dialogue between authors becomes significant (*Epoche-machen*) in a literary-historical sense through the appropriation and reassessment of the predecessor, who was recognized as being significant.[2]

From the perspective of the researcher, the summit-dialogue is significant for three reasons. The first is obvious; this is the level where the defining moments of a tradition's contours are located. The peaks, or high points, represent the more significant interpreters because of the impact they had on their contemporaries, the influence they exerted on later readers, or their innovative interpretation that was retrospectively recognized and accepted into the canon of exemplary commentators. The conscious appropriation and reassessment of a predecessor's work plays a significant role in the formation of an interpretive tradition since this is the level at which an active and reflective conversation within a tradition occurs.

In his essay, "The Dialogical and the Dialectical *Neveu de Rameau*: How Diderot Adopted Socrates and Hegel Adopted Diderot,"[3] Jauss attempted to demonstrate how Diderot and Hegel represent peaks in the tradition of Socratic interpretations. Diderot revived the openness of the Socratic dialogue in contrast to the philosophical monologism of the Enlightenment. The primary literary device that Diderot employed was through the two characters *Moi* (me) and *Lui* (he). In *Neveu de Rameau* the reader's expectations are subverted in that the teacher, *Moi*, finds himself challenged and questioned by the immoral musician, *Lui*, who is portrayed in a manner that recalls the figure of Socrates. Hegel adopted Diderot's use of *Moi* and *Lui* but reversed their positions once again. This time they represent the "honest" and "disrupted conscious-

---

2. "*Pascal als Leser Montaignes, Rousseau als Leser Augustins, Le'vi-Strauss als Leser Rousseaus sind Beispiele für die Gipfelebene eines Dialogs von Autoren, der mit der Aneignung und Umbewertung des als entscheidend erkannten Vorgängers literarhistorisch Epoche machen kann.*" Ibid., 336.

3. See also Jauss, *Question and Answer*, 118–47.

ness" respectively.[4] At the same time, Hegel reintroduced a latent Platonic impulse in Diderot's thought with his introduction of a third element, the dialectical resolution between the two characters. Hegel's interpretation of Diderot would not have been "adequate" in France before 1774, but was appropriate within the context of German idealism thirty years later. Each author opened new folds in the meaning of Plato's Socratic dialogues, and therefore belongs to the "summit-dialogue" of authors in the reception history of Plato's work.

Second, the summit-dialogue preserves the interpretive questions and answers that were considered valid from various historical periods. These accepted questions and answers served as boundary markers for the hermeneutical playing field for what counted as valid readings of a text during those time frames. These "peak" works demonstrate the influence and normative function that a particular reading of a text can exercise. Not every reading of a biblical text is received equally within a tradition. Some readings are found to be more productive for the practices of the Christian community at that time, whether for the sake of theological reflection, art, or explicating the meaning of the text.

According to Stephen Holmes, certain theologians have been historically recognized in the Christian tradition "as outstanding examples of how to think through the way in which God's all-sufficient gift of his Son is sufficient to meet the needs of a particular age or circumstance."[5] He terms these outstanding interpreters the "doctors" of the church. As such, a doctor is someone who the church has found to be particularly insightful in explicating the biblical text and the implications of the gospel for their particular historical context in a manner that is not restricted to their horizon but is significant for successive historical horizons as well. As a result, their writings are recognized as major resources for theological study.[6] For example, Luther's exposition of Romans 1:17 became one of the focal points of interpretative debate within the Christian tradition and helped to set in motion one of the most defining turning points in Christian history, the Reformation. Luther's reading disclosed a fold in the potential meaning of Romans 1:17 that was

---

4. Jauss noted that Diderot was the only author that Hegel quoted in *Phenomenology of the Spirit*. Hegel included three lengthy quotes from Diderot at crucial junctions in his discussion of the consciousness. Jauss, "The Dialogical and the Dialectical," 19–25.

5. Holmes, *Listening to the Past*, 28–29.

6. Ibid., 33, 156.

particularly provocative in his historical and cultural context. As such, his work underwent the process of reception whereby his reading of the text was acknowledged by others, accepted into the canon of exemplary commentators, and sanctioned by various cultural and ecclesiastical institutions. Whether we agree with his reading of Romans or not, his interpretation continues to present us with questions and answers that define what we count as an appropriate reading of Romans today. However, the summit-dialogue is not populated solely by the work of commentaries and theological treatises. Homilies, lectionaries, hymns, and artwork can serve as one of the defining points in a biblical text's reception history.[7]

Third, a disproportionate percentage of the best evidence that has been historically preserved for how a passage has been interpreted, taught and applied is located at the summit-dialogue level. One of the lamentable effects of history is that we preserve the "events and developments on the grand scale . . . and ignoring what has sometimes been called the history of 'ordinary life.'"[8] A vast amount of material has been lost or forgotten in the history of biblical interpretation. At the same time, we cannot overlook the sheer quantity of material which has accumulated over two thousand years; much of this at the institutional level in the form of homilies, theological treatises, and commentaries, as well as paintings, sculpture, music (e.g., Handel's *Messiah*), and other forms of literature (such as Milton's *Paradise Lost*). Given the overwhelming amount of material that has been preserved that either comments on the Bible or was inspired by it, our primary consideration, in many instances, should be given to the most influential interpretations. This is especially true if we only have a limited amount of time to invest in this type of study.

Fourth, the summit-dialogue often preserves and reveals the major defining points in an interpretive tradition. It is at this level that new disclosures in meaning or paradigm shifts for how a text is read are initiated.

---

7. Jauss, "*Der Leser*," 336.

8. As a result much of the effect and influence of the biblical texts and their commentaries on the church and society "is probably beyond recovery, and what little I can offer in this regard must remain anecdotal, at best suggestive of a vast iceberg submerged beneath the waves of history." Bochmuehl, "A Commentator's Approach," 66.

> Such changes are first felt socially in books, if the innovative understanding of the individual reader is publicly acknowledged, received in the academic canon of model authors or is sanctioned by cultural institutions. At the middle level of institutionalized reading the norm-violating power of the literature is weakened and transposed into norm-forming functions.[9]

However, what one generation of readers perceive as productive, stimulating, or provocative cannot be guaranteed to provoke the prejudices of the next generation. Each generation of readers does not blindly follow the aesthetic norms of their teachers or parents. What the next generation of readers find interesting arises from their horizon of expectations and can strike them equally at a pre-reflective or reflective level of reading.

One of the primary traits a work will possess if it considered a member of the summit-dialogue is what Jauss terms its "strength." The strength of a reading can be related to how that particular interpretation solves problems that previous interpretive paradigms could not resolve. At the same time, a strong interpretation does not necessarily need to negate or be novel, or have a great author; the 'strength' of a reading depends upon its reception. Not every interpretation is of equal value for reception studies, "but only those which I would call, along with my Konstanz colleagues, 'publicly recognized concretizations' or, if you like, strong interpretations. Strong does not depend on the originality of the interpreter but on being recognized by other readers."[10]

In our contemporary horizon the decision to publish a manuscript, and its reception in the popular press, is often based on whether it says something innovative or provocative. A new interpretation of the life of Jesus based on an obscure papyri gets more attention than a well researched and written text that affirms the orthodox teachings of the church. However, Jauss argues this is not always the case when it comes to summit-dialogue or strong interpretations. Productive receptions of a text do not depend on the author's originality, or how a work negates our expectations, but is also related to how it affirms or fulfills the norms of its readers.[11]

9. Jauss, "*Der Leser*" 336.

10. Jauss, "The Dialogical and the Dialectical," 60

11. Jauss argues against Adorno at this point (who denied that there were affirming genres and texts). "The Dialogical and the Dialectical," 63. A second point of clarifica-

The summit-dialogue is one of the means by which continuity is retrospectively created within a tradition. In regard to the previous point, Jauss attempts to walk a fine line. When Jauss writes about the potential for continuity within a tradition we should not read that as a static concept of continuity. Because the strength of any interpretation is based on its reception by successive generations of readers, once a text has been recognized as a member of the summit-dialogue there is no guarantee that it has permanent residency there. As long as a particular work is recognized by its readers as presenting a strong interpretation it will most likely continue to function at the level of the summit-dialogue. However, if the readers no longer perceive it as answering the questions they are asking then this text may find itself subject to the leveling power of tradition and relegated to a dark shelf in that tradition's library. As a result, the summit-dialogue is a heuristic tool that allows us to identify the competing trajectories of interpretation and at the same time observe the history of mediation within that tradition that creates continuity.

Principles for Tracing a Summit-Dialogue

The primary principle that Jauss advocates when researching the history of a text's effects is that we must not approach the task mechanically but comprehend it as part of the mediation process that occurs through the fusion of horizons. In order to accomplish this we must give consideration to both the text and its reception by readers.[12] Because a literary tradition is not characterized by a free play between texts and authors there is material that we can use for investigating a text's reception history. The primary avenue that Jauss pursues in this regard is through the logic of question and answer. This tradition-constituted conversa-

---

tion concerns the relationship of a summit-dialogue to a literary cannon or anti-canon. When he refers to a summit-dialogue, Jauss should not be understood as advocating a monological canon of accepted texts that determine a tradition. At any given point in time there will be competing trajectories of interpretation. These dialogues can occur at the level of genre, interpretations, and literary cannons. This is another area where Jauss feels significant research in literary history is needed. "The opposition between genre and anti-genre, canon and license, continuity and discontinuity is basic to the history of European Art and Literature, but till now a neglected field of research." Ibid. And thus, by extension, there is the very real possibility that the reception history for any given biblical passage could be composed of multiple summit-dialogues.

12. Jauss, *"Der Leser,"* 337–39.

tion is only activated when a later reader "reopens it by recognizing an earlier author as his predecessor, and by finding those questions of his own that lead beyond the answers provided by this 'source.'"[13] What we can learn of the readers' horizon of expectations at both the level of the prejudices that a reader brings and the institutional norms of the second level help to refine and illuminate what we can glean from the summit-dialogue of authors.[14]

The Reception of the Parable of the Wedding Feast: Origen, Augustine, Aquinas and Calvin

The *Wirkungsgeschichte* of Matthew 22:1–14, the parable of the Wedding Feast, presents an illustrative and illuminative case study for the practice of reception theory in biblical studies. This chapter is not intended to serve as a definitive or exhaustive history of the interpretation of the parable of the Wedding Feast in Matthew 22, nor is it intended to function as a proof for reception theory. Rather, I hope to demonstrate the relevance of reception theory by examining certain facets of this text's history of interpretation from the Patristic period up to and including Calvin's commentary on the parable.[15]

This parable was chosen for several reasons. First, because parables are largely fictional or internally representative by nature, they are closer to Jauss's concern with literary or poetical forms of texts. Second, the fictional or internally representative nature of parables has the potential for greater polyvalency in meaning than a text that is more didactic,

13. Jauss, *Question and Answer*, 54.

14. But also for that reason it is not purely intuitive, if one means by this a supposedly hermeneutic model of a subjective point of view, sympathetic interpretation and tradition bound sense of understanding. Rather through a method/procedure, which gives up the false opposition between empiricism and hermeneutics separate, by/of examining the process of aesthetic experience in the light of reflection concerning the hermeneutic conditions of these experiences. Jauss, *Der Leser,* 328, my notes and translation.

15. Perhaps the argument for this chapter could be made stronger if the flow of the chapter were to proceed from the most recent interpretations to the oldest. To ask, why did Calvin interpret this parable in the manner that he did and then look for evidence that lead him to read the parable in this manner. However, taking this approach would have limited the number and scope of the questions that could be raised in this chapter. For alternate ways this study could have been organized, see Parris, *Reading the Bible with the Giants*, 191–214.

historical, or externally representative in nature. Because a parable possesses greater potential for a wider range of interpretations, hopefully it will demonstrate the usefulness of reception theory in a more transparent manner. This latitude in the play of interpretation allows exegetes' prejudices to not only influence how they read the text but at the same time hopefully allow us to discern the nature of these prejudices.[16] And third, I have selected this particular parable because there is not a large amount of literature written on it compared to some of the other parables, such as the Good Samaritan.[17] At the same time, this parable touches on several important theological issues such as the Gentile mission, the eschatological judgment, and invitation to salvation. As such, the norm-forming potential of this parable appears to be considerable.

Limitations in the Field of Play: Early Trajectories of Interpretation

Even though the allegorical method was the most widely used to interpret the parables in church history, ever since Adolf Jülicher modern exegetes have mercilessly criticized it for producing misunderstandings of the text.[18] Jülicher's book, *Die Gleichnissreden Jesu*, is credited with initiating the paradigm shift from the allegorical to the historical-critical method in order to determine the "original and proper meaning of the parables."[19] One of the common complaints that modern theologians

16. "Norman Perrin has pointed out that there is perhaps no plainer example of the exegete's presuppositions affecting their exegesis than in the parables. Here one's theological position, fundamental concerns, and methodological presuppositions can play a surprisingly large role in the way in which the parables are finally understood." Kissinger, *The Parables of Jesus*, xvii–xviii.

17. Some of the more detailed studies on this parable can be found in Beare, "The Parable of the Guests at the Banquet," 1–14; Funk, *Language, Hermeneutics and Word of God*, 163–98; Linnemann, "*Überlegungen zur Parabel vom grossen Abendmahl*," 246–55; Trilling, "*Zur Überlieferungsgeschichte des Gleichnisses vom Hochzeitsmahl Mt 22.1–15*," 251–65; and Trench, *Notes on the Parables*, 219–47.

18. James Barr ascribes this prejudice against allegorical method of interpretation to the widely held view that allegorical correspondences are by nature non-historical and thus as a method it is held "to be entirely or almost entirely invalid." Barr, *Old and New in Interpretation*, 103–4. The idea that the parables were not originally allegories when Jesus taught them is a view which has been widely adopted as a result of Jülicher's work and has been debated in recent times. Blomberg, *Interpreting the Parables*, 15–19.

19. Kissinger, *The Parables of Jesus*, xiii; Hunter, *Interpreting the Parables*, 38; Little, "Parable Research in the Twentieth Century I," 357.

raise against the allegorical method concerns the way they believe that during the Patristic period the biblical text was reduced to a pre-text into which the allegorist read his preconceptions to make it mean anything he wanted.[20]

More recently, allegory has come under criticism from a more sophisticated biblical hermeneutic. The question no longer concerns whether a parable contains one point or moral, as Jülicher argued, or is open to multiple levels of meanings which the allegorists tended to find. Rather, the problem now revolves around the manner by which a parable projects a "narrative world." The allegorical method is chastised for fracturing this projected world into a collection of theological truths. It approaches a parable as a source of propositional truths or intertextual references and misses the projected world into which the reader or hearer is meant to enter.[21]

From the perspective of reception theory, the allegorical method of interpretation is significant for that fact that the interpreter is concerned with applying the text to his audience's situation. In this sense, the competing schools of Alexandria, which focused on the *sensus allegoricus,* and Antioch, with its emphasis on the *sensus litteralis,* shared a common goal: "the transposition of the canonical text . . . out of its historical past and into the present; rendering it not only understandable, but also, so to speak, up-to-date."[22] The school at Antioch tried to save the author's original meaning encoded in the text by translating it into a form that was understandable in the present. In Alexandria they did not set aside the literal meaning, but sought "to interpret the text for the recipient's changed situation in such a way that the new spiritual meaning is still justified as an adaptation of the old, literal meaning."[23] Jauss views both of these positions as two sides of the same coin. Both attempt to form the same link between the reader and the text, but one is more reconstructive by nature and the other more applied.

---

20. Louth, *Discerning the Mystery,* 96–97. Louth attributes the modern attitude towards allegory to the prejudices that theology inherited from the Enlightenment. These prejudices include the search for an objective meaning in a text through the use of methods, the Romantic concept of meaning located in the reconstruction of the author's intentions, and the attempt to break free from tradition. Ibid., 98–107.

21. Via, *The Parables,* 4, 25–42, 79–87.

22. Jauss, "Limits and Tasks of Literary Hermeneutics," 98.

23. Jauss, "The Theory of Reception," 55.

The diversity of interpretations offered during the Patristic period provides fertile ground to test the applicability of various hermeneutical aspects of reception theory to this form of biblical genre. However, the diversity of interpretation during the Patristic period begins to coalesce into a few distinct trajectories or traditions of interpretation. While it is not possible to label a particular interpretation according to only one particular trajectory because these trajectories often overlap each other, the following three trajectories of interpretation are offered as a means of classification and in order to help facilitate the discussion in the first section of this chapter.

A. Polemical-theological interpretation: Does the father who invites the guests to the feast in the parable represent a God who is both gracious and judgmental?
B. Kerygmatic or Ethnic-Ethical interpretation: How do the invited guests and their responses to the invitation represent different types of people and their relationship to salvation?
C. Soteriological interpretation: What is the significance of the wedding garment for the life and salvation of the Christian?

Polemical-Theological Interpretation

Various Gnostic interpreters, the Valentinians in particular, appealed to the parables in order to substantiate their doctrines.[24] Irenaeus clearly realized that the various parables and metaphors in the New Testament were open to the "crafty manipulations" of Gnostic teachers who forced the meaning of the text to reflect their theological position.[25] In response to this, Irenaeus and Origen argued that this parable should be understood as presenting the orthodox doctrine that there was one God who both saved and exercised judgment. Thus, when read correctly, the parable of the Wedding Feast contradicted Valentinian teachings that

---

24. For example, the Valentinians interpreted the symbolism of the numbers one, three, six, nine and eleven in the parable of the 'Workers in the Vineyard' (Matthew 20:1–16) as symbolizing the thirty aeons of the Pleroma since the sum of these numbers totaled thirty. Irenaeus, *Adverses Haereses*, 1.1.3 (*PG* 7.467–70; Harvey, 1.16–20). See also Tertullian, *Liber de Anima*, 18 (*PL* 15.449–54), for his refutation of the Valentinian interpretation of the parable of the 'Ten Virgins' (Matthew 25:1–13) to show that the intellect is not above or higher than the bodily senses and what we learn through them.

25. Irenaeus, *Adversus Haerses*, 1.3.6 (*PG* 7.467–70; Harvey, 1.16–20); Young, *Biblical Exegesis*, 19–20. Margerie, *An Introduction to the History of Exegesis*, 1.52–53.

the Old Testament and the New Testament spoke of two different gods. While Irenaeus did not mention the Valentinians directly, his concern to refute their teachings is clearly seen in the first lines of his exposition of this parable. "For he makes known through these his words, the Lord clearly declared all, that there is one king and Lord of all, the Father."[26] This theme runs through his explanation of the parable in the character of the father who prepared the wedding feast for his son, invited everyone, burnt the city of those who killed his messengers, and cast the guest without the wedding garment into the outer darkness. In particular, the action of the father casting the guest without the wedding garment into the outer darkness demonstrates that the same Lord that invites us to salvation also exercises judgment.[27]

Origen specifically addressed the Valentinian heresy that the God portrayed as judgmental in the Old Testament and the God of the New Testament were two different beings.[28] The fact that the king in the parable is portrayed as good (he invites all to the feast he has prepared) and just (he destroys the cities of those who killed his servants) confirms that God possesses both of these traits (mercy and righteousness) without contradiction, according to Origen. Thus, God is the same God in both Old and New Testaments. In his comments on Matthew 22:1–14, Origen picked up this line of argument at several points.[29] He asked, "What does this mean to you? Is the one who gets angry the same as the one preparing the feast for his son, the father of Christ, or is the one who gets angry different from his father?"[30] For Origen, the an-

26. "*Manifeste enim et per haec verba sua ostendit Dominus omnia, et quoniam unus rex et Dominus omnium Pater.*" Irenaeus, *Adversus Haereses,* 4.58.5 (PG 7.1095; Keble, 426). The idea that the same God is at work in both Testaments is one of the distinctive elements of Irenaeus' exegesis. Margerie, 1.53, 56.

27. Margerie, 1.53, 56.

28. Origen, *De principiis*, 5.2 (Butterworth, 101–3). According to Valentinian teachings, the God of the Old Testament was a demiurge while in the New Testament, we see redemption accomplished through the "aeon" of Christ who united himself with the man Jesus to bring the knowledge (gnosis) of salvation to mankind. The best Christian sources on Valentinianism are found in Irenaeus, *Adverses Haereses*, 1 and 3.4, and Tertullian, *Adverses Valentianos*. These and other documents on the Valentinians are collected in Foerster, *Gnosis: A Selection of Gnostic Texts*, especially 121–243.

29. Like Irenaeus, he does not mention the Valentinians by name in this section of his commentary but his attack on their theology corresponds with the same criticism he makes against them in *Commentary on Matthew,* 10.12, and *De principiis*.

30. Origen, *In Mattheium*, 17.18 (G.C.S. 10.637). A partial English translation of this parable is available in Smith, *Ante-Nicene Exegesis of the Gospels*, 21–25.

swer lies in the manner in which God accommodates himself to our understanding through anthropomorphisms and anthropopathism. While we will never be able to fully understand God apart from such human analogies until our sins and weaknesses have been done away with at the resurrection of the dead, we can still understand the deeper truths of God that are taught through these anthropomorphisms. The king's action of sending his army to burn the city of those who rejected the invitation should not be taken as teaching that God is a vindictive judge. Rather, it is an analogy to help us to understand something of God's righteousness and judgment. Therefore, we should not interpret these anthropomorphisms literally, but see them as starting points to reveal deeper spiritual truths about God.[31]

The polemical-theological trajectory of interpretation, in particular its anti-Gnostic polemical interpretation, died off once the questions that the Valentinians raised were no longer being asked. In other words, Irenaeus and Origen's interpretations were, in part, answers to questions that arose through confrontations with Valentinian teachings. Once these questions were no longer being asked, we no longer see answers along this line being found by later commentators in the text.

KERYGMATIC OR ETHNIC-ETHICAL INTERPRETATION

The main questions addressed in this trajectory of interpretation are (1) the issue of the kingdom of God being taken from the Jews and given to the Gentiles, and (2) the interpretation of what the different characters' responses to the invitation might signify. These may appear distinct categories but the degree to which these two issues overlap in the exegesis of the parable makes such a distinction difficult and possibly pointless.

The first point to be noticed in this trajectory of interpretation is that it arises from the answers that were given in the polemical-theological trajectory. When Irenaeus argued that the parable taught that God was the same God in both Testaments, part of his argument was based on the idea that the first servants sent by the king to invite the guests to the feast referred to the prophets in the Old Testament and the

---

31. Origen, 17.18–19 (G.C.S. 10.635–40). One of the errors of the Valentinians was that they interpreted these anthropomorphisms at a literal level. Origen, *De principiis*, 4.2.1–2 (Butterworth, 267–73); Simonetti, *Biblical Interpretation in the Early Church*, 42.

servants who were sent later represented the apostles.[32] In doing so, he employed the typological form of interpretation practiced in the early church. This allowed Irenaeus to recognize that there was a continuity between the two Testaments implicit within the parable. The three groups of servants sent to invite the guests to the feast were understood allegorically as referring to how Jesus was spoken of by Moses in the Law, by the prophets, and finally proclaimed clearly by the apostles.[33] The questions that Valentinianism raised were answered by Irenaeus and Origen, who argued that this parable demonstrated, at an inferential level, that God was the same in both Testaments. This answer then leads on to questions concerning the relationship between the Jewish nation in the Old Testament and the Gentiles in the New Testament within the context of this parable. These are not totally new issues being raised but are genetically related by the logic of question and answer to the previous interpretations.

Perhaps the point of greatest consensus in the history of this parable's interpretation is the view that this parable teaches the replacement of the Jewish nation with the Gentiles as the recipients of the Kingdom of God. This reading was almost universally held throughout the history of the church. Even today it is difficult to find a reader who would not understand the parable in this manner, which is all the more surprising when we consider that there is nothing within the parable that explicitly makes this point.[34] The dominant impetus for this view arises from the manner by which the intertextual relationships within the Gospel of Matthew function to enable or restrict the range of play of understanding.[35] For Origen, these intertextual relationships played

32. Irenaeus, *Adversus Haereses*, 4.58.6 (*PG* 7.1095–96; Harvey, 2.281).

33. Ibid., 4.14.2–3, 4.26.1 (*PG* 7.1011–12; Harvey, 2.185–86); Simonetti, *Biblical Interpretation,* 19–22.

34. "Contrary to what one is often led to believe, one discovers that, even when the so-called 'criterion of dissimilarity' is applied to these parables (Mt. 22, Lk. 14), they are remarkably free of what is otherwise clearly known of an evangelist's or the early church's christology, soteriology (together, the kerygma), ecclesiology or view of missions." Lemcio, "The Parables of the Great Supper and the Wedding Feast," 8, 14.

35. For a fuller discussion of intertextuality, see "Thesis 2" in chapter 4. A quote from Jonathan Culler on the role of intertextuality helps us to understand this process and as a result why the concept of replacement is consistently recognized by the various interpreters in the parable of the Wedding Feast. "'Intertextuality' thus has a double focus. On the one hand, it calls our attention to the importance of prior texts, insisting that the autonomy of texts is a misleading notion and that a work has the meaning

a central role in his allegorical method of interpretation. "Origenist allegory was controlled by a view of scripture's unity and consistency which allowed the exploitation of texts from all over scripture to throw light on one another and build up a working-model of a spiritual world to which biblical images consistently referred."[36]

The parable of the 'Wedding Feast' is read in light of the preceding parable of the 'Wicked Tenants' (Matthew 21:33–41). Between these two parables, Matthew inserted the following statement, "Therefore I tell you, the kingdom of God will be taken away from you and given to a people that produces the fruits of the kingdom." (Matthew 21:43, RSV)[37] These intertextual references enable the reader to recognize a replacement theme in the parable of the Wedding Feast.[38] The manner in which Matthew has arranged and redacted his material shapes the competency of the reader to understand the parables through their successive relationship within the text. This is especially important if we

---

it does only because certain things have previously been written. Yet in so far as it focuses on intelligibility, on meaning, 'intertextuality' leads us to consider prior texts as contributions to a code which makes possible the various effects of signification." Culler, *Structuralist Poetics*, 104.

36. Young, *Biblical Exegesis and the Formation of the Christian Culture*, 152.

37. It is interesting to note though, is that none of the commentaries prior to the Reformation referred to Matthew 21:43 in order to defend the replacement concept. I think this is not only because of this verse's proximity to the parable but also because the same concept is taught at several other locations in the New Testament and was a widely held doctrine in the history of the church. Therefore, such a reading would seem obvious and natural and would not need justification. When other passages are cited to justify or explain the replacement theme they tend to be either Matthew 8:11–13 or Romans 2:13–16. Irenaeus appealed to Matthew 8:11–13 to show that "through the preaching of the apostles many from the east and the west shall believe in him and recline in the kingdom of heaven with Abraham and Isaac and Jacob, participating with them in the banquet. In this regard, we see one and the same God who first chose the patriarchs, visited his people, and then called the Gentiles." Irenaeus, *Adversus Haereses*, 4.58.10 (Harvey, 2.284–85). Jerome is one of the few who defended the replacement interpretation. For him, Romans 2:13–16 provides the reference to explain why the Jews were rejected at this point in the parable. "When the Gentiles do the law by nature, they condemn the Jews who do not follow the written law." Jerome, *Commentariorum in Mattheum*, 3.1694–1704 (C.C.S.L. 77.201).

38. Trilling makes the case even stronger by attempting to show that the two parables are structurally parallel to each other at several points such as Lord/King, rejection of servants, the transferal of the vineyard/invitation, destruction of the unworthy. Trilling, "Zur Überlieferungsgeschichte des Gleichnisses vom Hochzeitsmahl Mt 22,1–15," 254–57.

consider that texts were experienced in a linear fashion in the ancient world. As they were read aloud, the meaning of the text developed in the linear succession of its elements.[39]

This would seem to indicate that aspects of the reader's horizon of expectation which arise from 'intertextuality' are more stable over time than those aspects of the reader's horizon that arise from the prejudices which are handed down through the effective history of a tradition.[40] On the one hand, we must admit that in a purely semantic manner the text is fixed, and thus, stable in one sense, in that its message is inscribed and can be passed on to countless generations with little change. On the other hand, we must remember that Gadamer and others have shown that every time we understand a text, we understand it within our horizon, and thus, differently. What this particular instance indicates is that 'intertextuality' can in certain instances play a very strong role in stabilizing the meaning of the text across successive horizons of understanding.

Not only is the theme of replacement recognized in the parable, but some of the commentators also perceive a reason why this took place. This line of interpretation most likely sprang from the early church's confrontation with Judaism and served as an apologetic argument not only for God's rejection of Israel but also for his election of a new people, the Gentile church. According to Origen, the different reactions to the invitation represent the different divisions between human souls. Those who were first invited represent the noble Isaelites whom God fed with strong teachings in the Old Testament and who desired to come to the feast.[41] However, they were not willing to accept

39. The practice of reading aloud extended to reading in private also. Kennedy, *New Testament Interpretation through Rhetorical Criticism*, 5–6. This is especially important if we consider the 'linear' nature by which texts were read during that period as opposed to the manner by which we approach the Bible according to the individual sections today. "A text was a 'linear' reality, like a piece of music, its secrets gradually unveiled through time, as the performance unfolds, depending for the communication of shape on conventional forms, on repetition and allusion, on *mimêsis* (imitation) and on the consequent *anamêsis* (recollection) of themes, phrases, narratives, that have gone before." Young, *The Art of Performance*, 108.

40. For a discussion of the manner in which a text is inscribed and fixed as opposed to spoken discourse, see Ricœur, *Interpretation Theory*, 25–44.

41. I have translated "εὐγενῶν τινων ψυχῶν Ἰσραηλιτκῶν" as "noble souls of the Israelite's." This phrase appears to point to their special relationship with God as the children of his covenant in the Old Testament. Origen, *In Mattheium*, 17.22 (*G.C.S.* 10.644).

the invitation and as a result are guilty of rejecting the food God has to offer.[42] Chrysostom takes a similar line of thought but pushes the point much further. Both before and after the crucifixion, God attempted to persuade the people of Israel and to win them over. Their unwillingness to accept the invitation demonstrates an ungrateful attitude towards God's providential care for them. "What then could be more ungrateful then they, when being bidden to a marriage, and that of a King's marriage, and of a King making a marriage for his son?"[43] Not only that, but he interprets the parable as teaching that they are guilty of having killed the prophets, then killing the son (making an intertextual connection between this parable and the Wicked Tenants), and then refusing the invitation. Thus, according to Chrysostom, their response to the invitation reveals an escalation from the lesser crime of negligence to the greater crime of murder.

The responses of those who reject the invitation and abuse the servants leads to a prophetic statement concerning the destruction of the nation of Israel, which Chrysostom perceived as having been historically fulfilled. The destruction of Jerusalem by the Romans was the fulfillment of Matthew 22:7, where the King sends his army to burn the city.[44] This historical-prophetic interpretation appears to have its roots in Irenaeus, who understood this section of the parable in light of the sovereignty of the Lord as taught in the Old Testament. All men, armies, and nations belong to God and are his instruments for judgment.[45] This shift from a salvation-history to a historical-prophetic interpretation

42. "τὸ ἑτοιμαζόμενον ἄριστον ἐκ στρεᾶς ἐν πνευματικοῖς λογίοις τροφῆς." Origen, *In Mattheium*, 17.22 (*G.C.S.* 10.643). In the context of his discussion of the parable, "the meal" refers to the "strong and eloquent teachings" found in the Bible. Jerome follows Origen when he understands the "bulls and the fattened ones" carnal metaphors which refer to the spiritual; the doctrines of God's law. Jerome, *Commentariorum in Mattheum* 3.1664–75 (*C.C.S.L.* 77.200).

43. Chrysostom, *Commentariorum in Matthaeum*, 69.1 (*PG* 58.647; *N.P.N.F.* 10.421).

44. Ibid.; also Eusebius, *Psalmos*, 44.4 (*PG* 86.1.19–24).

45. Quoting Psalm 24.1, Irenaeus, *Adversus Haereses*, 4.58.8 (*PG* 7.1066; Harvey, 2.282). In the eastern Greek tradition, Theophylact continued Chrysostom's interpretation of this point some seven hundred years later when he cited Josephus' narration of the destruction of Jerusalem as proof of the fulfillment of the prophetic element of this parable. Theophylacti, *Enarratio in Evangelium Matthaei*, 22.117 (*PG* 123.386–87). For Theophylact, one of the reasons why the Jews rejected the invitation was that they were not willing to listen to what the prophets had to teach them.

illustrates a common element between prophetical and allegorical interpretation: both require that the reader possess a code in order to determine the relationships between the text and its referent. In this instance, the two main elements in the replacement theme, the guilt of the nation of Israel and the city referring to Jerusalem, provides the common ground where the prophetic and the salvation-history codes overlap.

In contrast to the historical-prophetic view, Origen read this section according to a framework of spiritual teaching. Those who rejected the invitation were destroyed by God, not through human agency but through the host of God's angels. In this way the burning of the city in the parable represents the destruction of not only the ruler of this age but also of the false teachers and "what is falsely called knowledge."[46] In the Western church, Origen's more spiritual reading of the judgment by the king in the parable was received by Jerome, Gregory the Great, Leo the Great, and Thomas Aquinas.[47]

Once the reason for the transfer of the kingdom from the Jews to the Gentiles was recognized, it was understandable to proceed to ask questions about the other characters in the parable. If those who ignore and kill the messengers represent the Jewish nation, then who are those who return to their farms and businesses, or those found on the outer roads? For Origen, the excuses offered by these characters teach that some people place the cares and concerns of this world before the kingdom of God.[48] Because they have their hearts set on gaining wealth, they miss out on the meal that God has to offer them.[49] In this way, Origen

46. Origen *In Matthaeum* 17.23 (*G.C.S.* 10.648). While he does mention the destruction of the city of Jerusalem in his commentary it plays a secondary role to what he sees as the more important teaching of the parable at this point.

47. Jerome admits that this judgment may also refer to the destruction of Jerusalem by the Romans under Vespian and Tatian. Jerome *Commentariorum in Mattheum* 3.1688–93 (*C.C.S.L.* 77.200–201); Maldonati, *Commentarii in Quatuor Evangelistas*, 2.303–4 (Davie, 2.230); Leo the Great, *Sermon*, 50 (*P.L.* 54.305–8; *F.C.* 93.214–17); Aquinas, *Catena Aurea*, 1.2.22.7. Aquinas mentions Chrysostom's prophetical view and Jerome's possibility that it could be read both ways. However, in citing the fathers he places Gregory the Great and Origen's views after Chrysostom and Jerome. Thus, when reading the *Catena Aurea*, one is lead to the conclusion that Origen's view is the preferred interpretation as it comes at the conclusion to his discussion of this verse.

48. Origen *In Matthaeum* 27.15 (*G.C.S.* 10.629).

49. The parable of the Pearl of Great Price illustrates this point for Origen. He believes that parable demonstrates the correct disposition one should have: a person

introduced an ascetic dimension into the interpretation of this parable that gained almost universal acceptance by those who follow him.[50]

It is worth noting that the early commentators are fairly restrained in drawing out the allegorical significance of the excuses of those who turn away and return to their farms or businesses. This is most clearly seen if we compare the interpretation of this parable with Augustine's interpretation of the parable of the Great Feast in Luke 14. There, each of the excuses is allegorically explained. The man who goes to check on a farm he has purchased represents the spirit of domination. The five pair of oxen signify the five senses, and this, in turn, speaks about the things of this world and the seeking of physical proof for the gospel as Thomas did. Finally, the one who has married a wife is guilty of the lusts of the flesh.[51] Theophylact offers one of the more fanciful interpretations of Matthew 22:1–14, but in contrast to Augustine's interpretation of the parable of the Great Feast, he is very restrained. According to Theophylact, the one returning to his field denotes those who love the flesh, for the field functions as a symbol for the body. The one who returns to his business is a person who loves profits. "This parable shows those who fail in the spiritual wedding, and those who fail to have a friendship or relationship with Christ. If you fail in these two, you fail in all others either because of carnal hedonism or because of their desire for gain."[52] Hilary of Poitiers presents a good example of how most of the commentators understood the excuses of those who turned away from the invitation when he states that this section of the parable represents "those who are caught in the ambitions of this age . . . and many on account of the longing for wealth in business are held back."[53] This ascetic perspective persisted through the Medieval period.[54]

should be willing to forsake all in order to possess what God has to offer. Origen *In Matthaeum* 27.23 (*G.C.S.* 10.646).

50. For example, almost half of Chrysostom's discussion of this parable is dedicated to praising the virtues of the ascetic lifestyle. Chrysostom *Commentariorum in Matthaeum* 69.2–4 (*P.G.* 78.651–54; *N.P.N.F.* 10.423–26).

51. Augustine summarizes his discussion of the excuses with: "The lust of the flesh, I have married a wife. The lust of the eyes, I have bought five pairs of oxen. The ambition of life, I have bought a farm." Augustine *Sermo* 112.6 (*P.L.* 38.646; *Sermons*, 1.463).

52. Theophylacti, *Enarratio in Evangelium Matthaei*, 22.117 (*P.G.* 123.383–84)

53. Hilary of Poitiers, *In Matthaeum*, 22.5 (*S.C.* 258.148)

54. Strabi, *Glossa Ordinaria, Evangelium Matthaeum*, 22.5 (*P.L* 116.156); Aquinas, *Catena Aurea*, 22.5. And finally, some draw out the ethical point that those who

If the polemical-theological trajectory of interpretation died out because the questions posed by the heretics were no longer being asked, then the kerygmatic or ethnic-ethical trajectory demonstrates just the opposite. One of the conclusions this trajectory reveals is the manner by which Origen's interpretation of this passage was so widely received until the fifth century. It appears that each commentator was dialoguing with Origen's commentary during this period. In the eastern Greek tradition, Chrysostom's historical-prophetic reading of the king sending his army to burn the city represents a divergence from Origen's comments. The Latin church to a large extent followed Origen's spiritual understanding that this referred to God's judgment against false doctrines which is exercised through his host of angels.

SOTERIOLOGICAL INTERPRETATION

The parable of the Wedding Feast concludes with the incident of the king entering the feast only to encounter one guest who is not properly attired. The king then has this guest bound and cast into the 'outer darkness' (22:13). The severity of this action and its eschatological overtones quite naturally raised questions about the nature of this guest's transgression. In order to discuss the interpretation this action, I think it is best if we take a step back and consider the overall context of the wedding feast as it would have been understood within the horizon of Jesus' and Matthew's audiences. In the Old Testament, marriage often stood as a sign for the covenant relationship between God and Israel (Hosea 2:19, Isaiah 54:6, and Ezekiel 16:7). The Rabbis often spoke of the covenant at Mount Sinai in terms of a marriage contract, with Moses serving as the friend of the groom and Israel as the bride.[55] In the prophetic books of the Old Testament, this theme was given an eschatological dimension; with the arrival of the Messiah, the wedding bond would be renewed.[56]

---

turn back to their farms or businesses are guilty of the lesser crime than those who mistreat and kill the servants. Origen *In Matthaeum* 27.15 (*G.C.S.* 10.629); Jerome, *Commentariorum in Mattheum*, 3.1674–88 (*C.C.S.L.* 77.200); Hilary, *In Matthaeum*, 22.5 (*S.C.* 258.148)

55. Strack and Billerbeck, *Kommentar zum Neuen Testament aus Talmud und Midrasch*, 1.969, 2.393. See also Riesenfeld "The Parables in the Synoptic and Johannine Traditions," 37–61.

56. Strack and Billerbeck, *Kommentar zum Neuen Testament*, 1.517; Stauffer, "γαμέω," in Kittel and Friedrich, eds. *Theological Dictionary of the New Testament*, 1:654–55.

These eschatological inferences appear to have been an active element in both Jesus' and the author's use of this term.[57] However, as we saw with the replacement theme, it is not Israel who shall be the bride but those who are members of the new covenant community.[58]

Origen's commentary demonstrates that these concepts were part of his horizon of expectations. As he initiates his discussion of this passage, he writes, "In this parable we can clearly see the idea that the human king is God, the Father of our Lord Jesus Christ. And the wedding feast for the king's son signifies the restoration (ἀποκατά—στασις) of the bride, the church of Christ to Christ, her bridegroom."[59] ἀποκατάστασις (restoration) was a very theologically significant term in Origen's vocabulary. He used it to refer to the restoration of creation at the eschaton and also the present nature of the believer's restored relationship to Christ.[60] Given the dual temporal framework within which the "wedding" was understood, we can see how the interpretation of the significance of the wedding garment in the parable is open to wide speculation. Does the wedding garment relate to one's admission into the present church (Ephesians 5:32), or is it something that one needs for admission into the eschatological marriage feast (Revelation 19)?

Normally, with an image or symbol such as the "wedding garment," there will be multiple resonances as to how it can be understood. Symbols give rise to a surplus of meaning. This is the result of a tension between the literal interpretation of the symbol and its metaphorical interpretation. The "wedding garment" in this parable has almost never been read as referring to a literal item of clothing, but as metaphorically pointing to something else that concerns the guest's relationship

---

57. "In the symbolic language of the East, the wedding is the symbol of the day of salvation, as the language of the Apocalypse bears witness: 'The marriage of the Lamb is come.'" Jeremias, *The Parables of Jesus*, 117.

58. Stauffer, "γαμέω," 1:655.

59. Origen, *In Matthaeum*, 27.15 (*G.C.S.* 10.628).

60. Lampe, "ἀποκατάστασις," in *A Patristic Greek Lexicon*, 195. For the Jewish background to this term see Strack-Billerbeck, *Kommentar zum Neuen Testament*, 4:799–976. This term ultimately will play a decisive role in Origen's downfall, in both the Origenist controversy in the fourth century and especially the anathema published against Origen in 532 AD he is criticised for teaching that everything, including the demons, will be restored to the position they occupied before the fall. Margerie, *An Introduction to the History of Exegesis*, 1.96, 226; Simonetti, *Biblical Interpretation*, 51, n. 2.

to God. It is through the assimilation or mediation of these conflicting interpretations (the literal and the metaphorical) that an extension
of meaning takes place. This "tension is not translatable because they
[metaphors and symbols] create meaning. This is not to say that they
cannot be paraphrased, just that such a paraphrase is infinite and inca-
pable of exhausting the innovative meaning."[61] In other words, once an
interpretation is given for a symbol that interpretation comes up short
because the symbol is capable of giving rise to new significations.[62] At
the same time, a symbol's interpretations may extend the symbol into
something that is more than was previously recognized or collapse it
into something less through an attempt to clearly explicate the meaning
of the symbol by means of propositional language.

In the case of the 'wedding garment,' there were already certain
pre-established understandings concerning the meaning of this symbol
that were inherited from the Old Testament, Jewish, and early Christian
interpretive traditions. The interesting issue is which of the various interpretative choices are adopted and why. Early in the Patristic period,
the concept of the 'garment' or 'robe' took on connotative relationships
with the rite of baptism. Because the early interpreters approached the
New Testament with this functioning as part of their preunderstanding,
it is not surprising to find "that the sacramental theology attested in
the patristic catecheses was refracted in the exegesis" at various points.[63]
Post-baptismal reinvestment conveyed the idea of the restoration of the
individual to their proper relationship with God and inclusion in the
new covenant community.[64] Tertullian spoke of this in the following
manner: "He [the baptism candidate] receives the former garment, this
clearly points to that which Adam by transgressing had lost."[65] Baptism

---

61. Ricœur, *Interpretation Theory*, 52.

62. "There is no need to deny the concept in order to admit that symbols give rise
to an endless exegesis. If no concept can exhaust the requirement of further thinking
borne by symbols, this idea signifies only that no given categorization can embrace all
the semantic possibilities of a symbol." Ibid., 57.

63. Tissot, "Patristic Allegories," 377.

64. See also Jeremias' discussion that "investiture with a new garment is therefore a
symbol of the New Age." Jeremias, *The Parables of Jesus*, 130, 188–89.

65. While Tertullian is addressing the issue of the rebaptism of those who had fallen,
away his views at this point are similar to his view of baptism. Tertullian *De pudicitia*
9.16 (*P.L.* 2.1051). In this chapter, Tertullian focuses primarily on the parable of the
prodigal son, and his discussion of the garment/robe is that which the father com-

is the rite by which one receives the garment of forgiveness, which restores a person to his or her original relationship with God that Adam had forfeited. This is what allowed one to enter the wedding feast, the church. However, this view was not widely received and fell out of use by the end of the third century, with Cyril of Jerusalem being one of the last to expound this reading.[66]

Origen's discussion of the parable is divided into two sections. In the first section, he explains the interpretation of the parable in a fairly straightforward, yet allegorical manner. When the guests enter the wedding feast, they remove their old clothes (which represent their evil lives and what is foreign to the wedding feast) and put on the proper garment. This garment is a heart of compassion (quoting Colossians 3:12), "For this is the wedding garment."[67] The one not wearing the garment represents those who have not had their character transformed or put on the Lord Jesus Christ.[68] Origen attempts to bring together several New Testament metaphors relating to salvation in his interpretation of the wedding garment. On the one hand, he establishes cross-references to other New Testament metaphors in order to reinforce his point that the wedding garment speaks about the transformed life of the believer. On the other hand, he does not harmonize these different metaphors into one image, but rather preserves their distinctive contributions,

---

mands to be placed on the younger son when he returns. However, Tertullian explicitly linked this with the wedding garment in our parable in 9.11. Thus, the intertextual connection between the robe (στολὴν τὴν πρώτην in Luke 15:22) and the wedding garment (ἔνδυμα γάμου) forms a connection between his interpretation of the two parables.

66. In his "Lectures on Baptism," he cites this parable to teach that the wedding garment denotes baptism and even more significantly, it is the eschatological garment of salvation. The garment speaks of the remission of sins by which our souls are cleansed and we are adorned with salvation as Isaiah prophesied. "Let my soul rejoice in the Lord: for He hath clothed me with a garment of salvation, and a robe of gladness: He hath crowned me with a garland as a bridegroom, and decked me with ornaments as a bride." (quoting Isaiah 61:10) Cyril of Jerusalem, "On Baptism" §2, *The Catechetical Lectures*, 3 (*N.P.N.F.* 7.14). Jeremias argues that Isaiah 61:10 functions as the contextual background to the wedding garment but does not mention Cyril's earlier recognition of this same intertextual connection. Jeremias, *The Parables of Jesus*, 188–89.

67. Origen, *In Matthaeum*, 27.16 (*G.C.S.* 10.632).

68. Ibid., *G.C.S.* 10.632–34.

and thus, his interpretation of the wedding garment is polyphonic by nature.[69]

In the second section of his discussion of the parable of the Wedding Feast, Origen attempts to "draw out the deeper meaning of the parable according to the wisdom of the Spirit."[70, 71] Christ's incarnation and sacrificial death restored our relationship with God. This relationship should result in our growth in faith, godliness, and good works, which together constitute "the garment of virtue, the wedding garment made with radiant material."[72] The guest who is not wearing the wedding garment in the parable signifies those in the church who have not taken off their old life or partaken in this process of spiritual growth and transformation. The king's judgment of the guest without the proper attire serves as a warning to all in the church that we should never be satisfied with our spiritual life but should constantly press on to the more "mature and sweet fruit (grapes) of excellence

69. Young makes the point that Origen's use of cross references often bring out multiple referents for a passage. Young, *Biblical Exegesis*, 135–37. Origen did not reject the historical nature of the biblical accounts but rather searched for a meaning that was richer and fuller than a literal or historical approach would allow. The polyvalent nature of the Bible and the allegorical method allowed for this. "Origen declares the whole Scriptural record to be God's symphony, wherein the inexpert listener may think he perceives jarring notes whilst the man whose ear has been well trained realizes the fitness and grace with which the various notes are worked up into one harmonious composition." Milburn, *Early Christian Interpretation,* 17–30; Torjensen, "'Body', 'Soul' and 'Spirit' in Origen's Theory of Exegesis," 17–30.

70. Origen, *In Matthaeum*, 27.17ff. (*G.C.S.* 10.634 ff.). Origen follows the Rule of Faith which taught that the Bible was inspired by the Holy Spirit and possessed an obvious meaning and one that was deeper and hidden from most readers. Origen *De principiis* 1, Preface, 4.3.14 (*On First Principles*, Butterworth, 1–6, 310–12); Young, *Biblical Exegesis*, 23–24.

71. The idea of condescension serves to explain why the Gnostic sects misunderstood these figures of speech in the Bible, but more importantly it serves the hermeneutical function of explaining how the transcendent God can communicate with mankind. Origen *Contra Celsus* 4.15 (*P.G.* 11.1045); Origen *Sermon* 27 (*P.G.* 12.703).

72. Origen *In Matthaeum* 27.21–24 (G.C.S. 10.642–52), especially the start to §24. This same process of spiritual transformation performs an important role in Origen's hermeneutic. "The more the soul conforms, through the reception of grace and the practice of virtues, to the resurrection of Christ, the more it surrenders itself to the Logos growing within it, allowing the Word to transform it into his likeness, the more the divinity begins to show through the glorified humanity of Christ and the letter of the Scripture and the mysteries begin to be perceived beneath their clothing as image." Margerie, *An introduction to the History of Exegesis*, 1.104.

(ἀρετῆς)."[73] Origen's interpretation of the wedding garment is varied and rich, but at the same time the multiplicity of New Testament metaphors and references which he cites are clustered around the transformation which takes place in a believer's life.[74] As such, Origen preserves some latitude in the metaphorical surplus of meaning in his interpretation of the symbol of the wedding garment. From our perspective, Origen's multiplicity in references and meaning for the symbol of the wedding garment stands in contrast to modern exegetical practices that search for a clear or stable meaning to the text. However, I think one of the reasons why his work was so widely received in the Patristic church was for this very reason; his polyphonic interpretations provided a rich seed bed for subsequent interpreters' theological reflection on the passage.

Perhaps the greatest contrast between Origen's work and those who follow him is the manner by which they risk undo closure of the disclosive potential of the parable for the sake of clarity or precision of interpretation. Jerome follows Origen's general view of the wedding garment, but in a more legalistic manner. The new garment is woven or completed through obedience to the laws and commands of the Lord. The garment represents taking off the old defiled self at conversion and putting on the new man in Christ. The one entering the feast without the new garment is guilty of defiling the wedding feast by wearing sordid clothing (his old life).[75] The application Jerome draws from the parable is similar to Origen's; it teaches us that it is not the entrance, or beginning the new life that is important, but how one finishes his life.[76]

Hilary of Poitiers restricted Origen's interpretation also, but took an approach more textually than Jerome's. Hilary recognized the tension between the literal and metaphorical meanings behind the symbol of the wedding garment. He attempted to resolve this tension by asking a series of questions concerning how the guest entered the feast without the proper garment in order to show that the garment could not refer to something external to a person's life that would have been visible to

---

73. Origen *In Matthaeum* 27.24 (*G.C.S.* 10.651).

74. That a passage or idea in the Bible would have a multiplicity in meaning is not a problem for Origen. Rather for him, "the Word of God is inexhaustibly rich and the human reader cannot exhaust its meaning . . ." Simonetti, *Biblical Interpretation,* 43.

75. Jerome *Commentariorum in Mattheum* 3.1705–26 (*C.C.S.L.* 77.201–2).

76. Ibid., 3.1736–39 (*C.C.S.L.* 77.202).

others. It could not refer to a special type of garment worn on festive occasions since everyone, including the poor, were invited. The fact the king's servants did not notice the guest's impropriety, he argued, reinforced that it could not have been a physical garment. Therefore, it must refer to something internal. This is why the guest could deceive the servants but could not escape the notice of God.[77] Hilary concluded that "the wedding garment is the glory of the Holy Spirit and the radiance of the heavenly garment . . . which is reserved in immaculate condition until the feast in the kingdom of heaven."[78]

In both Hilary and Jerome, we see Origen's polyphonic understanding of the wedding garment being constrained. This demonstrates two important hermeneutical points. First, as Ricœur pointed out, the explication of a metaphor or symbol always results in an expansion and reduction in the possible meaning of that symbol or metaphor. The different trajectories that later commentators took from Origen represent an expansion of meaning at the collective level, but for each individual commentator there was a reduction in the signification of symbol. Second, according to the logic of question and answer, not every question can be asked within a horizon. The different answers these commentators found for the symbol of the wedding garment were the result of different the questions asked within their respective horizons.

The reduction or clarification of the meaning of the wedding garment reached its most forceful argument in the work of Augustine. In reading Augustine's fortieth sermon, one is struck by its parallels with Hilary's commentary, which raises the question of how familiar he was with Hilary's work. For Augustine, the garment must be worn in the heart, otherwise the servants would have stopped this guest from entering the feast improperly attired. Like Hilary, Augustine did not see the responsibility for inspecting the guests resting with the servants but saw it as God's prerogative alone. "The Master of the house saw him, the Master of the house inspected, the Master of the house separated him

---

77. Hilary of Poitiers, *In Matthaeum*, 22.7 (S.C. 258.148–50). Hilary's questions about the garment are an illustration of Ricœur's thought on the manner by which the tension between the literal and metaphorical meaning of a symbol or metaphor creates a surplus of meaning. Ricœur, *Interpretation Theory*, 52.

78. Hilary of Poitiers, *In Matthaeum*, 22.7 (S.C. 258.148). Once again this dual temporal reference of the wedding comes through.

out."[79] What the wedding garment stood for was an important question since it entailed such a serious punishment and separated the good
from the evil.[80] According to Augustine, it cannot refer to baptism or
faith since both good and evil have access to these and are what allow
one to enter the feast (the present church).[81] In a similar manner it could
not refer to the sacraments, fasting, church leadership, or the working
of miracles.[82] Love was the only indispensable thing Augustine could
conceive of which could differentiate the guests in this manner. Love is
the greatest commandment and without it we are nothing.[83] This love is
two fold: it must be exercised toward God and man. It is also dynamic
in that it must be constantly cultivated and extended.[84] "So let charity be
advanced, so be it nourished, that being nourished it may be perfected;
so be the wedding garment put on; so be the image of God, after which
we were created, by this our advancing, engraven anew in us."[85]

Augustine's interpretation of the wedding garment clearly defined
and also constrained the meaning of the wedding garment and set a
trajectory of interpretation for how this symbol was interpreted until
the Reformation.[86] Gregory the Great is one example of the reception
of Augustine's interpretation, as he argued that the garment could
not be faith or baptism but must be love. In the eastern Greek tradition, Theophylact's' commentary demonstrates Augustine's influence,
whether consciously or unconsciously, even though this tradition did
not follow Augustinian theology in other areas. The clearest indication
of Augustine's influence here is seen Theophylact's comments that the
wedding garment was not faith or good works but love in the heart.[87]

---

79. Augustine *Sermo* 90.4 (*P.L.* 38.566; *Sermons on Selected Lessons*, 1.336).

80. Ibid., 95.5–6 (*P.L.* 38.583; *S.S.L.* 1.337–39).

81. Ibid., 95.7 (*P.L.* 38.583–4; *S.S.L.* 1.369–70).

82. Ibid., 90.5 (*P.L.* 38.561–2; *S.S.L.* 1.338).

83. Ibid., 90.6 (*P.L.* 38.562; *S.S.L.* 1.338), citing Mt 22:37–39 and I Cor 13.

84. Ibid., 90.8, 10 (*P.L.* 38.564, 566; *Sermons on Selected Lessons*, 1.341, 344).

85. Ibid., 90.10 (*P.L.* 38.566; *S.S.L.* 1.334).

86. Leo the Great is one of the few who rejected Augustine's interpretation. He argued that the garment was the new self that conformed to the resurrection and was put
on by obeying God's commands and partaking in the spiritual feasts (the sacraments?).
Sermon, 50 (*P.L.* 54.305–8; *F.C.* 93.214–17).

87. "Ὁ μὴ ἐνδυσάμενος σπλάγχα οἰκτιρμων, χρηστότητα, φιλαδελφίαν."
Theophylact, *Enarratio in Evangelium Matthaei*, 22.118 (*P.G.* 123.387–88). This may

Perhaps the most important exception to this is Thomas Aquinas, who balanced Augustine's view by attempting to bring out some of the other resonances of meaning that Origen had raised.[88]

SUMMARY

In contrast to modern presumptions that the allegorical method was liable of yielding a free play of interpretation, the record of this parable's interpretation is remarkably restrained during this period. Origen, in particular, is often charged with taking an arbitrary allegorical approach that resulted in his reading all manner of meaning into the text. The combination of how the various symbols and characters in the parable were understood in several distinct exegetical trajectories (or concerns) resulted in what appears to be a very diverse collection of readings. However, it is possible to discern three primary trajectories of interpretation for the parable of the Wedding Feast during the Patristic period. The interpreters during this period were fairly restrained in their approach within the terms of their exegetical goals and tended to follow one of three distinct trajectories that arose from the prejudices they inherited and from the influence of previous interpreters.[89] Their interpretations were not wooden replications of previous interpretations, nor were they the result of the free play of an unrestrained allegorical approach.

Second, the prejudices the Patristic exegetes brought to the text shaped the field of play for their exegetical activities. For example, the intertextual reference to Matthew 21:43 directs the reader's expectations in relation to this parable, and thus, the replacement theme figures so strongly in their readings. The interpreter's theological prejudices functioned in the background as a guide that gives meaning to the individual

---

have come to Theophylact through Maximus, for whom charity was an important theme.

88. It is interesting to note that Aquinas attempts this by appealing to Hilary and Jerome's works in relation to citations from Origen's commentary. Aquinas, *Catena Aurea*, 22.11–12.

89. In the doctrinal development of the church, a set of agreed upon symbols arose which became "the basis for a refined allegorical treatment of scripture, so that dogma and spirituality were not divorced and spirituality was 'disciplined' by the 'orthodox' understanding of key texts." Young, *The Art of Performance*, 123. Metaphors and symbols are bounded by the world in which they occur, they are not open to unlimited play of interpretation. Ricœur, *Interpretation Theory*, 58–61.

parts of the Bible, such as this parable, and even to the individual items and characters within the parable. Their interpretations were shaped by their historical situation within the Christian tradition, but were genuine attempts to understand the parable in light of the questions of their particular horizon.

Third, not all interpretations were of equal validity, priority, or weight in relation to the text. Among those I have discussed so far, Origen's commentary was the most widely received and influential interpretation of the parable up to the fifth century.[90] The interpretation he offered and the questions his commentary raised (such as how later commentators wrestled with Origen's polyvalent interpretation of what the wedding garment referred to) demonstrate the importance of his work. The theological and referential richness of Origen's commentary facilitated the interpretation of future readers by allowing them to "recognize more" in the parable. In this sense, his commentary functions as one of the earliest members of the summit-dialogue for this parable (and perhaps also for the entire gospel of Matthew). This stands in contrast to the movement of other interpretive trajectories into cul-de-sacs that were not received by future interpreters. The abandonment of certain trajectories resulted from the fact that the questions those interpretations originally sought to answer were no longer being asked. Anti-Gnostic interpretations are one example of this historical pattern.

For the contemporary reader, the play of interpretation that the early interpreters realized within these trajectories provokes our modern theological prejudices. In particular, their allegorical readings question and raise to consciousness the value we assign to a text possessing an objective or stable meaning, which we inherited from the Enlightenment. However, for the Patristic fathers the text had multiple levels of signification or reference, but this did not lead to an unlimited field of play in their interpretations. Rather, because they were at home in their tradition they were able to discern which interpretations resonated with the text. This ability came from their participation in their tradition, specifically within the orthodox faith, their interaction with

---

90. This study substantiates Margerie's point that all of the great exegetes of the early church were dependent on Origen's exegetical works. "He is the first great master of exegesis. All who came after him, even those who reacted against him, such as Saint Jerome, owe nearly everything to him in every domain." Margerie, *An Introduction to the History of Exegesis*, 1.112–13.

the biblical text, the context in which they ministered, and the concepts and interpretations passed down to them from previous concretizations of the parable's meaning.

The Reception of Augustine's Ecclesiological Interpretation

The previous section focused on the broader diachronic trajectories in the history of a the parable's interpretation that led up to Origen, and how Origen's polyphonic interpretation preserved an openness to the meaning of the parable and which, in turn, became the seedbed for future commentators. This section will restrict its scope to Augustine's ecclesiological interpretation of the parable, which will then lead into Aquinas' and Calvin's appropriation of Augustine's interpretation in part three of this chapter.

Augustine made several very interesting and innovative exegetical moves in his interpretation of the parable of the Wedding Feast.[91] Not only did he read it as a paradigm for the church, but also discerned within it the justification for the use of force against heretics. In order to clarify the exegetical shifts he made, it is necessary to explore the background that shaped his, and his audience's, horizon of expectations.

When Augustine inherited the bishop's seat at Hippo, he stepped into the midst of a long standing and difficult conflict with the Donatists.[92] Far from being an old problem, the Donatist schism was a wide spread movement and possibly the dominant church in Augustine's see.[93] Without going into great detail on Donatism, there were two main questions that this situation raised for Augustine. First, what was the

91. In discussing Augustine's interpretation of this parable, we must keep in mind that he often harmonizes the accounts in Matthew 22:1–14 with the parable of the Great Feast in Luke 14. See Augustine, *De Consensu Evangelistarum* (*C.S.E.L.* 43; *Harmony of the Gospels*, in *N.P.N.F.* 6.65–236). At the same time, he differentiates between the two parables at other points.

92. Prior to Augustine's ascension to bishop, the Roman government had tried both force and toleration in its attempt to control the Donatist movement. However, neither approach was successful. This was most likely due to the fact that "it was an African movement and its members were determined to assert their own independence, not only of the Catholic church but, also in more subtle ways, of the power of imperial Rome." Dillistone, "The Anti-Donatist Writings," 178; Willis, *Saint Augustine*, 346–61.

93. For the most widely cited discussion on this issue, see Willis, *Saint Augustine*, especially 49, 176–79, 346–61.

nature of the church? And second, how should the church respond to schismatics such as the Donatists?

What Is the Nature of the Church?

The question concerning the nature of the church arose from the inability of Cyprian's teachings in the unity of the Catholic Church to answer new questions which the Donatist situation raised about the nature of the church. Both Donatists and orthodox theologians appealed to Cyprian to defend their position, each with a defensible cause. On the one hand, Cyprian taught that schisms were never justified. This was based on his doctrine that if a person left the church, they also stepped outside the possibility of salvation. Therefore, the church could never be divided, since there could only be one true church at any time. On the other hand, Cyprian held that a bishop who lapsed under persecution was no longer worthy to administer the sacraments or hold church office since he had stepped outside the church, and thus, forfeited his office.

The event that ignited the debate over Cyprian's teachings was the election of Caecilianus as the bishop of Carthage in 312 AD.[94] The rigorists opposed his appointment since he received his orders from Felix of Aptunga, who was alleged to have been a traitor during the Diocletianic persecution.[95] Therefore, Caecilianus' appointment was not valid, and the rigorist party appointed Majorinus as a rival bishop, who was quickly succeeded by Donatus. This resulted in a series of appeals and counter-appeals all the way up to the emperor and the bishop of Rome. In every case, Caecilianus was vindicated. The debate raged over a question Cyprian never addressed: What happened if a bishop who had betrayed the church repented? As a result, the Donatists read Cyprian as teaching that once a person betrayed the church he could never hold office in the church again. However, most of the bishops, most importantly the bishop of Rome, believed that once a person repented, he was restored by grace and could once again administer the

---

94. Augustine, *Epistle*, 185.4 (*C.S.E.L.* 57.3–4; *F.C.* 4.144–45).

95. Such an appointment was intolerable since Cyprian taught that once a member of the clergy had lapsed they could no longer hold a church office. Dillistone, "The Anti-Donatist Writings," 178.

sacraments and hold office.[96] At a deeper level, the problem revolved around the concept of holiness. The Donatists wanted to protect the purity of the church from being contaminated by the actions and influences of traitors, such as Felix.[97]

Augustine attempted to resolve the question the Donatist schism had raised over this ambiguity in Cyprian's teachings. In his solution, Augustine relied heavily on the parables, especially the parable of the Wedding Feast and the parables of the Dragnet and the Tares in Matthew 13. Augustine interpreted these three parables according to a realized eschatology (he gave more weight to the present realization of the wedding as the church) but at the same time he still maintained an eschatological dimension in God's judgment.[98]

The parables of the Dragnet and the Tares taught that the present church is composed of good and evil members just as the "good and evil" were invited to the wedding feast. This was also seen in the fact that the wheat and tares grow together until the harvest, that and the dragnet captures both good and bad fish.[99] In taking this position, Augustine followed Cyprian's view that the church is a mixed community. There will always be tares among the wheat.[100] In the future, God will winnow the wheat from the tares, separate the good fish from the bad, and expel the

96. In this section, I will use "Catholic church" according to Augustine's definition of the term as the "universal" or "world–wide" church. Augustine *Epistle* 185.2, 4 (*C.S.E.L.* 57.2–4; *F.C.* 4.142–45).

97. "In other words, every 'quisling,' every collaborator, everyone tainted with pro-traitor sympathies must ruthlessly be exposed and excluded from membership or office in the Church." Dillistone, "The Anti-Donatist Writings," 188.

98. For him, "the kingdom of heaven is the church now." Berkhof, *The History of Christian Doctrine*, 230.

99. According to Augustine, the Donatist position was unrealistic since they understood the church to be composed only of wheat and criticized the Catholic church for being infested with tares. Augustine attacked both of these points. On the one hand, the Donatists were not as pure as they claimed. "Look at the hordes of Circumcellions, look at the convivial drunkards, look at the lewd teachers. Do you call these wheat?" On the other hand, the Catholic church was being blamed for the sins of the few tares. Augustine *Epistle* 76.2–3 (*C.S.E.L.* 34.326–27), 43.14–15 (*C.S.E.L.* 34.96–97).

100. This is not a criticism of the church but rather should serve as an incentive to make sure that we are of the wheat. Augustine, *Epistle*, 51 (*C.S.E.L.* 34.143–49); Augustine *Sermo* 90.1 (*P.L.* 38.599; *S.S.L.* 1.333–34). Jerome may provide a link between Augustine and Cyprian when he had to deal with a similar problem concerning those who wanted to exclude clergy who were once associated with Arian teachings. Jerome *Dialogus Adversus Luciferianos* (*P.L.* 23.177).

guest who is not wearing the wedding garment.[101] This act of judgment is reserved for God alone; it is not something his servants in the church can perform. Thus, Jesus' command, "*sinite utraque crescere usque ad messem*" (permit them both to grow until the harvest [Matthew 13:30]), was the basis for tolerating heretics and sinners within the church. This is a meaningful theological contribution which Augustine made to ecclesiology. "Augustine's wider and more patient view of the nature of the Church's holiness, never condoning sin yet recognizing that men could not act as final judges, has commended itself to the conscience of the vast majority in the Church of subsequent generations."[102]

While the tares cannot be excluded from the church because of some outward manifestation, they are separated from the wheat on the inside according to Augustine. The fact that the servants did not notice the guest without the wedding garment is another illustration of this point.[103] It is in light of Augustine's confrontation with the Donatist schism that his argument that the wedding garment cannot refer to baptism, faith, the sacraments, or church offices takes on a greater significance. The true traits of the church and salvation do not consist in the proper administration of church offices and sacraments, but in whether one has been cleansed by God and has put on the garment of love. In this way, Augustine made a distinction between those who are formally members of the church and those who have cloaked their hearts with love and are members of the true Body of Christ.[104]

How to Handle the Schismatics?

It is difficult to succinctly summarize Augustine's position on how to deal with the Donatists because it position developed over time, and also because he did not exercise a blanket policy towards them but examined many cases on an individual basis.[105] Nevertheless, for the purposes of this study, I believe we can summarize his approach as follows.[106]

101. Augustine *Sermo* 90.4 (P.L. 38.560–1; S.S.L. 1.336–37); also *Epistle*, 53.21, 76.2–3, 93.15; *Contra litteras Petiliani*, 3.2.3.

102. Dillistone, "The Anti-Donatist Writings," 189.

103. Augustine *Sermo* 90.4 (P.L. 38.566; S.S.L. 1.336).

104. Ibid., 90.6–10 (P.L. 38.562–6; S.S.L. 1.338–44).

105. Brown, "St. Augustine's Attitude to Religious Coercion," 382–91.

106. Both Willis and Brown show how Augustine's approach developed over time and how he carefully applied it to different situations as they arose.

First, the Donatists should to be approached with love and through dialogue every attempt to win them over should be made.[107] If persuasion fails, coercion can be applied. But this raised a theological question about the use of force to bring about conversion. The traditional view held that freedom of choice (*voluntas*) was an essential aspect of true religious conversion and that any religion that resorted to force only constructed a man-made artifice. By contrast, Augustine realized that God used discipline and the impingement of divine and human laws to make a person wise. Examples of this could be seen in God's discipline and chastisement of Israel in the Old Testament, the function of the Law as a *paedagogus*, the apostle Paul's affliction with blindness, and one's personal fear of death and pain. Thus, Augustine saw two poles at work in a person's moral and spiritual life: external pressure and internal freedom.[108]

When we examine his interpretation of the parable of the Wedding Feast, we see how Augustine "finds material ready to hand" for dealing with the Donatists. The sending of the servants by the king to invite the guests shows the first approach: to reach out in love and persuasion. Augustine harmonized the parable of the Wedding Feast with the parable of the Great Feast in Luke 14. This allowed him to claim that an external, coercive element was introduced in the phrase, "*compelle intrare*" (Luke 14:23).[109] His understanding of this phrase reveals the polarity which operates in a person's inner life. "Compel them, saith he, to come in. Let compulsion be found outside, the will arise within."[110]

---

107. This would fit with his Manichean background, for they practiced public debate in order to spread their teachings. Brown, "St. Augustine's Attitude," 384.

108. Ibid., 386–87.

109. Augustine's comment "*compelle intrare*" occurs in his synthesis of the two parables in his harmony of the Gospels. However, at another point he takes the position that Matthew and Luke recorded two different parables spoken by Jesus. Augustine *De Consensu Evangelistarum* 2.62 (*C.S.E.L.* 43.242–43). While the Harmony of the Gospels is dated around 399, Congar notes that Augustine was already involved with the Donatist controversy and that his comments on this passage are specifically addressed to this problem. Congar, "Introduction," 24ff.

110. Brown quotes this passage from Augustine's *Sermo* 112.8, in the Latin as follows: "*Compelle eos intrare, foris inveniatur necessitas, nascitur intus voluntus.*" However, he does not give the source for which text he is quoting this from. The Migne edition contains a slightly different textual variation on this important sentence: "*Coge, inquit intrare, foris inveniatur necessitas, nascitur intus voluntus.*" Augustine *Sermo* 112.8 (*P.L.* 38.647–48). Since both Latin verbs *cogo* and *compello* convey within their semantic

This compulsion is directed at the heretics and schismatics, represented by those who are found along the hedges by the servants (Luke 14:23). However, this compulsion should be undertaken from a position of love in a manner similar to the way a father disciplines his child or a physician treats his patients.[111] Compulsion was for the good of the one being treated and should be withdrawn once it had achieved its beneficial effect. "The *compelle intrare* of the parable thus becomes the classic text of Saint Augustine at this time against the Donatists."[112]

How then does Augustine harmonize his interpretation of *'compelle intrare'* with the tolerance he saw in his interpretation of the parable of the Tares (*"sinite utraque crescere ad messem"*)? First, compulsion may be used by civil authorities to break an obstinate heart so that a person may freely embrace the truth.[113] The co-operation between the church and civil government on issues such as the Donatist schism represents a shift in church/state relations that occurred with Constantine. Irenaeus, who wrote before this cultural shift, viewed the civil government as an agent of God's judgment. The person who does good should have nothing to fear, but the one who does evil should be afraid, "For he does not bear the sword in vain."[114] For Irenaeus, civil government was an agent under God's sovereign control, much as the storm clouds were. By the time Augustine wrote, he could appeal to Christians who hold office in the civil government to enact Godly legislation.[115] Thus, Augustine's interpretation also involves answering new questions in the relation between church and state—questions which would arise again in the late Medieval period. Second, and perhaps even more significantly in

---

domains the ideas of gathering together, collecting, or compelling by force, there is not much difference between the meaning of these two variants.

111. Augustine *Epistle* 185.7 (*C.S.E.L.* 57.6; *F.C.* 4.147–48). Brown observes that Augustine's usual term for coercion is not *cohercitio* from which we derive our term with it negative overtones. But rather Augustine uses *correptio* which means "'rebuke'— defined by its aim, *correctio,* 'setting straight.'" Even in his choice of terms Augustine wanted his audience to understand that coercion was not a punishment but a corrective process. Brown, "St. Augustine's Attitude," 114.

112. Willis, *Saint Augustine,* 134; cf. Congar, "Introduction," 22–48.

113. Augustine gives examples of former Donatists whom he believes this policy has truly liberated. Augustine *Epistle* 185.7, 13 (*C.S.E.L.* 57.6, 12; *F.C.* 4.147–48, 154).

114. Irenaeus *Adversus Haereses* 4.58.8 (*P.G.* 7.1096–97; Harvey, 2.282–83)

115. His letter to tribune and count Boniface is an example of this. Augustine *Epistle* 185.1 (*C.S.E.L.* 57.1; *F.C.* 4.141)

the reception history of his interpretation, he made a fine distinction in his discussion of the parable of the Tares. As long as there was the possibility that some of the wheat may be injured the tares should not be rooted out. But once the wheat was firmly rooted, universally accepted, and there was no danger of schism, then severe discipline could be exercised against the schismatics.[116] Yet even in this extreme instance, the first approach should be to reach out in love and bear with patience their errors.

Aquinas and the Medieval Reception of Augustine's View

One to the first things one notices about interpretation during the Medieval period is that, as a whole, the impact of Augustine's work is hard to overstate. "The influence of Augustine on the later biblical exegesis of the Latin Middle Ages was enormous. With Jerome, Gregory the Great and the Venerable Bede he was one of four great authorities, and would probably have been reckoned the greatest of the four."[117] However, when we examine the reception of Augustine's interpretation of the parable of the Wedding Feast, we notice that the medieval scholars were very selective in their appropriation of his exegesis. In respect to the understanding of "*compelle intrare,*" none of the early medieval exegetes viewed Augustine's interpretation as normative.[118]

Gregory the Great's interpretation of the Wedding Feast is one example. In contrast to Augustine's ecclesial reading, Gregory interpreted the "wedding" as a reference to the incarnation (the wedding of the divine being with human flesh which took place in the virgin's womb).[119] Gregory's concept that the wedding took place in the incar-

116. Literally, "severe discipline should not sleep" (*non dormiat seueritas disciplinae*). Augustine *Contra Epistulam Parmeniani* 3.2.13 (*C.S.E.L.* 51.116–18).

117. Bonner, "Augustine as Biblical Scholar," 561.

118. Bede followed Gregory's interpretation rather than Augustine's. Bede, *In Matthaei Evangeilum exposito*, 13 (*P.L.* 92.68–69); Beare, "The Parable of the Guest at the Banquet," 10. Christian Druthmarus (also known as Christian of Stavelot) followed Augustine in recognizing the wedding garment as love, but not on the use of compulsion. Christiani Druthmari, *Expositio in Matthæum Evangelistam*, 52 (*P.L.* 106.1438–41, esp. 1440). In his commentary on this parable, Sedulius Scottus cites Jerome and Gregory the Great and only makes a passing reference to Augustine's comment that these parables are similar (Sedulius disagrees and sees them as different parables). Sedulius Scottus, *In Matthæum*, 221–222.

119. Gregory the Great, *Homilia in Evangelia*, 2.38.3 (*P.L.* 76.1283; Burke, 35).

nation was widely received during the Medieval period and can be seen in the manner in which it is one of the first points mentioned in both the *Glossa Ordiana* and in Aquinas' *Catena Aurea*. At the same time, Gregory agreed with Augustine that the invitation of the "good and the bad" represented the present mixed nature of the church.[120] However, he disagreed with Augustine's understanding of *"compelle intrare."* According to Gregory, some of the people who receive the invitation were held back from accepting it by their desire for satisfaction and success in the world. *"Compelle intrare"* does not refer to the use of physical coercion but speaks of the manner by which people's desires are constantly frustrated in this life, and as a result, they turn in brokenness to their Maker.[121] Thus, there is a shift from human (Augustine's view) to divine agency in regard to the phrase, "compel them to enter," in Luke 14:23.

HORIZONTAL SHIFTS

In order to understand the reception of Augustine's interpretation of the parable of the Wedding Feast during the late Medieval period, there are two factors we need to consider. The first concerns the historical changes in the shape of the church during this period. Europe was politically fragmented after the fall of the Western Empire in the fifth century. This meant that the church was faced with maintaining some form of episcopal continuity and converting pagans, which were greater challenges than those presented by competing theological positions.

Several important cultural shifts took place in the eleventh century that dramatically changed all this. Monastic reforms, for example at Cluny, introduced a renewed spiritual vigor in the church. At the same time, the papacy underwent institutional and doctrinal reform. A sense of spiritual unity grew both inside and outside the church during

120. *"Ecce jam ipsa qualitate convivantium aperte ostinditur quia per has regis nuptias praesen Ecclesia designatur, in qua cum bonis et malis conveniunt"* (The quality of the guests shows us clearly that this marriage of the king represents the present church, where the wicked mingle with the good). Gregory the Great, *Homilia in Evangelia*, 2.38.7 (P.L. 76.1285; Burke, 38). Gregory expands on this theme by comparing the church to the structure of a pyramid. The wide base represents those who are carnally minded in the church while the narrow top represents those who are spiritual.

121. "[W]hile they try to navigate the high seas in pursuit of important affairs, they are continually driven back by contrary currents towards the shores of humiliation." Gregory the Great, *Homilia in Evangelia*, 2.38.9 (P.L. 76.1271; Burke, 115).

this century.[122] As a result of this new sense of Christendom that unified society, heretics were now viewed as a threat to the cohesion of society.[123] The spread of Catharism in the twelfth century presented one of the first real heretical challenges to the medieval church and was perceived as a threat which would rupture the Christian foundation of society in southern France. At first, the secular authorities attempted to stem the spread of Catharism through legislation. But it was not long before the church recognized this as a secular intrusion into what it considered to be an essentially ecclesiastical domain.[124]

The second factor that needs to be considered are the shifts in the semiotic code by which medieval exegetes recognized unbelievers, heretics, and schismatics within the biblical texts. The background to the medieval semiotic code is found in the teachings of the church fathers. According to Chrysostom and Jerome the parable of the Tares taught that the heretics should be left alone lest some of the wheat be killed in an attempt to remove the tares.[125] In the East, Theophylact followed this line of thought. If Matthew had been killed before he was converted he would never have written his Gospel.[126] In the West, Bede almost copied Jerome's interpretation of this passage.[127] The result was that until the twelfth century, the "*sinite utraque crescere*" of Matthew 13:30 was read

122. For a detailed study on the cultural and religious shifts which took place during this period, see Lambert, *Medieval Heresy*, 3–104,

123. An example of this is seen in the manner in which Aquinas compares heresy with that of a counterfeiting money. However, heresy is much more dangerous since money only supports temporal life. Aquinas, *Summa Theologiæ* Q. 11, art. 3, 32.88–89.

124. In 1215, Innocent III called for episcopal councils to enforce the anti-heretical canons of the Fourth Lateran Council. However, it was the emperor Frederick II who incorporated these policies into official imperial legislation at his coronation in 1220. Heresy was now officially classified as treason, which could be punished with having the tongue cut out to burning at the stake for the more serious offenders. The Inquisition is recognized as having come into being either with the adoption of Frederick's imperial laws into ecclesial law in Rome in 1231, by Gregory the IX or with Innocent's bull *Ad extirpanda* (1252). Hamilton, *The Medieval Inquisition*.

125. Chrysostom *Commentariorum in Matthaeum* 46.1–2 (*P.G.* 58.477–78). Jerome appealed to the fact that a heretic may become a defender of the faith. Jerome, *Commentariorum in Mattheum*, 2.815–34 (*C.C.S.L.* 77.106–7).

126. Theophylacti *Enarratio in Evangelium Matthaei* 13.30 (*P.G.* 123.283–86)

127. Bede *In Matthaei Evangeilum exposito* 13 (*P.L.* 92.68–69). However, it is debated whether this commentary is the work of Bede or that of Rabanus. Bainton, "Religious Liberty and the Parable of the Tares," 101–4.

in such a manner that allowed a degree of toleration within the church concerning the treatment of heretics.[128]

The widely received interpretation of the parable of the Tares helps us to understand their interpretations of the parable of the Wedding Feast. This is especially evident in relation to the third invitation issued by the father in the parable to the people on the "highways." At a literal level, medieval scholars recognized this as a reference to the to roads outside the city of Jerusalem. At an allegorical level, Gregory the Great set a trajectory for reading this reference in terms of pagans (because they are outside the city of God) and those who are spiritually poor, sick, and down trodden.[129] Thus, compulsion is conceived as rescuing weak and sick souls so that they may enter the kingdom.[130]

This raised the question of why those invited in the third invitation were living in such a mean condition. The fact that they were distant from the king indicated that their lives were characterized by flawed morals or behavior.[131] The reason why the Gentiles were in this state was due to the religious and philosophical doctrines which they had been taught in ignorance.[132] Thus, the invitation to the wedding feast is a call to convert to Christianity and its teachings. Peter Comestor's comments on this passage in the *Historia Scholastica* summarized this view well. "The weak and the crippled, good and evil were induced/persuaded. For no one is excluded from the kingdom due to weakness in body, rather they are (as it were) frequently compelled."[133]

128. The persistence of this interpretation can be seen as late as the twelfth century when the Bishop of Liège, Wazo, was questioned about the forceful coercion of heretics. In his reply, he appealed to the fathers (most likely Chrysostom in particular) that the tares should be allowed to grow with the wheat since one who is a tare today may in the future become one of the wheat. Leodiensis *Vita Vasonis* 25B–C (*P.L.* 142.752). In stating this, I realize that such a generalized statement does not express every view from this period, but a full discussion of this would go beyond the confines of this chapter.

129. Gregory the Great *Homilia in Evangelia* 2.38.7–8 (*P.L.* 76.1269–70; Burke, 112).

130. Peter Comestor, *Historia Scholastica*, 128 (*P.L.* 198.1605).

131. "*Exitus autem uiarum defectus actionum intelligimus, quia illi plerunque facile ad Deum ueniunt. . .*" Sedulius Scottus *In Matthaeum* 22.8.

132. Paschasius Radbertus *Expositio in Evangelium Matthaei* 10.22.911 (*P.L.* 120.746); Anselm *Enarrationes in Evangelium Matthaei* 22.8–10 (*P.L.* 162.1437).

133. The way in which he parallels "*induxerunt bonos et malos*" with "*compellit*" indicates that he is using these verbs in a manner in which their semantic domain overlap each other. They are both referring to compelling people to accept the invita-

AQUINAS' RECEPTION OF AUGUSTINE'S POSITION

It is against this background that Aquinas' interpretation of the parable of the Wedding Feast stands out so dramatically. Before I discuss his comments on that parable, let us return to the parable of the Tares briefly. In the *Catena Aurea*, Aquinas identified the tares as heretics. He begins his discussion of the *"sinite utraque crescere"* clause in Matthew 13:30 by citing Augustine that the tares and the wheat should grow together so that the wheat will not suffer harmed in an attempt to remove the tares.[134] He buttressed this quote from Augustine with similar ones from Jerome and Chrysostom. The manner by which Aquinas places six different citations from these three authors in succession leads one to the premature conclusion that Aquinas is arguing for a position of 'toleration.' Then he introduces an abrupt turn of thought by returning to an extended series of citations from Augustine that begins with, "This was at first my own opinion, that no man was to be driven by force into the unity of Christ."[135] Aquinas concludes this line of enquiry with, "And it is wonderful to see him [referring to Paul's conversion] who entered into the gospel by the force of bodily affliction laboring therein more than all those who are called by word only."[136] The conclusion Aquinas wants the reader to draw is clear: when there is no danger of harming the wheat, the tares should be rooted out.

This thought is developed further in the *Summa Theologiæ* in questions ten and eleven under the topic, "Consequences of the Faith." Here Aquinas prescribed the guidelines for how compulsion was to be practiced in the church. One of the principles for the application of the use of coercion concerned the distinction between *hæretici* and *infideles*. Heretics were those within the church who have abandoned the orthodox position while infidels referred to unbelievers in general. By making the distinction between heretics and infidels, Aquinas was able to embrace Chrysostom's position that heretics should be tolerated, but not before he transposed the allegorical code for the tares from

---

tion by inducing or persuading them, not by force. Comestor, *Historia Scholastica*, 128 (*P.L.* 198.1605)

134. Aquinas, *Catena Aurea*, 13.30, citing Augustine *Contra Epistulam Parmeniani* 3.2, and *Quaest in Matthaeum* 12.

135. Ibid., citing Augustine *Epistle* 93.17.

136. Ibid., citing Augustine *Epistle* 185.22.

heretics to infidels.[137] This allowed him to synthesize Chrysostom's with Augustine's position.

Aquinas embraced Augustine's earlier position that faith was voluntary, and therefore true conversion could not be coerced. However, this only applied to infidels who were not hindering the faith.

> Nevertheless, the faithful, if they are able, should compel them not to hinder the faith whether by their blasphemies or evil persuasions or even open persecutions. It is for this reason that Christ's faithful often wage war on infidels, not indeed for the purpose of forcing them to believe, because even were they to conquer them and take them captive, they should still leave them free to believe or not, but for the purpose of stopping them obstructing the faith of Christ.[138]

While a person cannot, and should not, be compelled to believe, once someone had converted, they were under obligation to keep the faith and thus may be "compelled to hold to the faith." Augustine's "*compelle intrare*" is appropriated by Aquinas as a reference to heretics, not unbelievers.[139] Coercion should only be exercised when a person's heresy was publicly known and presented no danger of creating a schism if an attempt was to be made to remove the heretic.

Drawing on Augustine's interpretation of the parable of the Wedding Feast, Aquinas argued that an attempt to persuade the person of their error should be practiced first. In contrast to Peter Comestor and Anselm, Aquinas interpreted those on the outer roads as heretics, not as Gentiles in need of salvation. While this distinction may seem inconsequential, the conclusions that Aquinas drew from them were quite significant. If a heretic refused to return to the orthodox position when confronted, he or she should be excommunicated from the church and handed over to the secular court. "As for heretics their sin deserves banishment, not only from the Church by excommunication, but also from this world by death."[140] This was based on Augustine's balance of author-

---

137. Aquinas, *Summa Theologiæ*, Q. 10, art. 8 (Gilby, 32.60–61).

138. Ibid., 32.62–63. This section is most likely a reference to the Crusades which were occurring at that time (see n. A).

139. Once again Aquinas opens by discussing the position of toleration and uses Augustine's change of mind on this matter to introduce the practice of coercion. Aquinas, *Summa Theologiæ*, Q. 10, art. 8. (Gilby, 32.60–65).

140. Aquinas, Q. 11, art. 3 (Gilby 32.88–89).

ity between ecclesiastical and secular authorities. It also defended the position by which the office of the Inquisition operated. With Aquinas, the medieval church's concept of dealing with infidels, heretics, and schismatics reached its most articulate position. The enduring reception of Aquinas' exposition of these passages is demonstrated by the fact that even as late as the sixteenth century his interpretation of these parables was still being cited at inquisitorial trials.[141] Thus, it is through Aquinas that Augustine's interpretation of the parable of the Wedding Feast was re-appropriated during the late Middle Ages.

At the same time there are several significant differences between Augustine's position and Aquinas. Augustine attempted to formulate answers to the questions raised by the Donatist schism. His primary concern was not controlling or restraining Donatism as a heretical movement, rather it was the violence that resulted from this movement, especially in their attacks against the orthodox communities and clergy, and he exercised a great deal of care in the application of coercive force. However, once his text entered into the effective history of the Christian tradition it exceeded his intentions.

For several hundred years Augustine's interpretation was not received as normative. With the cultural shifts that took place during the eleventh and twelfth centuries, a horizon of expectations opened up which allowed Aquinas to once again recognize Augustine's comments on 'compelle intrare' as relevant. Even though the office of the Inquisition was established and the Crusades were taking place by the time Aquinas appropriated Augustine, his work in the *Catena Aurea* and *Summa Theologiæ* served to justify these institutions through his re-appropriation of Augustine's interpretation of the parable of the Wedding Feast.[142] Aquinas' appropriation of Augustine's interpretation resulted in a concretization of the meaning of the parable, which demonstrates the norm-building function of biblical commentaries and other forms of theological literature.

141. During the trial of Claes de Praet in 1556 the defendant appealed to Matthew 13:30, "Why do you not let me grow until the harvest?" To which the examiner replied, "Because the master of the field gave this command to his servants lest they hurt the wheat and pull it out along with the tares, but I can skirt along the edge and pluck out one or two here and there sometimes six or eight or even then or twelve, and sometimes a hundred without hurting the wheat." Bainton, "Religious Liberty," 106.

142. See the translator's note on Q. 10, art. 8.1 in Aquinas, *Summa Theologiæ*, 32.62–63.

While Augustine attempted to stipulate how compulsion should be applied, history has demonstrated that the reception and practice of his interpretations were not as careful or restrained. Augustine could never have envisioned the Crusades or the Inquisition, but his defense of the use of force to compel the obstinate clearly helped defend these institutions through Aquinas' reception of his interpretation. This should serve as a warning that biblical interpretation should be engaged with an eye to the future. The exegete should carefully consider the implications of their interpretations for future generations just as a marksman carefully considers the trajectory his projectile will take.

Reception During the Reformation

The Reformation presents us with several interesting aspects in the reception history of Matthew 22:1–14. It is not uncommon to find works on the history of biblical interpretation claiming that Luther and especially Calvin were not only the fore-runners to modern exegetical practices, but also that they shared more in common with modern exegetes than they did with their medieval predecessors.[143] However, recent work in this area has convincingly shown that work of the early Reformers demonstrates a high level of continuity in their exegetical interests with the medieval scholars.[144]

Martin Luther's *Expositions* and Bucer's *Enarrations*

Luther's cursing of the allegorical method employed by the fathers, and in particular the "clever tricks" of Origen, as being "nothing but rubbish" appears to give the impression that he was making a strong break from Patristic and medieval exegetical practices.[145] But in many respects, he is quite hospitable to their allegorical interpretations. This is particularly obvious in the introduction to his interpretation of the parable of the Wedding Feast. "This Gospel presents to us the parable of the wedding;

143. Perhaps the classic text to make this argument is Farrar, *History of Interpretation.* For more recent works which hold to this view, see Krauss, "Calvin's Exegetical Principles," 9–18; Klein, Blomberg, and Hubbard, *Introduction to Biblical Interpretation,* 39–41.

144. For an excellent collection of articles which demonstrates this view, see Muller and Thompson, *Biblical Interpretation in the Age of the Reformation.*

145. Luther, "Table Talk," in *Luther's Works,* 54.46–47, 406; Hunter, *Interpreting the Parables,* 32.

therefore we are compelled to understand it differently than it sounds and appears to the natural ear and eye. Hence we will give attention to the spiritual meaning of the parable and then notice how the text has been torn and perverted."[146] Like many of the previous commentators, he understood the invitation to the feast to have been extended to the Jewish nation first and then, because they rejected the invitation, to the Gentiles.[147] The thrust of the parable concerns the proclamation of this invitation, the gospel, throughout the whole world, even though only a small portion of those who hear will embrace it.

However, Luther broke with previous interpretations of the parable at three critical points: what the feast referred to, the significance of the excuses, and what the wedding garment symbolized. He did not see the feast to which the king invited the guests primarily as a reference to the church, but rather to the richness of the teachings in the Bible. If all the food from every kingdom were gathered together it could not compare with the "smallest word of God." This is why Jesus compared it to a marriage feast in the parable, according to Luther.[148] "Wherefore the supper here is nothing else, but a very rich and sumptuous feast, which God hath made through Christ by the Gospel, which setteth before us great good things and rich treasures."[149]

The excuses of those who declined the invitation reveal that our relationship to God should take priority over our relationship to the things of this world such as business or family.[150] Most of the Patristic and medieval scholars would have agreed with Luther's exposition of the excuses. The reason why those who were invited refused the invitation was because they did not possess enough faith in Christ to abandon their dependence on work, family, and other worldly concerns. As a result, Luther sees these characters as symbolizing those who think that

146. Beare, "The Parable of the Guests at the Banquet," 11, quoted from a sermon preached on the twentieth Sunday after Trinity.

147. Luther, "A Sermon of Dr. Martin Luther Concerning the Bidding of Guests to the Great Supper," in *Luther's Works*, 42:191.

148. Luther, "An Exposition of the Lord's Prayer," in *Luther's Works*, 42:56.

149. Luther, "A Sermon of Dr. Martin Luther Concerning the Bidding of Guests to the Great Supper," in *Luther's Works*, 42:191.

150. Luther did not go as far as Chrysostom and teach that the Christian should withdraw from the world. Instead, he took a softer position that we "should not cleave to them in our hearts." Ibid., 42:192.

they can obtain salvation through their own good works.[151] "Wherefore no man cometh to this supper, but he that bringeth with him a sincere faith, which God preferreth and loveth above all creatures."[152] Faith now becomes the central theme in the parable. The wedding garment was perceived in accordance with this theme; the lack of the wedding garment signifies the absences of sincere faith in that individual.[153] In this respect, Luther marks a sharp turn in this aspect of the parable's interpretation especially since the time of Augustine. The feast was no longer recognized as the church, but it referred to an invitation to feast on the rich truths of the gospel. Luther shifted from Augustine's ecclesiological approach to ask questions about what this parable taught in relation to salvation through faith.

Luther's approach to the parable appears to be characterized by the same degree of allegorical correspondences as those who came before him. However, what he counted as a suitable reference for the symbols in the parable underwent a significant shift due to the questions that were being raised by him and other Reformers. His interpretation of the parable is inferior to previous interpretations in two respects. First, in comparison to the unified and holistic interpretation that the Patristic and medieval scholars offered, Luther's interpretation is very fragmented. He draws out two distinct points, the gospel and faith. But it is difficult to see in his explication of the parable that gospel and faith relate to each other logically or in the narrative structure of the parable. By contrast, most of the interpretations we have examined to this point present the parable in a manner in which all the elements are related to each other within the overall structure and narrative. Second, his interpretation of the wedding garment as faith not only reflected the Reformer's emphasis on salvation by faith, but like Augustine, it reduced the possible surplus of meaning in this symbol to a single concept. This is a point for which John Maldonatus justifiably criticized Luther and other Reformers.[154]

One of the more significant exegetical moves that Luther made concerns the interpretation of *compelle intrare*. Luther argued that this

151. Hunter, *Interpreting the Parables*, 32.
152. Luther 42:193.
153. Beare, "The Parable of the Guests at the Banquet," 11.
154. See the section below, "Maldonatus, Not Everything is Faith."

phrase should not to be understood in terms of "outward compulsion, as some interpret it, that wicked and ungodly ones should be violently driven to the supper ..."—a reference most likely directed at the Catholic position on this passage that had come down from Aquinas. In fact, the use of force to compel the "wicked and ungodly" to the feast results in no benefits to either the church or the person being compelled.[155] There are two reasons for this. First, sincere faith required a free act of volition. And secondly, within the context of the parable itself, the feast no longer stood for the church but the gospel. While someone could be forced into the church or to comply with its teachings and practices, it is difficult to see how this could be applied to compelling a person to feast on the gospel. Instead, Luther understood this compulsion to refer "only to the conscience, and is inner and spiritual."[156]

While there is no evidence that suggests that Luther revised his interpretation of the parable of the Wedding Feast, his stance on toleration did shift over time. The threats presented by the radical Reformers at Müntzer, Karlstadt, and the Peasants' Revolt resulted in Luther seeking to protect the established Protestant churches. This shift is best seen in his interpretation of the parable of the Tares. In his earlier works, he wrote that there will always be some measure of heresy in the church and that some degree of toleration should be extended toward the heretics. As time progressed, he taught that Protestant princes should defend the unity of the church and the truth of the gospel preached within their jurisdictions. In his final position, he argued that the heretics should not only be refuted by the ministers teaching but disciplined by the civil magistrates as well.[157]

Martin Bucer's commentary followed Luther's interpretation of the parable of the Wedding Feast at almost every point. Towards the end of his discussion of Matthew 22:1–14, he makes a significant digression, and comments on the '*compelle intrare*' in Luke 14:23 for several pages.[158] Compulsion must be understood in relation to the sending of

155. Luther, "A Sermon . . . Concerning the Bidding of Guests," in *Luther's Works*, 42:194–95.

156. Ibid., 42:195.

157. Grell, "Introduction," in Grell and Scribner, *Tolerance and Intolerance*, 5; Bainton, "Religious Liberty and the Parable of the Tares," 110–13.

158. Bucer thought that the parables of the Wedding Feast in Matthew and the Great Feast in Luke 14 were the same parable, but did not remark on the relationship

the servants by the father. These servants went out to every part of the kingdom and found the poor, crippled and blind and through their diligence and perseverance commended the kingdom of God to everyone they found.[159] In a manner very similar to Comestor's comments on this phrase, Bucer wrote that the king had his servants compel them to enter the feast through persuasive speech.[160]

Whereas Luther only vaguely referred to "the others" who misinterpreted *compelle intrare*, Bucer attributed the abuse of this phrase to the popes who twisted its meaning in order to legitimatize their use of imprisonment and the death sentence as a means to enrich the church, not to bring glory to God. According to Bucer, the error of their interpretation was simple; the text says, *compelle intrare*, compel them to enter.[161] It does not speak about the use of force against those who create divisions or spread false teachings, but refers to the tireless effort by God's servants to exhort and persuade the people to accept the invitation to the heavenly feast which God has prepared. The apostle Paul's ministry serves as the prime example of this type of compulsion. On the recipient's side, only those who willingly and gladly accepted this invitation were worthy to receive it. Decisions made under the threat of force would be of no avail just as Luther claimed.[162]

CALVIN'S *HARMONY* AND *INSTITUTES*

Calvin enjoyed the advantage of having access to Luther's and Bucer's work before he wrote on this parable, and his reading of it raises some very interesting questions especially in light of their work.[163] Because

---

between the different accounts in his commentary. *Enarrationes per Petuae*, 165–67. See Parker, *Calvin's New Testament Commentaries*, 224.

159. "... *ad sua caena uelut compellerent, ut tande conuiuatu numerus impleretur.*" Bucer, *Enarrationes per Petuae*, 165.

160. The parallels with Comestar not only include the same argument and use of *compello/induco* but also "*quasi compellerent.*" Ibid.; Comestar *Historia Scholastica* cap. 128 (*P.L.* 198.1605).

161. "*Quidam abutuntur hoc dicto, ad comprobandam uim, qua carcerum & mortis metu, ad approbanda Papae commenta quoslibet compellunt. Scriptum est, inquiunt, Compelle intrare.*" Bucer, *Enarrationes per Petuae*, 166.

162. Ibid.

163. While I cannot date Luther's sermons that I cited above, nor prove that Calvin read them, he did have access to Luther's other works. In the case of Bucer and other Reformers such as Melanchthon and Bullinger, Calvin not only read their commen-

his discussion of the parable in the *Institutes* is both briefer than and chronologically prior to that in his *Harmony*, I shall examine it first.[164]

In the *Institutes* Calvin interpreted the parable around the twin themes of faith and the gospel, like Luther and Bucer. The feast referred to the gospel and the invitations signify the "outward preaching of the word."[165] The invitation to attend the feast corresponded to Calvin's doctrine that God extended a general call of salvation to everyone. At the same time, there was a special call issued only to believers and took place through the ministry of the Holy Spirit illuminating God's word in the believer's heart.[166]

The guest who lacked the wedding garment should "be understood as applying to those who enter the church on profession of faith but not clothed with Christ's sanctification."[167] The binding and casting of this guest into the outer darkness serves two purposes. The fate of this imprudent guest is as a warning against hypocrisy within the church. At the same time, the king's actions should serve as an encouragement to believers who are disheartened over the low moral or spiritual state of the church since it demonstrates that God will purge the church of all who are not true believers.[168] While the special call to salvation may have been extended to a person, God can withdraw the invitation because of ungratefulness on her part. "God will not forever bear such dishonors . . . but as their baseness deserves will cast them out."[169]

Calvin's *Harmony of the Evangelists* preserves a more detailed explanation of the parable of the Wedding Feast. Like Augustine, Calvin

---

taries but commented upon their work in his commentaries. Parker, *Calvin's New Testament Commentaries*, 60–77, 87–90.

164. Calvin's *In harmoniam* first appeared in 1555, and his *Institutio Christianae Religionis* was first published in 1539.

165. Calvin, *Institutes*, 4.24, §8 (Battles, 2.974).

166. "For this call is common also to the wicked, but the other bears with it the Spirit of regeneration [cf. Titus 3:5], the guarantee and seal of the inheritance to come [Eph. 1:13–14], with which our hearts are sealed [2 Cor. 1:22] unto the day of the Lord." Ibid., 2.974–5.

167. Ibid., 2.974.

168. Ibid., 2.975. This reflects Calvin's teaching on the nature of the church. The church was both visible and invisible: the invisible church comprised all true believers, the visible church was the actual, mixed church which included everyone who professed to be a Christian. Ibid., 2.1021–22.

169. Ibid., 2.974.

did not write individual commentaries on the synoptic gospels but compiled a harmony of them. It is only natural then that Calvin placed the Wedding Feast in Matthew 22 alongside the parable of the Great Feast in Luke 14. After an introductory section comparing the accounts of Matthew and Luke, Calvin begins his exposition of these parables.[170]

Like Luther, Calvin wanted to be seen as making a break from the previous trajectories of interpretation. His statement that "we ought not to attempt an ingenious explanation of every minute clause" at the conclusion of his discussion of the parable of the Wedding Feast is one indication of this.[171] His criticism appears to be a directed at the allegorical interpretations from the Patristic and medieval exegetes. Like Luther, Calvin is guilty of his own criticism when he examines each particular element of the parable as closely as those he criticized. His interpretation of the various characters and their action in the parable also agrees with the allegorical interpretations offered by the Patristic and medieval scholars.[172] Those who were invited to the feast but rejected the invitation and had their city burned symbolize the Jewish nation.[173] The different excuses that the business person and farmer gave represent how the cares of the world entangle and impede our entering the kingdom of God. This is a universal condition of humanity and not just a failure on the part of the Jewish nation. As a result, Calvin laments that "hardly one person in a hundred can be found who prefers the kingdom of God to the fading riches."[174] The lame and blind who were found on the outer roads are once again recognized as an allegorical reference to

---

170. Calvin argues that these two accounts relate the same parable. While Luke's setting is preferred and Matthew filled out more of the details "there is remarkable agreement between them on the main points of the parable." Calvini, *In harmoniam* 13.121 (Pringle, 1.167–9).

171. "... *unde colligimus, non esse subtiliter excutiendas singulas particulas*" Calvin, *In harmoniam*, 13.121 (Pringle, 1.175).

172. While much of Calvin's exegesis overlaps with Patristic interpretations, his use of the fathers differs from that of the medieval exegete. He uses their interpretations but he does not appeal to their authority in order to substantiate his argument. Steinmetz, *Calvin in Context*, 135–37.

173. Calvin, *In Harmoniam*, 13.121 (Pringle, 170–71).

174. Ibid., Pringle, 171. This echoes a similar lament made by Origen and Gregory the Great. Origen *In Matthaeum* 17.24 (G.C.S. 10.652); Gregory the Great *Homilia in Evangelia* 2.38.7 (P.L. 76.1285; Burke, 38).

the Gentiles. Their invitation to the feast points to the initiation of the Gentile mission and the inception of the church according to Calvin.

Given how Calvin followed his predecessors on these points, there are several significant points in Calvin's commentary that call for special attention. The first is the subtle manner by which he explicated the significance of the feast. As he begins his discussion of the parable, he wrote of the feast in terms of the kingdom of God. But when he reached verse 22:9, where the invitation is extended to the destitute on the outer roads, he no longer spoke of the feast in reference to the kingdom of God. Instead he explicitly identified the feast as the Church. "What the prophets had obscurely foretold about creating a new church is now plainly explained."[175]

The second point concerns his interpretation of the wedding garment. The king's casting of the guest without the garment into the outer darkness illustrates that God will judge and remove those who pollute the church. "The general truth conveyed is, that not all who have entered the Church will become partakers of everlasting life, but only those who are found to wear the dress which befits the heavenly palace."[176] So far his commentary agrees with his discussion in the *Institutes*.[177] The wedding garment symbolizes "putting on Christ" while the man without the wedding garment signifies a person who has not put off his old self with its pollution.[178] Thus, the lesson that should be gleaned from the parable is that an external profession of faith is not sufficient for salvation.

The third point in his commentary that deserves attention involves the differences between his *Harmony* and the *Institutes*. In the *Institutes*, the general and special call of God are the prominent teachings which Calvin recognized in the parable. However, these are not mentioned at all in his *Harmony*. In fact, in it he even states that he will not enter into a discussion of "the eternal election of God."[179] While these two works do not contradict each other, they do illustrate Collingwood and Gadamer's point that the meaning of a text is related to the questions one asks of it. In the *Institutes*, Calvin was concerned with questions

175. "*Ita quod obscurius de creanda nova Ecclesia praedictum fuerat a Prophetis, clare exprimit.*" Calvin, *In Harmoniam*, 13.121 (Pringle, 172).

176. Ibid., Pringle, 174.

177. Calvin, *Institutes*, 2.974.

178. Ibid.; Calvin, *In Harmoniam*, 13.121 (Pringle, 174).

179. Calvin, *In Harmoniam*, 13.121, Matt. 14 (43) (Pringle, 175).

organized around theological loci, while in the commentary he was addressing a different agenda, to explicate the meaning of the biblical text. This stands in contrast to Bucer who tried to combine both a discussion of the theological loci and a commentary into a single work, a solution that Calvin did not find satisfactory, and choose instead to write his *Institutes* and commentaries as complementary works.[180] The difference between Calvin's hermeneutical interests in the *Institutes* and in his commentaries resulted in different questions being asked that yielded different answers.

The most remarkable aspect of Calvin's commentary is his adoption of Augustine's '*compelle intrare.*' "It will excite more general surprises to find the great Reformer maintaining the right of the civil magistrate to punish heretics, and even to inflict on them the last sentence of the law."[181] On the one hand, the phrase, "compel them to enter," was an allusion to the fact that the gospel was not just a verbal invitation but was accompanied with "exhortations fitted to arouse our minds." On the other hand, he devoted more attention and force of argument to support his adoption of Augustine's position.[182]

> And yet, I do not disapprove of Augustine's frequent use of this passage against the Donatists, in order to recommend that godly princes may lawfully issue edicts to force the obstinate and rebellious to worship the true God and (maintain) the unity of the faith. Although faith is voluntary, nevertheless we see that such means are profitable for breaking their stubbornness, who unless they are forced will not be obedient (or submit).[183]

180. Parker, *Calvin's New Testament Commentaries*, 88–90.

181. Pringle, "Translator's Preface" in Calvin, *Commentary on a Harmony*, xv. Steinmetz's claim that "In every case, explicit and anonymous, in which Calvin has referred to Patristic exegesis, he has quarrelled with it," is clearly an overstatement, especially,when we consider Calvin's explicit approval of Augustine's view on this passage. Steinmetz, *Calvin in Context*, 136.

182. Calvin, *In Harmoniam*, 13.121 (Pringle, 173); Luther, "Concerning the Bidding of Guests," in *Luther's Works*, 42:195; Bucer, *Enarrationes perpetuae*, 165.

183. "*Interea non improbo, quod Augustus hoc testimonio saepius contra Donatistas usus est, ut probaret, piorum principum edictis ad veri Dei cultum et fidei unitatem licite cogi praefractos et rebelles: quia, etsi voluntaria est fides, videmus tamen, iis mediis utiliter domari eorum pervicacam, qui non nisi coacti parent.*" (I do not disapprove of the use which Augustine frequently made of this passage against the Donatists, to prove that godly princes may lawfully issue edicts for compelling obstinate and rebellious persons to worship the true God, and to maintain the unity of the faith; for, though

There are four significant aspects to Calvin's reception of Augustine's position. First, force may be used to "compel obstinate and rebellious to worship the true God." In Calvin's Geneva this meant the execution of Servetus and the repression of the Anabaptists movements. For Calvin, the purpose of compulsion is not conversion, as Augustine argued, but "to vindicate the honour of [God] by silencing those who sully His holy name."[184] Second, the goal of compulsion is to "maintain the unity of the faith." This reflects the medieval character of Calvin's thought-world. The Reformers could not fathom how a person could leave his family, community, and occupation and become a wandering evangelist. To ignore these social relationships was seen as introducing a destabilizing element into society, but for the Anabaptists these were worldly concerns.[185] Third, compulsion is to be exercised by godly princes. Christian rulers should extend toleration to others unless they are "firmly committed to making propaganda for error."[186] Inside the church, the truth is to be defended by means of proper teaching and the exercise of church discipline. Outside the walls of the church, the civil magistrate is in a different situation, in which he is "under obligation to repress error."[187] Once again Calvin appropriated Augustine. Since the magistrate was God's representative, he had authority to exercise the use of force, and the Christian magistrate in particular should have be ashamed if he was indulgent with heretics.[188] And finally, while he held to the Reformation's and the earlier church's view that faith was voluntary, he adopted Augustine's teaching that force can serve the purpose of subduing those who are obstinate. While many Protestants were divided over the idea of religious tolerance, Calvin was a strong advocate that civil magistrates should use their authority to defend the faith against heretics and schismatics. As the Protestant church established

---

faith is voluntary, yet we see that such methods are useful for subduing the obstinacy of those who will not yield until they are compelled.) Calvin, *In Harmoniam*, 13.121 (Pringle, 713).

184. Bainton, *Hunted Heretic*, 170.

185. Kasdorf, "The Anabaptist Approach to Mission," in Shenk, *Anabaptism and Mission*, 51–69; Littell, "The Anabaptist Theology of Mission," in ibid., 20.

186. Wooly, "Calvin and Toleration," in Bratt, *The Heritage of John Calvin*, 141.

187. Ibid., 141–45.

188. For an excellent discussion of the actual mechanics and workings of the secular and ecclesial government of Geneva, see Monter, *Calvin's Geneva*, 125–43, 144–64.

itself in northern Europe, the Reformers' role shifted from that of dissidents attempting to reform the church to ecclesiastical leaders seeking to consolidate and protect the Protestant gains. It was in this context that Calvin's appropriation of Augustine's '*compelle intrare*' was received and became a norm for church-state relations in Switzerland and parts of France, especially in relation to radical reformers and Anabaptists.[189]

Calvin's appropriation of Augustine's interpretation of the "*compelle intrare*" phrase was mediated through the prejudices he inherited from the medieval period, in particular from Aquinas, and not directly from Augustine. Calvin's goal of maintaining the unity of the faith was not the same as Augustine's desire to restore the wayward back to the church.[190] Christian rulers during the Medieval period swore an oath to advance the glory of God by suppressing doctrines contrary to his glory. The use of force to constrain heresy and induce heretics to abandon their views was part of canon and civil law in the late middle ages.[191] Rather, his reception of Augustine was shaped by the horizon in which he lived and his historical position in the Christian tradition, in particular by classic texts such as Aquinas' works. The manner by which Aquinas mediates Calvin's appropriation of Augustine is an example of the summit-dialogue between authors which Jauss discusses in relation to role of classic texts in a tradition.

A CRITIQUE OF CALVIN BY WAY OF HIS CONTEMPORARIES

In this section I will examine two texts which, through their relationship to Calvin (and the other Reformers at certain points), allow us to say something about the appropriateness of Calvin's exegesis. The first is John Maldonatus' commentary on Matthew and the second is the Geneva Bible.

MALDONATUS, NOT EVERYTHING IS FAITH—Maldonatus is significant not only because he was a Catholic exegete who was a contemporary

189. Grell, "Introduction," in Grell and Scribner, *Tolerance and Intolerance*, 3–6. Some Reformers, such as Jean Bonneau, who disagreed with this view were eventually forced to adopt Calvin's position. Benedict, "*Un roi, une loi, deux fois*," in ibid., 70–71.

190. Bainton, "Religious Liberty," 170.

191. Benedict discusses these responsibilities in relation to the duties of the medieval rulers. Benedict, "*Un roi, une loi, deux fois*," in Grell and Scribner, *Tolerance and Intolerance*, 68.

of the Reformers and familiar with their work, but also because he was regarded as a master of exegesis whose works were widely received for several hundred years.[192] Like Calvin and Luther, Maldonatus professed a distrust for the allegorical method.[193]

One of his common criticisms of the Reformers was their tendency to read all the parables according to the framework of salvation by faith. In his comments on the parable of the Dragnet in Matthew 13, Maldonatus wrote that all the fish caught in the net (which symbolizes the church) are Christians and have entered the church by faith. The fact that some are good and some are bad points to the conclusion that only those who practice good works are saved. This refutes Calvin and Luther, who he labeled modern heretics for teaching that "all who have faith will be saved."[194] To support his interpretation of the parable of the Dragnet, he appeals to Augustine.

> It may well be said that, although Saint Augustine refuted no class of heretics so completely as the Donatists, yet that he wrote his many works against them, and not only against them but also against the followers of Luther and Calvin long after. This is so great a matter, that whoever reads them may substitute the word 'Donatists' with the followers of Luther and Calvin.[195]

According to Maldonatus, the parable of the Wedding Feast teaches two main ideas: that many are called but few come, and that not all who enter the church will be saved.[196] In particular, he questioned

192. Often the Reformers called him *maledicentissimus* (evil speaking) Maldonatus but, at the same time, praised him for his learning and thinking. Davie, "Introduction," in Maldonado, *A Commentary on the Holy Gospels*, ix.

193. For example, in his discussion of the parable of the persistent widow he writes, "*Haec simplicia sunt et ad sensum literalem pertinent, alios sensus allegoricos si quis quaerit, legat Agustinum, Theophilum, Antiochenum, Anastasium.*" (This is the simple meaning. If you want an allegorical one, read Augustine or Theophylact.) Maldonado, *Joannis Maldonati Commentarii*, 2.316. Hunter, *Interpreting the Parables*, 34.

194. Maldonado, *Joannis Maldonati Commentarii*, 1.192–93 (Davie, 1.146). This same point is brought out in his discussion of the wedding garment. Ibid., 1.306 (Davie, 1.229).

195. Ibid., 1.192–3 (Davie, 1.146).

196. While he does not personally interpret the parable allegorically as Calvin and Luther did, he does discuss seven main elements of the parable by way of citing the church fathers' interpretations and then offering his opinion as to which he thought was best according to grammatical or theological grounds. Maldonado, *Joannis Maldonati Commentarii*, 1.304–6 (Davie, 1.224–29).

Calvin's interpretation of the significance of the wedding garment. "The followers of Calvin say that it is faith—for everything is faith with them when they themselves have no faith; nor . . . do they consider that that guest came only by faith, without which he could not have entered the guest-chamber—that is, the church."[197] Therefore, the marriage garment cannot symbolize faith. Maldonatus cited various church fathers to support his position much like a medieval exegete did, but he did so with a critical eye on their exegesis and the grammatical structure of the text.[198] To support his position he called on Tertullian, Origen, Chrysostom, Jerome, Gregory the Great, and Theophylact, who all viewed "that the wedding garment is charity, good works, and a life answering to the faith in Christ."[199] While Maldonatus recaptured some of the breadth of play to the interpretation of the wedding garment, he concluded his comments on the parable by restricting the play of meaning to "good works."[200] This was most likely a result of his polemical activity against the Reformation.

What is more significant is his mention of the question about *"compelle intrare."* If Calvin's reception of Augustine's position is striking, then so is Maldonatus's denial of it. For him, this phrase cannot mean that a person should literally be forced to convert. Rather, it is a metaphor for inducing and exhorting people to accept the gospel, "almost to appear in a manner compelled."[201] How this phrase is inter-

197. "*Neque considerant homines valde, ut sibi videntur, acuti, invitatum illum non nisi per fidem venire, aut in coenaculum, id est, in Ecclesiam ingredi potuisse. Venire enim est credere.*" Ibid., 1.306 (Davie, 1.229). Maldonatus does not treat Calvin's commentary fairly at this point. For Calvin does mention that the question whether it is faith or works is a "useless controversy; for faith cannot be separated from good works, nor do good works proceed from any other source than from faith." Calvin, *In Harmoniam*, 13.121 (Pringle, 174).

198. When he finds differing interpretations among the church fathers for a passage, Maldonatus goes with the one he thinks is best, often against tradition or the majority of commentators. In particular, he often rejects Augustine's interpretations on the grounds of grammar or theology. Davie, "Introduction," in Maldonado, *A Commentary on the Holy Gospels,* viii.

199. Maldonado, *Joannis Maldonati Commentarii,* 1.306 (Davie, 1.229).

200. Ibid.

201. "*Compelle intrare, non significat, ad fidem cogendos esse homines, sed adeo rogandos, adeo incitandos, ut quodammodo compelli videantur.*" Ibid., 1.307 (Davie, 1.232). In his discussion of the parable of the Great Feast in Luke 14, Maldonatus does not even mention this phrase at all. Ibid., 2.250–51.

preted by Luther, Bucer, and especially Maldonatus demonstrates, on a synchronic plane, that by the time of the Reformation the horizon of expectations had shifted so that Augustine's interpretation was not recognized as an appropriate reading. If this is so, then we must question whether Calvin's appropriation of Augustine's position forces an agenda upon the text that most commentators at that time would have realized was doing violence to the meaning of the text.

This is especially crucial since one of Calvin's hermeneutical criteria was that an interpretation should follow and explain the mind of the author. The degree to which the interpreter strayed from this principle is the degree to which "he leads his readers away from [the truth of the text]."[202] In the light of his contemporaries' commentaries, Calvin should have recognized that Matthew and Luke could not have had the use of coercive force in mind. As a result, his commentary did not address the subject matter of the parable. Instead, he adopted Augustine's ecclesiological interpretation, though modified through the history of its reception, to support his concept of church-state relations in Geneva and to maintain the medieval ideal of the unity of the faith in the midst of the changes of the sixteenth century. It appears Calvin is guilty of Luz's complaint that "because the reality of churches did not correspond to the reality of the texts, very often the interpretations served as an excuse or an alibi."[203] From the perspective of reception theory, if Calvin had been open to the claims of the text (or what his contemporaries recognized as the claims of the text) then his prejudices should have been provoked in his engagement with it. This should have caused him to question his appropriation of Augustine (and Aquinas') view.

THE GENEVA BIBLE'S ANNOTATIONS—The *Geneva Bible* makes an important contribution to our understanding of Calvin for several reasons.[204] Calvin was very interested in influencing the English authorities toward embracing the Reformation in a more whole-hearted

---

202. Parker, *Calvin's New Testament Commentaries,* 91, quoting Calvin's preface in his *Commentary on Romans.*

203. Luz, *Matthew in History,* 49.

204. The following article provides a clear outline of the significance of the Geneva Bible from the perspective of reception theory. Jensen, "'Simply' Reading the Geneva Bible," 30–45.

manner.[205] The *Geneva Bible* represents the reception of Calvin's theology by English scholars who sought refuge in Geneva from Queen Mary.[206] It's annotations were designed to (1) help the reader identify with the characters in the text, (2) show the reader how to apply lessons from the text, and (3) fill in the gaps in the text for the reader. The goal was to decode the Bible for the average reader, but in many places, such as the parable of the Wedding Feast, it also functioned by encoding the reader's expectations.[207] For example, the annotations inform the reader that the parables taught the mixed nature of the church and that God suffers hypocrites for a time but will in the future "fanne them out."[208] These are oncepts that represent a specific trajectory from Augustine to Calvin in the reception history of the parable.

The annotations on the Wedding Feast in Matthew 22:1–14 follow Calvin's *Harmony* at almost every point. Like Calvin, and contrary to Maldonatus, the annotators interpreted the wedding garment in terms of a changed life that proceeds from true faith. However, on the crucial question concerning compulsion in Luke 14:23, the annotations read, "The *conpulsiō* cometh of the feling of the power of Gods worde, after that his worde hathe bene preached."[209] Contrary to Calvin, the translators took Luther's position that "*compelle intrare*" refers to the exhortations of the evangelists and the inward illumination of the Spirit of the gospel message.[210]

The fact that the translators and commentators of the Geneva Bible were seeking refuge under Calvin displays a critical difference between their horizons of expectations and Calvin's, even though they were geographically and chronologically contemporary. They stood in the shoes of the Anabaptists, whose obstinacy Calvin sought to restrain. For them, the civil authorities in England represented a hindrance to

---

205. Parker, 8.

206. When Luther's and Calvin's commentaries were translated into English during the late sixteenth and seventeenth centuries the translators used the Geneva Bible as the biblical text. Thus, English understanding of the Reformers would have been colored though the perspective of this translation. Alexander, "The Genevan Version of the English Bible," 249–51.

207. Jensen, "'Simply' Reading the *Geneva Bible*," 40–4.

208. Matthew 22:11–13, n. f, *Geneva Bible*.

209. Luke 14:23, n. f, *Geneva Bible*.

210. Calvin, *Institutes*, 3.24, §8.

the Gospel, not a partner to the church as was Calvin's experience in Geneva. This difference between their horizons was reflected in the annotations at other points.

"The single most important feature of the Geneva Bible, to both the laity and the clergy, consisted in the marginal notes."[211] However these marginal notes were also very controversial. Archbishop Parker thought the Church of England should issue a new translation to replace the Geneva Bible because of its "bitter" notes.[212] The notes on Exodus 1:19, where the Egyptian midwives refused to obey Pharaoh's order to kill the Jewish babies when they were born, is a good example. They read, "Their disobiênce herein was lawful, but their dissembling evil." In 1603, Dr. John Reynolds argued for a new translation that did not contain any annotations, "hauing found in them which are annexed to the Geneua translation (which he sawe in a Bible giuen him by an English Lady) some notes very partiall, vntrue, seditious, and sauouring too much of daungerous, and trayterous conceites. As for example, Exod. 1,19, where the marginal note alloweth disobedience to Kings."[213]

If the translators of the Geneva Bible did not see fit to follow Calvin's commentary on the meaning of *"compelle intrare"* but turned to the other Reformers and the church fathers, then we must once again question Calvin's interpretation. In this case, Jauss's concept of "culinary art" can function as a critical tool against Calvin's appropriation of Augustine. Calvin's interpretation was so closely tied to his historical, cultural, and political/ecclesiological horizon that his appropriation of Augustine at this point reduced to "culinary art." It was not capable of being applied in different horizons of interpretation, but was rather an interpretation offered to meet the immediate needs of his situation. The rejection of his interpretation of "compel them to come in" by the translators and annotators of the John Maldonatus and the *Geneva Bible's*

211. Berry, "Introduction," in *Geneva Bible*, 15.

212. Pollard, *Records of the English Bible*, 297. Referring to the Geneva Bible Archbishop Parker wrote, that a new translation should be commissioned because the Geneva Bible is being used, "as for that in certaine places be pulikely vsed sum translations which have not byn Labored in your Realme having inspersed diverse preiudicall nots which might have ben also well spared." "Archbishop Parker to Queen Elizabeth," ibid., 295.

213. Ibid., 46.

translators demonstrates the inappropriateness of Calvin's understanding of this passage even within his cultural and historical situation.

Conclusion

It is hoped that I have been able to demonstrate in this chapter that reception theory offers several productive directions or methods for biblical interpretation and its history. Since I have offered a summary at the end of each section of this chapter, I will focus primarily on the Reformers in the conclusion. First, in the preceding section I have tried to show the role and significance which previous interpretations play in shaping new interpretations; specifically how medieval and Patristic interpretations played such an influential role in the commentaries of the Reformers. As such, it is difficult to separate the text from the history of its interpretations and the effects of those interpretations. The *Wirkungsgeschichte* of the biblical texts "belongs to the texts in the same way that a river flowing away from its source belongs to the source."[214]

Second, a 'summit dialogue' can be discerned in the Augustine-Aquinas-Calvin trajectory of interpretation. The impact of their readings on their communities and successive generations is hard to overstate. This trajectory not only demonstrates the norm-forming potential of a biblical interpretation but also the importance of a hermeneutic of consequences.

Third, several conclusions can be reached about Calvin's interpretation of the parable of the Wedding Feast by employing Jauss's idea of synchronic studies. Aquinas and Calvin's appropriation of Augustine's *"compelle intrare"* are counter-readings of this biblical passage when compared with those of their contemporaries. Calvin should have realized that his appropriation of *"compelle intrare"* was not a legitimate interpretation or application of the text because it was not closely related to the question which the author originally intended to answer. Or as Jauss would say, it would have been an idea foreign to the original horizon of reception. The questions we ask of the text must be appropriate to the answers that the text gives. Questions about the nature of the church and how to preserve its unity were central elements in Augustine's horizon of expectations when he approached the biblical texts. In the parable of the Wedding Feast, he found answers to these

214. Luz, *Matthew in History*, 24.

questions. Calvin most likely recognized that Augustine's questions and answers resonated with similar questions he was asking within his horizon about social unity and consolidating the gains of the Reformation. However, the inappropriateness of Calvin's questions falsify his answers.[215] Because Calvin's interpretation was tied to his immediate historical and cultural concerns in Geneva, his appropriation of Augustine's *"compelle intrare"* was not capable of being received by later interpreters situated within other horizons, especially once the Enlightenment's concept of toleration was accepted. One of the reasons why we find his adoption of Augustine's position so provocative today is that we are heirs of the Enlightenment and toleration is a virtue in contemporary society. As a result, not one commentator writing during the past two hundred years could be found who agreed with Calvin's reading of the phrase *"compelle intrare."* The summit-dialogue from Augustine through Aquinas to Calvin ends with the Reformation. Thus, Calvin's interpretation of this passage not only seems foreign, but it provokes our prejudices and calls them into play.

Finally, the acceptance of Calvin's interpretation by the early Reformation church in Switzerland reflected their shift from being 'outsiders' who sought to reform the church to 'insiders' who sought to protect the gains they had made. This demonstrates once again the norm-forming power occurring in the reception of any particular interpretation. Ideas have consequences.

---

215. "When a preceding interpretation can be falsified, for the most part this indicates neither historical errors nor objective 'mistakes,' but rather falsely posed or illegitimate questions on the part of the interpreter." Jauss, *Towards an Aesthetic*, 185; Ricœur, *Time and Narrative*, 3:173.

8

A Classic Conclusion

I WOULD LIKE TO CONCLUDE THIS STUDY BY WAY OF AN EXAMINATION of the concept of the classic. The idea of the classic is inseparably linked to questions about the historicity of a literary work and its transmission through a tradition, and as a result it plays an important role in reception theory. Perhaps most importantly for this study, the classic raises the question of how we account for certain works attracting the attention of readers and commentators generation after generation.[1]

Eighteen hundred years ago Aulus Gellus wrote *"Classicus adsiduusque aliquis scriptor, non proletarius"* (The classical writer is someone of the upper class not of the rabble or proletariat).[2] A classic was written by an ancient author and it stands above other literary works as a timeless standard.[3] Contemporary humanities and literary studies define the term "classic" in three different ways. First, it is used to designate works from a specific period of literary history, most often in reference to the classics of Greek and Latin literature. Second, the term "classic" is used to designate the great works of literature or those that are accepted as being the best representative works from a particular period. And finally, it refers to those texts that are considered part of the reading curriculum in an educational system; texts chosen for their value to teach

---

1. Martindale and Thomas, *Classics and the Uses of Reception,* contains a collection of recent articles that examine applicability of reception studies to classical works.

2. Aulus Gellius *Noctes Atticæ* 19.7.15. The English term "classic" is derived from Gellius' use of the Latin *classicus.* Gellius contrasted the *scriptor classicus* with the *scriptor proletarius.* This image appears to have been taken Servius Tullius who referred to the first class Roman citizens as *classici,* those under them the *infra classeni,* and the lowest class as *proletarii.*

3. Kermode, *The Classic,* 15; Lianeri, "The Homeric Moment?" 145.

morality, good taste, and the values of a tradition.[4] It is the second and third definitions of the classic which are the primary concern of this chapter, namely, to show that the concept of the classic can help us to understand how we view the Bible, defining points in the history of the Bible's reception, and how both of these function within the Christian tradition. The deliberative route by which I intend to arrive at those conclusions is to examine the contributions that Hans-Georg Gadamer, Hans Robert Jauss, and Alasdair MacIntyre have made to what constitutes a classic, and the significance of these definitions for biblical hermeneutics from the perspective of reception theory.

Classic Gadamer

Gadamer's section on the classic in *Truth and Method* is perhaps the most significant hermeneutical text on the classic in the past half century. As a student, Gadamer was educated in the study of the classics and his hermeneutic is, to a large extent, concerned with the relevance of classical texts as bearers of truth claims.[5] For Gadamer, the study of classic texts betrayed the weakness of the "naive scheme of history-as-research." While the historical critical method raised to consciousness the reader's historical distance from the classic text, at the same time, it also immobilized the classic.[6] The historical critical approach destroyed the normative and pedagogical value of classical texts by reducing them to mere 'relics' from the past. We may consider Augustine's *Confessions* a theological classic, but the historical-critical method only subjects it to "answer a thousand impertinent questions."[7]

---

4. Wellek, "The Term and Concept of 'Classicism' in Literary History," 105–28; Fleischmann, "Classicism," in Preminger, Warnke, and Hardison, *The Princeton Encyclopedia of Poetry and Poetics,* 136–41. For an excellent reader on the classic, see Bate, *Criticism: The Major Texts.*

5. Watson, *Text and Truth,* 45; Sullivan, *Political Hermeneutics,* 20 ff; Lawrence, "Translator's Introduction," in Gadamer, *Reason in the Age of Science,* xiii.

6. Nietzsche, *The Use and Abuse of History,* 97. Jauss agrees with Nietzsche's assessment and feels that the dominance of the historical method was largely responsible for creating the dissatisfaction with literary studies in the 1960's. Jauss, "Limits and Tasks of Literary Hermeneutics," 96.

7. Watson, *Text and Truth,* 49.

After World War I, various scholars began to recognize the normative value of the classic alongside its historicity.[8] One of Gadamer's concerns is how to give hermeneutical justice to both of the classic's dimensions: its historicity and its normativity. The normative element of a classic text is its most important trait according to Gadamer. Its authority cannot be exhausted through historical research because it is primarily not a statement about the past but an address to the present. "The classical represents an ideal of excellence that remains compelling to us in spite of critical reflection upon certain aspects of it."[9] Traditional definitions of the classic are inadequate because they failed to address the manner in which the classic addresses the present.

How then does Gadamer define the classic?

> It does not refer to a quality that we ascribe to a particular historical phenomena but to a mode of being historical: the historical process of preservation (*Bewahrung*) that, through constantly proving itself (*Bewährung*), allows something true (*ein Wahres*) to come into being.[10]

This appears to be a development of Hegel's maxim that "What is rational is real and what is real is rational."[11] What is revealed in history is filtered and tested through the rational process of thesis, antithesis, and sublation. What is rational, real, or true will prove itself in history and become embedded in the tradition.

The term classic does not primarily designate a text comes from a certain historical period or exemplifies a particular style. Rather, the term classic refers to how a text exists or is preserved through history. In the case of the classic though, it is not so much the preservation of what is real or actual that is significant but the manner in which an enduring element of the classic continues to address successive historical horizons. A classic constantly proves itself by the way it is able to address new generations of readers because it possesses a surplus of meaning. It retains its normative role in a tradition through the interpretation and reinterpretation to which it is subjected. "This is just what the word

---

8. Sullivan, *Political Hermeneutics,* 18–64; Gadamer, *Truth and Method,* 286–87.

9. Warnke, "Legitimate Prejudices," 98.

10. Gadamer, *Truth and Method,* 287.

11. Hegel, *Hegel's Philosophy of Right,* 10. See my discussion of this topic in the section, "Time is the Best Teacher," in chapter 2.

'classical' means: that the duration of a work's power to speak directly is fundamentally unlimited."[12]

While the classical is historical, it stands above the changes in taste and culture that restrict other works to the horizon in which they originated. The truth a classic conveys is accessible to every generation. "When we call something classical, there is a consciousness of something enduring, of significance that cannot be lost and that is independent of all circumstances of time—a kind of timeless present that is contemporaneous with every other present."[13] Gadamer attempts to walk a fine line here. On the one hand, a classic is more than a text from a certain period or historical style. On the other hand, it does not possess some supra-historical value but is still a historically constituted and understood cultural artifact.[14] However, the historical nature of a classic needs to be understood in terms of how it proves itself and is preserved *through* history.

In brief, there are three aspects to Gadamer's thought on the classic that are relevant for theological hermeneutics. First, the normative value of the classic is a function of its ability to address each generation with its truth claims because its meaning will never be exhausted. The normative claim of a classic text is not monological but polyvocal. Second, the manner by which the classic overcomes historical distance and addresses the present directly (not as an artifact from the past that requires interpretation) is an ideal case of effective historical consciousness in which the past and present horizons are fused. In such cases, "Understanding is to be thought of less as a subjective act than as participating in an event of tradition, a process of transmission in which past and present are constantly mediated."[15] And third, the classical exemplifies how tradition preserves the past. A tradition does not preserve or remember everything. Rather it preserves those elements of the past which have relevance for successive generations. "Thus the classical epitomizes a general character of historical being: preservation amid the ruins of time."[16] A classic's truth claims are constantly proven

12. Gadamer, *Truth and Method*, 290; Warnke, "Hermeneutics and the Social Sciences," 355.

13. Gadamer, *Truth and Method*, 288.

14. Ibid., 286–88.

15. Ibid., 290.

16. Ibid., 289.

and preserved as they are passed down in the tradition in a manner that not only forms connections between the past and present but does so in a way that addresses the present in a relevant and compelling manner. Thus, a classical text operates like a thread that preserves and gives continuity to the tapestry of a tradition's corporate knowledge. If we were to substitute the word 'Bible' for 'classic' in the above paragraph the significance of Gadamer's concept of the classic for biblical hermeneutics is readily apparent.

David Tracy: A Classic Gadamerian

David Tracy has, perhaps more than anyone else, adopted and applied Gadamer's concept of the classic in his work, *The Analogical Imagination*.[17] On the whole, Tracy faithfully follows Gadamer's thought and clearly demonstrates the relevance of the classic for theological study. In fact, one of the elements which Tracy thinks constitutes a theological text's future reception as a classic involves the manner in which it enters into conversation with the classics of the Christian tradition. "Barth's retrieval of Calvin; Lonergan and Rahner of Aquinas; Reinhold Niebuhr of Augustine; H. Richard Niebuhr of Jonathan Edwards; Paul Tillich and Rudolf Bultmann of Luther" are contemporary examples of how theologians have entered into dialogue with the classics of the Christian tradition.[18]

There are two aspects to Gadamer's thought which Tracy develops in particular. The classic (1) possesses an excess of meaning and (2) a form of timelessness that while rooted in its own historicity, addresses the contemporary reader.[19] The surplus of meaning that a classic text possesses means that the truth of the classic is open for possible disclosure in every reader's horizon. The classic not only possesses an excess of meaning, but it actually encourages this through its interpretations.[20] The ability of the classic to disclose its truth claims in a relevant

17. Tracy, *The Analogical Imagination*, especially chap. 3, "The Classic," 99–153.

18. This is one of the main traits by which Tracy considers them as candidates for being recognized in the future as theological classics. Ibid., 104.

19. Ibid., 102.

20. Ibid., 113, 133. For Stout, the classic is the ideal example of how texts promote a diversity of interpretations. "The more interesting the text, the more readings we shall be able to give without simply repeating ourselves and our predecessors, and the more readings we shall want to give." Stout, "What is the Meaning of a Text?" 9.

manner to each horizon is the basis for its timelessness. This is what gives the classic its normative status. "Thus do we name in these experiences, and these alone, 'classics.' Thus do we recognize, whether we name it so or not, a normative element in our cultural experience, experienced as a realized truth."[21] The experience of readers during the past two thousand years of realizing new possibilities for existence which have arisen from their reading of the Bible would, according to the criteria of disclosive potential, firmly categorize the Bible as a classic.[22]

If the timelessness of the classic is grounded in the manner by which it addresses successive generations of readers, then the endurance of the classic is dependent upon its continued reception by its readers.[23] On the one hand, each generation must enter anew into direct dialogue with the classic text. "I can never repeat the classic to understand them. I must interpret them."[24] Simply repeating how previous interpreters have understood a text like Romans does not constitute an active engagement with the text. To do so is to circumvent the disclosive potential of the text to address each horizon of readers. It is not just the literary, theological, or other qualities of the Bible that make it a classic but its reception by successive generations of believers.

On the other hand, the classic addresses us indirectly through our tradition. The classic's disclosure of truth is so compelling that it becomes normative the moment it is experienced and as a result, it enters into the memory and prejudices of our tradition through its readers. "Its memory enters as a catalyst into all our other memories and, now subtly, now compellingly, transforms our perceptions of the real."[25] The classic is handed down to us directly as a text and indirectly through its effect and influence on our tradition. Because a classic text has shaped our tradition and is part of our cultural legacy it is part and parcel of our prejudices. In this sense, our encounters with classics will often be

21. Tracy, *The Analogical Imagination*, 108, also 113.

22. Vanhoozer, "A Lamp in the Labyrinth," 50–51.

23. "The position defended here emphasizes, above all, the reception by the reader of the classical text." Tracy, *The Analogical Imagination*, 118. Stendahl makes a very similar point, "For it is recognition that makes a classic a classic, not its inner qualities." Stendahl, "The Bible as a Classic," 4.

24. Tracy, *The Analogical Imagination*, 103.

25. Ibid., 115.

indirect, through second and third hand sources or references.[26] They contribute to the formation of our prejudices. How a particular generation interprets Jesus' teachings as recorded in the Sermon on the Mount in Matthew plays a significant role in practices of the church for that generation. However, their interpretation of the Sermon on the Mount is not limited to their historical horizon but it exceeds that horizon. It has the potential to enter into the memory of successive generations of interpreters. The normative status of the Bible operates at both the reflective level, through the reader's experience of the Bible's truth claims, and at the pre-reflective level, through the prejudices of the Christian tradition which have been partially constituted and defined by the impact the biblical text has had upon previous generations.

If Tracy and Gadamer are correct, then the interpretation of a Bible as a classic should be composed of a three-way dialogue: the Bible, the reader, and the Christian tradition. The interpreter must engage the biblical text in an open dialogue and allow its truth claims to exert themselves upon the reader. At the same time, the interpreter must expand this dialogue to include the history of the text's reception, its *Wirkungsgeschichte*.[27]

There are two reasons why this third aspect of the dialogue is hermeneutically valuable. First, at the contemporary or synchronic level it allows us as readers to check our understanding of the text against the wider perspective of our contemporary community. Second, at the historical or diachronic level it allows us to verify or correct our understanding against those of our tradition. "If one's own experience has been verified by other readers, especially by the community of capable readers over the centuries, the reflective judgment should prove that much more secure."[28]

This is not an exercise in the kind of historical knowledge which Gadamer and Jauss criticize. Rather, the goal is to develop the interpreter's effective-historical consciousness (*wirkungsgeschichtliches*

---

26. "Every classic text, moreover, comes to any reader through the history of its effects (conscious and unconscious, enriching and ambiguous, emancipatory, and distorted) upon the present horizon of the reader." Ibid., 105; Hirsch, *Cultural Literacy*, xiv. See Frye, *The Great Code*, for a thorough investigation and documentation of how the Bible is the most influential source for the Western literary tradition.

27. Tracy, *The Analogical Imagination*, 131.

28. Ibid., 116.

Bewußtsein).[29] As the interpreter engages the *Wirkungsgeschichte* of a classic text the possibilities are introduced for her to realize her place within the history of this text's transmission, to verify her interpretation, to uncover ideological and theological distortions in the transmission of the classic, and to designate intersubjective "boundaries" that determine what counts as a valid interpretation.[30]

The manner in which this type of study opens us to the provocative and transformational power of the classic text is an important contribution which reception theory offers that should not be overlooked. This provocation occurs when we realize the historical distance between the classic and our horizon as we engage the reception history of a classic. This raises our prejudices to consciousness, brings them into play with the claims of the text, and opens the possibility for the fusing of horizons.[31]

> As a single interpreter, for example, I may recognize the challenge to my present preunderstanding of a text of Ignatius of Loyola which Roland Barthes' vitalizing reading now allows— even when I do not accept Barthes' reading of this text as the most adequate one. I may recognize as a second example, the challenge to my preunderstanding which T. S. Eliot's readings of Shelley, Milton or Vergil provide—even when I do not finally accept his rejection of Shelley, his ambivalence towards Milton, his astonishing awe in front of Vergil . . . Yet in their interpretations of these texts at once challenge mine and, by that challenge, they inevitably transform, however subtly, my own interpretations of the same texts.[32]

Jauss: When Is Classic a Classic?

Like Gadamer, Jauss' hermeneutical theory arose from his work on classical texts. Gadamer was primarily interested in classical Greek literature, especially Aristotle and Plato's work. Jauss, on the other hand,

---

29. At the historical level the interpreter should attempt to "render explicit the history of the influences, effects, and interpretations as well as the history—partly traditional, partly personal—of the interpreter's own preunderstanding of the tradition." Ibid., 120.

30. Eckert, "Hermeneutics in the Classroom," 15.

31. Weinsheimer, *Philosophical Hermeneutics and Literary Theory*, 142.

32. Ibid., 120–21.

tends to have a much wider field of interest, but it was his work on the literature of medieval animal epics, the *Songs of Roland*, which raised hermeneutical questions concerning classics. In particular, he was concerned with how the modern reader should approach medieval texts which were once widely received but are so foreign to the modern reader's horizon of expectations that they present the challenge of the "forgotten horizon of a closed past."[33]

The 'timelessness' of a classic reveals a significant point of difference between Jauss and Gadamer on the subject on this topic. Gadamer's formulation of the timelessness of the classic was troublesome according to Jauss.[34] For Gadamer, the classic text continues to speak to each horizon "as if it were saying something to me in particular."[35] The classical tragedies of Greece are an example of this. While they were originally performed for certain festivals, their power to endure meant they were performed in new and different situations, until they are no longer experienced as performances today but are primarily read as texts. The reason they have endured as classics is because the original questions they sought to answer possess a "superiority to and freedom from its origins" that allows them to address each horizon directly.[36] Tracy adapted this concept to a theological framework. Questions concerning human finitude, mortality, estrangement, sinfulness, and the need for reconciliation are examples of questions that possess this 'freedom for its origins' and address everyone.[37]

While Gadamer denies that his formulation of the 'timeless' character of a classic implies any type of 'supra-historical' character to the classic or to its question, Jauss claims that Gadamer has not adequately defended against his work being understood as implying this. If Tracy's work is a faithful extension of Gadamer's, then we can see how

---

33. Jauss, "The Identity of the Poetic Text," 159; see 159–65. The following illustrate Jauss' concern in this area: "The Alterity and Modernity of Medieval Literature," 181–229; "Thesis on the Transition," 144–47.

34. Godzich, "Introduction," in Jauss, *Aesthetic Experience*, xxxii; Holub, *Reception Theory*, 44.

35. Gadamer, *Truth and Method*, 577.

36. Ibid. Jauss claims that the superiority of the question over its origin is based on Gadamer's concept of mimesis as 'recognition.' In the classic, we recognize a question which resonates with our experience of the world. Jauss, *Towards an Aesthetic*, 30–31.

37. Tracy, *The Analogical Imagination*, 164.

Gadamer's view can open the door to a form of supra-historicalism.[38] Tracy asserts that a classic is "*always* retrievable, *always* in need of appreciative appropriation and critical evaluation, *always* disclosive and transformative with its truth of importance, *always* open to new applications and thereby new interpretations."[39] In contrast to the vast majority of literature that is meaningful for only a limited period of time, a classic is perceived as provocative and transformative in every horizon because it possesses a surplus of meaning as well as a certain form of timelessness. This is because the meaning that the classic bears is both particular (how it is understood in each horizon) and universal (received in every horizon).[40]

According to Jauss, the classic is more subject to the vicissitudes of history than either Gadamer or Tracy realize. Classics come and go with the passing of time. "Jauss refuses to see in the enduring character of great works anything other than a temporary stabilization of the dynamic of reception."[41] A good example of this is the reception of *Fanny* and *Madame Bovary*, which was covered in chapter 4. Even though many recognize *Madame Bovary* as a literary classic today, it took years before the reading public could appreciate Flaubert's narrative style and the manner in which his novel challenged the morals at that time.[42] This demonstrates one of the more interesting features concerning the classic: historical distance is required in order to recognize a text as a classic. "If 'it is only by hindsight,' as Eliot says, 'that a classic can be known as such' . . . that is because the classic has not distinguishing characteristics that enable one to recognize it in the contemporary."[43] In fact, a text

---

38. Ricœur, *Time and Narrative*, 3.172. Warnke recognizes this problem in Gadamer's work but still attempts to defend his view against this charge. Warnke, *Gadamer, Hermeneutics, Tradition and Reason*, 105. In his latest work, Gadamer appears to modify his view and suggests that historical distance is required for the reception of the classic. Gadamer, "Reflections on My Philosophical Journey," 45.

39. Tracy, *The Analogical Imagination*, 115. "When we read a classic . . . we find that our present horizon is *always* provoked, sometimes challenged, *always* transformed by the power extended by the classic's claim." Ibid., 134, emphasis adde in both quotes.

40. Ibid., 101–7, 115. Sanks, "David Tracy's Theological Project," 713.

41. Ricœur, *Time and Narrative*, 3.172.

42. See chapter 4, "Thesis 3." Jauss documents the various reactions of critics when *Fanny* and *Madame Bovary* were published in "Die beiden Fassungen," 96–7.

43. Weinsheimer, *Philosophical Hermeneutics*, 135. Tracy also implicitly realizes this when he discusses which modern theological works are candidates for becoming classics in the future. Tracy, *The Analogical Imagination*, 104–5.

that is immediately and widely received is often too closely aligned with the expectations of the horizon in which it appeared. As time passes and the horizons of expectations shift, such a work will quickly become irrelevant and forgotten as the reader's prejudices change. It is at risk of becoming intellectual "fast food" or "culinary art," as was the case with *Fanny*.[44] To assert that a text is a classic within the original horizon it appeared in is to misunderstand what a classic is.

The passing of time allows the disclosive potential of the text to shape the expectations of succeeding generations of readers so that they are able to appreciate the text more fully, and retrospectively recognize it as a classic. In the instance of *Madame Bovary*, it was through a small group of connoisseurs that this novel was first received and the norms of how to read it were introduced and spread to ever wider circles of readers, which created new literary norms and expectations in the process.[45]

> The "verdict of the ages" on a literary work is more than merely "the accumulated judgment of other readers, critics, viewers, and even professors"; it is the successive unfolding of the potential for meaning that is embedded in a work and actualized in the stages of its historical reception as it discloses itself to understanding judgment, so long as this faculty achieves in a controlled fashion the "fusion of horizons" in the encounter with tradition.[46]

The various concretizations of the meaning of the text present the interpreter with both appropriate and inappropriate understandings of the text, fruitful questions for further dialogue, or dead-ends to be avoided.

> Only as the horizon changes and expands with each subsequent historical materialization, do responses to the work legitimize particular possibilities of understanding, imitation, transformation, and continuation—in short, structures of exemplary

44. While Tompkins takes a more critical view of the concept of the classic, she does note how the literary qualities of Hawthorne's work took time to be realized. Even though his short stories are widely read and reprinted today, "to Hawthorne's contemporaries they were indistinguishable form the surrounding mass of magazine fiction." Tompkins, "Masterpiece Theater," 134.

45. Jauss, *Towards an Aesthetic*, 28.

46. Ibid, 30, quoting Wellek, *Concepts of Criticism*, 17.

character that condition the process of the formation of literary tradition.[47]

It is through the reception of a text through history that we recognize the normative status of a particular text, confer on it the status of "classic," and begin to realize what constitutes an appropriate understanding of its meaning as this unfolds in different horizons of expectations.[48]

The passing of time is a double-edged sword. Not only is it needed to recognize and appreciate a classic, but it can also reduce a classic to an obscure corner of a tradition. As Heidegger pointed out, tradition possesses a leveling down power that can neutralize the provocative or normative status of any text.[49] Collingwood also realized this when he wrote that the question a classic originally sought to answer could be forgotten over time.[50] As a tradition progresses, previous interpretations and other works on a classic shape the pre-understanding of successive generations of readers. While this gives them a point of entry for understanding the text, a tradition of interpretation may become so dominant that certain generations of readers may read the classic in a manner in which its message lines up very closely with their pre-understandings. As a result, the text loses its provocative or truth disclosing potential. If a classic is not presented in a manner that protects the "otherness" of the text, then it is in danger of being incorporated into the reader's horizon of expectations. They naively project their preunderstanding onto the classic, and as a result, their horizon of expectations is not enlarged, provoked, or changed from this form of interaction with the classic.[51] The classic, as a result, is read in a manner that confirms the prejudices, methods, and practices of the current community. Alternatively, the tradition may shift in the opposite direction and the questions, which the text originally sought to answer, are now so foreign to the readers

47. Jauss, *Towards an Aesthetic*, 64.

48. See the section, "Performance and Tradition Formation," in chapter 2. "This logic manifests itself in the formation and transformation of the aesthetical canons and, changing horizons of interpretations, renders possible the distinction between the arbitrary and consenting, between the merely 'original', and the normative interpretations." Jauss, "Limits and Tasks of Literary Hermeneutics," 118.

49. Heidegger, *Being and Time*, 165; Jauss, *Aesthetic Experience*, 16; Frede, "The Question of Being: Heidegger's Project," 60.

50. Collingwood, *Autobiography*, 39.

51. Merriman, "Minutes of the Colloquy," 53; Warnke, "Legitimate Prejudices," 98.

that it is perceived as obscure or obsolete. In either case, one must ask if the text should be considered a classic any longer.[52] In either case, what once enjoyed the status of a classic is relegated to the back shelves of history.

According to Jauss, one of the goals of reception theory is to provide a means by which classic texts, which have fallen from their classical status, may be rescued from the dust of history. Through the historical reconstruction of the original horizon of expectations we can grasp to some degree the manner in which the text provoked, denied or challenged its original audience's expectations. The recovery of the alterity of a classic text raises the 'otherness' of the text to the reader's consciousness and opens the possibility for the reader to engage in it a more meaningful, or appropriate manner.

> The classical character of the so-called masterworks especially belongs to this character of the second horizontal change; their beautiful form that has become self-evident, and their seemingly unquestionable "eternal meaning" bring them, according to an aesthetics of reception, dangerously close to the irresistibly convincing and enjoyable "culinary" art, so that it requires a special effort to read them "against the grain" of the accustomed experience to catch sight of their artistic character once again.[53]

The reception history of a text provides us with concrete instances of how previous readers have realized various elements of the text's surplus of meaning. In this way, the past can enable us to "read against the grain" of our own prejudices and horizon of expectations, and in this way open us to the claims of the text again.

Classics and Continuity

One of the strengths of Gadamer's position concerns the way in which classics are proven and preserved as they are passed down through his-

52. The diversity of questions and answers embodied within the tradition will be homogenized and the reader will most likely view his tradition as a linear accumulation of knowledge or progress from the earliest period until the present. Kuhn, *The Structure of Scientific Revolutions*, 165–67, 177; Kuhn, *The Essential Tension*, 228–31. See also Rush, "Reception Hermeneutics," 128; Gadamer, "The Continuity of History," 238.

53. Jauss, *Towards an Aesthetic*, 25–26, emphasis added. Weinsheimer, *Philosophical Hermeneutics*, 142.

tory. The classic creates connections between the past and the present in a manner that are relevant and compelling for the contemporary reader. In this section, They perform this role on both the synchronic and diachronic axes.

On a broadly synchronic axis, the classic gathers and defines the literature of its period. The heterogeneous collection of texts from any particular period coalesce into a fairly homogeneous family of texts as successive generations of readers relate them to their horizon of expectations and in this process these texts become part of the prejudices of a common horizon.[54] Certain works are retrospectively recognized as being the high point or "classic" expression of that period or style of literature or art. A classic can also create and define the norms for a genre by which successive works are judged. The "classic is also the seed that generates a line of successors and thus initiates a history."[55] As such, these texts gather the other texts of that period under them, even those that were originally alternatives or rivals to the text that was eventually recognized as a classic.[56]

> In either case, in retrospect or prospect, the advent of the classic is not just historical but is a historic event. It gathers a history to it, organizes and unifies history. The classic makes history and thus is not merely the object of historical research but also its condition. The locus of unity in diversity, the classic is the still point of sameness and continuity in the succession of generations.[57]

Calvin's commentaries demonstrate how classic texts contribute to continuity at the synchronic level. During the early phases of the Reformation, various Reformers experimented with different genres or styles for biblical commentaries. Philip Melanchthon approached the exposition of the Scriptures in order to expound theological loci. This

---

54. Jauss, "Literary History as a Challenge to Literary Theory," 38. See the discussion of Jauss's sixth thesis in chapter 4.

55. Weinsheimer, *Philosophical Hermeneutics*, 138.

56. The leveling effect of tradition is one of the dominant elements that creates continuity within a tradition. Heidegger, *Being and Time*, 164–65; Frede, "The Question of Being," 60.

57. Weinsheimer, *Philosophical Hermeneutics*, 139. The classic represents a unity in diversity in the manner that it gathers and organizes history. Ibid.; Ricœur, *Time and Narrative*, 3.173.

meant that the issues discussed were not primarily related to the subject matter of the text but were organized around and determined by theological loci. Martin Bucer perceived the weakness of Melanchthon's approach and attempted to synthesize it with a running commentary that followed the text biblical more closely. While his commentaries gave more weight to the content and order of the biblical text he often jumped to a theological discussions when relevant issues were mentioned in the text. "The result, however, was two books in one . . . The reader was not made to enter into an engagement with the document and its words, for the very length and difficulty of the work erected a formidable barrier between the apostle and his readers."[58]

Calvin, by contrast, adopted the same model he used for his earlier work on Seneca's *De Clementia*. His biblical commentaries are characterized by a structure which is immediately familiar to most reader's today: the original text opens each section of the commentary followed by his comments on the passage that follow the order of the text. The actual text of his commentary followed a verse-by-verse analysis of the text which Ulrich Zwingli had introduced. The combination of Calvin's exegetical style and his emphasis on clarity and brevity are three of the distinctive features which continue to function as norms for how commentaries are written today.[59] Even to this day, Calvin's commentaries are praised by authors such as Brevard Childs and C. E. B. Cranfield.[60] As classics, Calvin's commentaries 'gather and define' one's view of biblical

58. Parker, *Calvin's New Testament Commentaries*, 88. Calvin, while he respect Bucer's work, wrote, "For whatever the subject matter he [Bucer] sets himself to expound, so many things are suggested to his pen by the incredible fertility of his powerful mind that he does not know when to stop writing." Quoted in Wright, "Bucer, Martin," 249.

59. Karl Barth is a vivid illustration of this when he pleas for a return to Calvin's style of commentary. "For example, place the works of Jülicher side by side with that of Calvin: how energetically Calvin, having first established what stands in the text, sets himself to re-think the material and to wrestle with it, till the walls which separate the sixteenth century from the first become transparent! . . . If a man persuades himself that Calvin's method can be dismissed . . . he betrays himself as one who has never worked upon the interpretation of Scripture." Barth, *The Epistle to the Romans*, 7; Parker, *Calvin's New Testament Commentaries*, 85–93. Even the genre of a harmony, which Calvin adopted and modified from Osiander and Augustine, functioned as a norm for future commentators. Bugenhagen's *Monotessaron historiae evangelicae lationogermanicum* (1566) and Martin Chemnitz's *Harmoniae* (1641–45) are two examples of later commentaries which were patterned on Calvin's work. Kealy, *Matthew's Gospel*, 226, 238.

60. Puckett, "Calvin, John," 293.

interpretation during the Reformation, until one actually reads other commentaries from that period and realizes the diversity of commentary genres that were practiced among the Reformers.[61]

Classics preserve and bind a tradition together along the diachronic axis as well. Our dialogue with classical texts occurs at three different levels according to Jauss. First, the classic shapes our prejudices at a pre-reflective level. The classic's compelling disclosure of truth has entered into the memory and prejudices of our tradition through previous readers and interpreters. Classical commentaries and theological works partially constitute our preunderstanding of the Bible and determine to a certain degree what we recognize in the text, hence, they serve as pre-reflective criteria for the "correctness" of an interpretation.[62] At the same time, we are already familiar with the classic through secondary and tertiary sources, references, and illusions in other works.[63]

Second, at the institutional level, the classic often plays an important role in the educational curriculum. This is both a blessing and a curse. On the one hand, a classic text can be used to develop the *phronesis* and historically-effective consciousness of the individual and community as Gadamer argued. On the other hand, if the classic is not presented in a manner that protects its 'otherness,' then it is in danger of being assimilated into the present horizon of expectations. We naively re-project our pre-understandings onto the classic and as a result, our horizon of expectations is not enlarged, provoked, or changed from this type of interaction with it.[64] In this case, the classic's assimilation to the present horizon only serves to confirm the prejudices, methods, and practices of the current community. This is why the fusion or mediation

61. For examples of the different commentaries from that period see the section, "Reception During the Reformation" in the previous chapter.

62. For more on this, see the section, "Performance and Tradition Formation," in chapter 3.

63. Gadamer, "The Continuity of History and the Existential Movement," 238. "The corpus of classic texts constitutes an iterable linguistic praxis; and the so-called intertextuality of literature thus appears to be, at least in part, a recourse for overcoming chronic change and localism in the connotations of the vocabulary." Bonati, "The Stability of Literary Meaning," in Valdés and Miller, *Identity of the Literary Text*, 240.

64. Merriman, "Minutes of the Colloquy," 53. The ideological criticism that classics can function as tools for suppression or domination reveals the danger of assimilating such texts naively into our present horizon. However, a classical text can still function even within such distorted conditions of communication. Warnke, "Legitimate Prejudices," 98.

of horizons must remain an active synthesis by raising to consciousness the historical distance, and the tension it creates, between the classic and the present horizon of the reader.[65]

In this sense, the classic contributes to the continuity of a tradition in a manner similar to the "summit-dialogue" of authors.[66] Like the summit-dialogue, an open and active conversation with our tradition often occurs through the texts recognized as classics.[67] The way in which an author revives a concept or question from an earlier author is an example of the archaeological function of the classic.[68] The biblical commentary fulfils this function not only in the manner that it seeks to explicate the biblical text but also when it revives or enters into dialogue with a previous interpreter's commentary.[69] However, it would be a mistake to equate the classic with the members of the summit-dialogue.

Not every classic will serve as a defining point in a tradition of interpretation. Rather the defining trait of the classic is its reception by successive generations of readers. Even though Jülicher's commentary on the parables marks the paradigm shift from nineteen hundred years of interpreting the parables allegorically, and as such is one of the most significant contributions to the summit-dialogue of parable interpretation, it is not recognized as a classic on the parables. By contrast, even though R. C. Trench's *Notes on the Parables* does not represent a defining moment in the reception history of parable interpretation, his work enjoys the status of being a classic text on the parables today. This is remarkable given the fact that Trench takes an allegorical approach to the parables and his work was first published almost fifty years before Julicher signaled a paradigm shift away from the allegorical method.[70]

Not everyone accepts the archaeological function of the classic. Michel Foucault claims that any idea of a relationship we may think we possess with a classic is mistaken. When cultural paradigm shifts take place, our relationship with the classical texts is broken.[71] The main

65. Merriman, "Minutes of the Colloquy," 52; Jauss, *Towards an Aesthetic*, 25–26; Gadamer, "The Continuity of History," 239.

66. Jauss, "*Der Leser*," 336–37.

67. Gadamer, "The Continuity of History," 238–39.

68. Jauss, "Tradition, Innovation, and Aesthetic Experience," 383.

69. Tracy, *Analogical Imagination*, 104–5.

70. See the section, "Parables and Paradigms," in chapter 6.

71. Instead of paradigm shifts, Foucault coined the term '*episteme*' which referred to "the total set of relations that unite at a given period the discursive practices that give

example he employs is how our relationship with the classics of Greece and Rome was severed during the cultural shifts of the Enlightenment. For Foucault, history is not continuous but is a chain of broken epochs transitioned by wholesale transformations in the discursive practices which constitute our culture.[72] Texts that are recognized as classics are the result of political decisions to legitimate the existing social order. Their role is to ideologically condition the people.[73] There are two problems with Foucault's position. First, as Cornel West points out, this position is based on the concept of the unending play of interpretation, which is problematic at best.[74] If we accept Foucault's position, then no one can claim that their view is better than the accepted one.

> In a world where there is only the unending play of difference nothing can rightly be evaluated to a place of continuing validity, not even the equal entitlement of the conflicting differentia— their right to be heard, their right to equal participation in the field of discourse, and so forth. Nothing can claim permanent entitlement, nothing superiority, not even justice. The allowable result is what Fox-Genovese calls the "worst forms of political domination," namely, the rule of power.[75]

Second, this position misses the fact that in the humanities classics cross paradigm boundaries.[76]

Since every act of interpretation is provisional, a classical text anticipates successive acts of interpretation.[77] Its socially formative

---

rise to epistemological figures, sciences, and possibly formalized systems." Foucault, *The Archeology of Knowledge*, 191. See also Foucault, *The Order of Things*.

72. Weinsheimer, *Philosophical Hermeneutics*, 146.

73. Brown, *Boundaries of Our Habitations*, 68; Tompkins, "Masterpiece Theater," 145.

74. West, *The American Evasion of Philosophy*, 226; see also the discussion in chapter 2, "The Enlightenment: Pushing Play to One Side of the Field."

75. Brown, *Boundaries of Our Habitations*, 71.

76. Bonati, "The Stability of Literary Meaning," in Valdés and Miller, *Identity of the Literary Text*, 240–41; Kuhn, *The Structure of Scientific Revolutions*, 165–67.

77. See the section, "Pannenberg's Defense of Universal History" in chapter 1. According to Pannenberg, we can understand our present only in light of the future which is open to revision thus, every text and interpretation anticipates future texts. Weinsheimer makes a similar point to mine when he argues that classics are 'prophetical' in that they project a history of successive texts and interpretations which will engage the classic. Weinsheimer, *Philosophical Hermeneutics*, 138.

power can be seen in the way it can induce paradigm shifts or serve as a historical marker that defines a period. As such, the classic anticipates the future effects it will have upon its tradition. The enduring nature of the classic and its normative status combine so that its anticipatory and archaeological functions fulfill an important cohesive role within a tradition.

Classics and Reception Theory

So far we have examined how Gadamer rescued the classical text from historical positivism, which, while it was correct in locating the text in its historical context, objectified the classic and muted its ability to address contemporary readers. Gadamer attempted to reconcile the historicity of the classical text with its ability to address successive generations of readers directly. Tracy's work not only demonstrates the strengths of Gadamer's position but also raises a question about a potential weakness; transforming "classic" into an ahistorical category.

The work of Hans Robert Jauss brings a needed correction to Gadamer's hermeneutic in this area. In particular, he retains the normative element of the classic while at the same time conceiving of it in thoroughly historical terms. It takes time to realize the potential of a text in order for it to be recognized as a classic. Classics come and go, and sometimes they need to be retrieved from the leveling power of tradition. Though with the passage of time, a text which was once received as a classic may also lose that honor. Consequently, the notion of a "classic" is a function of the interplay among a text's disclosive potential, the tradition of that text's interpretation, and its reception by contemporary readers.

Classics, Holy Scripture, and Foundational Texts

The question of "What counts as a classic?" needs to be differentiated more than I have done so far. On the one hand, I agree with the main traits covered so far of what classifies as a classic. A classic text possesses some degree of normativity, is characterized by a surplus of meaning, sought to answer questions that succeeding generations have found meaningful, and has proven itself through it continued reception by readers over time. On the other hand, such broad strokes are not very useful for the practice of reception theory in relation to biblical interpretation; we need to consider how different types of classics function within a tradition.

Krister Stendahl's distinction between the Bible as a classic and the Bible as Holy Scripture helps us to differentiate the term classic in relationship to the Bible. Stendahl considers a classic a work that has been "considered worth attention beyond its time . . . beyond its space."[78] In a manner similar to Jauss, Stendahl argues that a work is accorded the status of a classic due to its reception. It is not based on some intrinsic quality of the work but it is the work's reception by a "wide constituency of a society that makes a certain work into a classic." Because the status of a classic depends on its reception by its readers Stendahl notes that there is probably no "truly global classic."[79]

While it is appropriate to classify the Bible as a classic, to say that it is a literary classic does not do full justice to how the Bible functions within the Jewish and Christian traditions. There are many different types of classics: literary, philosophical, or historical.[80] For example, Augustine's and Calvin's writings are often considered theological classics. While they have both proven themselves through history, the degree of authority attributed to them is very different from how most readers regard the Bible.[81] The Bible possesses a normative quality and function within the Jewish and Christian communities that differentiates it from other classics. Stendahl questions if the Bible would have been recognized as a classic if it did not perform a normative function within these communities.[82] "It is this element of the normative which

78. Stendahl, "The Bible as a Classic," 4–6.

79. Ibid.

80. Wittgenstein's question of "What is a game?" provides a helpful direction to pursue in relation to the question of "What is a classic?" For Wittgenstein a term such as "game" is a blurred concept, there is no one definition for what counts as a game. Rather there are similarities which games share that "crop up and disappear" depending on which instances of games you are considering. These similarities are best described as "family resemblances." In the same manner, there are many different forms which the classic may take and to look for one definition would, by necessity, restrict our investigation from the start. Rather we should "look and see" what is recognized as a classic and then consider why it is a classic, how it functions within its place in the tradition, and what it shares in common with other classics. Wittgenstein, *Philosophical Investigations*, 65–72.

81. Stendahl makes a similar comparison between how readers perceive Shakespeare and Homer in relation to the Bible. Stendahl, "The Bible as a Classic," 8.

82. Ibid., 6–7.

makes the Bible into a peculiar kind of classic."[83] But is this distinction between the categories of "classic" and "scripture" as strong as Stendahl implies?

It is at this point that Alasdair MacIntyre's concept "tradition-constituted enquiry" can help us to grasp Stendahl's split idea of the Bible as "classic" and mediate it with the Bible as "scripture." Traditions (religious as well as secular) are partially constituted through an extended argument over the meaning and significance of that tradition's authoritative texts. The shape and direction a tradition takes is often determined by the critical interpretations and application of those foundational texts.

> For such a tradition, if it is to flourish at all . . . has to be embodied in a set of texts which function as the authoritative point of departure for tradition-constituted enquiry and which remain as essential points of reference for enquiry and activity, for argument, debate, and conflict within that tradition. Those texts to which this canonical status is assigned are treated both as having a fixed meaning embodied in them and also as always open to rereading, so that every tradition becomes to some degree a tradition of critical reinterpretation in which one and the same body of texts . . . is put to the question, and to successively different sets of questions, as a tradition unfolds.[84]

MacIntyre's conception of foundational texts parallels Gadamer's thought on play and performance: each performance is a re-presentation of the same score and at the same time each performance will be different. On the one hand, MacIntyre asserts that a foundational text's meaning is perceived as being stable. This stability in meaning allows it to serve as a central point for research, interpretation, and debate within that tradition. If this were not the case then it is doubtful if such texts could operate in a normative manner within a tradition. On the other hand, these foundational texts are viewed as applicable to each generation and thus open to more than one meaning. With each change in the readers' horizon new questions and debates about the meaning and role of authoritative texts will be raised. The tension between the stability of the meaning of foundational texts and their perpetual openness to new readings is resolved through an extended debate over their meaning that lies at the heart of most traditions. This process of critical

83. Ibid., 9.
84. MacIntyre, *Whose Justice? Which Rationality?* 383.

reinterpretation shapes and, to a large extent, determines the health of a tradition. "Thus a major source of disagreement and debate within a tradition will be 'interpretative' in the older, narrow sense of textual exposition."[85]

The constant reinterpretation of the tradition's foundational texts and the application of these interpretations to the tradition's practices are what constitute the ongoing life of the tradition. Powell applies MacIntyre's ideas to the history of the interpretation of the U.S. Constitution. While the Constitution serves as the foundational text for what Powell terms the tradition of "Constitutionalism," the decisions rendered by the courts and the scholarly commentaries on the Constitution also serve a normative role.[86] In particular, legal interpretations and decisions (adjudications) do not serve merely as precedents for the practice of constitutional law in the future, but are related to the internal goods of the tradition.[87] Within this tradition, Powell identifies a handful of significant legal decisions which played an authoritative role in future decisions or which changed the course of the tradition of Constitutional interpretation.[88] It is because these decisions are constantly referred to in legal debate, the normative status they serve, and the manner in which they have become part of the dramatic narrative which defines the tradition of Constitutionalism, that they serve as classic texts within this tradition. In this sense, we can label the Bible as the foundational text for the Christian tradition, and commentaries such as Calvin's or Karl Barth's commentary on Romans as classic texts that shape the interpretive dialogue within the Christian tradition.

---

85. Powell, *The Moral Tradition of American Constitutionalism*, 28–29; Gadamer, *Truth and Method*, 263.

86. Powell, *The Moral Tradition*, 29–30, 49.

87. These internal goods include the respect for past interpretations, logical coherence, and adherence to the norms of legal argument. Powell, *The Moral Tradition*, 117–18.

88. Such cases include the Dred Scott case, in which a slave attempted to sue his master for freedom when they moved to the free state of Illinois; Lochner v. NY, which examined the issue of how long an employer may demand its employees work per week; and Brown v. The Board of Education, which struck down the segregation laws. Powell, *The Moral Tradition*, 120–32, 139–43, 165–72. Jauss would term these legal documents as members of the summit-dialogue of American 'Constitutionalism.'

The Bible as a Foundational Text and Classic Commentaries

If the Bible functions as the foundational text, one form of a classic, which serves to shape and define the Christian tradition, then how do classic commentaries and theological texts function within the tradition? First, as Thomas Kuhn observed, they are used within the educational and professional institutions. Kuhn makes this point in relation to the authority that certain textbooks possess within scientific paradigms. Particular textbooks are used to introduce the students and members of a research community to what counts as data, theories, and the body of articulated problems, "to which the scientific community is committed at the time they are written."[89] At the same time, these textbooks equip the members of a scientific community with a vocabulary to express their research and thought, and provides them with examples of what count as problems and solutions.[90]

If this is the case in the sciences, then the role that classic texts play within the humanities and theology is perhaps even more significant. The pedagogical value of the classic commentaries can function in a manner similar to scientific textbooks in Kuhn's model: they can be employed within seminaries and universities to introduce the students to what counts as a interpretive question and what is considered an appropriate reading. Classic commentaries serve to illustrate the bounds of what is considered appropriate performance of the score of the biblical text.

Theological classics serve an archaeological function in the way they are employed within the institutions and educational processes to introduce the history of the Christian tradition and its thought. While the institutional textbooks in the sciences are rewritten after a paradigm shift, in the humanities classical texts continue to be retained after paradigm shifts. This not only introduces an element of continuity in a tradition, but also familiarizes those who read them with alternative readings and interpretive solutions.[91] If textbooks develop technical

---

89. Kuhn, *The Structure of Scientific Revolutions*, 136; Kuhn, *The Essential Tension*, 230.

90. Ibid., 177, 187.

91. Ibid., 165.

reasoning within the scientific community, classic texts contribute to the *phronesis* and historically-effective consciousness in biblical studies.[92]

Second, classic commentaries often play a central role in defining and shaping the direction of a tradition. One of the first indications and expressions that a tradition has entered a period of epistemological crisis, according to Jauss, is evidenced in the arts and literature from that time.[93] Because commentaries and theological treatises are both a form of literature and play a central role in the interpretive debate concerning the Bible, they perform two roles at the same time. A classic commentary can serve as a fork in the road, either by inducing a paradigm shift in thought or by indicating that such a shift has already taken place. One of the most known examples of how a particular interpretation sparked a theological paradigm shift is Luther's interpretation of Romans 1:17. At the personal level, this biblical text transformed Luther's entire understanding of the Bible. At the corporate level, the contribution of Luther's reading of this passage to the interpretive debate is displayed in how it informed the Protestant Reformation's understanding of the Scriptures and doctrine of salvation.[94]

In other instances, a classic will follow a horizontal shift that has already occurred. William Carey's "An Enquiry into the Obligation of Christians to Use Means for the Conversion of Heathens" is an example of an exposition of Matthew 28:18–20 that followed a paradigm shift. However, the implications of that shift had not been clearly articulated until his work was published. When Carey wrote the essay, the Protestant church as a whole had already taken its first tentative steps in various missionary ventures. By contrast, William Carey came from a hyper-Calvinistic, dissenting Baptist church background which believed the command of Matthew 28:18–20 was no longer binding on the church because there were no successors to the apostles.[95] At a pastors' conference

92. For an extended discussion on the nature and role of *phronesis*, see the section, "Hermeneutical Knowledge and Tradition," in chapter 2.

93. Jauss, "The Literary Process of Modernism," 34–36; Jauss, "1912: Threshold to an Epoch," 56–58.

94. Thiselton, *New Horizons*, 35; MacIntyre, "Epistemological Crisis," 61.

95. Berg, *Constrained By Jesus' Love*, 165. This also demonstrates Jauss' point that any synchronic time frame will be made up of different 'time curves' of literature and its reception. In Carey's instance, his particular denominational background represents a "time curve" of the reception of Matthew 28:18–20, which was quite different from the larger Christian community. Jauss, "Literary History as a Challenge to Literary Theory," in *Towards an Aesthetic of Reception*, 36–37; Jauss, *Aesthetic Experience*, 269–70.

in 1786, Carey raised the question as to whether the Great Commission may still be binding upon the church. The president of the denomination, Dr. Ryland, reacted very strongly to his question. "You are a miserable enthusiast, to propose such a question. Nothing certainly can come to pass in this matter before a new Pentecost . . . promises success to the commission of Christ as in the beginning."[96] In order to counter the hyper-Calvinistic presuppositions of his particular denomination, Carey needed to present a more articulate and convincing argument than if he had been addressing the larger Protestant movement rather than his local church community. His argument was not based on new insights but rather involved a summary of previous positions concerning the nature of the church and knowledge about the various ethnic groups around the world which had come from British colonization.[97] While various Protestant leaders had argued that Matthew 28:18–20 was still binding on the church, it was not until Carey published his essay that this interpretation was widely accepted and the debate over the applicability of the Great Commission to the contemporary church was more or less settled.[98] "Since the time of William Carey it has been customary to take the closing verses of Matthew's Gospel as the fundamental mandate for mission."[99] Both of these aspects of the classic interpretation, inducing and indicating a shift in the horizon of expectations, are what we expect if the meaning of the text is something that is concretized when the horizon of the text is mediated with the horizon of the reader.

96. Warneck, *Outline of a History of Protestant Missions*, 75.

97. William Carey's tract was rather small and reflected his theological and geographical insights. Almost one fourth of its eighty-seven pages are statistical charts about the various nations (section 3). While his theological argument was not elaborate, he carefully set out a biblical and historical argument for missions in a clear and concise manner.

98. The Moravian movement's attempt to addressed the Enlightenment's spiritual coldness and call for the Protestant church to follow the mandate in Matthew 28 met with only limited reception. "But sixty-five years later, when Carey summoned Christians to missionary obedience, he spoke to hearts stirred by the Evangelical Awakening. The response that issued then has continued to grow." Hogg, "The Rise of Protestant Missionary Concern, 1517–1914," 106–7.

99. Newbigin, "Cross-currents in Ecumenical and Evangelical Understandings of Mission," 146; see also McGaveran, *Momentous Decisions in Missions Today*, 20

Saints, Doctors, and Classics

Stephen Holmes appeals to the concept of hagiography order to explore the significance that theological classics hold within the Christian tradition. A saint is someone who has recognized by the church as successfully imitating the life of Christ in a way that expands and enriches our understanding of what it means to be Christ-like.[100] In a similar manner, some interpreters have been acknowledged for how they expand and enrich the internal logic of the Scriptures.[101] Those who have been historically recognized as outstanding examples for how they expound God's gift of his son to their generation are the 'doctors' of the church. The fact that their reading of a biblical text was shaped by the particulars of their historical horizon does not diminish the role they play, rather it adds to the richness of the tradition of biblical interpretation.

There are three tangible benefits of listening to the doctors. First, their interpretations allow us to measure our readings of the Bible against theirs; this is valuable even though they were just as were prone to misreadings as we are. But if there is a wide agreement over a particular interpretation, especially if this agreement crosses a variety of historical and cultural contexts, then there is a presumption of correctness for that reading.[102] Second, these classics serve an important role in theological education. "That is there is a proper hagiography within the Church, just as there is a proper intellectual apostolate; it is appropriate to dwell long and lovingly on the writings of certain heroes, and it is by doing so that one becomes a theologian."[103] Finally, how the doctors read the Bible may conflict with our understanding of the same passage, which not only raises questions and provokes our understanding of the passage, but can also provide us with fresh disclosures of the text's meaning. "A respect for, and a disciplined listening to, the tradition can enable us to speak prophetically in our own day, calling our contemporaries to hear the challenge of the gospel."[104] Theological classics reveal to us the twists and turns of the Christian tradition and at the same time

---

100. Holmes, *Listening to the Past*, 28.

101. Ibid., 156.

102. Ibid., 157–58.

103. Ibid., 29.

104. Ibid., 136.

supply it with continuity.[105] They present us with accepted questions and answers which serve as boundaries of our hermeneutical playing field, and they can open our eyes to potential folds in the meaning of scriptural texts that have been forgotten.

Conclusion

Reception theory presents a hermeneutical model which involves a three-way dialogue. It integrates the history of the text's reception into the traditional hermeneutical model which is concerned with the dialogue between the interpreter the text. Dobschütz, Ebeling, and Froehlich were sensitive to the need to incorporate this third element into biblical hermeneutics and church history. The resources for con-structing an adequate framework for this hermeneutical model are found in the philosophical hermeneutics of Hans-Georg Gadamer and the literary hermeneutics of Hans Robert Jauss.

Is it worth the effort to apply reception theory to the biblical text? I believe it is for three reasons. First, the Christian tradition is filled with a rich treasury of biblical interpretation and application in a wide diversity of historical situations. Not only does this treasury provide the interpreter with a historical map that reveals legitimate and illegitimate interpretations of the text, but it also provides hermeneutical resources and insights which may have been forgotten in the transmission of the tradition. Second, the norm-forming power of texts helps to explain how the reception of biblical texts and previous interpretations of the Bible have shaped church history. Third, the practice of reception theory leads to the formation of the interpreter's *phronesis* and *wirkungsgeschichtliches Bewußtsein*. Historically-effected consciousness is characterized by an openness on the interpreter's part which consists in knowing that he still has something to learn from his tradition. We learn who we are as a result of our tradition and our position within it. But in order to learn how we belong to a tradition, we must first learn how to listen to it. This is perhaps the most significant contribution which reception theory presents to biblical hermeneutics; a means by which we can not only study how the Bible has been interpreted and applied but also listen and learn from the past as well.

---

105. Brown, *Boundaries of Our Habitations*, 75–78.

Classics not only play a central role in reception theory but also demonstrate the importance of this hermeneutical model. If we recognize the classical attributes of the Bible and how the tradition of biblical interpretation is partially constituted by classic commentaries and theological works then we are confronted with a challenge to engage in a three way dialogue when interpreting the Bible: the reader, the Bible, and the reception history of biblical interpretation.

Perhaps more importantly, Jauss' thought on the classics should provoke us as biblical readers. Classics come and go. It is only because successive generations read a classic in a manner that allows it to address them in an appropriate and relevant manner, through the effective mediation of horizons, that it remains a classic. The same challenge confronts us. We cannot merely repeat how the Bible has been interpreted by those who came before us, naively assimilate a biblical passage's meaning into the present, or subject the text to a methodological approach that transforms it into a relic from the past. We must engage the Bible along with its rich reception history in a relevant manner. Our ancestors and our descendents demand nothing less from us.

Bibliography

Abbreviations

CSEL   Corpus scriptorum ecclesiasticorum latinorum

LCL   Loeb Classical Library

PG   Patrologiae cursus completus: Series graeca. Edited by J. P. Migne. 162 vols. Paris: Garnier, 1857–86

PL   Patrologiae cursus completus: Series latina. Edited by J. P. Migne. 217 vols. Paris: Garnier, 1844–64

SC   Sources chrétiennes. Paris: Cerf, 1943–

SJT   *Scottish Journal of Theology*

WBC   Word Biblical Commentary

Works Cited

The Bible and Holy Scriptures Contained in the Olde and Newe Testament. Geneva: Routland Hall, 1560. Reproduced, *The Geneva Bible: A Facsimile of the 1560 Edition*. Introduction by Lloyd E. Berry. Madison: University of Wisconsin Press, 1969.

Ackroyd, P. R., and C. F. Evans. *The Cambridge History of the Bible*. 3 vols. Cambridge: Cambridge University Press, 1970.

Adorno, Theodore W. "On Tradition." *Telos* 94 (1992–93) 75–81.

Alexander, John David. "The Genevan Version of the English Bible." DPhil thesis. Oxford University, 1956.

Alexander, William Menzies. *Demonic Possession in the New Testament: Its Historical, Medical and Theological Aspects*. Edinburgh: T. & T. Clark, 1902.

Allen, Leslie C. *Psalms 101–150*. WBC 21. Waco, TX: Word, 1983.

Alter, Robert. "Mimesis and the Motive for Fiction." *Tri Quarterly*. 42 (Spring, 1978) 228–249.

Ambrose. *Expositio Evangelii secundum Lucam*. SC 52.

Anselm of Laon. *Enarrationes in Evangelium Matthaei*. PL 162.

Apel, Karl-Otto. "The A Priori of Communication and the Foundation of the Humanities" *Man and World* 5 (1972), 3–37.

————. *Towards a Transformation of Philosophy*. Translated by Glyn Adey and David Frisby. Boston: Routledge; London: Kegan Paul, 1980. Originally published as *Transformation der Philosophie*. Frankfurt: Suhrkamp, 1972–73.

————. "Types of Rationality Today: The Continuum of Reason between Science and Ethics." In *Rationality To-day*, edited by Théodore F. Geraets, 307–50. Ottawa: University of Ottawa Press, 1979.

————. *Understanding and Explanation: A Transcendental-Pragmatic Perspective.* Translated by Georgia Warnke. Studies in Contemporary German Social Thought. Cambridge, MA: MIT Press, 1984. Originally published as *Die Erklären-Verstehen-Kontroverse in Transzendental-Pragmatischer Sicht*. Frankfurt: Suhrkamp, 1979.

Aquinas, St. Thomas. *Catena Aurea: Commentary on the Four Gospels Collected out of the Works of the Fathers by S. Thomas Aquinas*. Translated by E.B. Pusey. Edited by John Henry Newman. Oxford: Parker, 1841–45.

————. *Summa Theologiæ*. Translated by Thomas Gilby. London: Eyre & Spottiswoode, 1975.

Arthur, Christopher E. "Gadamer and Hirsch: The Canonical Work and the Interpreter's Intention." *Cultural Hermeneutics* 4 (1977) 183–97.

Aristotle. *Nicomachean Ethics*. Translated by H. Rackham. LCL 73. Cambridge: Harvard University Press, 1934.

————. *Poetics*. 3rd Edition. Translated by Malcolm Heath. London: Penguin, 1996.

Auerochs, Bernd. "*Gadamer über Tradition*." *Zeitschrift für philosophische Forschung* 49 (1995) 294–311.

Augustine. *De consensu evangelistarum*. CSEL 43. Vienna: Tempsky, 1904. Translated as *The Harmony of the Gospels*, vol. 6, *Select Library of Nicene and Post-Nicene Fathers of the Christian Church*. Edited by Philip Schaff. Grand Rapids: Eerdmans, 1956.

————. *Epistulae*. SCEL 57. Vienna: Tempsky, 1923. Translated by Wilfrid Parsons as *Saint Augustine: Letters*, vol. 4, *The Fathers of the Church*. Washington. DC: Catholic University of America Press, 1955.

————. *Sancti Aurelii Augustini. Questionibus Evangelioromicum Appendice Quaestionum XVI in Matthaeum*. Edited by Almut Mutzenberger. Vol. 44B, Corpus Christianorum. Series Latina. Turnhout: Brepols, 1980.

————. *Sermo*. PL 38. Translated as *Sermons on Selected Lessons of the New Testament*, vol. 1, *S. Matthew. S. Mark, S. Luke* (London: John Henry Parker, J. G. F. and J. Rivington, 1844).

Bainton, Roland H. *Hunted Heretic: The Life and Death of Michael Servetus, 1511–1553*. Boston: Beacon, 1953.

————. "Religious Liberty and the Parable of the Tares." In *Early and Medieval Christianity* 1:95–121. The Collected Papers in Church History of Roland Bainton. London: Hodder & Stoughton, 1962.

Baird, J. Arthur. *Audience Criticism and the Historical Jesus*. Philadelphia: Westminster, 1969.

Barr, James. *Old and New in Interpretation: A Study on the Two Testaments*. London: SCM, 1966.

Barbour, Ian. "Paradigms in Science and Religion." In *Paradigms and Revolutions,* edited by Gary Gutting, 223–45. South Bend, IN: University of Notre Dame, 1980.

Barth, Karl. *Church Dogmatics.* Translated by G. W. Bromiley and T. F. Torrance. 13 vols. Edinburgh: T. & T. Clark, 1936-1969.

———. "An Exegetical Study of Mt. 28:18–20." In *The Theology of Christian Mission,* edited by Gerald H. Anderson, 55–71. Nashville: Abingdon, 1961.

———. *The Epistle to the Romans.* Translated by Edwyn C. Hoskyns. Oxford: Oxford University Press, 1968.

Barthes, Roland. *The Pleasure of the Text.* Translated by Richard Miller. Oxford: Blackwell, 1990.

Bate, W. J., editor. *Criticism: The Major Texts.* New York: Harcourt Brace Jovanovich, 1970.

Bauman, Zygmunt. *Hermeneutics and the Social Sciences.* London: Hutchinson, 1978.

Beare, Francis W. "The Parable of the Guests at the Banquet: A Sketch of the History of its Interpretation." In *The Joy of Study: Papers in Honor of F.C. Grant,* 1–14. New York: Macmillan, 1951.

Beasley-Murray, George R. *John.* WBC 36. Waco, TX: Word, 1987.

Bede, The Venerable. *In Matthaei Evangelium exposito.* PL 92.

Begbie, Jeremy S. *Theology, Music and Time.* Cambridge Studies in Christian Doctrine. Cambridge: Cambridge University Press, 2000.

Beiser, Frederick C., editor. *The Cambridge Companion to Hegel.* Cambridge: Cambridge University Press, 1993.

Benson, Joseph. *The New Testament of Our Lord and Savior Jesus Christ with Critical, Explanatory and Practical Notes.* New York: G. Lane and P.P. Sandford, 1843.

Berg, J. Van Den. *Constrained By Jesus' Love: An Inquiry into the Motives of the Missionary Awakening in Great Britain in the Period Between 1698 and 1815.* Kampen: J. H. Kok, 1956.

Berkhof, Louis. *The History of Christian Doctrine.* Grand Rapids: Baker, 1975.

Bernstein, Richard J. *Beyond Objectivism and Relativism: Science, Hermeneutics and Praxis.* Philadelphia: University of Pennsylvania Press, 1983.

———. "From Hermeneutics to Praxis." In *Hermeneutics and Modern Philosophy,* edited by Brice R. Wachterhauser, 87–110. Albany: State University of New York, 1986.

Bett, W. R., editor. *A Short History of Some Common Diseases.* London: Oxford University Press, 1934.

Blaug, Mark. "Kuhn Versus Lakatos, or Paradigms Versus Research Programmes in the History of Economics." In *Paradigms and Revolutions,* edited by Gary Gutting, 137–59. South Bend, IN: University of Notre Dame, 1980.

Blomberg, Craig L. *The Historical Reliability of the Gospels.* Downers Grove, IL: InterVarsity, 1987.

———. *Interpreting the Parables.* Leicester: Apollos, 1990.

Bockmuehl, Markus. "A Commentator's Approach to the 'Effective History' of Philippians." *Journal for the Study of the New Testament* 60 (1995) 57–88.

———. "'To Be Or Not To Be': The Possible Futures of New Testament Scholarship." *SJT* 51 (1998) 271–306.

Bonner, Gerald. "Augustine as Biblical Scholar." In *The Cambridge History of the Bible: From the Beginnings to Jerome*, edited by P. R. Ackroyd and C. F. Evans, 1:541–63. Cambridge: Cambridge University Press, 1970.

Boor, Friedrich de. "Kirchengeschichte oder Auslegungsgeschichte?" *Theologische Literaturzeitung* 6 (1972) 401–14.

Boudreaux, Petrus. *Codicum Parisinorum.* Catalogus Codicum Astrologorum Graecorum 8.4. Brussells: Mauritii Lamertin, 1921.

Bratt, John H., *The Heritage of John Calvin: Heritage Hall Lectures, 1960–70.* Grand Rapids: Eerdmans, 1973.

Brown, Delwin. *Boundaries of Our Habitations: Tradition and Theological Construction.* Series in Religious Studies. Albany: SUNY Press, 1994.

Brown, P. R. L. "St. Augustine's Attitude to Religious Coercion." In *Augustine*, edited by John Dunn and Ian Harris, 1:382–91. Great Political Thinkers. Cheltenham: Edward Elgar, 1997.

Bruce, Alexander B. *The Parabolic Teachings of Christ: A Systematic and Critical Study of the Parables of Our Lord.* 3rd ed. New York: A. C. Armstrong, 1908; London: Hodder & Stoughton, 1882.

Bruns, Gerald L. "Midrash and Allegory: The Beginnings of Scriptural Interpretation." In *The Literary Guide to the Bible*, edited by Robert Alter and Frank Kermode, 625–46. Cambridge: Harvard Univerity Press, 1987.

————. "What is Tradition?" *New Literary History.* 22 (1991) 1–21.

Bucer, Martin. *Enarrationes perpetuae in sacra quatuor euangelia ad Academiam Marpurgensem.* Argentorati: Georgium, 1530.

Buck, Günther. "The Structure of Hermeneutic Experience and the Problem of Tradition." Translated by Peter Heath. *New Literary History* 10 (1978) 31–47.

Bugge, Christian A. *Die Haupt-Parabeln Jesu.* Giessen: Rickerische, 1903.

Bultmann, Rudolf. *Essays Philosophical and Theological.* Translated by J. C. G. Greig. London: SCM, 1955.

————. *The History of the Synoptic Tradition.* Translated by John Marsh. New York: Harper & Row, 1963. Originally published as *Die Geschichte der Synoptischen Tradition.* Gottingen: Vandernhoeck and Ruprecht, 1931.

————. "Is Exegesis without Presuppositions Possible?" Translated by Schubert M. Ogden. In *Existence and Faith: Shorter Writings of Rudolf Bultmann*, edited by Schubert M. Ogden, 289–96. London: Hodder & Stoughton, 1960. Originally published as "Ist voraussetzungslose Exegese möglich?" *Theologische Zeitschrift* 13 (1957) 409–17.

————. *Kerygma and Myth: A Theological Debate.* Translated by Reginald H. Fuller. London: SPCK, 1953.

Calinescu, Matei. *Five Faces of Modernity.* 2nd ed. Durham. NC: Duke University Press, 1987.

Calvin, John. *In harmoniam ex Matthaeo, Marco et Luca compositam commentarii. ad editionem Amstelodamensem accuratissime exscripti.* Berolini: Apud Gustavum Eichler, 1833. Translated by William Pringle as *Commentary on a Harmony of the Evangelists, Matthew, Mark, and Luke,* 2 vols. Grand Rapids: Eerdmans, 1956–57.

————. *Institutes of the Christian Religion.* Translated by Ford Lewis Battles. Vols. 20–21, The Library of Christian Classics. Philadelphia: Westminster, 1975.

Campbell, William E. *Erasmus, Tyndale and More*. London: Eyre and Spottiswoode, 1949.

Capps, David. *Pastoral Care and Hermeneutics*. Edited by Don S. Browning. Theology and Pastoral Care Series. Philadelphia: Fortress, 1984.

Carey, William. *An Enquiry into the Obligation of Christians to Use Means for the Conversion of the Heathens: in Which the Different Nations of the World, the Success of Former Undertakings, and the Practicability of Further Undertakings are Considered*. Leicester: Ann Ireland, 1792.

Caygill, Howard. *A Kant Dictionary*. The Blackwell Philosopher Dictionaries. Oxford: Blackwell, 1995.

Childs, Brevard S. *The Book of Exodus: A Critical, Theological Commentary*. Old Testament Library. Philadelphia, Westminster, 1974.

Chrysostom. *Commentariorum in Matthaeum*. PG 58. Translated by George Prevost and M. B. Riddle as *Homilies on the Gospel of Matthew*, Select Library of Nicene and Post-Nicene Fathers of the Christian Church 10 (Grand Rapids: Eerdmans, 1956).

Clarke, Adam. *The Holy Bible, Containing the Old and New Testaments, the Text Carefully Printed from the Most Correct Copies of the Present Authorized Translation, Including the Marginal Readings and Parallel Texts: With a Commentary and Critical Notes Designed as a Help to a Better Understanding of the Sacred Writings*. London: Joseph Butterworth, 1810.

Collingwood, R.G. *An Autobiography*. With an Introduction by Stephen Toulmin. London: Oxford University Press, 1939.

———. *The Idea of History: With Lectures 1926–1928*. Rev. ed. Edited by Jan van der Dussen. Oxford: Clarendon, 1993.

Coltman, Rod. *The Language of Hermeneutics: Gadamer and Heidegger in Dialogue*. SUNY Series in Contemporary Continental Philosophy. Albany: State University of New York Press, 1998.

Comestor, Peter. *Historia Scholastica: Historia Evangelica*. PL 198.

Congar, Yves. "Introduction." In *Traités anti-Donatistes in Bibliotheque Augustinienne, Oeuvres de Saint Augustin 28*. n.p.: Desclée de Brouwer, 1963.

Copleston, Frederick. *Friedrich Nietzsche: Philosopher of Culture*. 2nd ed. London: Search, 1975.

Corbineau-Hoffmann, A. "Spiel." In *Historisches Worterbuch der Philosophie*, edited by Joachim Ritter and Karlfried Gründer, vol. 9. Basel: Schwabe, 1995.

Crossan, John Dominic. *The Dark Interval: Towards a Theology of Story*. Allen, TX: Argus Communications, 1975.

———. *In Parables: The Challenge of the Historical Jesus*. New York: Harper & Row, 1973.

Culler, Jonathan. *Structuralist Poetics: Structuralism, Linguistics, and the Study of Literature*. London: Routledge & Kegan Paul, 1975.

Dahood, Mitchell. *Psalms III: 101–150*. Anchor Bible 17A. Garden City, NY: Doubleday, 1970.

Dallmayr, Fred R. "Prelude—Hermeneutics and Deconstruction: Gadamer and Derrida in Dialogue." In *Dialogue and Deconstruction: The Gadamer–Derrida Encounter*, edited by Diane P. Michelfelder and Richard E. Palmer, 75–92. SUNY Series in Contemporary Continental Philosophy. Albany: SUNY Press, 1989.

Danto, Arthur C. *Analytic Philosophy and History.* Cambridge: Cambridge University Press, 1965.

Dau, William H. T., and Gerhard F. Gente. *Concordia Triglotta.* St. Louis: Concordia, 1921.

Descartes, René. *Discourses on Method and the Meditations.* Translated by F. E. Sutcliffe. New York: Penguin, 1968.

Detsch, Richard. "A Non-Subjectivist Concept of Play—Gadamer and Heidegger versus Rilke and Nietzsche." *Philosophy Today* 29 (1985) 156–72.

DiCenso, James. *Hermeneutics and the Disclosure of Truth: A Study in the Work of Heidegger, Gadamer, and Ricoeur. Studies in Religion and Culture.* Edited by Nathan A. Scott Jr. Charlottesville: University of Virginia Press, 1990.

Dillon, Richard J. "Towards a Tradition-History of the Parables of the True Israel (Matthew 21,33—22,14)." *Biblica.* 47 (1966) 1–42.

Dillistone, Frederick W. "The Anti-Donatist Writings." In *A Companion to the Study of St. Augustine.* Edited by Roy W. Battenhouse, 175–202. New York: Oxford University Press, 1956.

Dobschütz, Ernst von. "Bible in the Church." In *Encyclopaedia of Religion and Ethics,* edited by James Hastings, 2:579–615. Edinburgh: T. & T. Clark, 1909.

Doppelt, Gerald. "Kuhn's Epistemological Relativism: An Interpretation and Defense." *Inquiry* 21 (1978) 33–86.

Dreyfus, Hubert L. "Holism and Hermeneutics." *Review of Metaphysics* 34 (1980) 3–55.

———. *Being-in-the-World: A Commentary on Heidegger's Being and Time, Division I.* Cambridge, MA: MIT Press, 1991.

Druthmari, Christiani. *Expositio in Matthaeum Evangelistam.* PL 106.

Eagleton, Terry. *Literary Theory: An Introduction.* Oxford: Blackwell, 1983.

Ebeling, Gerhard. *The Word of God and Tradition: Historical Studies Interpreting the Divisions of Christianity.* Translated by S. H. Hooke. London: Collins, 1968. Originally published as *Wort Gottes und Tradition.* Göttingen: Vandenhoeck & Ruprecht, 1964.

Eckert, Michael. "Hermeneutics in the Classroom: An Application of Reception Theory." *College English Association Critic* 46 (1984) 5–16.

Eco, Umberto. *The Role of the Reader: Explorations in the Semiotics of Texts. Advances in Semiotics.* Edited by Thomas Sebeok. Bloomington: Indiana University Press, 1981.

———. *Semiotics and the Philosophy of Language.* London: Macmillan, 1988.

———. "Social Life as a Sign System." In *Structuralism: An Introduction,* edited by David Robey, 57–72. Oxford: Clarendon, 1973.

———. *A Theory of Semiotics.* Bloomington: Indiana University Press, 1976. Originally published as *Trattato di semiotica generale.* Milan: Bompiani, 1975.

Epstein, Isidore, editor. *Hebrew-English Edition of the Babylonian Talmud.* Translated by H. Freedman. London: Soncino, 1990.

Eusebius Pamphilus. *Ecclesiastical History.* Translated by Christian Frederick Cruse. Grand Rapids: Baker, 1990.

Farley, Edward. "Theology and Practice Outside the Clerical Paradigm." In *Practical Theology: The Emerging Field in Theology, Church, and World,* edited by Don S. Browning, 21–41. San Francisco: Harper & Row, 1983.

Farrar, Frederic W. *History of Interpretation*. Grand Rapids: Baker, 1961. First published 1886 by Dutton.

Feyerabend, Paul. *Farewell to Reason*. New York: Verso, 1987.

Fiebig, Paul. *Die Gleichnisreden Jesu im Licht der rabbinischen Gleichnisse des neutestamentlichen Zeitalters*. Tubingen: Mohr Siebeck, 1912.

Fish, Stanley. "Why No One's Afraid of Wolfgang Iser." *Diacritics* 11 (1981) 2–13.

Forster, Michael. "Hegel's Dialectical Method." In *The Cambridge Companion to Hegel*, edited by Frederick C. Beiser, 130–70. Cambridge: Cambridge University Press, 1993.

Foerster, Werner editor. *Gnosis: A Selection of Gnostic Texts*. Translated by R. McL. Wilson. Oxford: Clarendon, 1972. Originally published as *Die Gnosis*. Zurich: Artemis, 1969–71.

Foucault, Michel. *The Archeology of Knowledge*. Translated by A. M. Sheridan Smith. New York: Pantheon, 1972. Originally published as *L'Archéologie du savior*. Paris: Editions Gallimard, 1969.

———. *Madness and Civilization: A History of Insanity in the Age of Reason*. Translated by Richard Howard. New York: Pantheon, 1965. Originally published as *Folie et déraison: Historie de la folie à l'âge classique*. Paris: Editions Gallimard, 1961.

———. *The Order of Things*. New York: Random House, 1970. Originally published as *Les Mots et les chose: Une Archélogie des sciences humaines*. Paris: Editions Gallimard, 1966.

Fowl, Stephen. *Engaging Scripture: A Model for Theological Interpretation*. Challenges in Contemporary Theology. Oxford: Blackwell, 1998.

Frank, Manfred. "Limits of the Human Control of Language." In *Destruktion and Deconstruction*, edited by Diane P. Michelfelder and Richard E. Palmer, 150–61. Albany: SUNY Press, 1988.

Frede, Dorothea. "The Question of Being: Heidegger's Project." In *The Cambridge Companion of Heidegger*, edited by Charles B. Guignon, 42–69. Cambridge: Cambridge University Press, 1993.

Frye, Northrop. *The Great Code: The Bible and Literature*. New York: Harcourt, Brace, Jovanovich, 1982.

Froehlich, Karlfried. "Church History and the Bible." In *Biblical Hermeneutics in Historical Perspective: Studies in Honor of Karlfried Froehlich on His Sixtieth Birthday*, edited by Mark S. Burrows and Paul Rorem, 1–15. Grand Rapids: Eerdmans, 1991.

———. "The Doctrine of Tradition as a Doctrine about Scripture and the Church." *Journal of Ecumencial Studies* 28 (1991) 466–71.

———. "Which Paul? Observations on the Image of the Apostle in the History of Biblical Exegesis." In *New Perspectives on Historical Theology: Essays in Memory of John Meyendorff*, edited by Bradley Nassif, 279–99. Grand Rapids: Eerdmans, 1996.

Funk, Robert W. *Language, Hermeneutics and Word of God: The Problem of Language in the New Testament and Contemporary Theology*. New York: Harper & Row, 1966.

Gadamer, Hans-Georg. "The Continuity of History and the Existential Movement." Translated by Thomas Wren. *Philosophy Today* 16 (1972) 230–40. Originally

published as "*Die Kontinuität der Geschichte und der Augenblick der Existenz*."
*Geschichte—Element der Zukunft: Vorträge an den Hochschultagen 1965 der
Evangelischen Studentengemeide*, edited by Reinhard Wittram, Hans-Georg
Gadamer, and Jurgen Moltmann. Tübingen: Mohr Siebeck, 1965.

————. "Destruktion and Deconstruction." Translated by Geoff Waite and Richard
Palmer. In *Dialogue & Deconstruction: The Gadamer-Derrida Encounter*, edited
by Diane P. Michelfelder and Richard E. Palmer, 102–13. SUNY Series in
Contemporary Continental Philosophy. Albany: SUNY Press, 1989.

————. "The Eminent Text and Its Truth." *Bulletin of the Midwest Modern Language
Association* 13 (1980) 3–10.

————. *Hegel's Dialectic: Five Hemerneutical Studies*. Translated by P. Christopher
Smith. New Haven: Yale University Press, 1976. Originally published as *Hegels
Dialektik: Funf hermeneutische Studien*. Frankfurt: Suhrkamp, 1973.

————. "Hermeneutics and Social Science." *Cultural Hermeneutics* 2 (1975) 307–16.

————. "The Hermeneutics of Suspicion." In *Hermeneutics: Questions and
Prospects*, edited by Gary Shapiro and Alan Sica, 54–65. Amherst: University of
Massachusetts Press, 1984.

————. *Philosophical Hermeneutics*. Berkeley: University of California Press, 1976.

————. "Praktisches Wissen." In *Gesammelte Werke* 5:230–48. Tübingen: Mohr
Siebeck, 1985.

————. "The Problem of Historical Consciousness." Translated by Jeff L. Close. In
Interpretive Social Research: A Reader. Edited by Paul Rabinow and William
M. Sullivan, 103–60. Berkeley: University of California Press, 1979. Originally
published as *Le Problème de la conscience historique*. Louvain: Insitut Superieur
de Philosophie. Université Catholique de Louvain, 1963.

————. *Reason in the Age of Science*. Translated by Frederick G. Lawrence. Vol. 2,
Studies in Contemporary German Social Thought, edited by Thomas McCarthy.
Cambridge, MA: MIT Press, 1981. Originally published as *Vernunft im Zeitalter
der Wissenschaft*. Frankfurt: Suhrkamp, 1976.

————. "Reflections on My Philosophical Journey." In *The Philosophy of Hans-Georg
Gadamer*, edited by Lewis Edwin Hahn. Library of Living Philosophers 24.
Chicago: Open Court, 1997.

————. *The Relevance of the Beautiful and Other Essays*. Translated by Nicholas
Walker. Cambridge: Cambridge University Press, 1986.

————. "Text and Interpretation." Translated by Dennis J. Schmidt and Richard
Palmer. In *Dialogue & Deconstruction: The Gadamer-Derrida Encounter*,
edited by Diane P. Michelfelder and Richard E. Palmer, 21–51. SUNY Series in
Contemporary Continental Philosophy. Albany: SUNY Press, 1989.

————. *Truth and Method*. 2nd rev. ed. Translated by Joel Weinsheimer and Donald
G. Marshall. New York: Crossroad, 1989.

————. "Truth in the Human Sciences." Translated by Brice R. Wachterhauser. In
Hermeneutics and Truth, edited by Brice R. Wachterhauser, 25–32. Evanston, IL:
Northwestern University Press, 1994.

————. "*Vom Zirkel des Verstehens*." In *Martin Heidegger zum siebzigsten Geburtstag:
Festschrift*, 24–34. Pfullingen: Neske, 1959.

———. "What is Truth?" Translated by Brice R. Wachterhauser. In *Hermeneutics and Truth,* edited by Brice R. Wachterhauser, 33–46. Evanston, IL: Northwestern University Press, 1994.

Garrett, Jan Edward. "Hans-Georg Gadamer on 'Fusion of Horizons.'" *Man and World* 11 (1978) 392–400.

Gebauer, Gunter, and Christopher Wulf. *Mimesis: Culture, Art and Society.* Translated by Don Reneau. Berkeley: University of California Press, 1995.

Gerkin, Charles V. *The Living Human Document: Re-Visioning Pastoral Counseling in a Hermeneutical Mode.* Nashville: Abingdon, 1984.

Gellius, Aulius. *Attic Nights.* 3 vols. Translated by John Rolfe. LCL. Cambridge: Harvard University Press, 1927.

Gombrich, E. H. *Art and Illusion: A Study in the Psychology of Pictorial Representation.* London: Phaidon, 1959.

Gregory the Great. *Homilia in Evangelia.* PL 76. Translated by Nora Burke as *Pope Saint Gregory the Great: Parables of the Gospel.* Dublin: Scepter, 1960.

Grell, Ole Peter, and Bob Scribner, editors. *Tolerance and Intolerance in the European Reformation.* Cambridge: Cambridge University Press, 1996.

Grene, Marjorie. *Martin Heidegger.* London: Bowes & Bowes. 1957.

Grondin, Jean. "Gadamer on Humanism." In *The Philosophy of Hans-Georg Gadamer,* edited by Lewis Edwin Hahn, 157–70. Library of Living Philosophers 24. Chicago: Open Court, 1997.

Gutting, Gary, editor. *Paradigms and Revolutions: Appraisals and Applications of Thomas Kuhn's Philosophy of Science.* South Bend, IN: University of Notre Dame Press, 1980.

Habermas, Jürgen. "The Hermeneutic Claim to Universality." Translated by Josef Bleicher. In *Contemporary Hermeneutics: Hermeneutics as Method, Philosophy and Critique,* edited by Josef Bleicher, 181–211. London: Routledge & Kegan Paul, 1980.

———. "Knowledge and Interest." Translated by Guttorm Florstad. *Inquiry* 9 (1966) 285–300.

———. "A Review of Gadamer's *Truth and Method.*" In *Understanding and Social Inquiry,* edited by Fred R. Dallmayr and Thomas A. McCarthy, 335–63. Notre Dame: University of Notre Dame Press, 1977.

Hahn, Lewis Edwin, editor. *The Philosophy of Hans-Georg Gadamer.* Library of Living Philosophers 24. Chicago: Open Court, 1997.

Hamilton, Bernard. *The Medieval Inquisition.* London: Holmes & Meier, 1982.

Hegel, Georg Wilhelm Friedrich. *Hegel's Science of Logic.* Edited and translated by A. V. Miller. Muirhead Library of Philosophy. London: Allen & Unwin, 1969.

———. *Phenomenology of Spirit.* Translated by A. V. Miller. With analysis of the text and forward by J. N. Findlay. Oxford: Clarendon, 1977. Originally published as *Phanomenologie des Geistes.* 5th ed. Hamburg: Felix Meiner, 1952.

———. *Hegel's Philosophy of Right.* Translated by T. M. Knox. Oxford: Oxford University Press, 1952.

Heidegger, Martin. *The Basic Problems of Phenomenology.* Translated by Albert Hofstadter. Studies in Phenomenology and Existential Philosophy. Bloomington: Indiana University Press, 1982.

————. *Being and Time.* Translated by John Macquarrie and Edward Robinson. The Library of Philosophy and Theology. Edited London: SCM, 1962. Originally published as *Sein und Zeit.* Tübingen: Neomarius, 1926.

————. "Building Dwelling Thinking." Translated by Albert Hofstadter. In *Poetry, Language, Thought,* 143–162. Martin Heidegger Works. New York: Harper & Row, 1971. Originally published as "Bauen Wohnen Denken." In *Vorträge und Aufsätze.* Pfullingen: Neske, 1954.

————. *Der Satz vom Grund.* Pfullingen: Neske, 1957.

————. *Holzwege.* Frankfurt: Vittorio Klostermann, 1963.

————. "Language." Translated by Albert Hofstadter. In *Poetry, Language, Thougt,* 187–210. Martin Heidegger Works. New York: Harper & Row, 1971. Originally published as "Die Sprache" in *Unterwegs zur Sprache.* Pfullingen: Neske, 1959.

————. "Plato's Doctrine of Truth." Translated by William Barrett and H. D. Aiken. In *Philosophy in the Twentieth Century* 3:251–70. New York: Random House, 1962.

————. *Poetry, Language, Thought.* Translated by Albert Hofstadter. Martin Heidegger Works. New York: Harper & Row, 1971.

————. *The Principle of Reason.* Translated by Reginald Lilly. Studies in Continental Philosophy. Bloomington: Indiana University Press, 1991. Originally published as *Der Satz vom Grund* (Pfullingen: Neske, 1957).

————. *Was heisst Denken?* Tubingen: Neimeyer, 1954.

Heller, Peter. "Multiplicity and Unity in Nietzsche's Works and Thoughts on Thought." *The German Quarterly* 52 (1978) 319–38.

Henry, Matthew. *An Exposition of the Old and New Testaments.* 6 vols. Edited by George Burder and Joseph Hughes. New York: Haven, 1831.

Hilary of Poitiers. *In Evangelium Matthaei Commentarius.* Edited by H. de Lubac and Jean Daniélou. SC 254 and 258.

Himes, Michael J. "The Ecclesiological Significance of the Reception of Doctrine." *Heythrop Journal* 33 (1992) 146–60.

Hinman, Lawrence M. "*Quid Facti* or *Quid Juris*? The Fundamental Ambiguity of Gadamer's Understanding of Hermeneutics." *Philosophy and Phenomenological Research* 40 (1980) 512–35.

Hippocrates. Translated by W. H. S. Jones et al. LCL. Cambridge, MA: Harvard University Press, 1923.

Hirsch, E. D. Jr. *The Aims of Interpretation.* Chicago: University of Chicago Press, 1976.

————. *Cultural Literacy: What Every American Needs to Know.* Boston: Houghton Mifflin, 1987.

————. *Validity in Interpretation.* New Haven: Yale University Press, 1967.

Hodgson, Peter C. "Georg Wilhelm Friedrich Hegel." In *Nineteenth Century Religious Thought in the West,* edited by John Clayton, Ninian Smart, Patrick Sherry, and Steven T. Katz, 1: 81–121. Cambridge: Cambridge University Press, 1985.

Hogan, John P. "Hermeneutics and the Logic of Question and Answer: Collingwood and Gadamer." *Heythorp Journal* 28 (1987) 263–84.

Hogg, William Richey. "The Rise of Protestant Missionary Concern, 1517–1914." In *The Theology of Christian Mission,* edited by Gerald H. Anderson, 95–111. Nashville: Abingdon, 1961.

Holmes, Stephen R. *Listening to the Past: The Place of Tradition in Theology*. Grand Rapids, MI: Baker, 2002.

Holub, Robert C. *Crossing Borders: Reception Theory, Poststructuralism, Deconstruction*. Madison: University of Wisconsin Press, 1992.

———. "German Theory in the United States." In *Protocol of the Colloquy of the Center for Hermeneutical Studies in Hellenistic and Modern Culture*, edited by William R. Herzog II, 37–45. Berkeley: The Graduate Theological Union and the University of California, 1983.

———. *Reception Theory: A Critical Introduction. In New Accents*. Edited by Terence Hawkes. New York: Methuen, 1984.

———. "Reception Theory and Russian Formalism." *Germano-Slavica* 3 (1980) 271–86.

———. "Trends in Literary Theory: The American Reception of Reception Theory." *German Quarterly* 55 (1982) 80–96.

Hoy, David Couzens. "Heidegger and the Hermeneutic Turn." In *The Cambridge Comparion to Heidegger*, edited by Charles B. Guignon, 170–194. Cambridge: Cambridge University Press, 1993.

Hughes, Philip. *The King's Preceedings*. Vol. 1, *The Reformation in England*. London: Hollis & Carter, 1950.

Hume, David. *An Enquiry Concerning Human Understanding*. Edited by C. W. Wendel. New York: Bobbs-Merrill, 1955.

Hunter, A. M. *Interpreting the Parables*. London: SCM, 1960.

Husserl, Edmund. *Cartesian Meditations: An Introduction to Phenomenology*. Translated by Dorion Carins. The Hague: Nijhoff, 1960.

Inwood, Michael. *A Hegel Dictionary*. The Blackwell Philosopher Dictionaries. Oxford: Blackwell, 1992.

Irenaeus. *Adversus Haereses*. PG 7.

———. *Libros quinque adversus haereses*. Edited by W. W. Harvey. Cambridge: Typis Academicis, 1852. Translated by John Keble as *Five Books of S. Irenaeus Against Heresies*. A Library of the Fathers of the Holy Catholic Church. Oxford: James Parker, 1872.

Iser, Wolfgang. *The Act of Reading: A Theory of Aesthetic Response*. Baltimore: Johns Hopkins Uninversity Press, 1980. Originally published as *Der Act des Lesens: Theorie ästhetischer Wirkung*. Munich: Fink, 1976.

———. *Die Appellstruktur der Texte: Unbestimmtheit als Wirkungsbedingung literarischer Prosa*. Konstanz: Universitätsverlag, 1970.

———. "Indeterminacy and the Reader's Response in Prose Fiction." In *Aspects of Narrative: Selected Papers from the English Institute*, edited by J. Hillis Miller, 1–45. New York: Columbia University Press, 1971.

———. "The Current Situation of Literary Theory: Key Concepts and the Imaginary." *New Literary History* 11 (1979) 1–20.

———. *The Implied Readers: Patterns of Communication in Prose Fiction from Bunyan to Beckett*. Baltimore: Johns Hopkins University Press, 1974. Originally published as *Der implizite Leser: Kommunikationsformen des Romans von Bunyan bis Beckett*. Munich: Fink, 1972.

————. "Narrative Strategies as a Means of Communication." In *Interpretation of Narrative*, edited by Mario J. Valdes and Owen J. Miller, 100–117. Toronto: University of Toronto Press, 1978.

————. "The Reading Process: A Phenomenological Approach." In *New Directions in Literary History*, edited by Ralph Cohen, 211–28. Baltimore: Johns Hopkins University Press, 1974.

————. "Talk Like Whales: A Reply to Stanley Fish." *Diacritics* 11 (1981) 82–87.

Jauss, Hans Robert. "1912: Threshold to an Epoch. Apollinaire's Zone and Lundi Rue Christine." Translated by Roger Blood. *Yale French Studies* 74 (1988) 39–66.

————. *Aesthetic Experience and Literary Hermeneutics*. Translated by Michael Shaw. Theory and History of Literature 3. Minneapolis: University of Minnesota Press, 1982.

————. "The Alterity and Modernity of Medieval Literature." Translated by Timothy Bahti. *New Literary History* 20 (1979) 181–229.

————. "Die beiden Fassungen von Flauberts Education sentimentale." *Heidelberger Jahrbücher* 2 (1958) 96–116.

————. "The Dialogical and the Dialectical *Neveu de Rameau*: How Diderot Adopted Socrates and Hegel Adopted Diderot." Translated by Sara Brewer Berlowitz. In *Protocol of the Colloquy of the Center for Hermeneutical Studies in Hellenistic and Modern Culture*, edited by William R. Herzog II, 1–29. Berkeley: The Graduate Theological Union and the University of California, 1983.

————. "Einleitung." In *Text und Applikation: Theologie, Jurisprudenz und Literaturwissenschaft im hermeneutischen Gespräch*, edited by Manfred Furhmann, Hans Robert Jauss, and Wolfhart Pannenberg, 249–58. Poetik und Hermeneutik 9. Munich: Fink, 1981.

————. "Geschichte der Kunst und Historie." In *Geschichte—Ereignis und Erzählung*, edited by Reinhart Koselleck and Wolf-Dieter Stempel, 175–210. Poetik und Hermeneutik: Arbeitsergebnisse einer Forschungsgruppe 5. Munich: Fink, 1973.

————. "The Idealist Embarrassment: Observations on Marxist Aesthetics." *New Literary History* 7 (1975) 191–208.

————. "The Identity of the Poetic Text in the Changing Horizon of Understanding." In *Identity of the Literary Text*, edited by Mario J. Valdés and Owen Miller, 146–74. Toronto: University of Toronto Press, 1985.

————. "Der Leser als Instanz einer neuen Geschichte der Literatur." *Poetica* 7 (1975) 325–44.

————. "Limits and Tasks of Literary Hermeneutics." *Diogenes* 109 (1980) 92–119.

————. "The Literary Process of Modernism from Rousseau to Adorno." Translated by Lisa C. Roetzel. *Cultural Critique* (1988–1989) 27–61.

————. *Literaturgeschichte als Provokation*. Frankfurt: Suhrkamp, 1970.

————. "Paradigmawechsel in der Literaturwissenschaft." *Linguistische Berichte* 3 (1969) 44–56.

————. "Poiesis." *Critical Inquiry* 8 (1982).

————. *Question and Answer: Forms of Dialogic Understanding*. Translated by Michael Hays. Theory and History of Literature 68. Minneapolis: University of Minnesota Press, 1989. Originally published as *Ästhetische Erfahrung und literarische Hermenutik*. Frankfurt: Suhrkamp, 1982.

————. "Racines and Goethes Iphigenie: mit einem Nachwort über die Partialität der rezeptionsästhetischen Methode." In *Theorie literarischer Texte,* edited by Rüdiger Bubner et al, 1–47. Neue Hefte für Philosophie 4. Göttingen: Vandenhoeck & Ruprecht, 1973.

————. "The Theory of Reception: A Retrospective of its Unrecognized Prehistory." In *Literary Theory Today,* edited by Peter Collier and Helge Geyer-Ryan, 53–73. Oxford: Polity, 1990.

————. "Theses on the Transition from the Aesthetics of Literary Works to a Theory of Aesthetics of Experience." In *Interpretation of Narrative,* edited by Mario Valdes and Owen Miller, 137–47. Toronto: University of Toronto Press, 1978.

————. *Towards an Aesthetic of Reception.* Translated by Timothy Bahti. Theory and History of Literature 2. Minneapolis: University of Minnesota Press, 1982.

————. "Tradition, Innovation, and Aesthetic Experience." *Journal of Aesthetics and Art Criticism* 46 (1988) 375–88.

————. "Versuch einer Ehrenrettung der Ereignisbegriffs." In *Geschichte—Ereignis und Erzählung,* edited by Reinhart Koselleck and Wolf-Dieter Stempel, 554–60. Poetik und Hermeneutik: Arbeitsergebnisse einer Forschungsgruppe 5. Munich: Fink, 1973.

————. "Zur Analogie von literarischem und historischem Ereignis." In *Geschichte— Ereignis und Erzählung,* edited by Reinhart Koselleck and Wolf-Dieter Stempel, 535–36. Poetik und Hermeneutik: Arbeitsergebnisse einer Forschungsgruppe 5. Munich: Fink, 1973.

————. "Zur Abgrenzung und Bestimmung einer literarischen Hermeneutik." In *Text und Applikation: Theologie, Jurisprudenz und Literaturwissenschaft im hermeneutischen Gespräch,* edited by Manfred Furhmann, Hans Robert Jauss, and Wolfhart Pannenberg, 459–81. Poetik und Hermeneutik 9. Munich: Fink, 1981.

Jauss, Hans Robert, editor. *Die Nicht mehr schönen Künste.* Poetik und Hermeneutik: Grenzphänomene des Ästheticschen 3. Munich: Fink, 1968.

Jeanrond, Werner G. *Theological Hermeneutics: Development and Significance.* New York: Crossroad, 1991.

Jensen, Michael. "'Simply' Reading the Geneva Bible: The Geneva Bible and Its Readers." *Literature and Theology* 9 (1995) 30–45.

Jeremias, Joachim. *Jesus' Promise to the Nations.* Translated by S. H. Hooke. London: SCM, 1958. Originally published as *Jesu Verheissung für die Volker.* Stuttgart: Kohlhammer, 1956.

————. *The Parables of Jesus.* Translated by S. H. Hooke. Rev. ed. The New Testament Library. London: SCM, 1963. Originally published as *Die Gleichnisse Jesu.* Göttingen: Vandenhoeck and Ruprecht, 1962.

Jerome. *Commentariorum in Mattheum.* Corpus Christianorum: Series Latina 77. Turnhout: Brepols, 1959.

————. *Epistolae.* PL 22.

Jones, Geraint Vaughan. *The Art and Truth of the Parables: A Study in Their Literary Form and Modern Interpretation.* London: SPCK, 1964.

Jülicher, Adolf. *Die Gleichnissreden Jesu.* 2 vols. Darmstadt: Wissensschaftliche Buchgesellschaft, 1976. First published 1886 by Mohr Siebeck.

Kant, Immanuel. *Conflict of Faculties*. Translated by M. Gregor and Robert E. Anchor. New York: Abaris, 1979.

———. *Critique of Judgment*. Translated by James Creed Meredith. Oxford: Clarendon, 1952. Originally published as *Kritik der Urteilskraft*. Berlin: Lagrande und Friederich, 1790.

Kealy, Seán. *Matthew's Gospel and the History of Biblical Interpretation*. Vol. 55a and 55b. *Mellen Biblical Press Series*. Edited by Lewiston, NY: Mellen, 1997.

Kee, Howard Clark. *Medicine, Miracles, and Magic in New Testament Times*. Society for New Testament Studies Monograph Series 55. Cambridge: Cambridge University Press, 1986.

Kennedy, George. *New Testament Interpretation through Rhetorical Criticism*. Chapel Hill: University of North Carolina Press, 1984.

Keir, Howard. "New Testament Exorcism and Its Significance Today." *The Expository Times* 96.4 (1985) 105–9.

Kermode, Frank. *The Classic: Literary Images of Permanence and Change*. New York: Viking, 1975.

Kimmerle, Heinz. "Hermeneutical Theory or Ontological Hermeneutics." Translated by Friedrich Seifert. *Journal for Theology and the Church* 4 (1967) 107–121.

Kiple, Kenneth F. ed. *The Cambridge World History of Human Disease*. Cambridge: Cambridge University Press, 1993.

Kisiel, Theodore. "The Happening of Tradition: The Hermeneutics of Gadamer and Heidegger." *Man and World* 2 (1969) 359–385.

———. "Ideology Critique and Phenomenology: The Current Debate in German Philosophy." *Philosophy Today* 14 (1970) 151–60.

Kissinger, Warren S. *The Parables of Jesus: A History of Interpretation and Bibiliography*. ATLA Bibliography Series. Metuchen, NJ: Scarecrow, 1979.

Kittel, Gerhard, and Gerhard Friedrich, editors. *Theological Dictionary of the New Testament*. Translated by Geoffrey W. Bromiley. 10 vols. Grand Rapids: Eerdmans, 1964–76.

Klein, William H., Craig L. Blomberg, and Robert L. Hubbard Jr. *Introduction to Biblical Interpretation*. Dallas: Word, 1993.

Krauss, Hans-Joachim. "Calvin's Exegetical Principles." *Interpretation* 31 (1977) 9–18.

Krieger, Murray. *A Window to Criticism*. Princeton: Princeton University Press, 1964,

Kuhn, Thomas. *The Copernican Revolution: Planetary Astronomy in the Development of Western Thought*. Cambridge: Harvard University Press, 1957.

———. *The Essential Tension: Selected Studies in Tradition and Change*. Chicago: University of Chicago Press, 1977.

———. "Logic of Discovery or Psychology of Research?" In *Criticism and the Growth of Knowledge,* edited by Imre Lakatos and Allan Musgrave, 1–25. Cambridge: Cambridge University Press, 1970.

———. *The Structure of Scientific Revolutions*. 2nd ed. International Encyclopedia of Unified Science. Chicago: University of Chicago Press, 1970.

Lambert, Malcolm. *Medieval Heresy: Popular Movement from the Gregorian Reform to the Reformation*. 2nd ed. Oxford: Blackwell, 1977.

Lammi, Walter. "Hans-Georg Gadamer's 'Correction' of Heidegger." *Journal of History of Ideas* 52 (1991) 487–507.

Lampe, Geoffrey William Hugo. *A Patristic Greek Lexicon.* Oxford: Oxford University Press, 1961.

Larmore, Charles. "Tradition, Objectivity, and Hermeneutics." In *Hermeneutics and Modern Philosophy,* edited by Brice R. Wachterhauser, 147–67. Albany: SUNY Press, 1986.

Lash, Nicolas. *Change in Focus: A Study of Doctrinal Change and Continuity.* London: Sheed & Ward, 1973.

Lemcio, Eugene E. "The Parables of the Great Supper and the Wedding Feast: History, Redaction and Canon." *Horizons in Biblical Theology* 8 (1986) 1–26.

Lennox, William G. *Epilepsy and Related Disorders.* Boston: Little, Brown, 1960.

Leo the Great. *Sermon.* PL 54. *Patrologia Latina.* Translated by Jane Patricia Freeland and Agnes Josephine Conway as *St. Leo the Great: Sermons.* The Fathers of the Church 93. Washington. DC: The Catholic University of America Press, 1996.

Lianeri, Alexandra. "The Homeric Moment?: Translation, Historicity, and the Meaning of the Classics." In *Classics and the Uses of Reception,* edited by Charles Martindale and Richard F. Thomas, 141–52. Oxford: Blackwell, 2006.

Lichtenstein, E. "Bildung." In *Historisches Worterbuch der Philosophie,* edited by Joachim Ritter, 1:921–37. Basel: Scwabe, 1971.

Link, Hannelore. "'Die Appellstruktur der Text' und ein 'Paradigmawechsel in der Literaturwissenschaft'?" *Jahrbuch der deutschen Schillergesellschaft* 17 (1973) 532–83.

Linnemann, Eta. *Parables of Jesus: Introduction and Exposition.* Translated by John Sturdy. London: SPCK, 1966. Originally published as *Gleichnisse Jesu, Einführung und Auslegung.* Göttingen: Vandenhoeck & Ruprecht, 1961.

———. "Überlegungen zur Parabel vom grossen Abendmahl." *Zeitschrift für die neutestamentliche Wissenschaft* 51 (1960) 246–55.

Little, James C. "Parable Research in the Twentieth Century I: The Predecessors of J. Jeremias." *Expository Times* 87 (1976) 356–60.

———. "Parable Research in the Twentieth Century II: The Contribution of J. Jeremias." *Expository Times* 88 (1977) 40–43.

———. "Parable Research in the Twentieth Century III: Developments since J. Jeremias." *Expository Times* 88 (1977) 71–75.

Louth, Andrew. *Discerning the Mystery: An Essay on the Nature of Theology.* Oxford: Clarendon, 1983.

Lundin, Roger, Anthony C. Thiselton, and Clarence Walhout. *The Promise of Hermeneutics.* Grand Rapids: Eerdmans, 1999.

Luther, Martin. *Luther's Works.* 55 vols. Edited by Helmut T. Lehman and Jaroslav Pelikan. Philadelphia: Fortress, 1958–1986. Originally published as *D. Martin Luthers Werke: Kritische Gesamtausgabe.* Weimar: Hermann Böhlaus Nachfolger, 1883–.

Luz, Ulrich. *Matthew 1–7.* Translated by Wilhelm C. Linss. Continental Commentaries. Minneapolis: Augsburg, 1989. Originally published as *Das Evangelium nach Matthäus,* 4 vols. Zurich: Benziger, 1985–.

———. *Matthew.* 3 vols. Translated by James E. Crouch. Hermeneia. Minneapolis: Fortress, 2001–2007.

————. *Matthew in History: Interpretation, Influence, and Effects*. Minneapolis: Fortress, 1994.

MacIntyre, Alasdair. *After Virtue: A Study in Moral Theory*. 2nd ed. Notre Dame, IN: University of Notre Dame Press, 1984.

————. "Contexts of Interpretation: Reflections on Hans-Georg Gadamer's Truth and Method." *Boston University Journal* 27 (1976) 41–46.

————. "Epistemological Crisis, Dramatic Narrative, and the Philosophy of Science." In *Paradigms and Revolutions*, edited by Gary Gutting, 54–74. Notre Dame, IN: University of Notre Dame Press, 1980.

————. *Three Rival Versions of Moral Enquiry: Encyclopedia, Genealogy, and Tradition*. Norte Dame, IN.: University of Notre Dame Press, 1990.

————. *Whose Justice? Which Rationality?* Notre Dame, IN: University of Notre Dame Press, 1985.

Machor, James L., and Philip Goldstein, editors. *Reception Theory: From Literary Theory to Cultural Studies*. London: Routledge, 2001.

Makaryk, Irena R., editor. *Encyclopedia of Contemporary Literary Theory: Approaches, Scholars, Terms*. Toronto: University of Toronto Press, 1993.

Makkreel, Rudolf A. *Imagination and Interpretation in Kant: The Hermeneutical Import of the Critique of Judgment*. Chicago: University of Chicago Press, 1990.

Maldonado, Juan de (Maldonatus). *Joannis Maldonati Commentarii in Quatuor Evangelistas*. London: Moguntiae, 1853–54 [original 1596]. Translated by George J. Davie as *A Commentary on the Holy Gospels*. 2 vols. Catholic Standard Library. London: Hodges, 1888.

Man, Paul de. *The Rhetoric of Romanticism*. New York: Columbia University Press, 1984.

Mandel, Ross. "Heidegger and Wittgenstein: A Second Kantian Revolution." In *Heidegger and Modern Philosophy: Critical Essays*, edited by Michael Murray, 259–270. New Haven: Yale University Press, 1978.

Margerie, Bertrand de. *An Introduction to the History of Exegesis: The Greek Fathers*. Translated by Leonard Maluf. Vol. 1. Petersham, MA: Saint Bede's, 1993.

Martindale, Charles, and Richard F. Thomas, editors. *Classics and the Uses of Reception*. Oxford: Blackwell, 2006.

Matejka, Ladislav, and Krystyna Pomorska, editors. *Readings in Russian Poetics: Formalist and Structuralist Views*. Ann Arbor: Michigan Slavic Publications, 1978.

Mayr, Franz. "Language." In *Sacramentum Mundi: An Encyclopedia of Theology*, edited by Karl Rahner, 3: 268–74. New York: Burns & Oates, 1969.

McGaveran, Donald. *Momentous Decisions in Missions Today*. Grand Rapids: Baker, 1984.

McHann, James Clark Jr. "The Three Horizons: A Study in Biblical Hermeneutics with Special Reference to Wolfhart Pannenberg." PhD. dissertation, University of Aberdeen, 1987.

Merriman, Brigid. "Minutes of the Colloquy of 27 February 1983." In *Protocol of the Colloquy of the Center for Hermeneutical Studies in Hellenistic and Modern Culture*, edited by William R. Herzog II, 51–67. Berkeley: The Graduate Theological Union and the University of California, 1983.

Michelfelder, Diane P., and Richard E. Palmer, editors. *Deconstruktion and Deconstruction: The Gadamer-Derrida Encounter: Texts and Comments.* Albany: SUNY Press, 1988.

Milburn, R. L. P. *Early Christian Interpretations of History: The Bampton Lectures of 1952.* 1954. Reprint, Eugene, OR: Wipf & Stock, 2005.

Misgeld, Dieter. "On Gadamer's Hermeneutic." In *Hermeneutics and Praxis,* edited by Robert Hollinger, 143–70. South Bend, IN: University of Notre Dame, 1985.

———. "Modernity and Hermeneutics: A Critical-Theoretical Rejoinder." In *Gadamer and Hermeneutics,* edited by Hugh J. Silverman, 163–77. Continental Philosophy 4. New York and London: Routledge, 1991.

Mitscherling, Jeff. "The Historical Consciousness of Man." *History of European Ideas* 11 (1989) 733–41.

———. "Philosophical Hermeneutics and 'The Tradition.'" *Man and World* 22 (1989) 247–50.

———. "Resuming the Dialogue." In *Anti-Foundationalism and Practical Reasoning: Conversations between Hermeneutics and Analysis,* edited by Evan Simpson, 121–34. Edmonton: Academic, 1987.

Monter, E. William. *Calvin's Geneva.* Edited by Norman F. Cantor. New Dimensions in History: Historical Cities. New York: Wiley, 1967.

Mueller-Vollmer, Kurt, editor. *The Hermeneutics Reader: Texts of the German Tradition from the Enlightenment to the Present.* New York: Continuum, 1990.

Mulhall, Stephen. *Heidegger and Being and Time.* Routledge Philosophy Guidebooks. New York: Routledge, 1996.

Mukarovsky, Jan. *Aesthetic Function, Norm and Value as Social Facts.* Translated by Mark E. Suino. Michigan Slavic Contributions. Ann Arbor: University of Michigan Press, 1970.

———. "Standard Language and Poetic Language." Translated by Paul L. Garvin. In *Critical Theory Since Plato,* edited by Adam Hazard, 1050–57. New York: Harcourt Brace Jovanovich, 1971.

Muller, Richard A., and John L. Thompson, editors. *Biblical Interpretation in the Age of the Reformation: Essays Presented to David C. Steinmetz in Honor of His Sixtieth Birthday.* Grand Rapids: Eerdmans, 1996.

Murray, Michael, editor. *Heidegger and Modern Philosophy: Critical Essays.* New Haven: Yale University Press, 1978.

Naumann, Manfred. "Literary Production and Reception." *New Literary History* 8 (1976) 107–26.

Newbigin, Leslie. "Cross-currents in Ecumenical and Evangelical Understandings of Mission." *International Bulletin of Missionary Research* 6 (1982) 146–51.

Nicholson, Graeme. "Answers to Critical Theory." In *Gadamer and Hermeneutics,* edited by Hugh J. Silverman, 151–62. Continental Philosophy 4. New York: Routledge, 1991.

Nietzsche, Friedrich. *The Gay Science: With a Prelude and an Appendix of Songs.* Translated by Walter Kaufmann. New York: Random House, 1974. Originally published as *Die fröhliche Wissenschaft* (1887).

———. *The Use and Abuse of History.* Translated by Adrian Collins. 2nd revised edition. *Library of Liberal Arts.* New York: Macmillan, 1985. Originally published as *Von Nutzen und Nachteil der Historie für das Leben* (1874).

Nutton, Vivian. "From Galen to Alexander, Aspects of Medicine and Medical Practice in Late Antiquity." In *Dumbarton Oaks Papers: Symposium on Byzantine Medicine*, edited by John Scarborough, 38:1–36. Washington, DC: Meriden-Stinehour, 1984.

O'Kane, Martin. *Painting the Text: The Artist as Biblical Interpreter*. The Bible in the Modern World. Sheffield: Sheffield Phoenix, 2007.

Olafson, Frederick A. *Heidegger and the Philosophy of the Mind*. New Haven: Yale University Press, 1987.

Oppenheimer, Robert. "Tradition and Discovery." In *American Council of Learned Societies*, 3–19. Rochester, New York: American Council of Learned Societies, 1959.

Origen. *Contra Celsus*. Translated by Henry Chadwick. Cambridge: Cambridge University Press, 1986.

———. *Matthäuserklärung*. Translated by Erich Klostermann. Die griechischen christlichen Schriftsteller der ersten drei Jahrhunderte 10. Leipzig: Heinrichs, 1935.

———. "Commentary on Matthew: Books I., II., and X.–XIV." Translated by Allan Menzies. In vol. 10 of *Ante-Nicene Fathers.Additional Volume: Containing Early Christian Works Discovered Since the Completion of the Series, and Selections from the Commentaries of Origen*, edited by Allan Menzies, Grand Rapids: Eerdmans, 1951.

———. *First Principles*. Translated by G.W. Butterworth. Gloucester, MA: Peter Smith, 1973.

Palmer, Richard E. *Hermeneutics: Interpretation Theory in Schleiermacher, Dilthey, Heidegger, and Gadamer*. Evanston, IL. Northwestern University Press, 1969.

———. "Ritual, Rightness, and Truth in Two Later Works of Hans-Georg Gadamer." In *The Philosophy of Hans-Georg Gadamer*, edited by Lewis Edwin Hahn, 529–47. Library of Living Philosophers 24. Chicago: Open Court, 1997.

Pannenberg, Wolfhart. "Focal Essay: The Revelation of God in Jesus of Nazareth." In *Theology as History*, edited by James M. Robinson and John B. Cobb, 101–33. New Frontiers in Theology: Discussions among Continental and American Theologians 3. New York: Harper & Row, 1967.

———. "Hermeneutics and Universal History." Translated by Paul J. Achtemeier. In *Basic Questions in Theology: Collected Essays*, edited by George H. Kehm, 1: 96–136. Philadelphia: Fortress, 1970. Originally published as "Hermeneutik und Universalgeschichte," *Zeitschrift für Theologie und Kirche* 60 (1960) 90–121.

———. *Theology and the Philosophy of Science*. Translated by Francis McDonagh. Philadelphia: Westminster, 1976. Originally published as *Wissenschaftstheorie und Theologie*. Frankfurt: Suhrkamp, 1973.

———. "What is Truth?" Translated by George H. Kehm. In *Basic Questions in Theology*, 2:1–27. Philadelphia: Westminster, 1971.

Parker, Thomas H. L. *Calvin's New Testament Commentaries*. 2nd ed. Louisville: John Knox, 1993.

Parris, David P. *Reading the Bible with the Giants: How 2000 Years of Biblical Interpretation Can Shed New Light on Old Texts*. Carlisle, UK: Paternoster, 2007.

Paslick, Robert H. "The Ontological Context of Gadamer's 'Fusion': Boehme, Heidegger, and Non-Duality." *Man and World* 18 (1985) 405–22.

Patte, Daniel, editor. *Semiology and Parables: An Exploration of the Possibilities Offered by Structuralism for Exegesis.* Pittsburgh Theological Monograph Series 9. Pittsburgh: Pickwick, 1976.

Peppermüller, Rolf. *Abaelards: Auslegung des Römerbriefs.* Beiträge zur Geschichte und Philosophie des Mittelalters, Texte und Untersuchungen 10. Münster: Aschendorff, 1972.

Perrin, Norman. "The Modern Interpretation of the Parables of Jesus and the Problem of Hermeneutics." *Interpretation: A Journal of Bible and Theology* 25 (1971) 131–48.

Piccone, Paul. "The Actuality of Traditions." *Telos* 94 (1992–93) 89–102.

Pilch, John J. *Healing in the New Testament: Insights from Medical and Mediterranean Anthropology.* Minneapolis: Fortress, 2000.

Pollard, Alfred W., edito. *Records of the English Bible: The Documents Relating to the Translation and Publication of the Bible in English, 1525–1611.* London: Oxford University Press, 1911.

Popper, Karl R. *The Logic of Scientific Discovery.* London: Routledge, 1992. Originally published as *Logik der Forschung* (Springer, 1934).

Powell, H. Jefferson. *The Moral Tradition of American Constitutionalism: A Theological Interpretation.* Durham, NC: Duke University Press, 1993.

Powell, Mark Allan. *Chasing the Eastern Star: Adventures in Biblical Reader-Response Criticism.* Louisville: Westminster John Knox, 2001.

Preminger, Frank J., Alexander Warnke, and O. B. Hardison Jr. editors. *The Princeton Encyclopedia of Poetry and Poetics.* Princeton: Princeton University Press, 1974.

Puckett, David L. "Calvin, John." In *Dictionary of Major Biblical Interpreters,* edited by Donald K. McKim, 287–94. Downers Grove, IL: IVP Academic, 2007.

Radbertus, Paschasius. *Expositio in Evangelium Matthaei.* PL 120.

Räisänen, Heikki. "The Effective 'History' of the Bible: A Challenge to Biblical Scholarship?" *SJT* 45 (1992) 303–24.

Ricoeur, Paul. *The Conflict of Interpretations: Essays in Hermeneutics.* Edited by Don Ihde. Evanston: IL: Northwestern University Press, 1974. Originally published as *Le Conflit des interprétations: Essais d'herménéutique.* Paris: Seuil.

———. *Essays on Biblical Interpretation.* Edited by Lewis S. Mudge. Philadelphia: Fortress, 1980.

———. "Hermeneutics and the Critique of Ideology." In *Hermeneutics and Modern Philosophy,* edited by Brice R. Wachterhauser, 300–39. Albany: SUNY Press, 1986.

———. *Hermeneutics and the Human Sciences: Essays on Language, Action and Interpretation.* Translated by John B. Thompson. Cambridge: Cambridge University Press, 1981.

———. *Interpretation Theory: Discourse and the Surplus of Meaning.* Fort Worth, TX: Texas Christian University Press, 1976.

———. "The Model of the Text: Meaningful Action Considered as a Text." In *Interpretive Social Research: A Reader,* edited by Paul Rabinow and William M. Sullivan, 73–100. Berkeley: University of California Press, 1979.

———. "Schleiermacher's Hermeneutics." *The Monist* 60 (1977) 181–97.

———. *Time and Narrative.* 3 vols. Chicago: University of Chicago Press, 1984–88.

Riesenfeld, Harald. "The Parables in the Synoptic and Johannine Traditions." *Svensk Exegetisck Årsbok* 25 (1960) 37–61.

Risser, James. "The Remembrance of Truth: The Truth of Remembrance." In *Hermeneutics and Truth*, edited by Brice R. Wachterhauser, 123–36. Evanston, IL: Northwestern University Press, 1994.

Ritter, Joachim and Karlfried Gründer editors. *Historisches Wörterbuch der Philosophie.* Basel: Scwabe, 1971–1995.

Roberts, David D. *Nothing but History: Reconstruction and Extremity after Metaphysics.* Berkeley: University of California Press, 1995.

Robinson, James M., and John B. Cobb Jr., editors. *The Later Heidegger. New Frontiers in Theology* 1. New York: Harper & Row, 1963.

Rorty, Richard. *Contingency, Irony, and Solidarity.* Cambridge: Cambridge University Press, 1989.

———. *Philosophy and the Mirror of Nature.* Princeton: Princeton University Press, 1980.

Rupp, E. G. *Studies in the Making of the English Protestant Tradition, (Mainly in the Reign of Henry VIII).* Cambridge: Cambridge University Press, 1949.

Rush, Ormond. "Living Reception of the Living Tradition: Hermeneutical Principles for Theology." In *Banyo Studies: Commenorative Papers to Mark the Golden Jubilee of Pius XII Seminary*, edited by Neil J. Byrne, 242–90. Banyo, Queensland, AUS: Pius XII Seminary, 1991.

———. "Reception Hermeneutics and the 'Development' of Doctrine: An Alternative Model." *Pacifica* 6 (1993) 125–40.

Sanks, T. Howland. "David Tracy's Theological Project: An Overview and Some Implications." *Theological Studies* 54 (1993) 698–727.

Sawyer, John F. A. "The Ethics of Comparative Interpretation." *Currents in Research: Biblical Studies* 3 (1995) 151–68.

Scarborough, John, editor. *Dumbarton Oaks Papers: Symposium on Byzantine Medicine.* Vol. 38. Washington, DC: Meriden-Stinehour, 1984.

Scheffler, Israel. *Science and Subjectivity.* Indianapolis: Bobbs–Merrill, 1967.

Schleiermacher, Friedrich D. E. *Hermeneutics: The Handwritten Manuscripts.* Edited by Heinz Kimmerle. Translated by Jame Duke and Jack Forstman. American Academy of Religion: Text and Translation Series. Atlanta: Scholars, 1977. Originally published as *Hermeneutik und Kritik. Mit einem Anhang sprachphilosophischer Texte Schleiermachers.* Frankfurt: 1959.

Schiller, Friedrich. *On the Aesthetic Education of Man, in a Series of Letters.* Edited and translated by Elizabeth M. Wilkinson and L. A. Willoughby. Oxford: Clarendon, 1967.

Schuchman, Paul. "Aristotle's Phronēsis and Gadamer's Hermeneutic." *Philosophy Today* 23 (1979) 41–50.

Schweitzer, Albert, *The Quest of the Historical Jesus: A Critical Study of its Progress from Reimarus to Wrede.* Translated by W. Montgomery. London: A. & C. Black, 1910.

Searle, John R. *Expression and Meaning: Studies in the Theory of Speech Acts.* Cambridge: Cambridge University Press, 1979.

———. *Intentionality: An Essay in the Philosophy of Mind.* Cambridge: Cambridge University Press, 1983.

Sedulius Scottus. "In Matthaeum." In *Sedulius Scottus: Kommentar zum Evangelium nach Matthäus*, edited by Bengt Löfstedt. Freiburg: Herder, 1991.

Segers, Rien T. "An Interview with Hans Robert Jauss." *New Literary History* 11 (1979) 83–95.

———. "Readers, Text and Author: Some Implications of Rezeptionsästhetik." *Yearbook of Comparative and General Literature* 24 (1975) 15–23.

Seiden, Margaret R. "Epilepsy." In *International Encyclopedia of Psychiatry, Psychology, Psychoanalysis, and Neurology*, edited by Benjamin B. Wolman. New York: Aesculapius, 1977.

Serequeberhan, Tsenay. "Heidegger and Gadamer: Thinking as 'Meditative' and as 'Effective-historical Consciousness.'" *Man and World* 20 (1987) 41–64.

Shanker, Stuart G. "Wittgenstein's Solution to the Hermeneutic Problem." *Conceptus* 18 (1984) 50–61.

Shapere, Dudley. "The Structure of Scientific Revolutions." In *Paradigms and Revolutions: Appraisals and Applications of Thomas Kuhn's Philosophy of Science*, edited by Gary Gutting, 27–38. Notre Dame, IN: University of Notre Dame Press, 1980.

Shenk, Wilbert R., editor. *Anabaptism and Mission*. Scottdale, PA: Herald, 1984.

Simonetti, Manlio. *Biblical Interpretation in the Early Church: An Historical Introduction to Patristic Exegesis*. Translated by John A. Hughes. Edited by Anders Bergquist and Markus Bockmuehl. Edinburgh: T. & T. Clark, 1994. Originally published as *Profilo Storico dell' Esegesi Patristica*. Rome: Instituto Patristico Augustinianum Roma, 1981.

Slethaug, Gordon E. "Play/freeplay, theories of." In *Encyclopedia of Contemporary Literary Theory: Approaches, Scholars, Terms*, edited by Irena R. Mayaryk, 145–59. Toronto: University of Toronto Press, 1993.

Smalley, Beryl. *The Study of the Bible in the Middle Ages*. Oxford: Blackwell, 1952.

Smith, Harold. *Ante-Nicene Exegesis of the Gospels*. Translations of Christian Literature 6. London: SPCK, 1928.

Smith, John. "Response." In *Protocol of the Colloquy of the Center for Hermeneutical Studies in Hellenistic and Modern Culture*, edited by William R. Herzog II, 46–49. Berkeley: The Graduate Theological Union and the University of California, 1983.

Sorensen, Eric. *Possession and Exorcism in the New Testament and Early Christianity*. Wissenschaftliche Untersuchungen Zum Neuen Testament 2/157. Tübingen: Mohr/Siebeck, 2002.

Sparks, H. F. D. "Jerome as Biblical Scholar." In *The Cambridge History of the Bible: From the Beginnings to Jerome*, edited by P. R. Ackroyd and C. F. Evans, 1:510–41. Cambridge: Cambridge University Press, 1970.

Stendahl, Krister. "The Bible as a Classic and the Bible as Holy Scripture." *Journal of Biblical Literature* 103 (1984) 3–10.

Stout, Jeffrey. *The Flight from Authority: Religion, Morality, and the Quest for Autonomy*. Notre Dame: University of Notre Dame Press, 1981.

———. "What is the Meaning of a Text?" *New Literary History* 14 (1982) 1–12.

Strabi, Walafridi. *Glossa Ordinaria*. PL 116. *Patrologia Latina*.

Strack, H. L., and P. Billerbeck. *Kommentar zum Neuen Testament aus Talmud und Midrasch*. 6 vols. Munich: Beck, 1922–1961.

Stueber, Karsten R. "Understanding and Objectivity: A Dialogue between Donald Davidson and Hans Georg-Gadamer." In *Hermeneutics and Truth,* edited by Brice R. Wachterhauser, 172–89. Evanston, IL: Northwestern University Press, 1994.

Sullivan, Robert R. *Political Hermeneutics: The Early Thinking of Hans-Georg Gadamer.* University Park, PA: Pennsylvania State University Press, 1989.

Sussman, Max. "Sickness and Disease." In *The Anchor Bible Dictionary,* edited by David Noel Freedman, 6:6–15. New York: Doubleday, 1992.

Szondi, Peter. "Introduction to Literary Hermeneutics." Translated by Timothy Bahti. *New Literary History* 10 (1978) 17–29.

Temkin, Owsei. *The Falling Sickness: A History of Epilepsy from the Greeks to the Beginnings of Modern Neurology.* 2nd ed. Baltimore: John Hopkins, 1971.

———. *Galenism: Rise and Decline of Medical Philosophy.* Ithaca, NY: Cornell University Press, 1973.

Theophylacti. *Enarratio in Evangelium Matthaei.* PG 123.

Thiselton, Anthony C. "Authority and Hermeneutics: Some Proposals for a More Creative Agenda." In *A Pathway into the Holy Scriptures,* edited by P. E. Satterthwaite and D. F. Wright, 107–41. Grand Rapids: Eerdmans, 1994.

———. *The First Epistle to the Corinthians.* The New International Greek Testament Commentary. Grand Rapids: Eerdmans, 2000.

———. "Knowledge, Myth and Corporate Memory." In *Believing in the Church: The Corporate Nature of Faith. A Report by the Doctrine Commission of the Church of England,* 45–78. London: SPCK, 1981.

———. *New Horizons in Hermeneutics: The Theory and Practice of Transforming Biblical Reading.* Grand Rapids: Zondervan, 1992.

———. "The Parables as Language-Event: Some Comments on Fuchs's Hermeneutics in the Light of Linguistic Philosophy." *SJT* 23 (1970) 437–68.

———. *The Two Horizons: New Testament Hermeneutics and Philosophical Description.* Grand Rapids: Eerdmans, 1980.

Tissot, Yves. "Patristic Allegories of the Lukan Parable of the Two Sons (Luke 15:11–32)." Translated by Donald G. Miller. In *Exegesis: Problems of Method and Exercises in Reading (Genesis 22 and Luke 15),* edited by François Bovon and Grégoire Rouiller, 362–409. Pittsburg Theological Monograph Series 21. Pittsburgh: Pickwick, 1978.

Tomkins, Jane. "Masterpiece Theater: The Poilitics of Hawthorne's Literary Reception." In *Reception Study: From Literary Theory to Cultural Studies,* edited by James L. Machor and Philip Goldstein, 133–59. New York: Routledge, 2001.

Torjensen, Karen Jo. "'Body,' 'Soul' and 'Spirit' in Origen's Theory of Exegesis." *Anglican Theological Review* 67 1985) 17–30.

Tracy, David. *The Analogical Imagination: Christian Theology and the Culture of Pluralism.* London: SCM, 1981.

Trench, Richard Chenevix. *Notes on the Parables of our Lord.* 13th rev. ed. London: Macmillan, 1877.

Trexler, Richard C. *The Journey of the Magi: Meanings in History of a Christian Story.* Princeton: Princeton University Press, 1997.

Trilling, Wolfgang. "Zur Überlieferungsgeschichte des Gleichnisses vom Hochzeitmahl Mt 22, 1–14." *Biblische Zeitschrift* 4 (1960) 251–65.

Troeltsch, Ernst. "Historiography." In *Encyclopedia of Religion and Ethics,* edited by James Hastings, 6:716–23. Edinburgh: T. & T. Clark, 1913; reprinted 1953.

Trueman, Carl R. "Pathway of Reformation: William Tyndale and the Importance of the Scriptures." In *A Pathway into the Holy Scripture*, edited by P.E Satterthwaite and D. F. Wright. 11–29. Grand Rapids: Eerdmans, 1994.

Tugendhat, Ernst. "Heidegger's Idea of Truth." Translated by Christopher Macann. In *Hermeneutics and Truth*, edited by Brice R. Wachterhauser, 83–97. Evanston, IL: Northwestern University Press, 1994.

Tynjanov, J. "On Literary Evolution." In *Readings in Russian Poetics: Formalist and Structuralist Views*, edited by Ladislav Matejka and Krystyna Pomorska, 68–78. 1971. Reprint, Normal, IL: Dalkey Archive, 2002.

Via, Dan O. *The Parables: Their Literary and Existential Dimension*. 1967. Reprint, Eugene, OR: Wipf & Stock, 2007.

————. "The Relationship of Form to Content in the Parables: The Wedding Feast." *Interpretation* 25 (1971) 171–84.

Valdés, Mario J. and Owen Miller, editors. *Identity of the Literary Text*. Toronto: University of Toronto Press, 1985.

Valéry, Paul. "Poetry and Abstract Thought." Translated by Denise Folliot. In *Critical Theory since Plato*, edited by Adam Hazard, 915–26. New York: Harcourt Brace Jovanovich, 1971.

Vanhoozer, Kevin J. "A Lamp in the Labyrinth: The Hermeneutics of 'Aesthetic' Theology." *Trinity Journal* 8 (1987) 25–56.

Verene, Donald Phillip. "Gadamer and Vico on *Sensus Communis* and the Tradition of Humane Knowledge." In *The Philosophy of Hans-Georg Gadamer*, edited by Lewis Edwin Hahn, 24:137–53. *Library of Living Philosophers*. Chicago and London: Open Court, 1997.

Walhout, Clarence, Roger Lundin, and Anthony C. Thiselton. *The Responsibility of Hermeneutics*. Grand Rapids: Eerdmans, 1985.

Wailes, Stephen L. *Medieval Allegories of Jesus' Parables*. Publications for the Center for Medieval and Renaissance Studies 23. Berkeley: University of California Press, 1987.

Waismann, F. *The Principles of Linguistic Philosophy*. Edited by R. Harre. London: Macmillan, 1965.

Warneck, Gustav. *Outline of a History of Protestant Missions from the Reformation to the Present Time*. 3rd ed. Translated by George Robson. 1901. Reprint, New York: Fleming Revell, 1906.

Warnke, Georgia. *Gadamer, Hermeneutics, Tradition and Reason*. Cambridge: Polity, 1987.

————. "Hermeneutics and the Social Sciences: A Gadamerian Critique of Rorty." *Inquiry* 28 (1985) 339–57.

————. "Legitimate Prejudices." *Laval théologique et philosophique* 53 (1997) 89–102.

Watson, Francis. *Text and Truth: Redefining Biblical Theology*. Edinburgh: T. & T. Clark, 1997.

Weinsheimer, Joel C. *Gadamer's Hermeneutics: A Reading of "Truth and Method."* New Haven, CT: Yale University Press, 1985.

————. *Philosophical Hermeneutics and Literary Theory*. New Haven, CT: Yale University Press, 1991.

————. "Translator's Preface." In *Truth and Method*, 2nd rev. ed., by Hans-Georg Gadamer, translated by Joel Weinsheimer and Donald G. Marshall, xi–xiv. New York: Crossroad, 1989.

Wellek, René. *Concepts of Criticism*. Edited by Stephen G. Nichols Jr. New Haven: Yale Universtiy Press, 1963.

————. "The Term and Concept of 'Classicism' in Literary History." In *Aspects of the Eighteenth Century: Papers Presented at the John Hopkins University Humanities Seminar, 1963*, edited by Earl R. Wasserman, 105–28. Baltimore: John Hopkins University Press, 1965.

West, Cornel. *The American Evasion of Philosophy: A Genealogy of Pragmatism*. Madison: University of Wisconsin Press, 1989.

Westcott, Brooke Foss. *A General View of the History of the English Bible*. Revised and edited by William Aldis Wright. London: Macmillian, 1905.

Wiles, Maurice F. "Early Exegesis of the Parables." *SJT* 11 (1958) 287–301.

————. "Origen as Biblical Scholar." In *The Cambridge History of the Bible: From the Beginnings to Jerome*, edited by P. R. Ackroyd and C. F. Evans, 1:454–510. Cambridge: Cambridge University Press, 1970.

Wilkinson, John. "The Case of the Epileptic Boy." *Expository Times* 79 (1967) 39-42.

Willis, Geoffrey Grinshaw. *Saint Augustine and the Donatist Controversy*. London: SPCK, 1950.

Wittgenstein, Ludwig. *Culture and Value*. 2nd ed. Oxford: Blackwell, 1980.

————. *Philosophical Investigations. The English Text of the Third Edition*. Translated by G. E. M. Anscombe. New York: Macmillian, 1958.

————. *Remarks on the Foundation of Mathmatics*. Translated by G. E. M. Anscombe. Edited by Rush Rhees, G. H. von Wright, and G. E. M. Anscombe. Cambridge, MA: MIT Press, 1978.

————. *Zettel*. Translated by G. E. M. Anscombe. Edited by G. E. M. Anscombe and G. H. von Wright. Oxford: Blackwell, 1967.

Wright, David F. "Bucer, Martin." In *Dictionary of Major Biblical Interpreters*, edited by Donald K. McKim, 247–54. Downers Grove, IL: IVP Academic, 2007.

————. "Introduction: William Tyndale and the Tyndale Fellowship for Biblical and Theological Research." In *A Pathway into the Holy Scripture*, edited by P. E. Satterthwaite and D. F. Wright, 1–9. Grand Rapids: Eerdmans, 1994.

Young, Frances M. *The Art of Performance: Towards a Theology of Holy Scripture*. London: Darton, Longman & Todd, 1990.

————. *Biblical Exegesis and the Formation of the Christian Culture*. Cambridge: Cambridge University Press, 1997.